Beginning T-SQL 2008

Kathi Kellenberger

Apress®

Beginning T-SQL 2008

Lead Editors: Jonathan Gennick, Douglas Pundick
Technical Reviewer: Ken Simmons
Editorial Board: Clay Andres, Steve Anglin, Mark Beckner, Ewan Buckingham, Tony Campbell, Gary Cornell, Jonathan Gennick, Jonathan Hassell, Michelle Lowman, Matthew Moodie, Jeffrey Pepper, Frank Pohlmann, Douglas Pundick, Ben Renow-Clarke, Dominic Shakeshaft, Matt Wade, Tom Welsh
Project Manager: Kylie Johnston
Copy Editor: Kim Wimpsett
Production Support: Patrick Cunningham
Indexer: BIM Indexing
Artist: April Milne

Distributed to the book trade worldwide by Springer-Verlag New York, Inc., 233 Spring Street, 6th Floor, New York, NY 10013. Phone 1-800-SPRINGER, fax 201-348-4505, e-mail orders-ny@springer-sbm.com, or visit http://www.springeronline.com.

For information on translations, please contact Apress directly at 233 Spring Street, New York, NY 10013. E-mail info@apress.com, or visit http://www.apress.com.

Apress and friends of ED books may be purchased in bulk for academic, corporate, or promotional use. eBook versions and licenses are also available for most titles. For more information, reference our Special Bulk Sales–eBook Licensing web page at http://www.apress.com/info/bulksales.

The source code for this book is available to readers at http://www.apress.com.

This book is dedicated to Thomas Indiana, the most joyful person I have ever known. In his first three years, he has taught me to appreciate every moment of my life.

Contents at a Glance

Contents

About the Author

**Kathi Kellenberger** fell in love with computers the first time she touched a TRS-80 during her last year of college. Unfortunately, she was working on a degree in a health-care field that she stayed with for 16 years after college. During those years, she began programming as a hobby and eventually set up databases and wrote programs for several charity projects. Luckily, she was able to switch to computer programming during the Y2K craze, working on projects to update networks, workstations, and software for several small law firms. During that time, she programmed everything from ASP web sites to WordPerfect macros to Palm Pilot applications. She also began working with SQL Server.

After programming for a few years, she had the chance to become a SQL Server database administrator for Bryan Cave LLP, a prestigious law firm headquartered in St. Louis. The move proved to be a good one, and she made SQL Server the focus of her career.

In 2004 after reading a particularly bad article on her favorite SQL Server web site, she decided that even she could write a better article, and her writing career began. Writing articles led to the opportunity to contribute to one of Brian Knight's books, Professional SQL Server 2005 Integration Services (Wrox, 2006). She soon added speaking at user groups' meetings and conferences and getting involved with the PASS organization as a volunteer. In 2008, Kathi was awarded SQL Server MPV status for her many contributions to the SQL Server user community.

Kathi lives in Edwardsville, Illinois, with husband, Dennis. She enjoys singing, cycling, running, and spending time with family and friends.

About the Technical Reviewer

■**Ken Simmons** is a database administrator/developer specializing in SQL Server and .NET. He is the author of *Pro SQL Server 2008 Administration* (Apress, 2009) and *Pro SQL Server 2008 Mirroring* (Apress, 2009). He has been working in the IT industry since 2000 and currently holds certifications for MCP, MCAD, MCSD, MCDBA, and MCTS for SQL 2005.

Ken is active in the online community and often participates in the SQL forums on MSDN and SQLServerCentral.com. He enjoys sharing tips by writing articles for SQLServerCentral.com and MSSQLTips.com. When he is not working, Ken enjoys traveling with his wife, Susan, and son, Nathan, and can often be found on a cruise ship, at a Disney resort, or on the beach in his hometown of Pensacola, Florida.

Acknowledgments

When I was first approached by Apress to write a beginning T-SQL book, it was important to me to write the book myself. When I say that, I mean that it was important to me to be the only author on this book. Of course, I know that it takes many dedicated people to actually produce the book. Some of them I have met, like Apress editor Jonathan Gennick. Others I know through frequent e-mails: project manager Kylie Johnston and editors Ken Simmons, Douglas Pundick, and Kim Wimpsett. I am sure there are countless others who have worked behind the scenes to help get my book into your hands. I thank everyone for their hard work and dedication to help me write a better book.

It was important to me to write this book myself because I felt the book was already living inside my brain, just waiting for my fingers to type the words. I knew what I wanted to cover and could imagine you reading each chapter well before I began writing it. I'm not saying that writing the entire book was an easy task, especially with the busy life I lead, but I knew that this was what I needed to do.

So many people in my life have helped me along the way. My parents, Bill and Marilyn Morgan, taught me to believe that I could do anything in life that I wanted to do, and they were right! I thank them for everything they have done for me and my siblings. And, Mom, I promise I'll get to the campground for a weekend soon. I thank my brothers, Bill, Jeff, and Bob Morgan, for being computer geeks like me and for sharing their knowledge with me when I was getting started in this business. Thanks to my sisters, Jackie Laurie, Jeanne Morgan, and Chris Brandt, who aren't quite as geeky as I am but who are the most fun sisters anyone could ever have.

Thanks to Dennis, my love, for encouraging me, listening to me, and just putting up with me all these years. You are my prince. Thanks to Andy and Anna, my son and his wife, and to Denise and Ryan, my daughter and her husband. Thanks for being my kids and for being my friends. And to Thomas, my amazing grandson, you have made my life more fun than I knew possible.

As you can imagine, writing a book takes over one's life. I found myself just working and writing for months. I want to thank several friends, Justin Siess, Jason Rutherford, Stephen Harris, Luke Moore, and Pam King, for getting me away from my desk for awhile each day and back to the gym even when I didn't think I had time to go.

Several other people have been instrumental in my career. Doug Wilmsmeyer believed that I could leave my health professions career and become a programmer before I even knew that is what I wanted to do. Thanks, Doug, for your encouragement and advice throughout the years. Brian Knight, author, trainer, and SQL Server superstar, changed my life in 2005 when he asked me to write a couple of chapters for his Integration Services book. Thanks to Brian and to his business partners, Steve Jones and Andy Warren, who have encouraged me and nurtured my writing since I turned in my first article to SQLServerCentral.com almost five years ago. Thanks to Tom LaRock, SQLRockstar, for your encouragement and friendship.

Thanks, most of all, to my students and readers who have provided criticism and feedback, appreciation and praise. It is for you that I write this book.

Introduction

Welcome to *Beginning T-SQL 2008*. This book introduces you to the language known as T-SQL, also called Transact-SQL. It's the fundamental language that you need to know in order to work productively with Microsoft's database management system known as SQL Server. Almost everything that you do in SQL Server boils down to T-SQL commands, whether you write them yourself or whether a tool generates them for you. If you want to be successful in a career involving SQL Server, then it helps to master the underlying language.

To whet your appetite and to give you an idea of what you're in for, here is a simple example of a T-SQL statement. It's a simple query to list all the databases hosted on SQL Server:

```
SELECT name FROM sys.databases;
```

I wrote this book because I love working with T-SQL and love teaching others how to use it. I was introduced to SQL Server in the run up to year 2000. I was enamored with the power of SQL Server and with the expressiveness built into the T-SQL language. The amount of work that you can get done in a single statement of T-SQL versus large blocks of code in other languages is simply amazing. Using T-SQL, you can generate complex reports from a single statement, embed business logic in your database, create maintenance scripts to automate administrative tasks, and do much, much more.

The approach I take in this book is to begin with a review of some fundamental database concepts. Why? Because you need to understand how SQL Server stores the data before you begin to write queries against it. Then I move on to writing some simple queries, giving you the tools you need to begin extracting useful data from a database. From there we move on to manipulating data because most databases are not static; they are updated frequently. I then show you the programming logic features of T-SQL that you can use to create scripts and database objects so you can do more with T-SQL than just write single statements. Finally, I introduce you to some new, more advanced T-SQL features so that you can take advantage of cutting-edge techniques that many developers haven't even heard about.

Almost everything in SQL Server boils down to T-SQL sooner or later. Don't think you can escape T-SQL by using tools. Tools that generate code for you are great, but tools break. And when things go wrong, that's your chance to really shine—*if* you know T-SQL. Those who understand T-SQL can look at what a tool or a utility is doing and understand why the generated code is failing. Those without T-SQL knowledge will be seeking you out, because you'll be the one to diagnose and solve the problem. You'll also be able to get work done without fancy and expensive tool sets. With T-SQL, you can be productive in almost any circumstance.

Who This Book Is For

I have often found myself helping developers write T-SQL code. These developers usually know how to write simple queries, but they might need help writing an outer join or can't figure out which columns belong in the GROUP BY clause. I have also had the pleasure of teaching T-SQL to a few individuals who had never written a query before. This book is targeted to both groups: those with a bit of T-SQL experience and those who are absolute beginners when it comes to T-SQL.

How This Book Is Structured

About a year ago I got the opportunity to teach beginning T-SQL to a group of a dozen students. The catch was that I had to write the courseware in addition to teaching it. Because of that experience, the idea for this book was born, and the book is roughly based on the class I taught.

Within the book, each chapter or section builds on knowledge presented in the previous chapter or section. Most of the sections talk about a concept, give you an example to type in and execute, and then explain the results. You will also find exercises in Chapters 2 through 8 to reinforce what you have just learned.

If you are new to T-SQL, you will probably read this book beginning with Chapter 1 and continue to Chapter 11. You might just want to keep the book around as a reference to look up concepts that you don't use on a daily basis. Either way, the book contains many simple examples to illustrate the techniques covered and get you quickly using those techniques.

Chapter 1, "Getting Started": This chapter provides instructions for installing SQL Server Express edition and configuring it to be ready for the rest of the book. It also introduces database concepts such as normalization and indexes so that you understand how data is stored in SQL Server databases.

Chapter 2, "Writing Simple SELECT Queries": This chapter teaches you how to write your first T-SQL statements. It covers how to select, filter, and order data from a table.

Chapter 3, "Using Functions and Expressions": This chapter shows you how to use built-in functions and expressions to modify how the data is displayed, filtered, or ordered.

Chapter 4, "Querying Multiple Tables": This chapter demonstrates several techniques to use data from more than one table in the same query.

Chapter 5, "Grouping and Summarizing Data": This chapter teaches how to write aggregate queries. Aggregate queries allow you to group data and use special functions, such as SUM and COUNT, that operate over groups of data.

Chapter 6, "Manipulating Data": Because you will need to modify data as well as retrieve it, this chapter teaches how to insert new rows and update or delete existing rows.

Chapter 7, "Understanding T-SQL Programming Logic": This chapter demonstrates that T-SQL is more than just data retrieval and manipulation by teaching how to create scripts with programming logic.

Chapter 8, "Moving Logic to the Database": This chapter teaches how to create database objects such as stored procedures and views that allow you to store logic within the database. You will also learn about table constraints that control what data may be added to a table.

Chapter 9, "Working with New Data Types": This chapter covers the new data types introduced with SQL Server 2005 and 2008. You will learn about the XML data type, new large value data types, spatial data types, and more.

Chapter 10, "Writing Advanced Queries": This chapter introduces several new query types, such as the new pivot query, as well was some advanced techniques using common table expressions to solve complex problems efficiently.

Chapter 11, "Where to Go Next?": This chapter provides information about resources, many of them free, that you can use to enhance your skills.

Appendix, "Solutions to the Exercises": The appendix provides solutions to the exercises in Chapter 2 through Chapter 8.

Prerequisites

To run the code samples in this book, you will need a computer with the following:

1. Windows Server 2003 SP2, Windows Server 2008, Windows Vista, Windows XP SP2, or Windows XP SP3
2. 1GHz or faster processor (2GHz or faster is recommended)
3. 512MB RAM (1GB or more is recommended)
4. 1.9GB free hard disk space
5. An Internet connection to download SQL Server Express edition from Microsoft's web site

Downloading the Code

The source code for this book is available to readers at `http://www.apress.com` in the Downloads section of this book's home page. Please feel free to visit the Apress web site and download all the code there. You can also check for errata and find related titles from Apress.

Contacting the Author

Kathi can be contacted at kkellenbe@hotmail.com. You will find her blog and social networking pages at the following sites:

http://www.sqlservercentral.com/blogs/kathi_kellenberger/default.aspx

http://www.facebook.com/kathi.kellenberger

http://www.myspace.com/sqlgoddess

http://www.linkedin.com/in/kathikellenberger

CHAPTER 1

■■■

Getting Started

If you are reading this book, you probably know what T-SQL is. T-SQL, also known as Transact-SQL, is Microsoft's implementation of the Structured Query Language (SQL) for SQL Server. T-SQL is the language that is most often used to extract or modify data that is stored in a SQL Server database, regardless of the application or tool used. SQL Server 2008 T-SQL is based on standards created by the American National Standards Institute (ANSI), but Microsoft has added several functionality enhancements. You will find that T-SQL is a very versatile and powerful programming language.

T-SQL consists of Data Definition Language (DDL) and Data Manipulation Language (DML) statements. This book focuses primarily on the DML statements, which you will use to retrieve and manipulate data. The book also covers DDL statements, which you will use to create and manage objects. You will learn about table creation, for example, in Chapter 8.

In this chapter, you will learn how to install a free edition of SQL Server and get it ready for running the example code and performing the exercises in the rest of the book. This chapter also gives you a quick tour of SQL Server Management Studio and introduces a few concepts to help you become a proficient T-SQL programmer.

Installing SQL Server Express Edition

Microsoft makes SQL Server available in many different editions, including two that can be installed on a desktop computer or laptop. If you do not have access to SQL Server, you can download and install the SQL Server Express edition from Microsoft's web site at `http://www.microsoft.com/express/sql/download/default.aspx`. The Express edition also comes in three flavors. To fully take advantage of all the concepts covered in this book, download SQL Server 2008 Express with Advanced Services. Be sure to choose either the 64-bit or 32-bit download according to the operating system that you are running. The Express edition will run on the following operating systems available at the time of this writing: Windows Server 2003 SP2, Windows Server 2008, Windows Vista, and Windows XP SP2.

■ **Note** SP2 refers to Service Pack 2. A *service pack* is an update to the operating system or to other software that fixes bugs and security issues.

1

Here are the steps to follow to install SQL Server Express:

1. Once you have downloaded the SQL Server 2008 Express edition installation file from Microsoft's site, double-click the file to extract and start up the SQL Server Installation Center. Figure 1-1 shows the Planning pane of the SQL Server Installation Center once the extraction has completed.

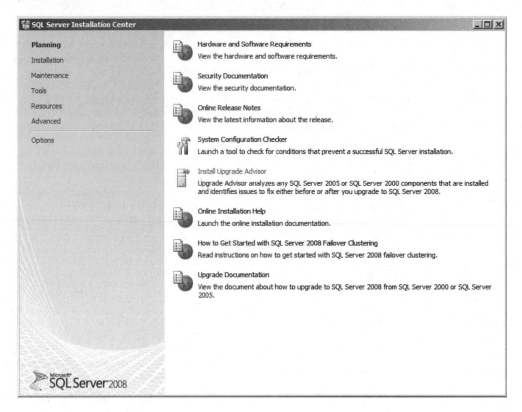

Figure 1-1. SQL Server Installation Center's Planning pane

2. To make sure that your system meets all the requirements to install SQL Server Express, click the System Configuration Checker link, which opens the Setup Support Rules screen (see Figure 1-2). Click "Show details" or "View detailed report" to see more information. Click OK to dismiss the screen when you are done.

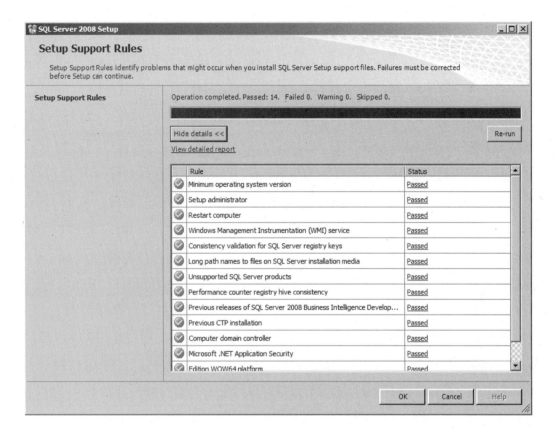

Figure 1-2. *The Setup Support Rules details page*

3. If your system does not meet the requirements, click the Hardware and Software Requirements link on the Planning pane of the SQL Server Installation Center, which will take you to a web page on Microsoft's site. Be sure to scroll down the web page to find the information for the Express edition. The hardware requirements are not difficult to meet with today's PCs.

4. Once you are certain that your computer meets all the requirements, switch to the Installation pane, shown in Figure 1-3, and click "New SQL Server stand-alone installation or add features to an existing installation." The Setup Support Rules screen you saw in step 2 will display again, but the behavior will be different this time. Click OK to dismiss the Setup Support Rules screen, and an installation wizard will begin.

3

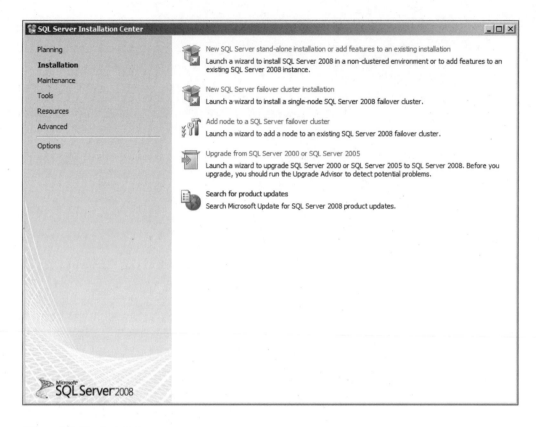

Figure 1-3. *The Installation pane*

5. You may or may not see a Setup Support Files screen at this point. If you do see it, click Install.

6. Some more checking of your system will take place. You may get a warning about your firewall (Figure 1-4), especially if you are installing on a workstation. The warning will say to open ports required for other systems to access your SQL Server. You can ignore that warning unless you do really want to open up your system. Click Next to continue.

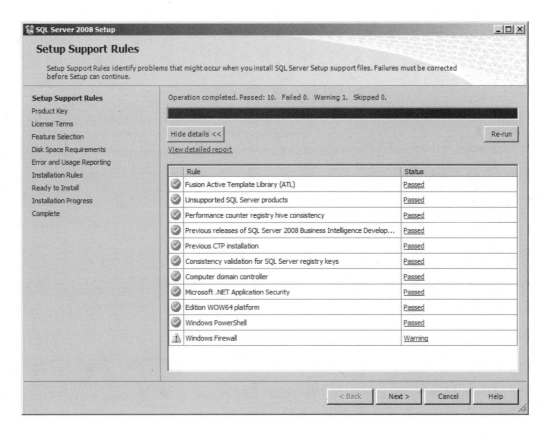

Figure 1-4. *More system checks*

7. If you have a previously installed instance of SQL Server on your computer, the installation will prompt you to either update an existing instance or install a new instance on the Installation Type screen. Select to install a new instance, and click Next.

8. Click Next on the Product Key screen when installing SQL Server Express edition. No need to have a key since this is a free edition!

9. Accept the license terms, and click Next.

10. On the Feature Selection screen (Figure 1-5), make sure that Database Engine Services, Full-Text Search, and Management Tools – Basic are selected before clicking Next. If a previous SQL Server 2008 installation is in place, the Management Tools check box might be grayed out since you need to install it only once per computer.

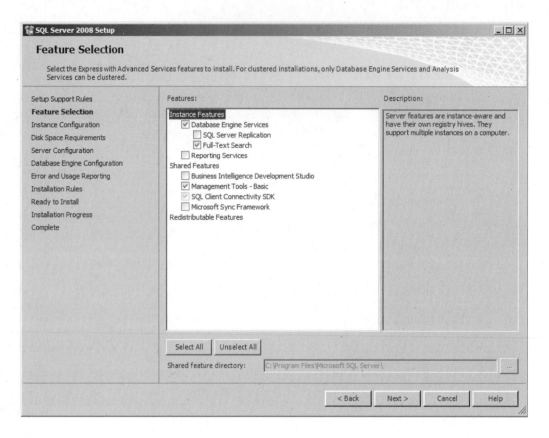

Figure 1-5. *The Feature Selection screen*

11. Figure 1-6 shows the Instance Configuration screen, and it is very important. Here you can choose to install a default instance or a named instance. If you have any SQL Server instances already installed, possibly an earlier version such as 2005, they will show up in the list on this screen. Each instance must have a unique name, so you must avoid using any existing instance names. See the sidebar "Named Instances" for more information about naming SQL Server instances. The Express edition installation installs the named instance SQLEXPRESS by default. Use the name SQLEXPRESS if you can; otherwise, type in a unique name. Figure 1-6 shows the screen when the SQLEXPRESS instance already exists and a new name is typed in. Click Next.

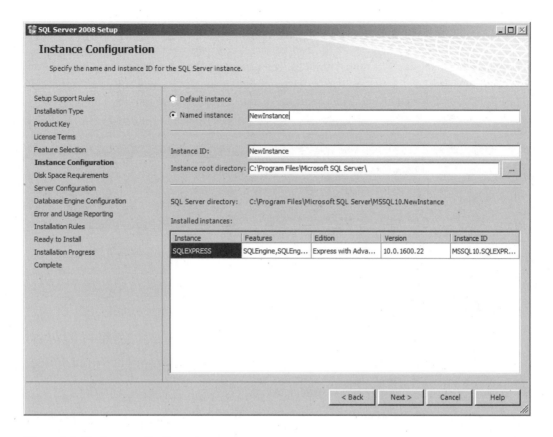

Figure 1-6. *The Instance Configuration screen*

NAMED INSTANCES

Multiple SQL Server installations can run on one physical computer as long as they are SQL Server 2000 or newer. Each installation is called an *instance*. You may have only one default instance on a computer. Any additional instances must be named. To connect to SQL Server, you must specify the physical computer name. When working with named instances, you must specify the instance name as well. To connect to a default instance, only the computer name is required. When connecting to name instances, the computer name plus the instance name are required: computer*Name\instanceName*.

12. The Disk Space Requirements screen (Figure 1-7) will ensure that you have enough disk space for the install. However, "space for the install" refers to having space for the executable and other files such as the system databases. The system databases start out small but can grow quite large in a production system. The space requirements do not include any user databases, which are the databases that will store your data, so make sure you have room for them as well before clicking Next.

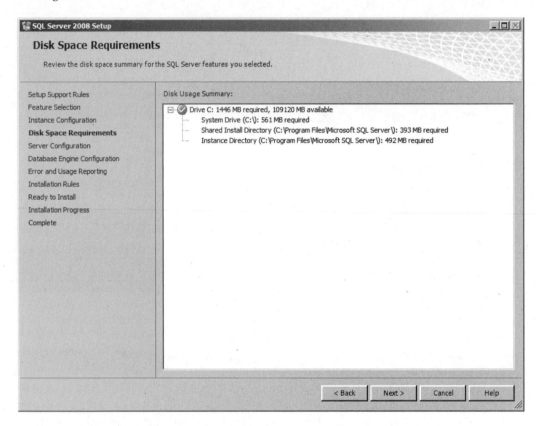

Figure 1-7. *The Disk Space Requirements screen*

13. On the Service Configuration screen, shown in Figure 1-8, you must specify accounts under which SQL Server will run. If you were setting up SQL Server for a production environment, you would probably have a special service account to use. Since you are just installing the Express edition for learning purposes here, choose NT Authority\System for the database engine account name, and accept the defaults for the other services.

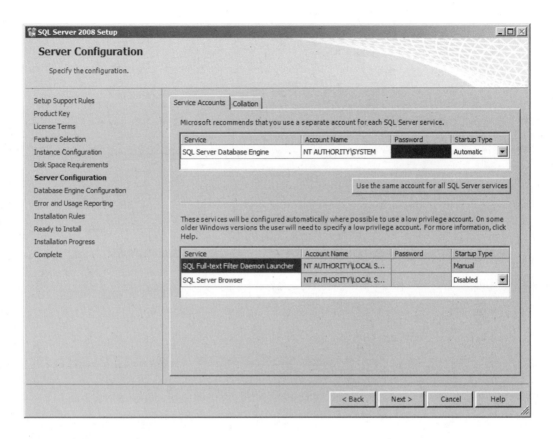

Figure 1-8. *Server Configuration screen*

14. On the Database Engine Configuration screen's Account Provisioning tab (Figure 1-9), you will either select the "Windows authentication mode" option or the Mixed Mode option. If you select "Windows authentication mode," SQL Server can accept connections only from Windows-authenticated accounts; if you selected Mixed mode, it can additionally allow accounts set up within SQL Server. For the purposes of the book, you can leave the authentication mode as "Windows authentication mode." Click the Add Current User button near the bottom of the page to make sure that the account you are using is added as an administrator.

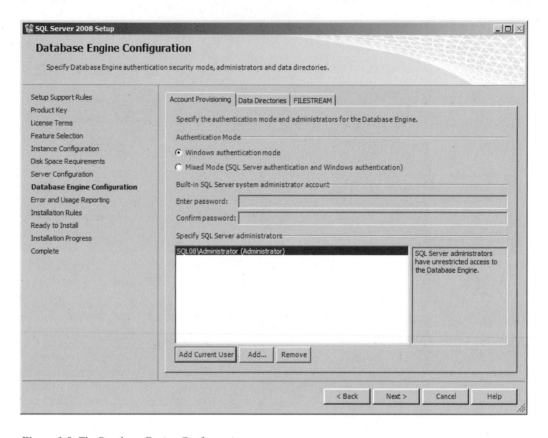

Figure 1-9. *The Database Engine Configuration screen*

15. On the Data Directories tab, you can specify directories for database and log files as well as all the other directories needed for your SQL Server instance. In a learning environment, the defaults are fine. On a production system, the database administrator will strategically place files for best performance.

16. Click the FILESTREAM tab on the current screen to enable FILESTREAM functionality as in Figure 1-10. FILESTREAM is an exciting new feature of SQL Server 2008 that you will learn more about in Chapter 9.

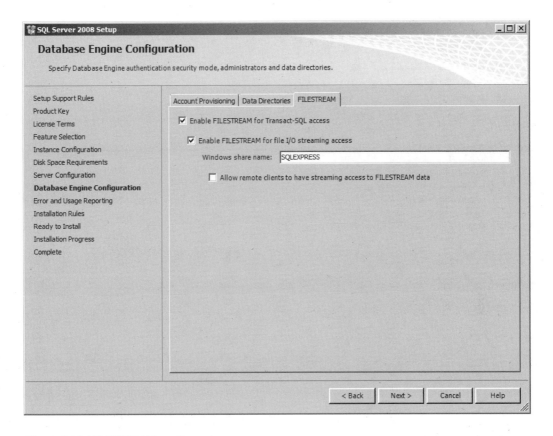

Figure 1-10. *FILESTREAM configuration*

17. Click Next after configuring FILESTREAM. You'll see an Error and Usage Reporting screen. Check the buttons on that screen to send reports to Microsoft if you choose to do that, and click Next again.

18. The installation performs more checks from the Installation Rules page that appears next, such as making sure that the settings you have selected will work. Click Next to continue.

19. A summary screen of what will be installed displays. Click Install, and the installation begins.

20. Once the install is complete, you can view a report to help you solve any issues with the installation. Figure 1-11 shows the report from a successful installation.

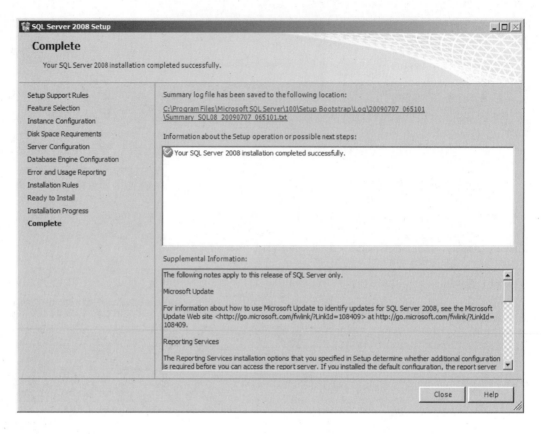

Figure 1-11. *A successful installation report*

21. Click the Close button. Congratulations! You have just installed SQL Server Express.

After the installation completes, the SQL Server Installation Center displays once more. You may be interested in viewing some of the resources available in this application at a later time. Luckily, you don't have to start the install again. You can run the Installation Center by selecting Start ➤ All Programs ➤ Microsoft SQL Server 2008 ➤ Configuration Tools ➤ SQL Server Installation Center at any time.

Installing the Sample Databases

Sample databases are very useful to help beginners practice writing code. Several databases, such as Pubs, Northwind, and AdventureWorks, have been available for this purpose over the many releases of SQL Server. Beginning with SQL Server 2005, you must purposely install the sample databases. You can download the sample databases from the CodePlex samples web site at `http://www.codeplex.com`. Because the link will change frequently as updated samples become available, search for *SQL Server*

2008 sample databases. Make sure you are downloading the latest version of the 2008 sample databases. Figure 1-12 shows a portion of the download page that was current the day that this section was written.

Figure 1-12. *The source for the AdventureWorks databases*

The following steps will guide you through installing the sample databases:

1. After clicking the appropriate link for your processor type and operating system, click I Agree to accept the license agreement.
2. Click Save to download the files.
3. Navigate to a location that you will remember, and click Save.
4. Once the download completes, click Run to start the installation if the download dialog box is still displayed. Otherwise, navigate to the file, and double-click to run it.
5. Click Next on the welcome screen (Figure 1-13).

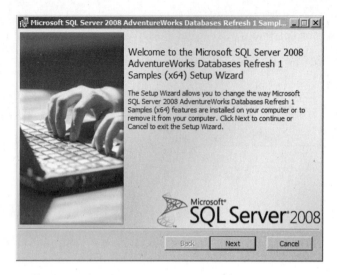

Figure 1-13. *The sample database welcome screen*

6. Accept the license agreement, and click Next.

7. Accept the defaults (Figure 1-14) on the Custom Setup page, and click Next.

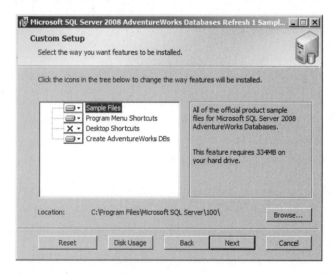

Figure 1-14. *Custom Setup page*

8. Choose the instance of SQL Server where you want the databases installed, as in Figure 1-15. The Read Carefully message mentions that FILESTREAM and Full-Text search must be installed. If you followed the earlier instructions for installing SQL Server Express, these features will be enabled. Click Next.

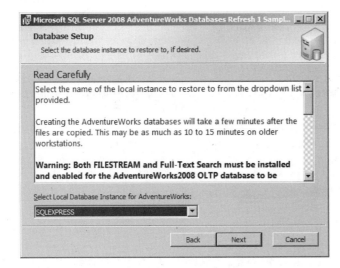

Figure 1-15. *Choosing the SQL Server instance*

9. Click Install, and wait while the installation does its work.
10. A final page displays (Figure 1-16) to confirm that the install is complete. Click Finish to dismiss the dialog box.

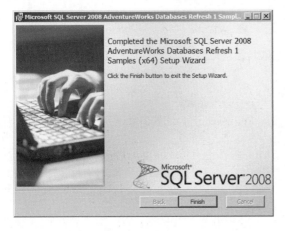

Figure 1-16. *The completed page*

You should now have several databases from the AdventureWorks family installed on your SQL Server instance. Your next step is to install SQL Server's help system, Books Online. Then I'll show you how to look at the AdventureWorks databases in the "Using SQL Server Management Studio" section.

Installing Books Online

If you have installed SQL Server Express edition, you will have to install the help system, SQL Server Books Online. From time to time Microsoft will offer an updated version of Books Online, much like updates to software, with corrections and new information.

Follow these steps to install SQL Server Books Online:

1. Navigate to `http://msdn.microsoft.com/en-us/sqlserver/cc514207.aspx` to find the latest release of Books Online, and download the file where you will be able to find it in the next step.

2. Double-click the file to start the installation.

3. After clicking Next, if you have a previous version of Books Online installed, you will have to uninstall it, as in Figure 1-17.

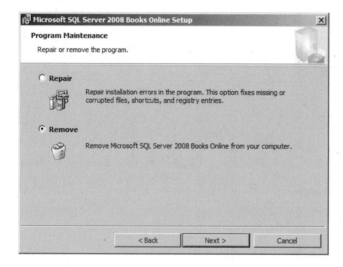

Figure 1-17. *Uninstalling a previous version*

4. If you had to uninstall the previous version, double-click the file to start the installation once again.

5. Continue clicking through the wizard until Books Online is installed (Figure 1-18) and click Finish.

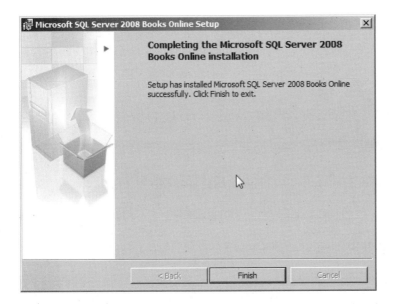

Figure 1-18. *Books Online install complete*

Using Books Online

Once SQL Server isBooks Online is installed, you can launch it by selecting Start ➤ All Programs ➤ Microsoft SQL Server 2008 ➤ Documentation and Tutorials ➤ SQL Server Books Online. You will also be able to launch it from SQL Server Management Studio, which I'll cover in the next section.

The screen for SQL Server Books Online is divided into two sections, as shown in Figure 1-19. On the left pane the contents are displayed. You can expand each entry to see the sections and double-click a topic to view each article on the right.

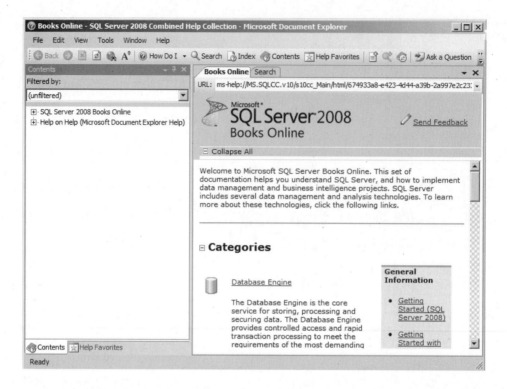

Figure 1-19. *The two panes of SQL Server Books Online*

The pane on the right has a tab for viewing the articles and a tab for searching. Type in a term, such as **query**, to see the results found in the local help system and articles posted online. On the right you'll see four links (Figure 1-20) where you can switch between Local Help, MSDN Online, Codezone Community, or Questions. The Codezone Community link features articles from web sites such as SQLServerCentral.com and SQLTeam.com.

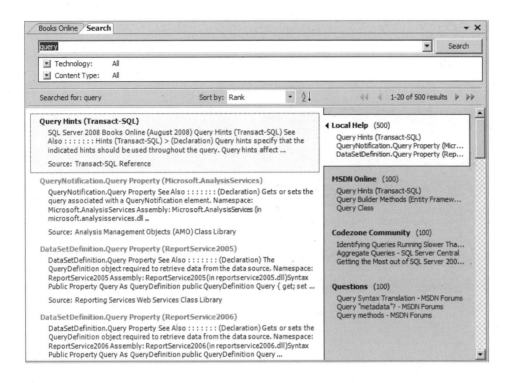

Figure 1-20. *Four links for different information sources*

Once you find an article or help topic you think you will want to view periodically, you can right-click and choose Add to Help Favorites. The Help Favorites tab is located on the left side of the screen. Click the Sync with Table of Contents button to find the actual location of the local article in the contents. If you decide that you would rather not see the online articles, you can select Tools ➤ Options and modify these settings.

You will learn how to write T-SQL from reading this book, but I recommend that you check Books Online frequently to learn even more!

Using SQL Server Management Studio

Now that you you have SQL Server, SQL Server Books Online, and thehave SQL Server, SQL Server Books Online, and the sample databases installed, it is time to get acquainted with SQL Server Management Studio (SSMS)). SSMS is the tool that ships with most editions of SQL Server, and you can use it to manage SQL Server and the databases as well as write T-SQL code. If you have installed SQL Server Express with Advanced Services as outlined earlier, you should be able to find SSMS by selecting Start ➤ All Programs ➤ Microsoft SQL Server 2008 ➤ SQL Server Management Studio. SSMS is your window into SQL Server. You can manage your database, create scripts, and—most importantly—execute T-SQL code and see the results.

Launching SQL Server Management Studio

Launch SSMS by selecting Start ➤ All Programs ➤ Microsoft SQL Server 2008 ➤ SQL Server Management Studio. After the splash screen displays, you will be prompted to connect to an instance of SQL Server, as shown in Figure 1-21.

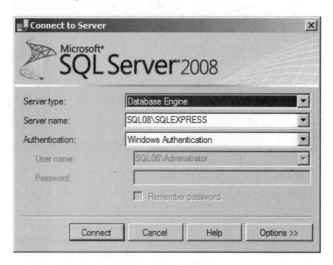

Figure 1-21. *Connect to Server dialog box*

Notice that in this example the computer name is SQL08 and the instance name is SQLEXPRESS. If you installed a default instance, you will need to specify only the computer name. You can also use (local), Localhost, or a period in place of the computer name as long as you are logged on locally and not trying to connect to a remote SQL Server. Make sure that the appropriate server name is filled in, and click Connect.

Once connected to an instance of SQL Server, you can view the databases and all the objects in the Object Explorer. The Object Explorer is located the left side of the screen by default. You can expand each item to see other items underneath. For example, once you expand the Databases folder, you can expand one of the databases. Then you can expand the Tables folder for that database. You can expand a table name and drill down to see the columns, indexes, and other properties. In the right pane, you can see details about the selected item. If you do not see the details, press the F7 key. Figure 1-22 shows the Object Explorer window and details.

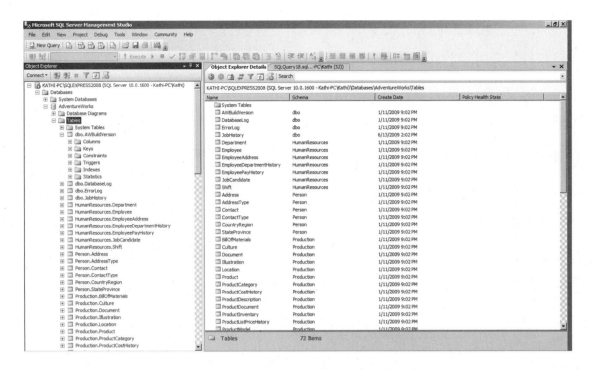

Figure 1-22. *The Object Explorer*

Running Queries

One SSMS feature that you will use extensively during this book is the Query Editor. In this window you will type and run queries as you learn about T-SQL. The following steps will guide you through writing your first query in the Query Editor:

1. Make sure your SQL Server instance is selected in the Object Explorer, and click New Query, which is located right above the Object Explorer to open the Query Editor window.

2. Select the AdventureWorks2008 database from the drop-down list on the left if it is not already selected, as in Figure 1-23.

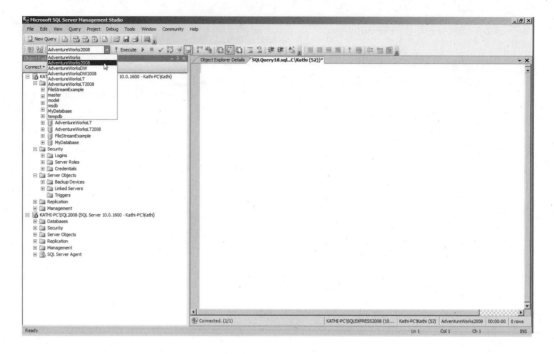

Figure 1-23. *The AdventureWorks2008 database*

3. Type the following code in the Query Editor window on the right. It's a query to display all the data in the Employee table.

```
SELECT * FROM HumanResources.Employee;
```

You will notice as you type that IntelliSense (Figure 1-24) is now available in the Query Editor window. IntelliSense helps you by eliminating keystrokes to save you time. It also validates the code before the code is compiled. IntelliSense is new for SQL Server 2008. It does not work when connecting to earlier versions of SQL Server.

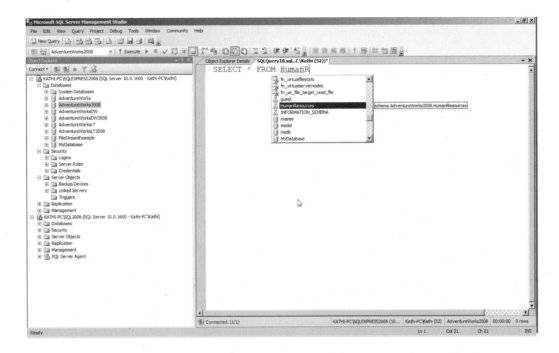

Figure 1-24. *IntelliSense*

4. Click Execute or press the F5 key to see the results, as in Figure 1-25.

	BusinessEntityID	NationalIDNumber	LoginID	OrganizationNode	OrganizationLevel	JobTitle
1	1	295847284	adventure-works\ken0	0x	0	Chief Executive Officer
2	2	245797967	adventure-works\terri0	0x58	1	Vice President of Engineering
3	3	509647174	adventure-works\roberto0	0x5AC0	2	Engineering Manager
4	4	112457891	adventure-works\rob0	0x5AD6	3	Senior Tool Designer
5	5	695256908	adventure-works\gail0	0x5ADA	3	Design Engineer
6	6	998320692	adventure-works\jossef0	0x5ADE	3	Design Engineer
7	7	134969118	adventure-works\dylan0	0x5AE1	3	Research and Development Manager
8	8	811994146	adventure-works\diane1	0x5AE158	4	Research and Development Engineer
9	9	658797903	adventure-works\gigi0	0x5AE168	4	Research and Development Engineer
10	10	879342154	adventure-works\michael6	0x5AE178	4	Research and Development Manager
11	11	974026903	adventure-works\ovidiu0	0x5AE3	3	Senior Tool Designer

Figure 1-25. *Results of running your first T-SQL query*

SSMS has several scripting features to help you write code. Follow these steps to learn how to create a query without typing:

1. Make sure that the Tables folder is expanded, and select the `HumanResources.Employee` table, as in Figure 1-26.

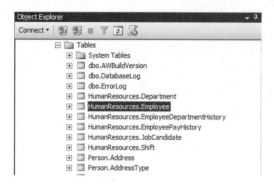

Figure 1-26. *The HumanResources.Employee table*

2. Right-click the `HumanResources.Employee` table, and select Script Table as ➤ Select to ➤ New Query Editor Window.

3. A new window will automatically open with some code (Figure 1-27). Click Execute.

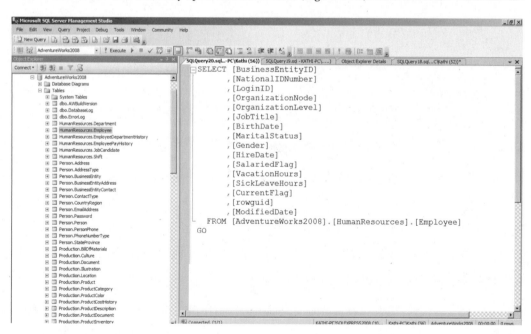

Figure 1-27. *Automatically generated code*

Sometimes you will end up with multiple statements in one Query Editor window. To run only some of the statements in the window, select what you want to run, and click Execute or press F5. Figure 1-28 shows an example. When you execute, only the first query will run.

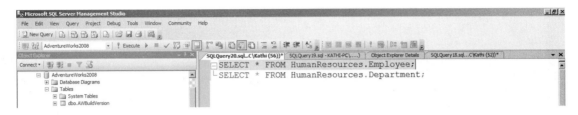

Figure 1-28. *Selected code*

Sections of code can be collapsed to get it out of your way by clicking the minus sign to the left of the code. You can search and replace just like a regular text editor, and, of course, you have IntelliSense to help you write the code.

Results can be saved to text files by clicking the Results to Text icon shown in Figure 1-29 before you execute the code. You can also select and copy the results for pasting into Excel or Notepad.

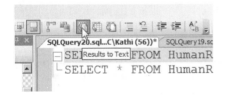

Figure 1-29. *Results to Text icon*

You can add documentation to your code or just keep code from running by adding comments. To comment a section of code, begin the section with **/*** and end the section with */. You can comment out a line of code or the end of a line of code with two . hyphens (**--**). To automatically comment out code, select the lines you want to comment, and click the Comment button shown in Figure 1-30. Uncomment by selecting commented lines and clicking the Uncomment button next to the Comment button.

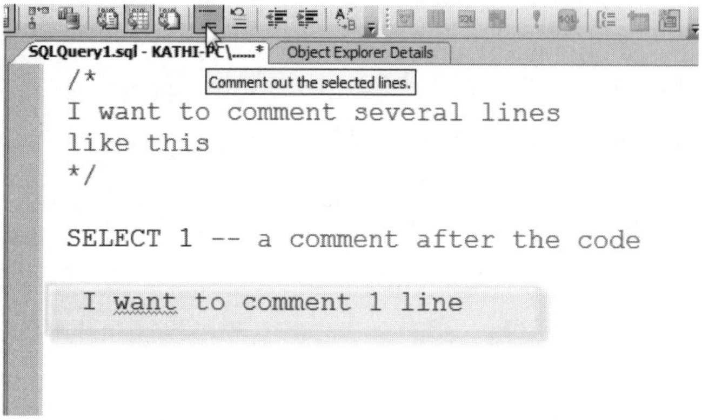

Figure 1-30. *Commented code*

The Object Explorer allows you to manage the databases, security, maintenance jobs, and other aspects of SQL Server. Most of the tasks that can be performed are in the realm of database administrators, so we will not explore them in this book.

Exploring Database Concepts

In this section, you will learn just what SQL Server is and about databases and objects that make up databases. You will learn how data is stored in a database, and you'll learn about objects, called *indexes*, that help SQL Server return the results of your queries quickly.

What Is SQL Server?

SQL Server is Microsoft's)relational database management system (RDBMS). A relational database management system stores data in tables according to the relational model. The relational model is beyond the scope of this book, but to learn more, read *Beginning Relational Data Modeling*, Second Edition, by Sharon Allen and Evan Terry (Apress, 2005).

Editions

Microsoft makes SQL Server available in many editions, including a free version (Express edition) that can be distributed with applications or used to learn about SQL Server as well as an expensive full-featured version (Enterprise edition) that is used to store terabytes of data in the most demanding enterprises. There is even a version that can be installed on smart phones (Compact edition). Search for the article "Features Supported by the Editions of SQL Server 2008" in SQL Server Books Online for more information about the editions and features of each. Table 1-1 gives an overview of the editions available.

Table 1-1. *SQL Server Editions*

Edition	Usage	Expense
Compact	Occasionally connected systems including mobile devices	Free
Express	Great for learning SQL Server and can be distributed with applications	Free
Web	Used for small web sites	Inexpensive
Workgroup	Used for workgroups or small database applications	Inexpensive
Developer	Full featured but used for development only	Inexpensive
Standard	Complete data platform with some high-availability and business intelligence features	Expensive
Enterprise	All available features	Very expensive

Many well-known companies trust SQL Server with their data. To read case studies about how some of these companies use SQL Server 2008, visit `http://www.microsoft.com/sqlserver/2008/en/us/case-studies.aspx`.

Service vs. Application

SQL Server is a service, not just an application. Even though you can install some of the versions on a regular workstation, it generally runs on a dedicated server and will run when the server starts; in other words, usually no one needs to manually start SQL Server. To minimize or practically eliminate downtime for critical systems, SQL Server boasts high-availability features such as clustering, log shipping, and database mirroring. Think about your favorite shopping web site. You expect it to be available any time day or night and every day. Behind the scenes, a database server, possibly a SQL Server instance, must be running and performing well at all times. Even during downtime for maintenance—when applying security patches, for example—administrators must keep downtime to a minimum.

SQL Server is feature rich, providing a complete business intelligence suite, impressive management tools, sophisticated data replication features, and much, much more. These features are well beyond the scope of this book, but I invite you to visit `http://www.apress.com` to find books to help you learn about these other topics if you are interested.

SQL Server does not come with a data-entry interface for regular users or even a way to create a web site or a Windows application. To do that, you will most likely use a programming language such as Visual Basic .NET or C#. Calls to SQL Server via T-SQL can be made within your application code or through a middle tier such as a web service. Regardless of your application architecture, at some point you'll use T-SQL. SQL Server does have a very nice reporting tool called Reporting Services that is part of the business intelligence suite. Otherwise, you will have to use another programming language to create your user interface.

Figure 1-31 shows the architecture of a typical web application. The web server requests data from the database server. The clients communicate with the web server.

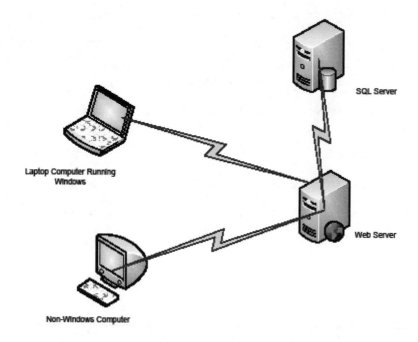

Figure 1-31. *The architecture of a typical web application*

Database As Container

A database in SQL Server is basically a container that holds several types of objects and data in an organized fashion. Generally, one database is used for a particular application or purpose, though this is not a hard and fast rule. For example, some systems have one database for all the enterprise applications required to run a business. On the other hand, one application could access more than one database.

Start SQL Server Management Studio if it is not already running, and connect to the SQL Server instance you installed in the "Installing SQL Server Express Edition" section. Expand the Databases folder to see the databases installed on the SQL Server. You should be able to see several sample databases, as in Figure 1-32.

Figure 1-32. *The databases*

Within a database, you will find several objects, but only one type of object, the table, holds the data that we usually think about. In addition to tables, a database can contain indexes, views, stored procedures, user-defined functions, and user-defined types among other objects. Later chapters in this book will cover most of the other objects that are used to make up a database. You'll find an introduction to indexes later in this chapter.

SQL SERVER FILES

A SQL Server database must be comprised of at least two files. One is the data file with the extension .mdf, and the other is the log file, with the extension .ldf. Additional data files, if they are used, will usually have the extension .ndf. Data files can be organized into multiple file groups. File groups are useful for strategically backing up only portions of the database at a time or to store the data on different drives for increased performance.

The log file in SQL Server stores transactions, or changes to the data, to ensure data consistency. Database administrators take frequent backups of the log files to allow the database to be restored to a point in time in case of data corruption, disk failure, or other disaster.

Data Is Stored in Tables

The most important objects in a database are tables because the tables are the objects that store the data and allow you to retrieve the data in an organized fashion. You can represent a table as a grid with columns and rows. The terminology used to describe the data in a database varies depending on the system, but in this book, I will stick with the terms *table*, *row*, and *column*. The following is an example of a table created to hold data about store owners:

CustomerID	Title	FirstName	MiddleName	LastName	Suffix	CompanyName
1	Mr.	Orlando	N.	Gee	NULL	A Bike Store
2	Mr.	Keith	NULL	Harris	NULL	Progressive Sports
3	Ms.	Donna	F.	Carreras	NULL	Advanced Bike Components
4	Ms.	Janet	M.	Gates	NULL	Modular Cycle Systems

In a properly designed database, each table holds information about one type of entity. An entity type might be a student, customer, or vehicle, for example. Each row in a table contains the information about one instance of the entity represented by that table. For example, a row will represent one student, one customer, or one vehicle. Each column in the table will contain one piece of information about the entity. In the vehicle table, there might be a VIN column, a make column, a model column, a color column, and a year column, among others.

Each column within a table has a definition specifying a data type along with rules, called *constraints*, ,that enforce the values that can be stored. Constraints include whether a column can be left blank, whether it must be unique, whether it is limited to a certain range of values, and so on. You will learn more about constraints in Chapter 8.

In a well-designed database, each table will have a primary key that is used to uniquely identify each row. In the previous example, the primary key is CustomerID.

■ **Note** You will learn what NULL means in Chapter 2.

Data Types

SQL Server has a rich assortment of data types for storing strings, numbers, money, XML, binary, and temporal data. Start SQL Server Management Studio if it is not running already, and connect to the SQL Server you installed in the "Installing SQL Server Express Edition" section. Expand the Databases section. Expand the AdventureWorks2008 database and the Tables section. Locate the HumanResources.Employee table, and right-click it. Select the Design option to view the properties (see Figure 1-33).

	Column Name	Data Type	Allow Nulls
🔑	BusinessEntityID	int	☐
	NationalIDNumber	nvarchar(15)	☐
▶	LoginID	nvarchar(256)	☐
	OrganizationNode	hierarchyid	☑
	OrganizationLevel		☑
	JobTitle	nvarchar(50)	☐
	BirthDate	date	☐
	MaritalStatus	nchar(1)	☐
	Gender	nchar(1)	☐
	HireDate	date	☐
	SalariedFlag	Flag:bit	☐
	VacationHours	smallint	☐
	SickLeaveHours	smallint	☐
	CurrentFlag	Flag:bit	☐
	rowguid	uniqueidentifier	☐
	ModifiedDate	datetime	☐
			☐

Figure 1-33. *The properties of the* HumanResources.Employee *table*

The HumanResources.Employee table contains a variety of data types and one column, OrganizationalLevel, with no data type defined. The OrganizationalLevel column is a computed column consisting of a formula.

SalariedFlag and CurrentFlag have the Flag user-defined data type, which is defined within the database. Developers can create user-defined data types to simplify table creation and to ensure consistency. For example, the AdventureWorks2008 database has a Phone data type used whenever a column contains phone numbers. To see the Phone data type definition, expand the Programmability section, the Type section, and the User Defined Data Types section. Locate and double-click the Phone data type to see the properties (see Figure 1-34).

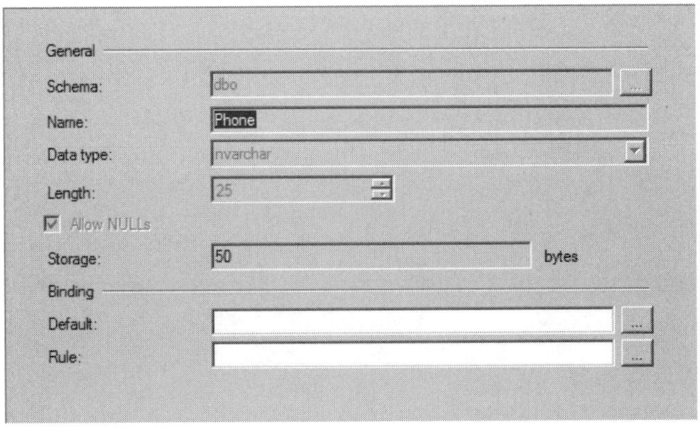

Figure 1-34. *The properties of the Phone user-defined data type*

Beginning with SQL Server 2005, developers can create custom data types, called *CLR data types*, with multiple properties and methods using a .NET language such as C#. Creating CLR data types is beyond the scope of this book, but Chapter 9 covers three built-in CLR data types: `HIERARCHYID`, `GEOMETRY`, and `GEOGRAPHY`. The `OrganizationNode` column is a `HIERARCHYID`. You will find a wealth of information about data types in SQL Server Books Online by searching on the data type that interests you.

Normalization

Normalization is the process of designing database tables in a way that makes for efficient use of disk space and that allows the efficient manipulation and updating of the data. Normalization is especially important in online transaction processing (OLTP) databases, such as those used in e-commerce. Database architects usually design reporting-only databases to be denormalized to speed up data retrieval since they do not have to worry about frequent data updates.

The process of normalization is beyond the scope of this book, but it is helpful to understand why databases are normalized. To learn more about normalization, see the book *Pro SQL Server 2008 Relational Database Design and Implementation* by Louis Davidson, Kevin Kline, Scott Klein, and Kurt Windisch (Apress, 2008).

Figure 1-35 shows how a database design might look before it is normalized. The example is of an order-entry database. There is one table, and that table consists of data about both customers and orders. One problem that you can probably see straightaway is that there is room only for three items per order and only three orders per customer.

CustomerOrders
CustomerID
Title
FirstName
LastName
CompanyName
AddressLine1
AddressLine2
City
State_Province
Country
PostalCode
OrderID1
OrderDate1
OrderItem1_1
OrderQty1_1
OrderItem1_2
OrderQty1_2
OrderItem1_3
OrderQty1_3
OrderItem2_1
OrderQty2_1
OrderItem2_2
OrderQty2_2
OrderItem2_3
OrderQty2_3
OrderItem3_1
OrderQty3_1
OrderItem3_2
OrderQty3_2
OrderItem3_3

Figure 1-35. *The denormalized database*

Figure 1-36 shows how the database might look once it is normalized. In this case, the database contains a table to hold information about the customer and a table to contain information about the order, such as the order date. The database contains a separate table to hold the items ordered. The order table contains a `CustomerID` that determines the customer instead of containing all the customer information. The `orderDetail` table allows as many items as needed per order. The `OrderDetail` table contains the `OrderID` column to specify the correct order.

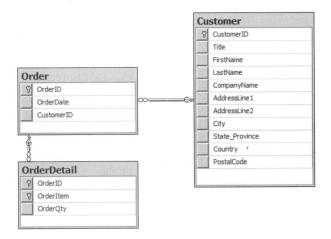

Figure 1-36. The normalized database

It may seem like a lot of trouble to properly define a database up front. However, it is well worth the effort to do so. I was called in once to help create reports on one of the most poorly designed databases I have ever seen a few years ago. This was a small Microsoft Access database that was used to record information from interviewing users at a medium-sized company about the applications that the employees used. Each time a new application was entered into the database, a new Yes/No column for that application was created, and the data-entry form had to be modified. The developer, who should have known better, told me that she just didn't have time to create a properly normalized database. Much more time was spent fighting with this poor design than would have been spent properly designing the database.

Understanding Indexes

When a user runs a query to retrieve a portion of the rows from a table, how does the database engine determine which rows to return? If the table has indexes defined on it, SQL Server may use the indexes to find the appropriate rows.

There are several types of indexes, but this section covers two types: clustered and nonclustered. A *clustered index* stores and organizes the table. A *nonclustered index* is defined on one or more columns of the table, but it is a separate structure that points to the actual table. Both types of indexes are optional, but they can greatly improve the performance of queries when properly designed and maintained. A couple of analogies will help explain how indexes work.

A printed phone directory is a great example of a clustered index. Each entry in the directory represents one row of the table. A table can have only one clustered index. That is because a clustered index is the actual table organized in order of the cluster key. At first glance, you might think that inserting a new row into the table would require all the rows after the inserted row to be moved on the disk. Luckily, this is not the case. The row will have to be inserted into the correct data page. A list of pointers maintains the order between the pages, so the rows in other pages will not have to actually move.

The primary key of the phone directory is the phone number. Usually the primary key is used as the clustering key as well, but this is not the case in our example. The cluster key in the phone directory is a combination of the last name and first name. How would you find a friend's phone number if you knew the last and first name? Easy—you would open the book approximately to the section of the book that contains the entry. If your friend's last name starts with an *F*, you search near the beginning of the book; if it starts with an *S*, you search toward the back. You can use the names printed at the top of the page to quickly locate the page with the listing. You then drill down to the section of the correct page until you find the last name of your friend. Now you can use the first name to choose the correct listing. The phone number is right there next to the name. It probably takes more time describe the process than to actually do it. Using the last name plus the first name to find the number is called a *clustered index seek*.

The index in the back of a book is an example of a nonclustered index. A nonclustered index has the indexed columns and a pointer or bookmark pointing to the actual row. In the case of our example, it contains a page number. Another example could be a search done on Google, Bing, or another search engine. The results on the page contain links to the original web pages. The thing to remember about nonclustered indexes is that you may have to retrieve part of the required information from the rows in the table. When using a book index, you will probably have to turn to the page of the book. When searching on Google, you will probably have to click the link to view the original page. If all the information you need is included in the index, you have no need to visit the actual data.

Although you can have only one clustered index per table, you can have up to 999 nonclustered indexes per table. If you ever need that many, you might have a design problem! An important thing to keep in mind is that although indexes can improve the performance of queries, indexes take up disk space and require resources to maintain. If a table has four nonclustered indexes, every write to that table may require four additional writes to keep the indexes up-to-date.

I just mentioned that 999 nonclustered indexes is too many. When talking about databases, an answer I hear all the time is "It depends." The number of indexes allowed per table increased with the release of SQL Server 2008 to take advantage of a couple of new features: sparse columns and filtered indexes. You will learn more about sparse columns in Chapter 9.

Database Schemas

Schemas are part of a new security model introduced in SQL Server 2005. A schema is a container that you can use to organize database objects.

■ **Note** Objects in earlier versions of SQL Server were owned by database users. In SQL Server 2005 and later, a user can own a schema, but not individual objects.

Historically, database designers have often created all objects to be owned by the dbo user, or the database owner. This practice simplifies the naming of objects and makes managing security easier. You can take the same approach in SQL Server 2005 and 2008. The difference is that now you'll create those objects all in the dbo schema. You will designate the schema by using the fully qualified name of the object. A schema is a way to organize the tables and object within the database. For example, the AdventureWorks2008 database contains several schemas based on the purpose: HumanResources, Person, Production, Purchasing, and Sales. Each table or other object belongs to one of the schemas.

A user can have a default schema. When accessing an object in the default schema, the user does not have to specify the schema name; however, it is a good practice to do so. If the user has permission to create new objects, the objects will belong to the user's default schema unless specified otherwise. To access objects outside the default schema, the schema name must be used. Table 1-2 shows several objects along with the schema.

Table 1-2. *Schemas Found in AdventureWorks2008*

Name	Schema	Object
HumanResources.Employee	HumanResources	Employee
Sales.SalesOrderDetail	Sales	SalesOrderDetail
Person.Address	Person	Address

Summary

This chapter provided a quick tour of SQL Server. You learned how databases are structured and designed and how SQL Server uses indexes to efficiently return data. If you followed the instructions in this chapter, you now have an instance of SQL Server running on your workstation or laptop so that you have a place to practice the queries you are about to learn.

In Chapter 2 you will get a chance to write your own queries. You'll learn the **SELECT** statement, the next step in your journey to T-SQL mastery.

■ ■ ■

CHAPTER 2

Writing Simple SELECT Queries

In Chapter 1 you prepared prepared your computeryour computer by installing SQL Server Express and the AdventureWorks2008 sample databases. You learned how to get around in SQL Server Management Studio and learned a few other tips to help make writing queries easier.

Now that you are ready, it is time to learn how to retrieve data from a SQL Server database. You will retrieve data from SQL Server using the **SELECT** statement, starting with the simplest syntax. This chapter will cover the different parts, called *clauses*, of the **SELECT** statement so that you will be able to not only retrieve data but also filter and order it. The ultimate goal is to learn to get exactly the data you need from your database—no more, no less.

Beginning in this chapter, you will find many code examples. Even though all the code is available from this book's catalog pages at `http://www.apress.com`, you will probably find that by typing the examples yourself you will learn more quickly. As they say, practice makes perfect! In addition, exercises follow many of the sections so that you can practice using what you have just learned. You can find the answers for each set of exercises in the appendix.

■ **Note** If you take a look at SQL Server Books Online, you will find the syntax displayed for each kind of statement. Books Online displays every possible parameter and option, which is not always helpful when learning about a new concept for the first time. In this book, you will find only the syntax that applies to the topic that is being discussed at the time.

Using the SELECT Statement

You use the **SELECT** statement to retrieve data from SQL Server. T-SQL requires only the word **SELECT** followed by at least one item in what is called a *select-list*.

If SQL Server Management Studio is not running, go ahead and start it. When prompted to connect to SQL Server, enter the name of the SQL Server instance you installed while reading Chapter 1 or the name of your development SQL Server. You will need the AdventureWorks2008 sample databases installed to follow along with the examples and to complete the exercises. You will find instructions for installing the sample databases in Chapter 1.

Selecting a Literal Value

Perhaps the simplest form of a **SELECT** statement is that used to return a literal value that you specify. Begin by clicking New Query to open a new query window. Listing 2-1 shows two **SELECT** statements that both return a literal value. Notice the single quote mark that is used to designate the string value. Type each line of the code from Listing 2-1 into your query window.

Listing 2-1. Statements Returning Literal Values

```
SELECT 1
SELECT 'ABC'
```

After typing the code in the query window, press F5 or click Execute to run the code. You will see the results displayed in two windows at the bottom of the screen, as shown in Figure 2-1. Because you just ran two statements, two sets of results are displayed.

■ **Tip** By highlighting one or more statements in the query window, you can run just a portion of the code. For example, you may want to run one statement at a time. Use the mouse to select the statements you want to run, and press F5.

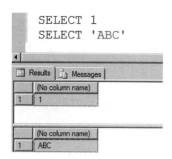

Figure 2-1. The results of running your first T-SQL statements

Notice the Messages tab next to the Results tab. Click Messages, and you will see the number of rows affected by the statements, as well as any error or informational messages. If an error occurs, you will see the Messages tab selected by default instead of the Results tab when the statement execution completes. You can then find the results, if any, by clicking the Results tab.

Retrieving from a Table

You will usually want to retrieve data from a table instead of literal values. After all, if you already know what value you want, you probably don't need to execute a query to get that value.

In preparation for retrieving data from a table, either delete the current code or open a new query window. Change to the example database by typing and running **Use AdventureWorks2008** or by selecting the AdventureWorks2008 database from the drop-down list, as shown in Figure 2-2.

Figure 2-2. *Choosing the AdventureWorks2008 database*

You use the **FROM** clause to specify a table name in a **SELECT** statement. The **FROM** clause is the first part of the statement that the database engine evaluates and processes. Here is the syntax for the **SELECT** statement with a **FROM** clause:

```
SELECT <column1>, <column2> FROM <schema>.<table>;
```

Type in and execute the code in Listing 2-2 to learn how to retrieve data from a table.

Listing 2-2. *Writing a Query with a FROM Clause*

```
USE AdventureWorks2008;
GO
SELECT BusinessEntityID, JobTitle
FROM HumanResources.Employee;
```

The first statement in Listing 2-2 switches the connection to the AdventureWorks2008 database if it is not already connected to AdventureWorks2008. The word **GO** doesn't really do anything except divide the code up into separate distinct code batches.

When retrieving from a table, you still have a select-list as in Listing 2-1; however, your select-list typically contains column names from a table. The select-list in Listing 2-2 requests data from the **BusinessEntityID** and **JobTitle** columns, which are both found in the **Employee** table. The **Employee** table is in turn found in the **HumanResources** schema.

Figure 2-3 shows the output from executing the code in Listing 2-2. There is only one set of results, because there is only one **SELECT** statement.

Results

	BusinessEntityID	Job Title
1	1	Chief Executive Officer
2	2	Vice President of Engineering
3	3	Engineering Manager
4	4	Senior Tool Designer
5	5	Design Engineer
6	6	Design Engineer
7	7	Research and Development Manager
8	8	Research and Development Engineer
9	9	Research and Development Engineer
10	10	Research and Development Manager
11	11	Senior Tool Designer
12	12	Tool Designer
13	13	Tool Designer
14	14	Senior Design Engineer
15	15	Design Engineer
16	16	Marketing Manager
17	17	Marketing Assistant
18	18	Marketing Specialist
19	19	Marketing Assistant
20	20	Marketing Assistant

Figure 2-3. The partial results of running a query with a FROM clause

Notice that the **FROM** clause in Listing 2-2 specifies the table name in two parts: **HumanResources.Employee**. The first part—**HumanResources**—is a schema name. In SQL Server 2008, groups of related tables can be organized together as schemas. You don't always need to provide those schema names, but it's a best practice to do so. Two schemas can potentially each contain a table named **Employee**, and those would be different tables with different data. Specifying the schema name as part of your table reference eliminates a source of potential confusion and error.

To retrieve all the columns from a table, you can use the * symbol, also known as *asterisk, star,* or *splat.* Run the following statement to try this shortcut: **SELECT * FROM HumanResources.Employee**. You will see that all the columns from the table are returned.

The asterisk technique is useful for performing a quick query, but avoid it in a production application or process. Retrieving more data than you really need may have a negative impact on performance. Why retrieve all the columns from a table and pull more data across the network when you need only a few columns? Application code may break if an additional column is added to or removed from the table. Additionally, there might be security reasons for returning only some of the columns. Best practice is to write select-lists specifying exactly the columns that you need.

Generating a Select-List

You might think that typing all the required columns for a select-list is tedious work. Luckily, SQL Server Management Studio provides a shortcut for writing good **SELECT** statements. Follow these instructions to learn the shortcut:

1. In the Object Explorer, expand Databases.
2. Expand the AdventureWorks2008 database.
3. Expand Tables.
4. Right-click the HumanResources.Employee table.
5. Choose Script Table as ➤ Select To ➤ New Query Editor Window.

You now have a properly formed **SELECT** statement, as shown in Listing 2-3, that retrieves all the columns from the **HumanResources.Employee** table. You can easily remove any unneeded columns from the query.

Listing 2-3. A Scripted SELECT Statement

```
SELECT [BusinessEntityID]
      ,[NationalIDNumber]
      ,[LoginID]
      ,[OrganizationNode]
      ,[OrganizationLevel]
      ,[JobTitle]
      ,[BirthDate]
      ,[MaritalStatus]
      ,[Gender]
      ,[HireDate]
      ,[SalariedFlag]
      ,[VacationHours]
      ,[SickLeaveHours]
      ,[CurrentFlag]
      ,[rowguid]
      ,[ModifiedDate]
  FROM [AdventureWorks2008].[HumanResources].[Employee]
GO
```

Notice the brackets around the names in Listing 2-3. Column and table names need to follow specific naming rules so that SQL Server's parser can recognize them. When a table, column, or database has a name that doesn't follow those rules, you can still use that name, but you must enclose it within square brackets ([]). Automated tools often enclose *all* names within square brackets as a "just-in-case" measure.

Also notice that the **FROM** clause in Listing 2-3 mentions the database name: [AdventureWorks2008]. You need to specify a database name only when accessing a database other than the one to which you are currently connected. For example, if you are currently connected to the master database, you can access data from AdventureWorks2008 by specifying the database name. Again, though, automated tools often specify the database name regardless.

Mixing Literals and Column Names

You can mix literal values and column names in one statement. Listing 2-4 shows an example. Notice the keyword **AS** after the literal value. You use the keyword **AS** to specify an alias for the column. An *alias* is a column name that you create on the fly.

Listing 2-4. Mixing Literal Values and Column Names

```
USE AdventureWorks2008;
GO
SELECT 'A Literal Value' AS "Literal Value",
    BusinessEntityID AS EmployeeID,
    LoginID JobTitle
FROM HumanResources.Employee;
```

Go ahead and execute the query in Listing 2-4. You should see results similar to those in Figure 2-4. Notice the column names in your results. The column names are the aliases that you specified in your query. You can alias any column, giving you complete control over the headers for your result sets.

	Literal Value	EmployeeID	Job Title
1	A Literal Value	225	adventure-works\alan0
2	A Literal Value	193	adventure-works\alejandro0
3	A Literal Value	163	adventure-works\alex0
4	A Literal Value	109	adventure-works\alice0
5	A Literal Value	287	adventure-works\amy0
6	A Literal Value	214	adventure-works\andreas0
7	A Literal Value	47	adventure-works\andrew0
8	A Literal Value	164	adventure-works\andrew1
9	A Literal Value	149	adventure-works\andy0
10	A Literal Value	115	adventure-works\angela0
11	A Literal Value	137	adventure-works\anibal0
12	A Literal Value	260	adventure-works\annette0
13	A Literal Value	33	adventure-works\annik0
14	A Literal Value	252	adventure-works\arvind0
15	A Literal Value	222	adventure-works\ascott0
16	A Literal Value	265	adventure-works\ashvini0
17	A Literal Value	183	adventure-works\barbara0
18	A Literal Value	245	adventure-works\barbara1
19	A Literal Value	131	adventure-works\baris0

Figure 2-4. The results of using aliases

The keyword **AS** is optional. You can specify an alias name immediately following a column name. If an alias contains a space or is a reserved word, you can surround the alias with square brackets, single quotes, or double quotes. If the alias follows the rules for naming objects, the quotes or square brackets are not required.

Be aware that any word listed immediately after a column within the select list is treated as an alias. If you forget to add the comma between two column names, the second column name will be used as the alias for the first. Omitting the comma like that is a common error. Look carefully at the query in Listing 2-4, and you'll see that the intent is to display the **LoginID** and **JobTitle** columns. Because the comma was left out between those two column names, the name of the **LoginID** column was changed to **JobTitle**. **JobTitle** was treated as an alias rather than as an additional column. Watch for and avoid that common mistake.

Reading about T-SQL and typing in code examples are wonderful ways to learn. The best way to learn, however, is to figure out the code for yourself. Imagine learning how to swim by reading about it instead of jumping into the water. Practice now with what you have learned so far. Follow the instructions in Exercise 2-1, and write a few queries to test what you know.

Exercise 2-1

For this exercise, switch to the AdventureWorksLT2008 database. That database is a very simplified version of AdventureWorks2008, but it is perfect for learning queries that access only one table. You can find the solutions in the appendix.

Remember that you can expand the tables in the Object Explorer to see the list of table names and then expand the table to see the list of column names.

Now, try your hand at writing the following tasks:

1. Write a **SELECT** statement that lists the customers along with their ID numbers. Include the last names, first names, and company names.
2. Write a **SELECT** statement that lists the name, product number, and color of each product.
3. Write a **SELECT** statement that lists the customer ID numbers and sales order ID numbers from the **SalesLT.SalesOrderHeader** table.
4. Answer this question: why should you specify column names rather than an asterisk when writing the select-list? Give at least two reasons.

Filtering Data

Usually an application requires only a fraction of the rows from a table at any given time. For example, an order-entry application that shows the order history will need to display the orders for only one customer at a time. There might be millions of orders in the database, but the operator of the software will view only a handful of rows instead of the entire table. Filtering data is a very important part of T-SQL.

Adding a WHERE Clause

To filter the rows returned from a query, you will add a **WHERE** clause to your **SELECT** statement. The database engine processes the **WHERE** clause second, right after the **FROM** clause. The **WHERE** clause will contain expressions, called *predicates*, that can be evaluated to **TRUE**, **FALSE**, or **UNKNOWN**. You will learn more about **UNKNOWN** in the "Working with Nothing" section later in the chapter. The **WHERE** clause syntax is as follows:

```
SELECT <column1>,<column2>
FROM <schema>.<table>
WHERE <column> = <value>;
```

Listing 2-5 shows the syntax and some examples demonstrating how to compare a column to a literal value. The following examples are from the AdventureWorks2008 database unless specified otherwise. Be sure to type each query into the query window and execute the statement to see how it works. Make sure you understand how the expression in the **WHERE** clause affects the results returned by each query. Notice that tick marks, or single quotes, have been used around literal strings and dates.

Listing 2-5. How to Use the WHERE Clause

```
USE AdventureWorks2008;
GO
--1
SELECT CustomerID, SalesOrderID
FROM Sales.SalesOrderHeader
WHERE CustomerID = 11000;


--2
SELECT CustomerID, SalesOrderID
FROM Sales.SalesOrderHeader
WHERE SalesOrderID = 43793;


--3
SELECT CustomerID, SalesOrderID, OrderDate
FROM Sales.SalesOrderHeader
WHERE OrderDate = '2001-07-01';


--4
SELECT BusinessEntityID, LoginID, JobTitle
FROM HumanResources.Employee
WHERE JobTitle = 'Chief Executive Officer';
```

Each query in Listing 2-5 returns rows that are filtered by the expression in the **WHERE** clause. Be sure to check the results of each query to make sure that the expected rows are returned (see Figure 2-5). Each query returns only the information specified in that query's **WHERE** clause.

Results

	CustomerID	SalesOrderID
1	11000	43793
2	11000	51522
3	11000	57418

	CustomerID	SalesOrderID
1	11000	43793

	CustomerID	SalesOrderID	OrderDate
1	29825	43659	2001-07-01 00:00:00.000
2	29672	43660	2001-07-01 00:00:00.000
3	29734	43661	2001-07-01 00:00:00.000
4	29994	43662	2001-07-01 00:00:00.000
5	29565	43663	2001-07-01 00:00:00.000
6	29898	43664	2001-07-01 00:00:00.000
7	29580	43665	2001-07-01 00:00:00.000
8	30052	43666	2001-07-01 00:00:00.000

	BusinessEntityID	LoginID	JobTitle
1	1	adventure-works\ken0	Chief Executive Officer

Figure 2-5. *The results of using the* `WHERE` *clause*

Using WHERE Clauses with Alternate Operators

Within `WHERE` clause expressions, you can use many comparison operators, not just the equal sign. Books Online lists the following operators:

> (greater than)

< (less than)

= (equals)

<= (less than or equal to)

>= (greater than or equal to)

!= (not equal to)

<> (not equal to)

!< (not less than)

!> (not greater than)

Type in and execute the queries in Listing 2-6 to practice using these additional operators in the `WHERE` clause.

Listing 2-6. Using Operators with the WHERE Clause

```
USE AdventureWorks2008;
GO
--Using a DateTime column
--1
SELECT CustomerID, SalesOrderID, OrderDate
FROM Sales.SalesOrderHeader
WHERE OrderDate > '2001-07-05';


--2
SELECT CustomerID, SalesOrderID, OrderDate
FROM Sales.SalesOrderHeader
WHERE OrderDate < '2001-07-05';


--3
SELECT CustomerID, SalesOrderID, OrderDate
FROM Sales.SalesOrderHeader
WHERE OrderDate >= '2001-07-05';


--4
SELECT CustomerID, SalesOrderID, OrderDate
FROM Sales.SalesOrderHeader
WHERE OrderDate <> '2001-07-05';


--5
SELECT CustomerID, SalesOrderID, OrderDate
FROM Sales.SalesOrderHeader
WHERE OrderDate != '2001-07-05';


--Using a numeric column
--6
SELECT SalesOrderID, SalesOrderDetailID, OrderQty
FROM Sales.SalesOrderDetail
WHERE OrderQty > 10;


--7
SELECT SalesOrderID, SalesOrderDetailID, OrderQty
FROM Sales.SalesOrderDetail
WHERE OrderQty <= 10;
```

```
--8
SELECT SalesOrderID, SalesOrderDetailID, OrderQty
FROM Sales.SalesOrderDetail
WHERE OrderQty <> 10;


--9
SELECT SalesOrderID, SalesOrderDetailID, OrderQty
FROM Sales.SalesOrderDetail
WHERE OrderQty != 10;


--Using a string column
--10
SELECT BusinessEntityID, FirstName
FROM Person.Person
WHERE FirstName <> 'Catherine';


--11
SELECT BusinessEntityID, FirstName
FROM Person.Person
WHERE FirstName != 'Catherine';


--12
SELECT BusinessEntityID, FirstName
FROM Person.Person
WHERE FirstName > 'M';


--13
SELECT BusinessEntityID, FirstName
FROM Person.Person
WHERE FirstName !> 'M';
```

Take a look at the results of each query to make sure that the results make sense and that you understand why you are getting them. Remember that both != and <> mean "not equal to" and are interchangeable. Using either operator should return the same results if all other aspects of a query are the same.

You may find the results of query 12 interesting. At first glance, you may think that only rows with the first name beginning with the letter *N* or later in the alphabet should be returned. However, if any **FirstName** value begins with *M* followed by at least one additional character, the value is greater than *M*, so the row will be returned. For example, *Ma* is greater than *M*.

Using BETWEEN

BETWEEN is another useful operator to be used in the WHERE clause. You can use it to specify an inclusive range of values. It is frequently used with dates but can be used with string and numeric data as well. Here is the syntax for BETWEEN:

```
SELECT <column1>,<column2>
FROM <schema>.<table>
WHERE <column> BETWEEN <value1> AND <value2>;
```

Type in and execute the code in Listing 2-7 to learn how to use BETWEEN.

Listing 2-7. Using BETWEEN

```
USE AdventureWorks2008
GO
--1
SELECT CustomerID, SalesOrderID, OrderDate
FROM Sales.SalesOrderHeader
WHERE OrderDate BETWEEN '2001-07-02' AND '2001-07-04';


--2
SELECT CustomerID, SalesOrderID, OrderDate
FROM Sales.SalesOrderHeader
WHERE CustomerID BETWEEN 25000 AND 25005;


--3
SELECT BusinessEntityID, JobTitle
FROM HumanResources.Employee
WHERE JobTitle BETWEEN 'C' and 'E';


--An invalid BETWEEN expression
--4
SELECT CustomerID, SalesOrderID, OrderDate
FROM Sales.SalesOrderHeader
WHERE CustomerID BETWEEN 25005 AND 25000;
```

Pay close attention to the results of Listing 2-7 shown in Figure 2-6. Query 1 returns all orders placed on the two dates specified in the query as well as the orders placed between the dates. You will see the same behavior from the second query—all orders placed by customers with customer IDs within the range specified. What can you expect from query 3? You will see all job titles that start with *C* or *D*. You will not see the job titles beginning with *E*, however. A job title composed of *only* the letter *E* would be returned in the results. Any job title beginning with *E* and at least one other character is greater than *E* and therefore not within the range. For example, the *Ex* in *Executive* is greater than just *E*, so any job titles beginning with *Executive* get eliminated.

	CustomerID	SalesOrderID	OrderDate
1	27645	43702	2001-07-02 00:00:00.000
2	16624	43703	2001-07-02 00:00:00.000
3	11005	43704	2001-07-02 00:00:00.000
4	11011	43705	2001-07-02 00:00:00.000
5	27621	43706	2001-07-03 00:00:00.000

	CustomerID	SalesOrderID	OrderDate
1	25000	73018	2004-06-15 00:00:00.000
2	25001	61662	2004-01-08 00:00:00.000
3	25002	61397	2004-01-03 00:00:00.000
4	25003	60269	2003-12-18 00:00:00.000
5	25004	74889	2004-07-24 00:00:00.000

	BusinessEntityID	Job Title
1	1	Chief Executive Officer
2	5	Design Engineer
3	6	Design Engineer
4	15	Design Engineer
5	217	Document Control M…

	CustomerID	SalesOrderID	OrderDate

Figure 2-6. The partial results of queries with BETWEEN

Query 4 returns no rows at all because the values listed in the **BETWEEN** expression are switched. No values meet the qualification of being greater than or equal to 25,005 and also less than or equal to 25,000. Make sure you always list the lower value first and the higher value second when using **BETWEEN**.

Using NOT BETWEEN

To find values outside a particular range of values, you write the **WHERE** clause expression using **BETWEEN** along with the **NOT** keyword. In this case, the query returns any rows outside the range. Try the examples in Listing 2-8, and compare them to the results
from Listing 2-7.

Listing 2-8. Using NOT BETWEEN

```
Use AdventureWorks2008
GO
--1
SELECT CustomerID, SalesOrderID, OrderDate
FROM Sales.SalesOrderHeader
WHERE OrderDate NOT BETWEEN '2001-07-02' AND '2001-07-04';
```

```
--2
SELECT CustomerID, SalesOrderID, OrderDate
FROM Sales.SalesOrderHeader
WHERE CustomerID NOT BETWEEN 25000 AND 25005;

--3
SELECT BusinessEntityID, JobTitle
FROM HumanResources.Employee
WHERE JobTitle NOT BETWEEN 'C' and 'E';

--An invalid BETWEEN expression
--4
SELECT CustomerID, SalesOrderID, OrderDate
FROM Sales.SalesOrderHeader
WHERE CustomerID NOT BETWEEN 25005 AND 25000;
```

Query 1 displays all orders placed before July 2, 2001 (`2001-07-02`), or after July 4, 2001 (`2001-07-04`)—in other words, any orders placed outside the range specified (see Figure 2-7). Query 2 displays the orders placed by customers with customer IDs less than 25,000 or greater than 25,005. When using the `NOT` operator with `BETWEEN`, the values specified in the expression do not show up in the results. Query 3 returns all job titles beginning with *A* and *B*. It also displays any job titles beginning with *E* and at least one more character, as well as any job titles starting with a letter greater than *E*. If a title consists of just the letter *E*, it will not show up in the results. This is just the opposite of what you saw in Listing 2-7.

Results

	CustomerID	SalesOrderID	OrderDate
1	29825	43659	2001-07-01 00:00:00.000
2	29672	43660	2001-07-01 00:00:00.000
3	29734	43661	2001-07-01 00:00:00.000
4	29994	43662	2001-07-01 00:00:00.000
5	29565	43663	2001-07-01 00:00:00.000

	CustomerID	SalesOrderID	OrderDate
1	29825	43659	2001-07-01 00:00:00.000
2	29672	43660	2001-07-01 00:00:00.000
3	29734	43661	2001-07-01 00:00:00.000
4	29994	43662	2001-07-01 00:00:00.000
5	29565	43663	2001-07-01 00:00:00.000

	BusinessEntityID	JobTitle
1	2	Vice President of Engineering
2	3	Engineering Manager
3	4	Senior Tool Designer
4	7	Research and Development Manager
5	8	Research and Development Engineer

	CustomerID	SalesOrderID	OrderDate
1	29825	43659	2001-07-01 00:00:00.000
2	29672	43660	2001-07-01 00:00:00.000
3	29734	43661	2001-07-01 00:00:00.000
4	29994	43662	2001-07-01 00:00:00.000
5	29565	43663	2001-07-01 00:00:00.000

Figure 2-7. *The partial results of queries with* `NOT BETWEEN`

Query 4 with the incorrect BETWEEN expression returns all the rows in the table. Since no customer ID values can be less than or equal to 25,005 and also be greater than or equal to 25,000, no rows meet the criteria in the BETWEEN expression. By adding the NOT operator, every row ends up in the results, probably not the original intent.

Filtering On Date and Time

Some temporal data columns store the time as well as the date. If you attempt to filter on such a column specifying only the date, you may retrieve incomplete results. Type in and run the code in Listing 2-9 to create and populate a temporary table that will be used to illustrate this issue. Don't worry about trying to understand the table creation code at this point.

Listing 2-9. Table Setup for Date/Time Example

```
CREATE TABLE #DateTimeExample(
    ID INT NOT NULL IDENTITY PRIMARY KEY,
    MyDate DATETIME2(0) NOT NULL,
    MyValue VARCHAR(25) NOT NULL
);
GO
INSERT INTO #DateTimeExample
    (MyDate,MyValue)
VALUES ('1/2/2009 10:30','Bike'),
    ('1/3/2009 13:00','Trike'),
    ('1/3/2009 13:10','Bell'),
    ('1/3/2009 17:35','Seat');
```

Now that the table is in place, type in and execute the code in Listing 2-10 to see what happens when filtering on the MyDate column.

Listing 2-10. Filtering On Date and Time Columns

```
--1
SELECT ID, MyDate, MyValue
FROM #DateTimeExample
WHERE MyDate = '2009-01-03';

--2
SELECT ID, MyDate, MyValue
FROM #DateTimeExample
WHERE MyDate BETWEEN '2009-01-03 00:00:00' AND '2009-01-03 23:59:59';
```

Figure 2-8 shows the results of the two queries. Suppose you want to retrieve a list of entries from January 3, 2009 (**2009-01-03**). Query 1 tries to do that but returns no results. Results will be returned only for entries where the **MyDate** value is precisely **2009-01-03 00:00:00**, and there are no such entries. The second query returns the expected results—all values where the date is **2009-01-03**. It does that by taking the time of day into account. To be even more accurate, the query could be written using two expressions: one filtering for dates greater than or equal to **2009-01-03** and another filtering for dates less than **2009-01-04**. You will learn how to write **WHERE** clauses with multiple expressions in the "Using WHERE Clauses with Two Predicates" section later in this chapter.

Figure 2-8. *Results of filtering on a date and time column*

You may be wondering what would happen if you formatted the date differently. Will you get the same results if slashes (/)(/)are used or if the month is spelled out (in other words, as **January 3, 2009**)? SQL Server does not store the date using any particular character-based format but rather as an integer representing the number of days between **1901-01-01** and the date specified. If the data type holds the time, the time is stored as the number of clock ticks past midnight. As long as you pass a date in an appropriate format, the value will be recognized as a date.

Writing **WHERE** clauses is as much an art as a skill. Take the time to practice what you have learned so far by completing Exercise 2-2.

Exercise 2-2

Use the AdventureWorks2008 database to complete this exercise. Be sure to run each query and check the results. You can go back and review the examples in the section if you don't remember how to write the queries. You can find the solutions in the appendix.

1. Write a query using a **WHERE** clause that displays all the employees listed in the **HumanResources. Employee** table who have the job title Research and Development Engineer. Display the business entity ID number, the login ID, and the title for each one.
2. Write a query using a **WHERE** clause that displays all the names in **Person.Person** with the middle name J. Display the first, last, and middle names along with the ID numbers.
3. Write a query displaying all the columns of the **Production.ProductCostHistory** table from the rows that were modified on June 17, 2003. Be sure to use one of the features in SQL Server Management Studio to help you write this query.
4. Rewrite the query you wrote in question 1, changing it so that the employees who do not have the title Research and Development Engineer are displayed.

5. Write a query that displays all the rows from the `Person.Person` table where the rows were modified after December 29, 2000. Display the business entity ID number, the name columns, and the modified date.
6. Rewrite the last query so that the rows that were not modified on December 29, 2000, are displayed.
7. Rewrite the query from question 5 so that it displays the rows modified during December 2000.
8. Rewrite the query from question 5 so that it displays the rows that were not modified during December 2000.
9. Explain why a `WHERE` clause should be used in many of your T-SQL queries.

Pattern Matching with LIKE

Sometimes you know only part of the value that will match the data stored in the table. For example, you may need to search for one word within a description. You can perform searches with pattern matching using wildcards to find one value within another value.

Pattern matching is possible by using the keyword `LIKE` in the expression instead of equal to or one of the other operators. Most of the time, the percent (**%**) character is used as a wildcard along with `LIKE` to represent any number of characters. Even though not used as often, you will also see the underscore (_) used as a wildcard to replace just one character. Type in and run the code from Listing 2-11 to learn how to use `LIKE`.

Listing 2-11. Using LIKE with %

```
USE AdventureWorks2008;
GO
--1
SELECT DISTINCT LastName
FROM Person.Person
WHERE LastName LIKE 'Sand%';


--2
SELECT DISTINCT LastName
FROM Person.Person
WHERE LastName NOT LIKE 'Sand%';


--3
SELECT DISTINCT LastName
FROM Person.Person
WHERE LastName LIKE '%Z%';


--4
SELECT DISTINCT LastName
FROM Person.Person
WHERE LastName LIKE 'Bec_';
```

The queries in Listing 2-11 contain the keyword **DISTINCT** to eliminate duplicates in the results shown in Figure 2-9. Query 1 returns all rows where the last name starts with *Sand*. Query 2 returns the opposite—it returns all the rows not returned by query 1, which are those rows where the last name does not start with *Sand*. Query 3 returns all rows that contain a *Z* anywhere in the last name. Query 4 will return only the last name *Beck* or any last name starting with *Bec* and one more character, but not the last name *Becker* since the underscore can replace only one character.

Figure 2-9. *The partial results of queries with* LIKE

Restricting the Characters in Pattern Matches

The value replacing a wildcard may be restricted to a list or range of characters. To do this, surround the possible values or range by square brackets ([ ]). Alternately, include the ^ symbol to list characters or the range of characters that you don't want to use as replacements. Here is the syntax for using brackets as the wildcard:

```
SELECT <column1>,<column2>
FROM <schema>.<table>
WERE <column> LIKE 'value[a-c]';

SELECT <column1>,<column2>
FROM <schema>.<table>
WERE <column> LIKE 'value[a,b,c]';
```

```
SELECT <column1>,<column2>
FROM <schema>.<table>
WERE <column> LIKE 'value[^d]';
```

Type in and execute the code from Listing 2-12, which shows some examples. You will probably not encounter the square bracket technique very often, but you should be familiar with the syntax in case you run into it.

Listing 2-12. Using Square Brackets with LIKE

```
USE AdventureWorks2008;
GO


--1
SELECT DISTINCT LastName
FROM Person.Person
WHERE LastName LIKE 'Cho[i-k]';


--2
SELECT DISTINCT LastName
FROM Person.Person
WHERE LastName LIKE 'Cho[i,j,k]';


--3
SELECT DISTINCT LastName
FROM Person.Person
WHERE LastName LIKE 'Cho[^i]';
```

Figure 2-10 displays the results of Listing 2-12. Queries 1 and 2 returns unique rows with a last name of *Choi, Choj,* or *Chok* because the pattern specifies the range *i* to *k*. Query 1 specifies the range of values, while query 2 explicitly lists the allowable values that may be replaced. Query 3 returns unique rows that have a last name beginning with *Cho* and ending with any character except for *i*.

Figure 2-10. The results of queries restricting characters in matches

Combining Wildcards

You may combine wildcards to create even more elaborate patterns. Remember that the percent sign (%) replaces any number of characters, the underscore (_) replaces one character, and the square brackets ([]) replace one character based on the values within the brackets. Listing 2-13 demonstrates some examples. Type in and execute the code to see how this works.

Listing 2-13. Combining Wildcards in One Pattern

```
USE AdventureWorks2008;
GO
--1
SELECT LastName
FROM Person.Person
WHERE LastName LIKE 'Ber[r,g]%';


--2
SELECT LastName
FROM Person.Person
WHERE LastName LIKE 'Ber[^r]%';


--3
SELECT LastName
FROM Person.Person
WHERE LastName LIKE 'Be%n_';
```

View Figure 2-11 to see the results. Query 1 returns all rows with a last name beginning with *Ber* followed by either *r* or *g* (which is signified by the characters within the brackets) and then by any number of characters. Query 2 returns all rows with a last name beginning with *Ber* followed by any letter except for *r* and then by any number of characters. Query 3 returns all rows with a last name beginning with *Be* followed by any number of characters, except that the next-to-last character must be an *n*.

Figure 2-11. *The results of queries with multiple wildcards*

You will probably find **LIKE** used frequently in queries, so it is important to understand how it works. Practice the skills you have just learned by completing Exercise 2-3.

Exercise 2-3

Use the AdventureWorks2008 database to complete this exercise. Follow the steps in this exercise to test your knowledge of pattern matching and wildcard queries. You can find the solutions in the appendix.

1. Write a query that displays the product ID and name for each product from the **Production.Product** table with a name starting with *Chain*.
2. Write a query like the one in question 1 that displays the products with *helmet* in the name.
3. Change the last query so that the products without *helmet* in the name are displayed.
4. Write a query that displays the business entity ID number, first name, middle name, and last name from the **Person.Person** table for only those rows that have *E* or *B* stored in the middle name column.
5. Explain the difference between the following two queries:

```
SELECT FirstName
FROM Person.Person
WHERE LastName LIKE 'Ja%es';
SELECT FirstName
FROM Person.Person
WHERE LastName LIKE 'Ja_es';
```

Using WHERE Clauses with Two Predicates

So far, the examples have shown only one condition or predicate in the WHERE clause, but the WHERE clause can be much more complex. It can have multiple predicates by using the logical operators AND and OR. Type in and execute the code in Listing 2-14 that demonstrates how to use AND and OR to combine two predicates.

Listing 2-14. How to Use AND and OR

```
USE AdventureWorks2008;
GO


--1
SELECT BusinessEntityID,FirstName,MiddleName,LastName
FROM Person.Person
WHERE FirstName = 'Ken' AND LastName = 'Myer';

--2
SELECT BusinessEntityID,FirstName,MiddleName,LastName
FROM Person.Person
WHERE LastName = 'Myer' OR LastName = 'Meyer';
```

Figure 2-12 shows the results. Query 1 returns any rows with the first name *Ken* and the last name *Myer* because both expressions must evaluate to true. Query 2 returns any rows with either the last name *Myer* or the last name *Meyer* because only one of the expressions must evaluate to true.

	BusinessEntityID	FirstName	MiddleName	LastName
1	1525	Ken	NULL	Myer
2	203	Ken	L	Myer

	BusinessEntityID	FirstName	MiddleName	LastName
1	1459	Deanna	NULL	Meyer
2	1455	Eric	B.	Meyer
3	1457	Helen	M.	Meyer
4	2140	Ken	NULL	Meyer
5	1523	Dorothy	J.	Myer
6	1525	Ken	NULL	Myer
7	203	Ken	L	Myer
8	2319	Linda	NULL	Myer

Figure 2-12. The results of queries with two predicates in the WHERE clause

Using WHERE Clauses with Three or More Predicates

A WHERE clause can contain more than two predicates combined by the logical operators AND and OR. If a WHERE clause contains more than two predicates using both AND and OR, you must be careful to ensure that the query returns the expected results. Type in and execute the code in Listing 2-15 to see how the order of the predicates affects the results and how to use parentheses to enforce the correct logic.

Listing 2-15. WHERE Clauses with Three Predicates

```
USE AdventureWorks2008;
GO


--1
SELECT BusinessEntityID,FirstName,MiddleName,LastName
FROM Person.Person
WHERE FirstName = 'Ken' AND LastName = 'Myer'
    OR LastName = 'Meyer';


--2
SELECT BusinessEntityID,FirstName,MiddleName,LastName
FROM Person.Person
WHERE LastName = 'Myer' OR LastName = 'Meyer'
    AND FirstName = 'Ken';


--3
SELECT BusinessEntityID,FirstName,MiddleName,LastName
FROM Person.Person
WHERE LastName = 'Meyer'
    AND FirstName = 'Ken' OR LastName = 'Myer';


--4
SELECT BusinessEntityID,FirstName,MiddleName,LastName
FROM Person.Person
WHERE FirstName = 'Ken' AND (LastName = 'Myer'
    OR LastName = 'Meyer');
```

You can see the results of Listing 2-15 in Figure 2-13. Once both logical operators **AND** and **OR** are used in the **WHERE** clause, things can get complicated. The logical operator **AND** takes precedence over **OR**; therefore, the database engine evaluates **AND** first. For example, suppose you want to find a name in the **Person.Person** table, *Ken Meyer*, but you cannot remember the spelling of the last name. It could be *Myer*. Listing 2-15 shows four attempts to solve this problem, but only the last one is correct.

Results

	BusinessEntityID	First Name	Middle Name	Last Name
1	1459	Deanna	NULL	Meyer
2	1455	Eric	B.	Meyer
3	1457	Helen	M.	Meyer
4	2140	Ken	NULL	Meyer
5	1525	Ken	NULL	Myer
6	203	Ken	L	Myer

	BusinessEntityID	First Name	Middle Name	Last Name
1	2140	Ken	NULL	Meyer
2	1523	Dorothy	J.	Myer
3	1525	Ken	NULL	Myer
4	203	Ken	L	Myer
5	2319	Linda	NULL	Myer

	BusinessEntityID	First Name	Middle Name	Last Name
1	2140	Ken	NULL	Meyer
2	1523	Dorothy	J.	Myer
3	1525	Ken	NULL	Myer
4	203	Ken	L	Myer
5	2319	Linda	NULL	Myer

	BusinessEntityID	First Name	Middle Name	Last Name
1	2140	Ken	NULL	Meyer
2	1525	Ken	NULL	Myer
3	203	Ken	L	Myer

Figure 2-13. The results of queries that force precedence to ensure the correct results

Query 1 returns the rows with the name *Ken Myer* but also returns any row with the last name *Meyer*. Queries 2 and 3 return identical results—the row with *Ken Meyer* and any rows with the last name *Myer*. Finally, by using the parentheses, query 4 returns the correct results.

When using multiple conditions, you must be very careful about the *precedence*, or order, that the expressions are evaluated. The database engine evaluates the conditions in the WHERE clause from left to right, but AND takes precedence over OR. Rearranging the terms can produce different but possibly still invalid results as in the previous example. To guarantee that the query is correct, always use parentheses to enforce the logic once the logical operator OR is added to the WHERE clause.

Using NOT with Parentheses

Another interesting twist when using parentheses is that you can negate the meaning of the expression within them by specifying the keyword NOT. For example, you could try to find the rows where the first name is *Ken* and the last name cannot be *Myer* or *Meyer*. Type in and execute Listing 2-16 to see two ways to write the query.

Listing 2-16. Using NOT with Parentheses

```
USE AdventureWorks2008;
GO
--1
SELECT BusinessEntityID,FirstName,MiddleName,LastName
FROM Person.Person
WHERE FirstName='Ken' AND LastName <> 'Myer'
    AND LastName <> 'Meyer';


--2
SELECT BusinessEntityID,FirstName,MiddleName,LastName
FROM Person.Person
WHERE FirstName='Ken'
    AND NOT (LastName = 'Myer' OR LastName = 'Meyer');
```

Often multiple ways exist to solve the same problem, as in this case. Query 1 contains three expressions. One expression restricts the rows to those where **FirstName** is *Ken*. The other two expressions compare **LastName** to a value using not equal to (<>). In query 2, the expressions within the parentheses are evaluated first. Next that result is negated by the **NOT** operator to find all last names that are not *Myer* or *Meyer*. Finally, only the rows that also have the first name *Ken* are returned. You can see the results in Figure 2-14.

As a best practice, always employ parentheses to enforce precedence when the **WHERE** clause includes the logical operator **OR**. Not only will this decrease the possibility of an incorrect **WHERE** clause, but it will increase the readability of the query.

	BusinessEntityID	FirstName	MiddleName	LastName
1	2300	Ken	NULL	Kwok
2	1726	Ken	NULL	Sánchez
3	1	Ken	J	Sánchez

	BusinessEntityID	FirstName	MiddleName	LastName
1	2300	Ken	NULL	Kwok
2	1726	Ken	NULL	Sánchez
3	1	Ken	J	Sánchez

Figure 2-14. The identical results of two queries with different techniques

Using the IN Operator

The **IN** operator is very useful when multiple values must be compared to the same column. Query 4 in Listing 2-15 could have been written in a more straightforward way using the **IN** operator. Follow the **IN** operator with a list of possible values for a column within parentheses. Here is the syntax:

```
SELECT <column1>,<column2>
FROM <schema>.<table>
WHERE <column> IN (<value1>,<value2>);
```

Type in and execute the code from Listing 2-17. The queries in that listing demonstrate how to use the **IN** operator. Review the results to be sure that you understand them.

Listing 2-17. Using the IN Operator

```
USE AdventureWorks2008
GO

--1
SELECT BusinessEntityID,FirstName,MiddleName,LastName
FROM Person.Person
WHERE FirstName = 'Ken' AND
    LastName IN ('Myer','Meyer');

--2
SELECT TerritoryID, Name
FROM Sales.SalesTerritory
WHERE TerritoryID IN (2,1,4,5);

--3
SELECT TerritoryID, Name
FROM Sales.SalesTerritory
WHERE TerritoryID NOT IN (2,1,4,5);
```

You will probably find that the operator **IN** can simplify many queries. Query 1 solves the same problem as in Listing 2-15. The original query used two expressions to compare two values to the same column within parentheses: **(LastName = 'Myer' OR LastName = 'Meyer')**. By using the **IN** operator, you were able to eliminate one expression by including both values in the **IN** list. You can also use **IN** with numbers and dates. Query 2 returns all rows with **TerritoryID** 2, 1, 4, or 5. By using **NOT**, query 3 returns the opposite results. Figure 2-15 shows the results of the three queries from Listing 2-17.

Figure 2-15. *The results of queries using the* IN *operator*

As the WHERE clause becomes more complicated, it becomes very easy to make a mistake. Complete Exercise 2-4 to practice writing with multiple predicates andWHERE clauses with multiple predicates and the IN operator.

Exercise 2-4

Use the AdventureWorks2008 database to complete this exercise. Be sure to check your results to assure that they make sense. You can find the solutions in the appendix.

1. Write a query displaying the order ID, order date, and total due from the `Sales.SalesOrderHeader` table. Retrieve only those rows where the order was placed during the month of September 2001 and the total due exceeded $1,000.
2. Change the query in question 1 so that only the dates September 1–3, 2001, are retrieved. See whether you can figure out three different ways to write this query.
3. Write a query displaying the sales orders where the total due exceeds $1,000. Retrieve only those rows where the salesperson ID is 279 or the territory ID is 6.
4. Change the query in question 3 so that territory 4 is included.
5. Explain when it makes sense to use the IN operator.

Working with Nothing

Probably nothing causes more aggravation to T-SQL developers than NULL values. NULL means that a value has not been entered for a particular column in a row. Suppose you have an e-commerce application that requires the customer to fill in information such as name and address. In this example, the phone number is optional. What does it mean if the customer does not enter a phone number and the table ends up with **NULL** in the **PhoneNumber** column of the **Customer** table? Does it mean that the customer does not have a phone? That's one possibility. Another is that the customer has at least one phone number but chose not to supply it since it was not required. Either way, the end result is that you have no phone number value to work with.

Think now about what would happen if you had a list of 1,000,000 phone numbers and tried to figure out whether any of the phone numbers belonged to the customer. Even if you compared each phone number to the customer's row, one by one, you would never know whether any of the phone numbers were the right one. You would never know, because you would be comparing 1,000,000 values to nothing. Conversely, can you guarantee that every one of your 1,000,000 phone numbers is not the missing phone number? No, you cannot do that either, since the customer's phone number is unknown.

This example should give you an idea about the challenges of working with **NULL** values. Type in and execute the code in Listing 2-18 to work on some examples using real data.

Listing 2-18. An Example Illustrating NULL

```
USE AdventureWorks2008;
GO


--1) Returns 19,972 rows
SELECT MiddleName
FROM Person.Person;


--2) Returns 291 rows
SELECT MiddleName
FROM Person.Person
WHERE MiddleName = 'B';


--3) Returns 11,182 but 19,681 were expected
SELECT MiddleName
FROM Person.Person
WHERE MiddleName != 'B';


--4) Returns 19,681
SELECT MiddleName
FROM Person.Person
WHERE MiddleName IS NULL
    OR MiddleName !='B';
```

Query 1 with no **WHERE** clause returns 19,972 rows, the total number of rows in the table. Query 2 returns 291 rows with the middle name *B*. Logic follows that query 3 will return the difference of the two numbers: 19,681 rows. When you check the results of query 3, you will find that more than 8,000 rows are not accounted for. That is because the rows with **NULL** values cannot be found by the expression containing not equal. Comparing **NULL** to *B* returns **UNKNOWN**, so the rows are not returned. You must specifically check for **NULL** values by using the **IS NULL** operator, as shown in query 4, which returns the correct number of rows.

Usually comparing the data in a column to a value or comparing the values from two columns returns either **TRUE** or **FALSE**. If the expression evaluates to **TRUE**, then the row is returned. If the expression evaluates to **FALSE**, then the row is not returned. If a value in the expression contains **NULL**, then the expression is resolved to **UNKNOWN**. In some ways, the behavior is like **FALSE**. When an expression resolves to **UNKNOWN**, the row is not returned. The problems begin when using any operator except for equal to (=). The opposite of **FALSE** is **TRUE**, but the opposite of **UNKNOWN** is still **UNKNOWN**.

Neglecting to take possible **NULL** values into consideration can often cause incorrect results. Always remember to think about **NULL** values, especially whenever writing any expression containing **NOT**. Do the **NULL** values belong in the results? If so, you will have to check for **NULL**. You will also need to keep **NULL** values in mind when using less than. **NULL** values will be left out of those results as well. Chapter 3 will show you some other options for working with **NULL**.

Understanding how **NULL** values can affect the results of your queries is one of the most important skills you will learn. Even experienced T-SQL developers struggle from time to time when working with **NULL** values. Be sure to complete Exercise 2-5 to practice what you have just learned.

Exercise 2-5

Use the AdventureWorks2008 database to complete this exercise. Make sure you consider how **NULL** values will affect your results. You can find the solutions in the appendix.

1. Write a query displaying the **ProductID**, **Name**, and **Color** columns from rows in the **Production.Product** table. Display only those rows where no color has been assigned.
2. Write a query displaying the **ProductID**, **Name**, and **Color** columns from rows in the **Production.Product** table. Display only those rows in which the color is not blue.
3. Write a query displaying **ProductID**, **Name**, **Style**, **Size**, and **Color** from the **Production.Product** table. Include only the rows where at least one of the **Style**, **Size**, or **Color** columns contains a value.

Performing a Full-Text Search

You have learned how to use **LIKE** to find a character match in data. Full-Text Search provides the ability to search for words or phrases within string or binary data columns similar to a web search such as Google or Bing. You can use **LIKE** for pattern matching only and not for searching binary data. Full-Text Search has support for multiple languages and other features such as synonym searches. Full-Text Search is especially beneficial for documents stored as binary data in the database.

Full-Text Search must be installed during the SQL Server setup, and a special full-text index needs to be created on the table. This book doesn't intend to teach you how to set up and manage Full-Text Search, but it will show you how to write some of the basic queries. For more information about Full-Text Search, see the book *Pro Full-Text Search in SQL Server 2008* by Hillary Cotter and Michael Coles (Apress, 2008). The AdventureWorks2008 database ships with three full-text indexes already in place. Table 2-1 lists the columns with full-text indexes included by default in AdventureWorks2008.

Table 2-1. *Tables with Full-Text Indexes*

TableName	ColumnName
Production.ProductReview	Comments
Production.Document	DocumentSummary
Production.Document	Document
HumanResources.JobCandidate	Resume

Using CONTAINS

CONTAINS is one of the functions used to search full-text indexes. You will learn more about functions in Chapter 3. The simplest way to use CONTAINS is to search a column for a particular word or phrase. Here is the syntax for CONTAINS:

```
SELECT <column1>,<column2>
FROM <schema>.<tablename>
WHERE CONTAINS(<indexed column>,<searchterm>);
```

Listing 2-19 shows how to use CONTAINS. Notice that the second query has a regular predicate in the WHERE clause as well. Be sure to type in and execute the code to learn how to use CONTAINS.

Listing 2-19. *Using CONTAINS*

```
USE AdventureWorks2008;
GO


--1
SELECT FileName
FROM Production.Document
WHERE Contains(Document,'important');

--2
SELECT FileName
FROM Production.Document
WHERE Contains(Document,' "service guidelines " ')
    AND DocumentLevel = 2;
```

Figure 2-16 displays the results. Notice how double quotes are used within single quotes to designate a phrase in query 2. Query 2 also demonstrates that both a full-text predicate and a regular predicate can be used in the same query. You may be wondering why the **Document** column is not part of the results since that is the search term. The document is actually a binary file, such as a Microsoft Word document, that must be opened by the appropriate application.

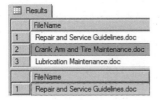

	FileName
1	Repair and Service Guidelines.doc
2	Crank Arm and Tire Maintenance.doc
3	Lubrication Maintenance.doc

	FileName
1	Repair and Service Guidelines.doc

Figure 2-16. *The results of a Full-Text Search operation*

Using Multiple Terms with CONTAINS

You can use **CONTAINS** to find words in data that are not even next to each other by using **AND**, **OR**, and **NEAR**. You can use the operator **AND NOT** to find results with one term and not another. This syntax is similar to searches with Google or other search engines. Listing 2-20 demonstrates this technique.

Listing 2-20. Multiple Terms in CONTAINS

```
USE AdventureWorks2008;
GO


--1
SELECT FileName, DocumentSummary
FROM Production.Document
WHERE Contains(DocumentSummary,'bicycle AND reflectors');


--2
SELECT FileName, DocumentSummary
FROM Production.Document
WHERE CONTAINS(DocumentSummary,'bicycle AND NOT reflectors');


--3
SELECT FileName, DocumentSummary
FROM Production.Document
WHERE CONTAINS(DocumentSummary,'maintain NEAR bicycle AND NOT reflectors');
```

Figure 2-17 shows the results. In this case, a regular string data column, **DocumentSummary**, is searched so that you can verify the results.

	FileName	DocumentSummary
1	Front Reflector Bracket Installation.doc	Reflectors are vital safety components of your bicycle. Always ...

	FileName	DocumentSummary
1	Repair and Service Guidelines.doc	It is important that you maintain your bicycle and keep it in goo...
2	Lubrication Maintenance.doc	Guidelines and recommendations for lubricating the required c...
3	Installing Replacement Pedals.doc	Detailed instructions for replacing pedals with Adventure Work...

	FileName	DocumentSummary
1	Repair and Service Guidelines.doc	It is important that you maintain your bicycle and keep it in goo...

Figure 2-17. *The results from using multiple search terms*

Searching Multiple Columns

You can search multiple columns or all full-text indexed columns at once without multiple **CONTAINS** predicates in the **WHERE** clause. Use the asterisk to specify that all possible columns are searched, or use a comma-delimited list in parentheses to specify a list of columns. Type in and execute the code in Listing 2-21, which demonstrates these techniques.

Listing 2-21. Using Multiple Columns

```
USE AdventureWorks2008;
GO

--1
SELECT FileName, DocumentSummary
FROM Production.Document
WHERE CONTAINS((DocumentSummary,Document),'maintain');

--2
SELECT FileName, DocumentSummary
FROM Production.Document
WHERE CONTAINS((DocumentSummary),'maintain')
      OR CONTAINS((Document),'maintain')

--3
SELECT FileName, DocumentSummary
FROM Production.Document
WHERE CONTAINS(*,'maintain');
```

The list of columns to be searched in query 1 is explicitly listed and contained within an inner set of parentheses. Query 2 is equivalent to query 1 by using two **CONTAINS** expressions, each searching a different column for the same term. By using the asterisk in query 3 within the **CONTAINS** expression, all columns with a full-text index are searched.

Using FREETEXT

FREETEXT is similar to **CONTAINS** except that it returns rows that do not exactly match. It will return rows that have terms with similar meanings to your search terms by using a thesaurus. **FREETEXT** is less precise than **CONTAINS**, and it is less flexible. The keywords **AND**, **OR**, and **NEAR** cannot be used with **CONTAINS**. Avoid using double quotes that specify an exact phrase with **FREETEXT**, because then SQL Server won't use the thesaurus and will search only for the exact phrase. The same rules about multiple columns apply. Type in and execute the code in Listing 2-22, which compares **FREETEXT** to **LIKE**.

Listing 2-22. Using FREETEXT

```
USE AdventureWorks2008
GO

--1
SELECT FileName, DocumentSummary
FROM Production.Document
WHERE FREETEXT((DocumentSummary),'provides');

--2
SELECT FileName, DocumentSummary
FROM Production.Document
WHERE DocumentSummary LIKE '%provides%'
```

Figure 2-18 displays the results from Listing 2-22. The **DocumentSummary** value in the rows returned from query 1 do not contain the word *provides*. Query 1 returns the rows anyway because **FREETEXT** will find similar words as well as exact matches.

	FileName	Document Summary
1	Repair and Service Guidelines.doc	It is important that you maintain your bicycle and ...
2	Lubrication Maintenance.doc	Guidelines and recommendations for lubricating t...
	FileName	Document Summary

Figure 2-18. The results from using FREETEXT

Full-Text Search operations can get much more complicated than the information provided here. This was meant to be an overview of the basic syntax. Be sure to see the book *Pro Full-Text Search in SQL Server 2008* by Hillary Cotter and Michael Coles (Apress, 2008) to learn more about Full-Text Search. Practice what you have just learned about Full-Text Search by completing Exercise 2-6.

Exercise 2-6

Use the AdventureWorks2008 database to complete the following tasks. Be sure to take advantage of the full-text indexes in place when writing the queries. You can find the solutions in the appendix.

1. Write a query using the `Production.ProductReview` table. Use `CONTAINS` to find all the rows that have the word *socks* in the `Comments` column. Return the `ProductID` and `Comments` columns.
2. Write a query using the `Production.Document` table. Use `CONTAINS` to find all the rows that have the word *reflector* in any column that is indexed with Full-Text Search. Display the `Title` and `FileName` columns.
3. Change the query in question 2 so that the rows containing *seat* are not returned in the results.
4. Answer this question: when searching a `VARBINARY(MAX)` column that contains Word documents, a `LIKE` search can be used, but the performance will be worse. True or false?

Sorting Data

So far, you have learned how to retrieve a list of columns from a table and filter the results. This section covers how to sort the data that is retrieved using the **ORDER BY** clause. The **ORDER BY** clause is the last part of the **SELECT** statement that the database engine will process.

You can specify one or more columns in the **ORDER BY** clause separated by commas. The sort order is ascending by default, but you can specify descending order by using the keyword **DESCENDING** or **DESC** after the column name. Here is the syntax for **ORDER BY**:

```
SELECT <column1>,<column2>
FROM <schema>.<tablename>
ORDER BY <column1>[<sort direction>],<column2> [<sort direction>]
```

Type in and execute the code in Listing 2-23 to learn how to use the **ORDER BY** clause.

Listing 2-23. How to Use ORDER BY

```
USE AdventureWorks2008;
GO


--1
SELECT ProductID, LocationID
FROM Production.ProductInventory
ORDER BY LocationID;

--2
SELECT ProductID, LocationID
FROM Production.ProductInventory
ORDER BY ProductID, LocationID DESC
```

Figure 2-19 shows the partial results. The rows from query 1 display in order of **LocationID**. Query 2 returns the results ordered first by **ProductID**, and then the results are further sorted by **LocationID** in descending order.

	ProductID	LocationID
1	1	1
2	2	1
3	3	1
4	4	1
5	317	1
6	318	1
7	319	1
8	320	1

	ProductID	LocationID
1	1	50
2	1	6
3	1	1
4	2	50
5	2	6
6	2	1
7	3	50
8	3	6

Figure 2-19. The results when using the ORDER BY clause

You may find that you learn to use the **ORDER BY** clause easily, but you should still practice what you have learned about sorting the results of your queries by completing Exercise 2-7.

Exercise 2-7

Use the AdventureWorks2008 database to complete this exercise and practice sorting the results of your queries. You can find the solutions in the appendix.

1. Write a query that returns the business entity ID and name columns from the `Person.Person` table. Sort the results by `LastName`, `FirstName`, and `MiddleName`.
2. Modify the query written in question 1 so that the data is returned in the opposite order.

Thinking About Performance

Reading this book and performing the exercises found in each chapter will enable you to become a proficient T-SQL programmer. You will learn how to write the queries, often in more than one way, to get the results. Often T-SQL developers do not learn the best way to write a query, and the performance of their applications and reports suffer. Several chapters of this book, beginning with this chapter, feature a section on performance to get you thinking about how the statements you write can affect performance.

Taking Advantage of Indexes

Indexes help the database engine locate the rows that must be returned by a query. In fact, the database engine will retrieve all the required columns from the index instead of accessing the table if possible. I am not advocating creating an index on every column, but strategically designed indexes immensely improve the performance of queries.

When a table contains an index on a column, the database engine will usually use that index to find the rows for the results if the column appears in the `WHERE` clause. For example, the `Person.Person` table contains an index called `IX_Person_LastName_FirstName_MiddleName`, which consists of the `LastName`, `FirstName`, and `MiddleName` columns. To see the index properties, follow these steps:

1. Using SQL Server Management Studio, connect to your SQL Server instance if you are not connected already.
2. Expand Databases.
3. Expand AdventureWorks2008.
4. Expand Tables.
5. Expand Person.Person.
6. Expand Indexes.
7. Locate the IX_Person_LastName_FirstName_MiddleName index, and double-click it to view the properties.

View the index properties in Figure 2-20. Notice that the **LastName** column appears first in the list. To take full advantage of this index, the **WHERE** clause must filter on **LastName**. Imagine searching a phone book by searching for a first name when you do not know the last name! SQL Server must do the same thing, looking at each entry in the index, when the query filters on **FirstName** but not **LastName**.

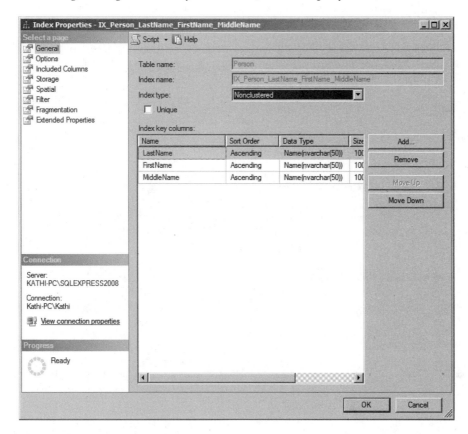

Figure 2-20. *The properties of an index*

What happens when filtering on only a nonindexed column? The database engine must check the value of the column in each row of the table to find the rows meeting the criteria. Again, I am not advocating creating an index on every column, and index creation and tuning are both well beyond the scope of this book. I just intend to make you aware that the indexes defined on the table will affect the performance of your queries.

Viewing Execution Plans

By using execution plans, you can determine whether the database engine utilizes an index to return the rows in the query. You can also compare the performance of two or more queries to see which one performs the best. Again, this book does not intend to make you an expert on execution plans but instead just gets you started using them to help you understand how your query performs. To learn more about execution plans, see the book *SQL Server Execution Plans* by Grant Fritchey (Apress, 2008).

While you have a query window open, click the Include Actual Execution Plan icon (see Figure 2-21) to turn on this feature for the current session. The setting must be toggled on for each query window; it is not a permanent setting.

Figure 2-21. *Clicking the Include Actual Execution Plan icon*

Listing 2-24 contains three queries to demonstrate the differences in performance found depending on whether SQL Server can take advantage of an index to return the results. Type in and execute the code in Listing 2-24.

Listing 2-24. *Learning How to View Execution Plans*

```
USE AdventureWorks2008;
GO


--1
SELECT LastName, FirstName
FROM Person.Person
WHERE LastName = 'Smith';


--2
SELECT LastName, FirstName
FROM Person.Person
WHERE FirstName = 'Ken';


--3
SELECT ModifiedDate
FROM Person.Person
WHERE ModifiedDate BETWEEN '2000-01-01' and '2000-01-31';
```

Once the query execution completes, click the Execution Plan tab. Figure 2-22 shows the graphical execution plans for the three queries. First take a look at the query cost for each query shown at the top of each section. The query cost gives you an estimated weight of each query compared to the total. The numbers should add up to 100 percent.

Query 1, which has a relative query cost of 0 percent, filters the results on the LastName column. Recall that an index comprised of the LastName, FirstName, and MiddleName columns exists on the Person.Person table. Because the query filters on the first column in the index, the database engine can take full advantage of the index; it performs an *index seek* without scanning the entire index. This is similar to looking at the phone book when you know the last name; you will not look at every page or every entry to find the name you are looking for. Query 2, which has a relative query cost of 3 percent, filters the results on the FirstName column. The table has an index that contains the FirstName column, but since it appears second in the index, SQL Server must perform an *index scan*. This means that the database engine must compare the string *Ken* to every FirstName value in the index. The database was able to take advantage of the index but not to the fullest extent. Because the index contains both columns found in the results, the database engine did not have to touch the actual table, pulling all the needed data from the index. The execution plan also suggests a new index that will make this query perform better.

Query 3, which has a relative query cost of 96 percent, filters the results on the ModifiedDate column. The table does not have an index containing this column. To filter the rows, the database engine must perform a *clustered index scan*. The *clustered index* is the actual table. In this case, the database engine had to look at each row of the table to retrieve the results, which causes the worst possible performance. Review the "Understanding Indexes" section in Chapter 1 to learn more about clustered indexes and indexes in general.

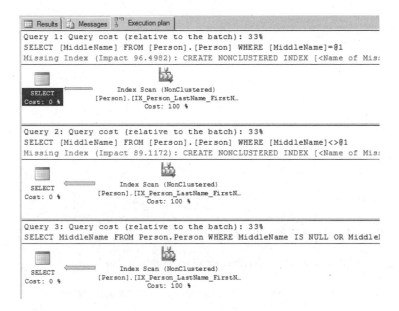

Figure 2-22. The actual execution plans generated from Listing 2-24

Viewing and understanding execution plans will help you learn how writing queries will affect the performance of your applications and reports. Don't rush to your database administrator demanding changes to the database indexes in your production database; this section doesn't intend to teach index tuning. Think of execution plans as another tool you can use to write better code. To learn more about how execution plans affect performance, complete Exercise 2-8.

Exercise 2-8

Use the AdventureWorks2008 database to complete this exercise. Be sure to turn on the Include Actual Execution Plan setting before you begin. Type the following code into the query window, and then complete each question. You can find the solutions in the appendix.

```
USE AdventureWorks2008;
GO


--1
SELECT LastName
FROM Person.Person
WHERE LastName = 'Smith';


--2
SELECT LastName
FROM Person.Person
WHERE LastName LIKE 'Sm%';


--3
SELECT LastName
FROM Person.Person
WHERE LastName LIKE '%mith';


--4
SELECT ModifiedDate
FROM Person.Person
WHERE ModifiedDate BETWEEN '2000-01-01' and '2000-01-31';
```

1. Highlight and run queries 1 and 2. Explain why there is no difference in performance between the two queries.
2. Highlight and run queries 2 and 3. Determine which query performs the best, and explain why you think that is the case.
3. Highlight and run queries 3 and 4. Determine which query performs the best, and explain why you think that is the case.

Summary

The **SELECT** statement is used to retrieve data from tables stored in SQL Server databases. The statement can be broken down into several parts called *clauses*. The **FROM** clause specifies the table where the data is stored. The **SELECT** clause contains a list of columns to be retrieved. To filter the data, use the **WHERE** clause. To sort the data, use the **ORDER BY** clause.

This chapter covered a lot of ground, especially all the nuances of the **WHERE** clause. Make sure you understand the material covered in the chapter well before continuing. Everything you learn throughout the rest of the book will depend on a thorough knowledge of the basics. The next chapter explores many of the built-in functions you can use to make data retrieval even more interesting.

CHAPTER 3

■ ■ ■

Using Functions and Expressions

Now that you have the knowledge to write simple **SELECT** statements, it is time to explore some of the other features of T-SQL that allow you to manipulate how the data is displayed, filtered, or ordered. To create expressions in T-SQL, you use functions and operators along with literal values and columns. The reasons for using expressions in T-SQL code are many. For example, you may want to display only the year of a column of the **DATETIME** data type on a report, or you may need to calculate a discount based on the order quantity in an order-entry application. Any time the data must be displayed, filtered, or ordered in a way that is different from how it is stored, you can use expressions and functions to manipulate it.

You will find a very rich and versatile collection of functions and operators available to create expressions that manipulate strings and dates and much more. You can use expressions in the **SELECT**, **WHERE**, and **ORDER BY** clauses as well as in other clauses you will learn about in Chapter 5.

Expressions Using Operators

You learned how to use several comparison operators in the **WHERE** clause in Chapter 2. In this section, you will learn how to use operators to concatenate strings and perform mathematical calculations in T-SQL queries.

Concatenating Strings

The concatenation operator (+) allows you to add together two strings. The syntax is simple: **<string or column name> + <string or column name>**. Start up SQL Server Management Studio if it is not already running, and connect to your development server. Open a new query window, and type in and execute the code in Listing 3-1.

Listing 3-1. Concatenating Strings

```
USE AdventureWorks2008;
GO


--1
SELECT 'ab' + 'c';


--2
SELECT BusinessEntityID, FirstName + ' ' + LastName AS "Full Name"
FROM Person.Person;
```

```
--3
SELECT BusinessEntityID, LastName + ', ' + FirstName AS "Full Name"
FROM Person.Person;
```

Figure 3-1 shows the results of Listing 3-1. Query 1 shows that you can concatenate two strings. Queries 2 and 3 demonstrate concatenating the **LastName** and **FirstName** columns along with either a space or a comma and space. Notice that you specified the alias, **Full Name**, to provide a column header for the result of the expressions combining **FirstName** and **LastName**. If you did not provide the alias, the column header would be **(No column name)**, as in query 1.

	(No column name)
1	abc

	BusinessEntityID	Full Name
1	285	Syed Abbas
2	293	Catherine Abel
3	295	Kim Abercrombie
4	2170	Kim Abercrombie
5	38	Kim Abercrombie
6	211	Hazem Abolrous
7	2357	Sam Abolrous
8	297	Humberto Ace...

	BusinessEntityID	Full Name
1	285	Abbas, Syed
2	293	Abel, Catherine
3	295	Abercrombie, K...
4	2170	Abercrombie, K...
5	38	Abercrombie, K...
6	211	Abolrous, Hazem
7	2357	Abolrous, Sam

Figure 3-1. *The results of queries concatenating strings*

Concatenating Strings and NULL

In Chapter 2 you learned about the challenges when working with **NULL** in **WHERE** clause expressions. When concatenating a string with a **NULL**, **NULL** is returned. Listing 3-2 demonstrates this problem. Type the code in Listing 3-2 into a new query window, and execute it.

Listing 3-2. *Concatenating Strings with NULL Values*

```
USE AdventureWorks2008;
GO

SELECT BusinessEntityID, FirstName + ' ' + MiddleName +
    ' ' + LastName AS "Full Name"
FROM Person.Person;
```

Figure 3-2 shows the results of Listing 3-2. The query combines the FirstName, MiddleName, and LastName columns into a Full Name column. The MiddleName column is optional; that is, NULL values are allowed. Only the rows where the MiddleName value has been entered show the expected results. The rows where MiddleName is NULL return NULL.

	BusinessEntityID	Full Name
1	285	Syed E Abbas
2	293	Catherine R. Abel
3	295	NULL
4	2170	NULL
5	38	Kim B Abercrombie
6	211	Hazem E Abolrous
7	2357	NULL
8	297	NULL
9	291	NULL
10	299	NULL
11	121	Pilar G Ackerman
12	16867	Aaron B Adams
13	16901	NULL
14	16724	Alex C Adams
15	10263	Alexandra J Adams
16	10312	Allison L Adams

Figure 3-2. The results of concatenating a string with NULL

ISNULL and COALESCE

Two functions are available to replace NULL values with another value. The first function, ISNULL, requires two parameters: the value to check and the replacement for NULL values. COALESCE works a bit differently. COALESCE will take any number of parameters and return the first non-NULL value. T-SQL developers often prefer COALESCE over ISNULL because COALESCE meets ANSI standards, while ISNULL does not, and because COALESCE is more versatile. Here is the syntax for the two functions:

```
ISNULL(<value>,<replacement>)
COALESCE(<value1>,<value2>,...,<valueN>)
```

Type in and execute the code in Listing 3-3 to learn how to use ISNULL and COALESCE.

Listing 3-3. Using ISNULL and COALESCE

```
USE AdventureWorks2008;
GO


--1
SELECT BusinessEntityID, FirstName + ' ' + ISNULL(MiddleName,'') +
    ' ' + LastName AS "Full Name"
FROM Person.Person;
```

```
--2
SELECT BusinessEntityID, FirstName + ISNULL(' ' + MiddleName,'') +
    ' ' + LastName AS "Full Name"
FROM Person.Person;


--3
SELECT BusinessEntityID, FirstName + COALESCE(' ' + MiddleName,'') +
    ' ' + LastName AS "Full Name"
FROM Person.Person;
```

Figure 3-3 shows a partial result of running the code. Query 1 uses the ISNULL function to replace any missing MiddleName values with an empty string in order to build Full Name. Notice in the results that whenever MiddleName is missing, you end up with two spaces between FirstName and LastName. Line 3 in the results of query 1 contains two spaces between *Kim* and *Ambercrombie* because a space is added both before and after the ISNULL function. To correct this problem, move the space inside the ISNULL function instead of before it: ISNULL(' ' + MiddleName,''). Adding a space to NULL returns NULL. When the MiddleName value is NULL, the space is eliminated, and no extra spaces show up in your results. Instead of ISNULL, query 3 contains the COALESCE function. If MiddleName is NULL, the next non-NULL value, the empty string, is returned.

	Results	
3	295	Kim Abercrombie
4	2170	Kim Abercrombie
5	38	Kim B Abercrombie
6	211	Hazem E Abolrous
7	2357	Sam Abolrous
8	297	Humberto Acevedo

	BusinessEntityID	FullName
1	285	Syed E Abbas
2	293	Catherine R. Abel
3	295	Kim Abercrombie
4	2170	Kim Abercrombie
5	38	Kim B Abercrombie
6	211	Hazem E Abolrous

	BusinessEntityID	FullName
1	285	Syed E Abbas
2	293	Catherine R. Abel
3	295	Kim Abercrombie
4	2170	Kim Abercrombie
5	38	Kim B Abercrombie
6	211	Hazem E Abolrous
7	2357	Sam Abolrous

Figure 3-3. The results of using ISNULL and COALESCE when concatenating strings

Concatenating Other Data Types to Strings

To concatenate nonstring values to strings, the nonstring value must be converted to a string. If the string value can be implicitly converted to a number, the values will be added together instead. Run this statement to see what happens: SELECT 1 + '1';. If the desired result is 11 instead of 2, the numeric value must be converted to a string using either the CAST or CONVERT function. If you attempt to concatenate a non-numeric string and a number without converting, you will receive an error message. Run this example to see the error: SELECT 1 + 'a';.

Use one of the functions, CAST or CONVERT, to convert a numeric or temporal value to a string. Here is the syntax:

```
CAST(<value> AS <new data type>)
CONVERT(<new data type>,<value>)
```

Listing 3-4 demonstrates how to use these functions. Type in and execute the code in a query window.

Listing 3-4. Using CAST and CONVERT

```
USE AdventureWorks2008
GO


--1
SELECT CAST(BusinessEntityID AS NVARCHAR) + ': ' + LastName
    + ', ' + FirstName AS ID_Name
FROM Person.Person;


--2
SELECT CONVERT(NVARCHAR(10),BusinessEntityID) + ': ' + LastName
    + ', ' + FirstName AS ID_Name
FROM Person.Person;


--3
SELECT BusinessEntityID, BusinessEntityID + 1 AS "Adds 1",
    CAST(BusinessEntityID AS NVARCHAR(10)) + '1'AS "Appends 1"
FROM Person.Person;
```

Figure 3-4 shows the partial results of running the code. The functions in queries 1 and 2 have very different syntaxes, but they accomplish the same results in this situation. They both change the BusinessEntityID values from integers into a string data type (NVARCHAR) so that it can be concatenated to a string. Many programmers prefer CAST over CONVERT because CAST is compliant with the ANSI SQL-99 standard. Query 1 specifies just NVARCHAR as the data type without a size. By default, the length will be 30 characters. Query 3 demonstrates the difference between converting the numeric value and not converting it. For more information about CONVERT, take a look at the "CONVERT" section later in the chapter.

Figure 3-4. The partial results of using CAST and CONVERT

Developers must often concatenate strings for reports or for loading data from one system to another. Now practice what you have learned about concatenating strings within a T-SQL query by completing Exercise 3-1.

Exercise 3-1

Use the AdventureWorks2008 database to complete this exercise. You can find the solutions to Exercise 3-1 in the appendix.

1. Write a query that displays in the "AddressLine1 (City PostalCode)" format from the `Person.Address` table.
2. Write a query using the `Production.Product` table displaying the product ID, color, and name columns. If the color column contains a `NULL` value, replace the color with *No Color*.
3. Modify the query written in question 2 so that the description of the product is displayed in the "Name: Color" format. Make sure that all rows display a value even if the `Color` value is missing.
4. Write a query using the `Production.Product` table displaying a description with the "ProductID: Name" format. Hint: You will need to use a function to write this query.
5. Explain the difference between the `ISNULL` and `COALESCE` functions.

Using Mathematical Operators

You can use several operators to perform simple mathematical operations on numeric values. Use the plus symbol (+) to perform addition, the minus symbol (–) to perform subtraction, the asterisk (*) to perform multiplication, and the slash (/) to perform division. One operator that may be new to you is the modulo (%) operator. The modulo operator returns the remainder when division is performed on the two values. For example, 5 % 2 returns 1 because 1 is the remainder when you divide 5 by 2. One common use for modulo is to determine whether a number is odd or even when the second value in the expression is 2. If the result is 1, then the value is odd; if the result is 0, then the value is even. Listing 3-5 shows how to use some of the mathematical operators. Type in and execute the code to see the results.

Listing 3-5. Using Mathematical Operators

```
USE AdventureWorks2008;
GO


--1
SELECT 1 + 1;


--2
SELECT 10 / 3 AS DIVISION, 10 % 3 AS MODULO;


--3
SELECT OrderQty, OrderQty * 10 AS Times10
FROM Sales.SalesOrderDetail;


--4
SELECT OrderQty * UnitPrice * (1.0 - UnitPriceDiscount)
    AS Calculated, LineTotal
FROM Sales.SalesOrderDetail;


--5
SELECT SpecialOfferID,MaxQty,DiscountPct,
    DiscountPct * ISNULL(MaxQTY,1000) AS MaxDiscount
FROM Sales.SpecialOffer;
```

Take a look at the results shown in Figure 3-5. Queries 1 and 2 show how to perform calculations on literal values. Query 3 shows the result of multiplying the values stored in the OrderQty column by 10. Query 4 compares the precalculated LineTotal column to calculating the value by using an expression. The LineTotal column is a "computed column." Computed columns have a property, PERSISTED, that allows the calculated value to be stored in the table. If the PERSISTED property of the column is set to FALSE, the value is calculated each time the data is accessed. The advantage of storing the calculated value is that you can add an index on the computed column. The actual formula used in the table definition looks a bit more complicated than the one I used since it checks for NULL values. The simplified formula I used requires parentheses to enforce the logic, causing subtraction to be performed before multiplication. Since multiplication has a higher precedence than subtraction, use parentheses to enforce the intended logic. Query 5 shows how to use the ISNULL function to substitute the value 1000 when the MaxQTY is NULL before multiplying by the DiscountPct value.

Results

	(No column name)
1	2

	DIVISION	MODULO
1	3	1

	OrderQty	Times10
1	1	10
2	3	30
3	1	10

	Calculated	LineTotal
1	2024.994000	2024.994000
2	6074.982000	6074.982000
3	2024.994000	2024.994000
4	2039.994000	2039.994000
5	2039.994000	2039.994000

	SpecialOfferID	MaxQty	DiscountPct	MaxDiscount
1	1	NULL	0.00	0.00
2	2	14	0.02	0.28
3	3	24	0.05	1.20
4	4	40	0.10	4.00
5	5	60	0.15	9.00
6	6	NULL	0.20	200.00
7	7	NULL	0.35	350.00
8	8	NULL	0.10	100.00

Figure 3-5. *The results of using mathematical operators*

Practice what you have learned about mathematical operators to complete Exercise 3-2.

Exercise 3-2

Use the AdventureWorks2008 database to complete this exercise. You can find the solutions in the appendix.

1. Write a query using the Sales.SpecialOffer table. Display the difference between the MinQty and MaxQty columns along with the SpecialOfferID and Description columns.
2. Write a query using the Sales.SpecialOffer table. Multiply the MinQty column by the DiscountPct column. Include the SpecialOfferID and Description columns in the results.
3. Write a query using the Sales.SpecialOffer table that multiplies the MaxQty column by the DiscountPCT column. If the MaxQty value is NULL, replace it with the value 10. Include the SpecialOfferID and Description columns in the results.
4. Describe the difference between division and modulo.

Data Type Precedence

When using operators, you must keep the data types of the values in mind. When performing an operation that involves two different data types, the expression will return values with the data type with the highest precedence if possible. What value can be rolled into the other value? For example, an INT can be converted to a BIGINT, but not the other way around. In other words, if a value can be a valid INT, it is also a valid BIGINT. However, many valid BIGINT values are too big to be converted to INT. Therefore, when an operation is performed on a BIGINT and an INT, the result will be a BIGINT.

It is not always possible to convert the lower precedence data type to the higher precedence data type. A character cannot always be converted to a numeric value. For a list of possible data types in order of precedence, see the article "Data Type Precedence" in SQL Server's help system, Books Online.

Using Functions

So far, this chapter has covered using operators along with columns and literal values to create expressions. To get around issues concerning NULL values and incompatible data types within an expression, you were introduced to several functions: ISNULL, COALESCE, CAST, and CONVERT. This section covers many other built-in functions available with SQL Server 2008.

The functions you will learn about in this chapter return a single value. The functions generally require one or more parameters. The data to be operated on can be a literal value, a column name, or the results of another function. This section covers functions to manipulate strings, dates, and numeric data. You will also learn about several system functions and how to nest one function within another function.

Using String Functions

You will find a very rich set of T-SQL functions for manipulating strings. You often have a choice of where a string will be manipulated. If the manipulation will occur on one of the columns in the select-list, it might make sense to utilize the client to do the work if the manipulation is complex, but it is possible to do quite a bit of manipulation with T-SQL. You can use the string functions to clean up data before loading it into a database.

This section covers many of the commonly used string functions. You can find many more in Books Online.

RTRIM and LTRIM

The RTRIM and LTRIM functions remove spaces from the right side (RTRIM) or left side (LTRIM) of a string. You may need to use these functions when working with fixed-length data types (CHAR and NCHAR) or to clean up flat-file data before it is loaded from a staging database into a data warehouse. The syntax is simple:

```
RTRIM(<string>)
LTRIM(<string>)
```

Type in and execute the code in Listing 3-6. The data in the AdventureWorks2008 does not contain any extra spaces, so the first part of the code creates and populates a temporary table. Don't worry about understanding that part of the code at this point.

Listing 3-6. Using RTRIM and LTRIM

```
--Create the temp table
CREATE TABLE #trimExample (COL1 VARCHAR(10));
GO
--Populate the table
INSERT INTO #trimExample (COL1)
VALUES ('a'),('b  '),('  c'),('  d  ');

--Select the values using the functions
SELECT COL1, '*' + RTRIM(COL1) + '*' AS "RTRIM",
    '*' + LTRIM(COL1) + '*' AS "LTRIM"
FROM #trimExample;

--Clean up
DROP TABLE #trimExample;
```

Figure 3-6 shows the results of the code. The **INSERT** statement added four rows to the table with no spaces (a), spaces on the right (b), spaces on the left (c), and spaces on both (d). Inside the **SELECT** statement, you will see that asterisks surround the values to make it easier to see the spaces in the results. The **RTRIM** function removed the spaces from the right side; the **LTRIM** function removed the spaces from the left side. T-SQL does not contain a native function that removes the spaces from both sides of the string, but you will learn how to get around this problem in the section "Nesting Functions" later in the chapter.

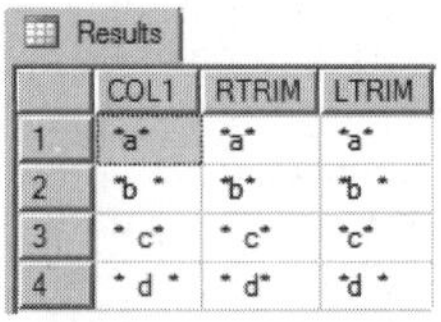
Results

	COL1	RTRIM	LTRIM
1	*a*	*a*	*a*
2	*b *	*b*	*b *
3	* c*	* c*	*c*
4	* d *	* d*	*d *

Figure 3-6. *The results of using RTRIM and LTRIM*

LEFT and RIGHT

The **LEFT** and **RIGHT** functions return a specified number of characters on the left or right side of a string. Developers use these functions to parse strings. For example, you may need to retrieve the three-character extension from file path data by using **RIGHT**. Take a look at the syntax:

```
LEFT(<string>,<number of characters)
RIGHT(<string>,<number of characters)
```

Listing 3-7 demonstrates how to use these functions. Type in and execute the code.

Listing 3-7. The LEFT and RIGHT Functions

```
USE AdventureWorks2008;
GO
SELECT LastName,LEFT(LastName,5) AS "LEFT",
    RIGHT(LastName,4) AS "RIGHT"
FROM Person.Person
WHERE BusinessEntityID IN (293,295,211,297,299,3057,15027);
```

Figure 3-7 shows the results. Notice that even if the value contains fewer characters than the number specified in the second parameter, the function still works to return as many characters as possible.

	LastName	LEFT	RIGHT
1	Abolrous	Abolr	rous
2	Abel	Abel	Abel
3	Abercrombie	Aberc	mbie
4	Acevedo	Aceve	vedo
5	Ackerman	Acker	rman
6	Alexander	Alexa	nder
7	Bell	Bell	Bell

Figure 3-7. The results of using LEFT and RIGHT

LEN and DATALENGTH

Use **LEN** to return the number of characters in a string. Developers sometimes use another function, **DATALENGTH**, incorrectly in place of **LEN**. **DATALENGTH** returns the number of bytes in a string. **DATALENGTH** returns the same value as **LEN** when the string is a **CHAR** or **VARCHAR** data type, which takes one byte per character. The problem occurs when using **DATALENGTH** on **NCHAR** or **NVARCHAR** data types, which take two byes per characters. In this case, the **DATALENGTH** value is two times the **LEN** value. This is not incorrect; the two functions measure different things. The syntax is very simple:

```
LEN(<string>)
DATALENGTH(<string>)
```

Type in and execute the code in Listing 3-8 to learn how to use **LEN** and **DATALENGTH**.

Listing 3-8.Using the LEN and DATALENGTH Functions

```
USE AdventureWorks2008;
GO

SELECT LastName,LEN(LastName) AS "Length",
    DATALENGTH(LastName) AS "Data Length"
FROM Person.Person
WHERE BusinessEntityID IN (293,295,211,297,299,3057,15027);
```

Figure 3-8 shows the results. The **Length** column displays a count of the characters, while the **Data Length** column displays the number of bytes.

	LastName	Length	Data Length
1	Abolrous	8	16
2	Abel	4	8
3	Abercrombie	11	22
4	Acevedo	7	14
5	Ackerman	8	16
6	Alexander	9	18
7	Bell	4	8

Figure 3-8. The results of using LEN and DATALENGTH

CHARINDEX

Use **CHARINDEX** to find the numeric starting position of a search string inside another string. By checking to see whether the value returned by **CHARINDEX** is greater than zero, you can use the function to just determine whether the search string exists inside the second value. Developers often use **CHARINDEX** to locate a particular character, such as the at symbol (@) in an e-mail address column, along with other functions when parsing strings. You will learn more about this in the "Nesting Functions" section later in the chapter. The **CHARINDEX** function requires two parameters: the search string and the string to be searched. An optional parameter, the start location, instructs the function to ignore a given number of characters at the beginning of the string to be searched. The following is the syntax; remember that the third parameter is optional (square brackets surround optional parameters in the syntax).

```
CHARINDEX(<search string>,<target string>[,<start location>])
```

Listing 3-9 demonstrates how to use **CHARINDEX**. Type in and execute the code to learn how to use this function.

Listing 3-9. Using CHARINDEX

```
USE AdventureWorks2008;
GO
SELECT LastName, CHARINDEX('e',LastName) AS "Find e",
    CHARINDEX('e',LastName,4) AS "Skip 4 Characters",
    CHARINDEX('be',LastName) AS "Find be"
FROM Person.Person
WHERE BusinessEntityID IN (293,295,211,297,299,3057,15027);
```

Figure 3-9 shows the results. The **Find e** column in the results displays the first location of the letter *e* in the **LastName** value. The **Skip 4 Characters** column displays the first location of the letter *e* when the first four characters of the **LastName** value are ignored. Finally, the **Find be** column demonstrates that you can use the function with search strings that are more than one character in length.

	LastName	Find e	Skip 4 Characters	Find be
1	Abolrous	0	0	0
2	Abel	3	0	2
3	Abercrombie	3	11	2
4	Acevedo	3	5	0
5	Ackerman	4	4	0
6	Alexander	3	8	0
7	Bell	2	0	1

Figure 3-9. The results of using CHARINDEX

SUBSTRING

Use **SUSTRING** to return a portion of a string starting at a given position and for a specified number of characters. For example, an order-entry application may assign a customer ID based on the first seven letters of the customer's last name plus digits 4–9 of the phone number. The **SUBSTRING** function requires three parameters, the string, a starting location, and the number of characters to retrieve. If the number of characters to retrieve is greater than the length of the string, the function will return as many characters as possible. Here is the syntax of **SUBSTRING**:

```
SUBSTRING(<string>,<start location>,<length>)
```

Type in and execute the code in Listing 3-10 to learn how to use **SUBSTRING**.

Listing 3-10. Using SUBSTRING

```
USE AdventureWorks2008;
GO
SELECT LastName, SUBSTRING(LastName,1,4) AS "First 4",
    SUBSTRING(LastName,5,50) AS "Characters 5 and later"
FROM Person.Person
WHERE BusinessEntityID IN (293,295,211,297,299,3057,15027);
```

Notice in the results (Figure 3-10) that if the starting point is located after the available characters (*Abel* and *Bell*), an empty string is returned. Otherwise, in this example, the `FirstName` column is divided into two strings.

	LastName	First 4	Characters 5 and later
1	Abolrous	Abol	rous
2	Abel	Abel	
3	Abercrombie	Aber	crombie
4	Acevedo	Acev	edo
5	Ackerman	Acke	rman
6	Alexander	Alex	ander
7	Bell	Bell	

Figure 3-10. The results of using SUBSTRING

REVERSE

`REVERSE` returns a string in reverse order. I often use it along with the `RIGHT` function to find a file name from the file's path. I use `REVERSE` to find the last backslash in the path, which then tells me how many characters, minus 1, on the right side of the string I need to grab. To see how to do this, see the example in the "Nesting Functions" later in the chapter. Type in and execute this code to learn how to use `REVERSE`: `SELECT REVERSE('!dlroW ,olleH')`.

UPPER and LOWER

Use `UPPER` and `LOWER` to change a string to either uppercase or lowercase. You may need to display all uppercase data in a report, for example. The syntax is very simple:

```
UPPER(<string>)
LOWER(<string>)
```

Type in and execute the code in Listing 3-11.

Listing 3-11. Using UPPER and LOWER

```
USE AdventureWorks2008;
GO
SELECT LastName, UPPER(LastName) AS "UPPER",
    LOWER(LastName) AS "LOWER"
FROM Person.Person
WHERE BusinessEntityID IN (293,295,211,297,299,3057,15027);
```

Take a look at the results in Figure 3-11. All **LastName** values appear in uppercase in the **UPPER** column, while they appear in lowercase in the **LOWER** column.

	LastName	UPPER	LOWER
1	Abolrous	ABOLROUS	abolrous
2	Abel	ABEL	abel
3	Abercrombie	ABERCROMBIE	abercrombie
4	Acevedo	ACEVEDO	acevedo
5	Ackerman	ACKERMAN	ackerman
6	Alexander	ALEXANDER	alexander
7	Bell	BELL	bell

Figure 3-11. The partial results of using UPPER and LOWER

> ■ **Note** You may think that you will use UPPER or LOWER often in the WHERE clause to make sure that the case of the value does not affect the results, but usually you do not need to do this. By default, searching in T-SQL is case insensitive. The collation of the column determines whether the search will be case sensitive. This is defined at the server, but you can specify a different collation of the database, table, or column. See "Working with Collations" in Books Online for more information.

REPLACE

Use **REPLACE** to substitute one string value for another. **REPLACE** has three required parameters, but it is very easy to use. Use **REPLACE** to clean up data; for example, you may need to replace slashes (/) in a phone number column with hyphens (-) for a report. Here is the syntax:

```
REPLACE(<string value>,<string to replace>,<replacement>)
```

Type in and execute the code in Listing 3-12 to learn how to use **REPLACE**.

Listing 3-12. Using REPLACE

```
USE AdventureWorks2008;
GO

--1
SELECT LastName, REPLACE(LastName,'A','Z') AS "Replace A",
    REPLACE(LastName,'A','ZZ') AS "Replace with 2 characters",
    REPLACE(LastName,'ab','') AS "Remove string"
FROM Person.Person
WHERE BusinessEntityID IN (293,295,211,297,299,3057,15027);

--2
SELECT businessentityid,LastName,MiddleName,
    REPLACE(LastName,'a',MiddleName) AS "Replace with MiddleName",
    REPLACE(LastName,MiddleName,'a') AS "Replace MiddleName"
FROM Person.Person
WHERE BusinessEntityID IN (285,293,10314);
```

Notice in the results (Figure 3-12) that the **REPLACE** function replaces every instance of the string to be replaced. It doesn't matter if the strings in the second and third parameter are not the same length, as shown in **Replace with 2 characters**. The **Remove string** example shows a convenient way to remove a character or characters from a string by replacing with an empty string represented by two single quotes. Because the last name *Bell* doesn't contain any of the values to be replaced, the value does not change.

Query 2 demonstrates that the second and third parameters do not have to be literal values by using the **MiddleName** column either as the string to replace in the **Replace MiddleName** column or as the replacement in the **Replace with MiddleName** column.

	LastName	Replace A	Replace with 2 characters	Remove string
1	Abolrous	Zbolrous	ZZbolrous	olrous
2	Abel	Zbel	ZZbel	el
3	Abercrombie	Zbercrombie	ZZbercrombie	ercrombie
4	Acevedo	Zcevedo	ZZcevedo	Acevedo
5	Ackerman	ZckermZn	ZZckermZZn	Ackerman
6	Alexander	ZlexZnder	ZZlexZZnder	Alexander
7	Bell	Bell	Bell	Bell

	LastName	MiddleName	Replace with MiddleName	Replace MiddleName
1	Abbas	E	EbbEs	Abbas
2	Abel	R.	R.bel	Abel
3	Adams	M	MdMms	Adaas

Figure 3-12. The partial results of using REPLACE

Nesting Functions

The previous section showed how to use one function at a time to manipulate strings. If the results of one expression must be used as a parameter of another function call, you can nest functions. For example, you can nest the **LTRIM** and **RTRIM** functions to remove the spaces from the beginning and ending of a string like this: **LTRIM(RTRIM(' test '))**. Type in and execute the example shown in Listing 3-13 to display the domains in a list of e-mail addresses and the file name from a list of file paths.

Listing 3-13. Nesting Functions

```
USE AdventureWorks2008;
GO


--1
SELECT EmailAddress,
    SUBSTRING(EmailAddress,CHARINDEX('@',EmailAddress) + 1,50) AS DOMAIN
FROM Production.ProductReview;


--2
SELECT [FileName] AS Path,RIGHT([FileName],
    CHARINDEX('\',REVERSE([FileName]))-1) AS Name
FROM AdventureWorks.Production.Document;
```

Figure 3-13 shows the results. Query 1 uses the **CHARINDEX** function to find the location of the at symbol (@). The results of that expression are used as a parameter to the **SUBSTRING** function. To display the characters after the @ symbol, add 1 to the position of the @ symbol.

Query 2 finds the file name from a file path. First the **REVERSE** function reverses the string value. Then the **CHARINDEX** finds the first backslash character in the reversed string. This corresponds to the location of the backslash from the right end of the string if it wasn't reversed. Since the backslash doesn't belong in the results, subtract 1 from the value returned by the **CHARINDEX** function. By using that result as the second parameter of the **RIGHT** function, the query returns the file name. When writing a query like this, take it a step at a time. You may have to experiment a bit to get it right.

	EmailAddress	DOMAIN
1	john@fourthcoffee.com	fourthcoffee.com
2	david@graphicdesigninstitute.com	graphicdesigninstitute.com
3	jill@margiestravel.com	margiestravel.com
4	laura@treyresearch.net	treyresearch.net

	Path	Name
1	C:\Program Files\Microsoft SQL Server\MSSQL.1\Sa...	Crank Arm and Tire Maintenance.doc
2	C:\Program Files\Microsoft SQL Server\MSSQL.1\Sa...	Front Reflector Bracket and Reflector Assembly 3...
3	C:\Program Files\Microsoft SQL Server\MSSQL.1\Sa...	Front Reflector Bracket Installation.doc
4	C:\Program Files\Microsoft SQL Server\MSSQL.1\Sa...	Installing Replacement Pedals.doc
5	C:\Program Files\Microsoft SQL Server\MSSQL.1\Sa...	Introduction 1.doc
6	C:\Program Files\Microsoft SQL Server\MSSQL.1\Sa...	Lubrication Maintenance.doc
7	C:\Program Files\Microsoft SQL Server\MSSQL.1\Sa...	Repair and Service Guidelines.doc
8	C:\Program Files\Microsoft SQL Server\MSSQL.1\Sa...	Seat Assembly.doc
9	C:\Program Files\Microsoft SQL Server\MSSQL.1\Sa...	Training Wheels 2.doc

Figure 3-13. The results of using nested functions

This section covered a sample of the many functions available to manipulate strings in T-SQL. Complete Exercise 3-3 to practice using these functions.

Exercise 3-3

Use the AdventureWorks2008 database to complete this exercise. Be sure to refer to the discussion of the functions to help you figure out which ones to use if you need help. You can find the solutions to these questions in the appendix.

1. Write a query that displays the first 10 characters of the `AddressLine1` column in the `Person.Address` table.
2. Write a query that displays characters 10 to 15 of the `AddressLine1` column in the `Person.Address` table.
3. Write a query displaying the first and last names from the `Person.Person` table all in uppercase.
4. The product number in the `Production.Product` table contains a hyphen (-). Write a query that uses the `SUBSTRING` function and the `CHARINDEX` function to display the characters in the product number following the hyphen. Note: there is also a second hyphen in many of the rows; ignore the second hyphen for this question. Hint: Try writing this statement in two steps, the first using the `CHARINDEX` function and the second adding the `SUBSTRING` function.

Using Date Functions

Just as T-SQL features a rich set of functions for working with string data, it also boasts an impressive list of functions for working with date and time data types.

In this section, you'll take a look at some of the most commonly used functions for date and time data.

GETDATE and SYSDATETIME

Use `GETDATE` or `SYSDATETIME` to return the current date and time of the server. The difference is that `SYSDATETIME` returns seven decimal places after the second, while `GETDATE` returns only three places. You may see zeros filling in some of the right digits if your SQL Server is installed on Vista-64 istead of another operating system.

`GETDATE` and `SYSDATETIME` are . *nondeterministic* functions. This means that they return different values each time they are called. Most of the functions in this chapter are *deterministic*, which means that a function always returns the same value when called with the same parameters and database settings. For example, the code `CHARINDEX('B','abcd')` will always return 2 if the collation of the database is case insensitive. In a case-sensitive database, the expression will return 0.

Run this code several times to see how these functions work: `SELECT GETDATE(), SYSDATETIME();`.

DATEADD

Use **DATEADD** to add a number of time units to a date. The function requires three parameters: the date part, the number, and a date. T-SQL does not have a **DATESUBTRACT** function, but you can use a negative number to accomplish the same thing. You might use **DATEADD** to calculate an expiration date or a date that a payment is due, for example. Table 3-1 from Books Online lists the possible values for the date part parameter in the **DATEADD** function and other date functions. Here is the syntax for **DATEADD**:

```
DATEADD(<date part>,<number>,<date>)
```

Table 3-1. *The Values for the Date Part Parameter*

Date Part	Abbreviation
Year	yy, yyyy
Quarter	qq, q
Month	mm, m
Dayofyear	dy, y
Day	dd, d
Week	wk, ww
Weekday	dw
Hour	hh
Minute	mi, n
Second	ss, s
Millisecond	ms
Microsecond	mcs
Nanosecond	ns

Type in and execute the code in Listing 3-14 to learn how to use the **DATEADD** function.

Listing 3-14. Using the DATEADD Function

```
Use AdventureWorks2008
GO
--1
SELECT OrderDate, DATEADD(year,1,OrderDate) AS OneMoreYear,
    DATEADD(month,1,OrderDate) AS OneMoreMonth,
    DATEADD(day,-1,OrderDate) AS OneLessDay
FROM Sales.SalesOrderHeader
WHERE SalesOrderID in (43659,43714,60621);
--2
SELECT DATEADD(month,1,'1/29/2009');
```

Figure 3-14 shows the results of Listing 3-14. In query 1, the **DATEADD** function adds exactly the time unit specified in each expression to the **OrderDate** column from the **Sales.SalesOrderHeader** table. Notice in the results of query 2 that since there is no 29th day of February 2009, adding one month to January 29, 2009, returns February 28, the last possible day in February that year.

	OrderDate	OneMoreYear	OneMoreMonth	OneLessDay
1	2001-07-01 00:00:00.000	2002-07-01 00:00:00.000	2001-08-01 00:00:00.000	2001-06-30 00:00:00.000
2	2001-07-05 00:00:00.000	2002-07-05 00:00:00.000	2001-08-05 00:00:00.000	2001-07-04 00:00:00.000
3	2003-12-23 00:00:00.000	2004-12-23 00:00:00.000	2004-01-23 00:00:00.000	2003-12-22 00:00:00.000

	(No column name)
1	2009-02-28 00:00:00.000

Figure 3-14. The results of using the DATEADD function

DATEDIFF

The **DATEDIFF** function allows you to find the difference between two dates. The function requires three parameters: the date part and the two dates. The **DATEDIFF** function might be used to calculate how many days have passed since unshipped orders were taken, for example. Here is the syntax: **DATEDIFF(<datepart>,<early date>,<later date>)**. See Table 3-1 for the list of possible date parts. Listing 3-15 demonstrates how to use **DATEDIFF**. Be sure to type in and execute the code.

Listing 3-15. Using DATEDIFF

```
Use AdventureWorks2008;
GO

--1
SELECT OrderDate, GETDATE() CurrentDateTime,
    DATEDIFF(year,OrderDate,GETDATE()) AS YearDiff,
    DATEDIFF(month,OrderDate,GETDATE()) AS MonthDiff,
    DATEDIFF(day,OrderDate,GETDATE()) AS DayDiff
FROM Sales.SalesOrderHeader
WHERE SalesOrderID in (43659,43714,60621);

--2
SELECT DATEDIFF(year,'12/31/2008','1/1/2009') AS YearDiff,
    DATEDIFF(month,'12/31/2008','1/1/2009') AS MonthDiff,
    DATEDIFF(day,'12/31/2008','1/1/2009') AS DayDiff;
```

Figure 3-15 shows the results. Your results from query 1 will be different from mine since the query uses **GETDATE()**, a nondeterministic function, instead of hard-coded dates or dates from a table. Even though query 2 compares the difference between two dates that are just one day apart, the differences in years and months are both 1. The **DATEDIFF** rounds up the result to the nearest integer and does not display decimal results.

	OrderDate	CurrentDateTime	YearDiff	MonthDiff	DayDiff
1	2001-07-01 00:00:00.000	2009-03-18 19:44:34.367	8	92	2817
2	2001-07-05 00:00:00.000	2009-03-18 19:44:34.367	8	92	2813
3	2003-12-23 00:00:00.000	2009-03-18 19:44:34.367	6	63	1912

	YearDiff	MonthDiff	DayDiff
1	1	1	1

Figure 3-15. *The results of using DATEDIFF*

DATENAME and DATEPART

The **DATENAME** and **DATEPART** functions return the part of the date specified. Developers use the **DATENAME** and **DATEPART** functions to display just the year or month on reports, for example. **DATEPART** always returns a numeric value. **DATENAME** returns the actual name when the date part is the month or the day of the week. Again, you can find the possible date parts in Table 3-1. The syntax for the two functions is similar:

```
DATENAME(<datepart>,<date>)
DATEPART(<datepart>,<date>)
```

Type in and execute the code in Listing 3-16 to learn how to use **DATENAME**.

Listing 3-16. Using DATENAME and DATEPART

```
Use AdventureWorks2008
GO
--1
SELECT OrderDate, DATEPART(year,OrderDate) AS OrderYear,
    DATEPART(month,OrderDate) AS OrderMonth,
    DATEPART(day,OrderDate) AS OrderDay,
    DATEPART(weekday,OrderDate) AS OrderWeekDay
FROM Sales.SalesOrderHeader
WHERE SalesOrderID in (43659,43714,60621);


--2
SELECT OrderDate, DATENAME(year,OrderDate) AS OrderYear,
    DATENAME(month,OrderDate) AS OrderMonth,
    DATENAME(day,OrderDate) AS OrderDay,
    DATENAME(weekday,OrderDate) AS OrderWeekDay
FROM Sales.SalesOrderHeader
WHERE SalesOrderID in (43659,43714,60621);
```

Figure 3-16 displays the results. You will see that the results are the same except for spelling out the month and weekday in query 2. One other thing to keep in mind is that the value returned from **DATEPART** is always an integer, while the value returned from **DATENAME** is always a string, even when the expression returns a number.

	OrderDate	OrderYear	OrderMonth	OrderDay	OrderWeekDay
1	2001-07-01 00:00:00.000	2001	7	1	1
2	2001-07-05 00:00:00.000	2001	7	5	5
3	2003-12-23 00:00:00.000	2003	12	23	3

	OrderDate	OrderYear	OrderMonth	OrderDay	OrderWeekDay
1	2001-07-01 00:00:00.000	2001	July	1	Sunday
2	2001-07-05 00:00:00.000	2001	July	5	Thursday
3	2003-12-23 00:00:00.000	2003	December	23	Tuesday

Figure 3-16. Results of using DATENAME and DATEPART

DAY, MONTH, and YEAR

The **DAY**, **MONTH**, and **YEAR** functions work just like **DATEPART**. These functions are just alternate ways to get the day, month, or year from a date. Here is the syntax:

```
DAY(<date>)
MONTH(<date>)
YEAR(<date>)
```

Type in and execute the code in Listing 3-17 to see that this is just another way to get the same results as using the **DATEPART** function.

Listing 3-17. Using the DAY, MONTH, and YEAR Functions

```
Use AdventureWorks2008
GO

SELECT OrderDate, YEAR(OrderDate) AS OrderYear,
    MONTH(OrderDate) AS OrderMonth,
    DAY(OrderDate) AS OrderDay
FROM Sales.SalesOrderHeader
WHERE SalesOrderID in (43659,43714,60621);
```

Figure 3-17 displays the results of the code from Listing 3-17. If you take a look at the results of query 1 from Listing 3-16 that used the **DATEPART** function, you will see that they are the same.

	OrderDate	OrderYear	OrderMonth	OrderDay
1	2001-07-01 00:00:00.000	2001	7	1
2	2001-07-05 00:00:00.000	2001	7	5
3	2003-12-23 00:00:00.000	2003	12	23

Figure 3-17. The result of using YEAR, MONTH, and DAY

CONVERT

You learned about **CONVERT** earlier in the chapter when I talked about concatenating strings. To append a number or a date to a string, the number or date must first be cast to a string. The **CONVERT** function has an optional parameter called **style** that can be used to format a date.

I have frequently seen code that used the **DATEPART** function to break a date into its parts and then cast the parts into strings and concatenate them back together to format the date. It is so much easier just to use **CONVERT** to accomplish the same thing! Here is the syntax:

```
CONVERT(<data type, usually varchar>,<date>,<style>)
```

Type in and execute the code in Listing 3-18 to compare both methods of formatting dates. Take a look at the SQL Server Books Online article "CAST and CONVERT" for a list of all the possible formats.

Listing 3-18. Using CONVERT to Format a Date/Time Value

```
--1 The hard way!
SELECT CAST(DATEPART(YYYY,GETDATE()) AS VARCHAR) + '/' +
    CAST(DATEPART(MM,GETDATE()) AS VARCHAR) +
    '/' + CAST(DATEPART(DD,GETDATE()) AS VARCHAR);
```

```
--2 The easy way!
SELECT CONVERT(VARCHAR,GETDATE(),111);
--3
USE AdventureWorks2008
GO
SELECT CONVERT(VARCHAR,OrderDate,1) AS "1",
    CONVERT(VARCHAR,OrderDate,101) AS "101",
    CONVERT(VARCHAR,OrderDate,2) AS "2",
    CONVERT(VARCHAR,OrderDate,102) AS "102"
FROM Sales.SalesOrderHeader
WHERE SalesOrderID in (43659,43714,60621);
```

Figure 3-18 shows the results of Listing 3-18. Notice in query 1 that we not only had to use DATEPART three times, but we also had to cast each result to a VARCHAR in order to concatenate the pieces back together. Query 2 shows the easy way to accomplish the same thing. This method is often used to remove the time from a DATETIME data type. Query 3 demonstrates four different formats. Notice that the three-digit formats always produce four-digit years.

Results			
(No column name)			
1	2009/3/18		

(No column name)			
1	2009/03/18		

1	101	2	102
1	07/01/01	07/01/2001	01.07.01	2001.07.01
2	07/05/01	07/05/2001	01.07.05	2001.07.05
3	12/23/03	12/23/2003	03.12.23	2003.12.23

Figure 3-18. *The results of formatting dates*

This section covered a sample of the functions available for manipulating dates. Practice what you have learned by completing Exercise 3-4.

Exercise 3-4

Use the AdventureWorks2008 database to complete this exercise. You can find the solutions to the questions in the appendix.

1. Write a query that calculates the number of days between the date an order was placed and the date that it was shipped using the Sales.SalesOrderHeader table. Include the SalesOrderID, OrderDate, and ShipDate columns.

2. Write a query that displays only the date, not the time, for the order date and ship date in the Sales.SalesOrderHeader table.

3. Write a query that adds six months to each order date in the `Sales.SalesOrderHeader` table. Include the `SalesOrderID` and `OrderDate` columns.
4. Write a query that displays the year of each order date and the numeric month of each order date in separate columns in the results. Include the `SalesOrderID` and `OrderDate` columns.
5. Change the query written in question 4 to display the month name instead.

Using Mathematical Functions

You can use several several mathematical functions on numericmathematical functions on numeric values. These include trigonometric functions such as **SIN** and **TAN** and logarithmic functions that are not used frequently in business applications. I discuss some of the more commonly used mathematical functions in this section.

ABS

The **ABS** function returns the absolute value of the number, in other words, the difference between the number and zero. Type in and execute this code to see how to use **ABS**: `SELECT ABS(2) AS "2", ABS(-2) AS "-2"`.

POWER

The **POWER** function returns the power of one number to another number. The syntax is simple: `POWER(<number>,<power>)`. There may not be many uses for **POWER** in business applications, but you may use it in scientific or academic applications. Type in and execute the code in Listing 3-19.

Listing 3-19. Using POWER

```
SELECT POWER(10,1) AS "Ten to the First",
    POWER(10,2) AS "Ten to the Second",
    POWER(10,3) AS "Ten to the Third";
```

Figure 3-19 displays the results. The **POWER** function returns a **FLOAT** value. Caution must be taken, however, with this function. The results will increase in size very quickly and can cause an overflow error. Try finding the value of 10 to the 10th power to see what can happen.

Results		
Ten to the First	Ten to the Second	Ten to the Third
10	100	1000

Figure 3-19. The results of using POWER

SQUARE and SQRT

The **SQUARE** function returns the square of a number, or the number multiplied to itself. The **SQRT** function returns the opposite, the square root of a number. Type in and execute the code in Listing 3-20 to see how to use these functions.

Listing 3-20. Using the SQUARE and SQRT Functions

```
SELECT SQUARE(10) AS "Square of 10",
    SQRT(10) AS "Square Root of 10",
    SQRT(SQUARE(10)) AS "The Square Root of the Square of 10";
```

Figure 3-20 shows the results. Notice that the third expression in the query is a "nested" function that squares 10 and then takes the square root of that result.

	Square of 10	Square Root of 10	The Square Root of the Square of 10
1	100	3.16227766016838	10

Figure 3-20. The results of using SQUARE and SQRT

ROUND

The **ROUND** function allows you to round a number to a given precision. The **ROUND** function is used frequently to display only the number of decimal places required in the report or application. The **ROUND** function requires two parameters, the number and the length, which can be either positive or negative. It also has an optional third parameter that causes the function to just truncate instead of rounding if a nonzero value is supplied. Here is the syntax:

```
ROUND(<number>,<length>[,<function>])
```

Type in and execute the code in Listing 3-21 to learn how to use **ROUND**.

Listing 3-21. Using ROUND

```
SELECT ROUND(1234.1294,2) AS "2 places on the right",
    ROUND(1234.1294,-2) AS "2 places on the left",
    ROUND(1234.1294,2,1) AS "Truncate 2",
    ROUND(1234.1294,-2,1) AS "Truncate -2";
```

You can view the results in Figure 3-21. When the expression contains a negative number as the second parameter, the function rounds on the left side of the decimal point. Notice the difference when 1 is used as the third parameter, causing the function to truncate instead of rounding. When rounding 1234.1294, the expression returns 1234.1300. When truncating 1234.1294, the expression returns 1234.1200. It doesn't round the value; it just changes the specified digits to zero.

	2 places on the right	2 places on the left	Truncate 2	Truncate -2
1	1234.1300	1200.0000	1234.1200	1200.0000

Figure 3-21. *The results of using ROUND*

RAND

RAND returns a float value between 0 and 1. **RAND** can be used to generate a random value. This might be used to generate data for testing an application, for example. The **RAND** function takes one optional integer parameter, **@seed**. When the **RAND** expression contains the seed value, the function returns the same value each time. If the expression does not contain a seed value, SQL Server randomly assigns a seed, effectively providing a random number. Type in and execute the code in Listing 3-22 to generate a random numbers.

Listing 3-22. *Using RAND*

```
SELECT CAST(RAND() * 100 AS INT) + 1 AS "1 to 100",
    CAST(RAND()* 1000 AS INT) + 900 AS "900 to 1900",
    CAST(RAND() * 5 AS INT)+ 1 AS "1 to 5";
```

Since the function returns a float value, multiply by the size of the range, and add the lower limit (see Figure 3-22). The first expression returns random numbers between 1 and 100. The second expression returns random numbers between 900 and 1900. The third expression returns random values between 1 and 5.

	1 to 100	900 to 1900	1 to 5
1	45	1556	2

Figure 3-22. *The results of generating random numbers with RAND*

If you supply a seed value to one of the calls to **RAND** within a batch of statements, that seed affects the other calls. The value is not the same, but the values are predictable. Run this statement several times to see what happens when a seed value is used: **SELECT RAND(3),RAND(),RAND()**.

Just like strings and dates, you will find several functions that manipulate numbers. Practice using these functions by completing Exercise 3-5.

Exercise 3-5

Use the AdventureWorks2008 database to complete this exercise. You can find the solutions to the questions in the appendix.

1. Write a query using the `Sales.SalesOrderHeader` table that displays the `SubTotal` rounded to two decimal places. Include the `SalesOrderID` column in the results.
2. Modify the query from question 1 so that the `SubTotal` is rounded to the nearest dollar but still displays two zeros to the right of the decimal place.
3. Write a query that calculates the square root of the `SalesOrderID` value from the `Sales.SalesOrderHeader` table.
4. Write a statement that generates a random number between 1 and 10 each time it is run.

System Functions

T-SQL features many other built-in functions. Some are specific for administering SQL Server, while others are very useful in regular end-user applications, returning information such as the database and current usernames. Be sure to review the "Functions" topic in Books Online often to discover functions that will make your life easier.

The CASE Function

Use the **CASE** function to evaluate a list of expressions and return the first one that evaluates to true. For example, a report may need to display the season of the year based on one of the date columns in the table. **CASE** is similar to `Select Case` or `Switch` used in other programming languages, but it is used inside the statement.

There are two ways to write a **CASE** expression: simple or searched. The following sections will explain the differences and how to use them.

Simple CASE

To write the "simple" **CASE** statement, come up with an expression that you want to evaluate, often a column name, and a list of possible values. Here is the syntax:

```
CASE <test expression>
    WHEN <comparison expression1> THEN <return value1>
    WHEN <comparison expression2> THEN <return value2>
    [ELSE <value3>] END
```

Type in and execute the code in Listing 3-23 to learn how to use the simple version of **CASE**.

Listing 3-23. Using Simple CASE

```
USE AdventureWorks2008;
GO
SELECT Title,
    CASE Title
    WHEN 'Mr.' THEN 'Male'
    WHEN 'Ms.' THEN 'Female'
    WHEN 'Mrs.' THEN 'Female'
    WHEN 'Miss' THEN 'Female'
    ELSE 'Unknown' END AS Gender
FROM Person.Person
WHERE BusinessEntityID IN (1,5,6,357,358,11621,423);
```

Figure 3-23 shows the results. Even though the **CASE** statement took up a lot of room in the query, it is producing only one column in the results. For each row returned, the expression evaluates the **Title** column to see whether it matches any of the possibilities listed and returns the appropriate value. If the value from **Title** does not match or is **NULL**, then whatever is in the **ELSE** part of the expression is returned. If no **ELSE** exists, the expression returns **NULL**.

	Title	Gender
1	NULL	Unknown
2	Ms.	Female
3	Mr.	Male
4	Ms.	Female
5	Sr.	Unknown
6	Mrs.	Female

Figure 3-23. *The results of using simple CASE*

Searched CASE

Developers often used the "searched" **CASE** syntax when the expression is too complicated for the simple **CASE** syntax. For example, you might want to compare the value from a column to several **IN** lists or use greater-than or less-than operators. The **CASE** statement returns the first expression that returns true. This is the syntax for the searched **CASE**:

```
CASE WHEN <test expression1> THEN <value1>
WHEN <test expression2> THEN <value2>
[ELSE <value3>] END
```

Type in and execute the code in Listing 3-24 to learn how to use this more flexible method of using **CASE**.

Listing 3-24. Using Searched CASE

```
SELECT Title,
    CASE WHEN Title IN ('Ms.','Mrs.','Miss') THEN 'Female'
    WHEN Title = 'Mr.' THEN 'Male'
    ELSE 'Unknown' END AS Gender
FROM Person.Person
WHERE BusinessEntityID IN (1,5,6,357,358,11621,423);
```

This query returns the same results (see Figure 3-24) as the one in Listing 3-23. The **CASE** function evaluates each **WHEN** expression independently until finding the first one that returns true. It then returns the appropriate value. If none of the expressions returns true, the function returns the value from the **ELSE** part or **NULL** if no **ELSE** is available.

	Title	Gender
1	NULL	Unknown
2	Ms.	Female
3	Mr.	Male
4	Ms.	Female
5	Sr.	Unknown
6	Mrs.	Female

Figure 3-24. *The results of using searched CASE*

One very important note about using **CASE** is that the return values must be of compatible data types. For example, you cannot have one part of the expression returning an integer while another part returns a non-numeric string. Precedence rules apply as with other operations.

Listing a Column as the Return Value

It is also possible to list a column name instead of hard-coded values in the **THEN** part of the **CASE** function. This means that you can display one column for some of the rows and another column for other rows. Type in and execute the code in Listing 3-25 to see how this works.

Listing 3-25. Returning a Column Name in CASE

```
USE AdventureWorks2008;
GO

SELECT VacationHours,SickLeaveHours,
    CASE WHEN VacationHours > SickLeaveHours THEN VacationHours
    ELSE SickLeaveHours END AS 'More Hours'
FROM HumanResources.Employee;
```

In this example (see Figure 3-25), if there are more **VacationHours** than **SickLeaveHours**, the query displays the **VacationHours** column from the **HumanResources.Empoyee** table in the **More Hours** column. Otherwise, the query returns the **SickLeaveHours**.

	VacationHours	SickLeaveHours	More Hours
1	99	69	99
2	1	20	20
3	2	21	21
4	48	80	80
5	5	22	22
6	6	23	23
7	61	50	61
8	62	51	62
9	63	51	63
10	16	64	64

Figure 3-25. The results of returning a column from CASE

COALESCE

You learned about **COALESCE** earlier in the chapter in the "Concatenating Strings and NULL" section. You can use **COALESCE** with other data types as well and with any number of arguments to return the first non-**NULL** value. You can use the **COALESCE** function in place of **ISNULL**. If a list of values must be evaluated instead of one value, you must use **COALESCE** instead of **ISNULL**. **COALESCE** may be used when concatenating strings or any time that a replacement for **NULL** must be found. Type in and execute the code in Listing 3-26 to learn more about **COALESCE**.

Listing 3-26. Using COALESCE

```
USE AdventureWorks2008;
GO

SELECT ProductID,Size, Color,
    COALESCE(Size, Color,'No color or size') AS 'Description'
FROM Production.Product
where ProductID in (1,2,317,320,680,706);
```

Figure 3-26 displays the results. The **COALESCE** expression first checks the **Size** value and then the **Color** value to find the first non-**NULL** value. If both values are **NULL**, then the string **No color or size** is returned.

	ProductID	Size	Color	Description
1	1	NULL	NULL	No color or size
2	2	NULL	NULL	No color or size
3	317	NULL	Black	Black
4	320	NULL	Silver	Silver
5	680	58	Black	58
6	706	58	Red	58

Figure 3-26. *The results of using COALESCE*

Admin Functions

T-SQL contains many administrative functions that are useful for developers. SQL Server also has many functions that help database administrators manage SQL Server. These functions are beyond the scope of this book. Listing 3-27 shows a few examples of functions that return information about the current connection such as the database name and application.

Listing 3-27. *A Few System Functions*

```
SELECT DB_NAME() AS "Database Name",
    HOST_NAME() AS "Host Name",
    CURRENT_USER AS "Current User",
    USER_NAME() AS "User Name",
    APP_NAME() AS "App Name";
```

Take a look at Figure 3-27 for my results; your results will probably be different. When I ran the query, I was connected to the master database on a computer named KATHI-PC as the dbo user while using Management Studio.

	Database Name	Host Name	Current User	User Name	App Name
1	AdventureWorks2008	KATHI-PC	dbo	dbo	Microsoft SQL Server Management Studio - Query

Figure 3-27. *The results of using system functions*

In addition to the functions used to manipulate strings, dates, and numbers, you will find many system functions. Some of these work on different types of data, such as **CASE**, while others provide information about the current connection. Administrators can manage SQL Server using dozens of system functions not covered in this book. Complete Exercise 3-6 to practice using the system functions covered in this section.

Exercise 3-6

Use the AdventureWorks2008 database to complete this exercise. You can find the solutions to the questions in the appendix.

1. Write a query using the `HumanResources.Employee` table to display the `BusinessEntityID` column. Also include a `CASE` statement that displays "Even" when the `BusinessEntityID` value is an even number or "Odd" when it is odd. Hint: Use the modulo operator.
2. Write a query using the `Sales.SalesOrderDetail` table to display a value ("Under 10" or "10–19" or "20–29" or "30–39" or "40 and over") based on the `OrderQty` value by using the `CASE` function. Include the `SalesOrderID` and `OrderQty` columns in the results.
3. Using the `Person.Person` table, build the full names using the `Title`, `FirstName`, `MiddleName`, `LastName`, and `Suffix` columns. Check the table definition to see which columns allow `NULL` values and use the `COALESCE` function on the appropriate columns.
4. Look up the `SERVERPROPERTY` function in Books Online. Write a statement that displays the edition, instance name, and machine name using this function.

Using Functions in the WHERE and ORDER BY Clauses

So far you have seen functions used in the **SELECT** list. You may also use functions in the **WHERE** and **ORDER BY** clauses. Take a look at Listing 3-28 for several examples.

Listing 3-28. Using Functions in WHERE and ORDER BY

```
USE AdventureWorks2008;
GO


--1
SELECT FirstName
FROM Person.Person
WHERE CHARINDEX('ke',FirstName) > 0;


--2
SELECT LastName,REVERSE(LastName)
FROM Person.Person
ORDER BY REVERSE(LastName);


--3
SELECT BirthDate
FROM HumanResources.Employee
ORDER BY YEAR(BirthDate);
```

Figure 3-28 shows the results of Listing 3-28. Even though it is very easy to use a function on a column in the **WHERE** clause, it is important to note that performance may suffer. If the database designer created an index on the searched column, the database engine must evaluate each row one at a time when a function is applied to a column.

Figure 3-28. *The results of using functions in the* WHERE *and* ORDER BY *clauses*

Practice using functions in the **WHERE** and **ORDER** by clauses by completing Exercise 3-7.

Exercise 3-7

Use the AdventureWorks2008 database to complete this exericse. You will find the solutions to the questions in the appendix.

1. Write a query using the `Sales.SalesOrderHeader` table to display the orders placed during 2001 by using a function. Include the `SalesOrderID` and `OrderDate` columns in the results.
2. Write a query using the `Sales.SalesOrderHeader` table listing the sales in order of the month the order was placed and then the year the order was placed. Include the `SalesOrderID` and `OrderDate` columns in the results.
3. Write a query that displays the `PersonType` and the name columns from the `Person.Person` table. Sort the results so that rows with a `PersonType` of `IN`, `SP`, or `SC` sort by `LastName`. The other rows should sort by `FirstName`. Hint: Use the `CASE` function.

Thinking About Performance

In Chapter 2 you learned how to use execution plans to compare two or more queries and determine which query uses the least resources or, in other words, performs the best. In this chapter, you will see how using functions can affect performance. Review the "Thinking About Performance" section in Chapter 2 if you need to take another look at how to use execution plans or to brush up on how SQL Server uses indexes.

Using Functions in the WHERE Clause

In the section "Using Functions in the WHERE and ORDER BY Clauses," you learned that functions can be used in the WHERE clause to filter out unneeded rows. Although I am not saying that you should never include a function in the WHERE clause, you need to realize that including a function that operates on a column may cause a decrease in performance.

The Sales.SalesOrderHeader table does not contain an index on the OrderDate column. Run the following code to create an index on the column. Don't worry about trying to understand the code at this point.

```
USE [AdventureWorks2008]
GO
--Add an index
IF  EXISTS (SELECT * FROM sys.indexes WHERE object_id =
    OBJECT_ID(N'[Sales].[SalesOrderHeader]')
    AND name = N'DEMO_SalesOrderHeader_OrderDate')
DROP INDEX [DEMO_SalesOrderHeader_OrderDate]
    ON [Sales].[SalesOrderHeader] WITH ( ONLINE = OFF );
GO
CREATE NONCLUSTERED INDEX [DEMO_SalesOrderHeader_OrderDate]
    ON [Sales].[SalesOrderHeader]
([OrderDate] ASC);
```

Toggle on the Include Actual Execution Plan setting before typing and executing the code in Listing 3-29.

Listing 3-29. Compare the Performance When Using a Function in the WHERE Clause

```
USE AdventureWorks2008;
GO

--1
SELECT SalesOrderID, OrderDate
FROM Sales.SalesOrderHeader
WHERE OrderDate >= '2001-01-01 00:00:00'
    AND OrderDate <= '2002-01-01 00:00:00';
```

```
--2
SELECT SalesOrderID, OrderDate
FROM Sales.SalesOrderHeader
WHERE YEAR(OrderDate) = 2001;
```

Query 1 finds all the orders placed in 2001 without using a function. Query 2 uses the **YEAR** function to return the same results. Take a look at the execution plans (Figure 3-29) to see that query 1 performs much better with a query cost of 7 percent. When executing query 2, the database engine performs a scan of the entire index to see whether the result of the function applied to each value meets the criteria. The database engine performs a seek of the index in query 1 because it just has to compare the actual values, not the results of the function for each value.

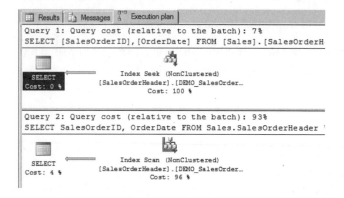

Figure 3-29. *The execution plans showing that using a function in the* WHERE *clause can affect performance*

Remove the index you created for this demonstration by running this code:

```
IF  EXISTS (SELECT * FROM sys.indexes WHERE object_id =
    OBJECT_ID(N'[Sales].[SalesOrderHeader]')
    AND name = N'DEMO_SalesOrderHeader_OrderDate')
DROP INDEX [DEMO_SalesOrderHeader_OrderDate]
    ON [Sales].[SalesOrderHeader] WITH ( ONLINE = OFF );
```

Run Listing 3-29 again now that the index is gone. Figure 3-30 shows that with no index on the **OrderDate** column, the performance is almost identical. Now the database engine must perform a scan of the table, in this case the clustered index, to find the correct rows in both of the queries. Notice that the execution plan suggests an index to help the performance of query 1. It doesn't suggest an index for query 2 since an index won't help.

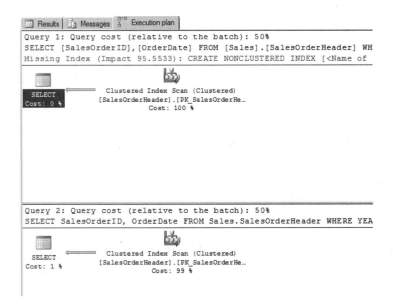

Figure 3-30. *The execution plans after removing the index*

You can see from these examples that writing queries is more than just getting the correct results; performance is important, too. Complete Exercise 3-8 to learn how using a function compares to a wildcard search.

Exercise 3-8

Use the AdventureWorks2008 database to complete this exercise. Make sure you have the Include Actual Execution Plan setting toggled on before starting this exercise. You can find the solutions in the appendix.

1. Type in and execute the following code. View the execution plans once query execution completes, and explain whether one query performs better than the other and why.

```
USE AdventureWorks2008;
GO


--1
SELECT Name
FROM Production.Product
WHERE Name LIKE 'B%';
```

```
--2
SELECT Name
FROM Production.Product
WHERE CHARINDEX('B',Name) = 1;
```

2. Type in and execute the following code. View the execution plans once query execution completes, and explain whether one query performs better than the other and why.

```
USE AdventureWorks2008;
GO

--1
SELECT LastName
FROM Person.Person
WHERE LastName LIKE '%i%';

--2
SELECT LastName
FROM Person.Person
WHERE CHARINDEX('i',LastName) > 0;
```

Summary

Using expressions in T-SQL with the built-in functions and operators can be very convenient. There is a rich collection of functions for string and date manipulation as well as mathematical and system functions and more. It's possible to use expressions and functions in the **SELECT**, **WHERE**, and **ORDER BY** clauses. You must use caution when using functions in the **WHERE** clause; it is possible to decrease performance.

Querying Multiple Tables

Now that you know how to write simple queries using one table and how to use functions and expressions in queries, it is time to learn how to write queries involving two or more tables. In a properly designed relational database, a table contains data about one thing or entity. For example, an order-entry application will have a table storing customer information, a table containing data about orders, and a table containing detail information about each item ordered. The order table has a column, called a *foreign key*, that points to a row in the customer table. The detail table has a foreign key column that points to the order table. By using *joins*, you can link these tables together so that you can display columns from each table in the same result set.

You can also use multiple tables with subqueries and union queries. You might use a subquery in place of an **IN** list in the **WHERE** clause, for example. A union query allows you to combine the result of two or more queries into one result set. For example, a database may contain archive tables with old sales data. By using a **UNION** query, you can combine the data from both the production tables and the archived tables so that it looks like the results are from the same table.

Finally, this chapter demonstrates two useful techniques, derived tables and common table expressions. These techniques allow you to isolate the logic used to query one table from the rest of the main query.

Learning how to join tables is a critical skill for T-SQL developers because it allows you to combine the relational data stored in multiple tables and present it as a single result set. Make sure you understand all the example code and complete the exercises in this chapter before moving on to the next chapter.

Writing Inner Joins

Most of the time, to join tables together, you will use **INNER JOIN**. When connecting two tables with **INNER JOIN**, only the rows from the tables that match on the joining columns will show up in the results. If you join the customer and order tables, the query will return only the customers who have placed orders, along with the orders that have been placed. Only the rows where the customer ID is common in both tables will show up in the results.

Joining Two Tables

To join tables together, you might think that another clause will be added to the **SELECT** statement. This is not the case. Instead, the **FROM** clause contains information about how the tables join together. Here is the syntax for joining two tables (the keyword **INNER** is optional):

```
SELECT <select list>
FROM <table1>
[INNER] JOIN <table2> ON <table1>.<col1> = <table2>.<col2>
```

Figure 4-1 shows how the **Sales.SalesOrderHeader** and **Sales.SalesOrderDetail** tables connect and shows some of the columns in the tables. You will see these tables joined in the first example query, so make sure you understand how they connect before typing Listing 4-1.

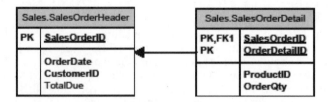

Figure 4-1. *The Sales.SalesOrderHeader and Sales.SalesOrderDetail tables*

The **Sales.SalesOrderHeader** table has a primary key called **SalesOrderID**. The **Sales.SalesOrderDetail** table has a composite primary key, one that is made up of more than one column, consisting of **SalesOrderID** and **OrderDetailID**. The **SalesOrderID** column in the **Sales.SalesOrderDetail** table is also a foreign key pointing back to the **Sales.SalesOrderHeader** table. The arrow points from the foreign key in the **Sales.SalesOrderDetail** table to the primary key in the **Sales.SalesOrderHeader** table.

Take a look at the code in Listing 4-1. Type in and execute the code to learn how to join the two tables.

Listing 4-1. *Joining Two Tables*

```
USE AdventureWorks;
GO
SELECT s.SalesOrderID, s.OrderDate, s.TotalDue, d.SalesOrderDetailID,
    d.ProductID, d.OrderQty
FROM Sales.SalesOrderHeader AS s
INNER JOIN Sales.SalesOrderDetail AS d ON s.SalesOrderID = d.SalesOrderID;
```

Figure 4-2 displays the results. The **SELECT** list may contain columns from either of the tables. In the **FROM** clause, you list one of the tables followed by the words **INNER JOIN** and the second table name. To define how the two tables join together, use the keyword **ON** and an equality expression. Each **Sales.OrderHeader** row contains a unique **SalesOrderID**. Each **Sales.SalesOrderDetail** row contains a **SalesOrderID** column that determines to which order the detail belongs. When you join these two tables together, the query displays every row from the **Sales.SalesOrderHeader** table that matches a row in the **Sales.SalesOrderDetail** table.

	SalesOrderID	OrderDate	TotalDue	SalesOrderDetailID	ProductID	OrderQty
1	43659	2001-07-01 00:00:00.000	27231.5495	1	776	1
2	43659	2001-07-01 00:00:00.000	27231.5495	2	777	3
3	43659	2001-07-01 00:00:00.000	27231.5495	3	778	1
4	43659	2001-07-01 00:00:00.000	27231.5495	4	771	1
5	43659	2001-07-01 00:00:00.000	27231.5495	5	772	1
6	43659	2001-07-01 00:00:00.000	27231.5495	6	773	2
7	43659	2001-07-01 00:00:00.000	27231.5495	7	774	1
8	43659	2001-07-01 00:00:00.000	27231.5495	8	714	3
9	43659	2001-07-01 00:00:00.000	27231.5495	9	716	1
10	43659	2001-07-01 00:00:00.000	27231.5495	10	709	6
11	43659	2001-07-01 00:00:00.000	27231.5495	11	712	2
12	43659	2001-07-01 00:00:00.000	27231.5495	12	711	4
13	43660	2001-07-01 00:00:00.000	1716.1794	13	762	1
14	43660	2001-07-01 00:00:00.000	1716.1794	14	758	1
15	43661	2001-07-01 00:00:00.000	43561.4424	15	745	1
16	43661	2001-07-01 00:00:00.000	43561.4424	16	743	1

Figure 4-2. *The partial results of joining two tables*

Take a look at the data from the Sales.SalesOrderHeader columns in the query results. The information from the Sales.SalesOrderHeader table repeats for each matching row in the Sales.SalesOrderDetail table. If a row exists in the Sales.SalesOrderHeader table with no matches in the Sales.SalesOrderDetail table, the Sales.SalesOrderHeader row will not show up in the results.

Because the column name, SalesOrderID, is the same in both tables, it must be fully qualified with the table name anywhere it is used in the query. To save typing, use an alias for each table. Notice that the query uses the table alias for all the columns in the SELECT list. Fully qualifying the column name is not required except for the columns with the same name; however, fully qualifying all of the column names will make the query more readable. Six months after you write a query, you can immediately see which table each column comes from without spending a lot of time figuring it out.

Avoiding an Incorrect Join Condition

Although you must specify join criteria with ON in the FROM clause when using INNER JOIN, nothing keeps you from writing the join incorrectly. Take a look at Listing 4-2. If you decide to run the code, you may have to click the red, square Cancel Executing Query icon to the right of the Execute icon to stop query execution, or the query will run for several minutes.

Listing 4-2. Writing an Incorrect Query

```
USE AdventureWorks;
GO
SELECT s.SalesOrderID, OrderDate, TotalDue,SalesOrderDetailID,
    d.ProductID, d.OrderQty
FROM Sales.SalesOrderHeader AS s
INNER JOIN Sales.SalesOrderDetail d ON 1 = 1;
```

119

Figure 4-3 displays a portion of the results after scrolling down more than 3,000 rows. When comparing the results to those in Figure 4-2, you will see that the rows from **Sales.SalesOrderHeader** join inappropriate rows from **Sales.SalesOrderDetail**. Both sets of results show **SalesOrderID** 43659, but the results are correct only in Figure 4-2. Because **1=1** is always true, *every* row from the first table joins *every* row from the second table to produce these incorrect results, which is also called a *Cartesian product*.

	SalesOrderID	OrderDate	TotalDue	SalesOrderDetailID	ProductID	OrderQty
3060	43659	2001-07-01 00:00:00.000	27231.5495	3060	729	3
3061	43659	2001-07-01 00:00:00.000	27231.5495	3061	750	1
3062	43659	2001-07-01 00:00:00.000	27231.5495	3062	761	4
3063	43659	2001-07-01 00:00:00.000	27231.5495	3063	766	3
3064	43659	2001-07-01 00:00:00.000	27231.5495	3064	763	1
3065	43659	2001-07-01 00:00:00.000	27231.5495	3065	708	3
3066	43659	2001-07-01 00:00:00.000	27231.5495	3066	758	1
3067	43659	2001-07-01 00:00:00.000	27231.5495	3067	715	5
3068	43659	2001-07-01 00:00:00.000	27231.5495	3068	738	1
3069	43659	2001-07-01 00:00:00.000	27231.5495	3069	757	2
3070	43659	2001-07-01 00:00:00.000	27231.5495	3070	765	2
3071	43659	2001-07-01 00:00:00.000	27231.5495	3071	760	2

Figure 4-3. *The partial results of an incorrect join*

Whenever you write a query with **INNER JOIN**, make sure you understand the relationship between the two tables. For example, you could join the **OrderQty** column from the **Sales.SalesOrderDetail** table to the **SalesOrderID** column in the **Sales.SalesOrderHeader** table. The query would run, but the results would not make any sense at all.

Joining on a Different Column Name

In the previous two examples, the key column names happen to be the same, but this is not a requirement. The **Person.Person** table contains information about people from several tables in the AdventureWorks2008 database. Figure 4-4 shows how the **Person.Person** and the **Sales.Customer** table connect. The **PersonID** from the **Sales.Customer** table joins to the **BusinessEntityID** in the **Person.Person** table. The **PersonID** column in the **Sales.Customer** table is the foreign key.

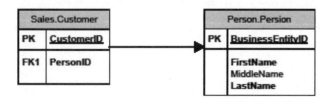

Figure 4-4. *How to connect the* Sales.Customer *and* Person.Person *tables*

Listing 4-3 shows an example that joins these two tables.

Listing 4-3. Joining Two Tables with Different Column Names

```
USE AdventureWorks2008;
GO
SELECT c.CustomerID, c.PersonID, p.BusinessEntityID, p.LastName
FROM Sales.Customer AS C
INNER JOIN Person.Person AS p ON c.PersonID = p.BusinessEntityID;
```

Figure 4-5 shows the partial results. The **Person.Person** table contains information about people from several tables in the database. In this case, the columns joining the two tables have different names. The **PersonID** from the **Sales.Customer** table joins to the **BusinessEntityID** in the **Person.Person** table. This works even though the columns have different names.

	CustomerID	PersonID	BusinessEntityID	LastName
1	29485	293	293	Abel
2	29486	295	295	Abercrombie
3	29487	297	297	Acevedo
4	29484	291	291	Achong
5	29488	299	299	Ackerman
6	28866	16867	16867	Adams
7	13323	16901	16901	Adams
8	21139	16724	16724	Adams

Figure 4-5. The partial results of joining tables with different key column names

Joining on More Than One Column

Although a join frequently involves joining a column from one table to a column from another table, sometimes you must join multiple columns. The AdventureWorks2008 database contains only one example in which multiple columns must be used in a single join: **Sales.SalesOrderDetail** to **Sales.SpecialOfferProduct**. Figure 4-6 shows how these two tables connect.

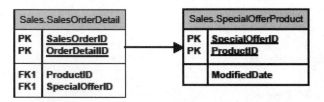

Figure 4-6. How to connect the Sales.SalesOrderDetail table to the Sales.SpecialOfferProduct table

The **Sales.SalesSpecialOfferProduct** table has a composite primary key composed of **SpecialOfferID** plus **ProductID**. To identify a row in this table, you must use both columns. When joining **Sales.SalesOrderDetail** to the **Sales.SpecialOfferProduct** table, you specify both columns in the join. Here is the syntax for joining on more than one column:

```
SELECT <SELECT list>
FROM <table1>
[INNER] JOIN <table2> ON <table1>.<col1> = <table2><col2>
    AND <table1>.<col3> = <table2>.<col4>
```

Type in and execute the code in Listing 4-4 to learn how to join on two columns.

Listing 4-4. Joining on Two Columns

```
USE AdventureWorks2008;
GO

SELECT sod.SalesOrderID, sod.SalesOrderDetailID,
    so.ProductID, so.SpecialOfferID,so.ModifiedDate
FROM Sales.SalesOrderDetail AS sod
INNER JOIN Sales.SpecialOfferProduct AS so
    ON so.ProductID = sod.ProductID AND
    so.SpecialOfferID = sod.SpecialOfferID
WHERE sod.SalesOrderID IN (51116,51112);
```

Take a look at the results (see Figure 4-7). Two columns, **ProductID** and **SpecialOfferID**, comprise the join condition. To determine which row matches the rows from **Sales.SalesOrderDetail**, both columns are used in the join condition. If the join contained only one of the columns, the results would be similar to the incorrect results in the section "Avoiding an Incorrect Join." If the join contained only the **ProductID**, the results would show every possible **SpecialOfferID** row for each **ProductID**, not just the correct rows. Try modifying the join yourself by leaving out one of the conditions to see what happens.

	SalesOrderID	SalesOrderDetailID	ProductID	SpecialOfferID	ModifiedDate
1	51112	36341	956	14	2003-06-01 00:00:00.000
2	51112	36342	965	13	2003-06-01 00:00:00.000
3	51112	36343	885	1	2001-05-02 00:00:00.000
4	51112	36344	948	1	2001-05-02 00:00:00.000
5	51112	36345	960	13	2003-06-01 00:00:00.000
6	51112	36346	886	1	2001-05-02 00:00:00.000
7	51112	36347	994	1	2001-05-02 00:00:00.000
8	51112	36348	966	1	2001-05-02 00:00:00.000
9	51112	36349	959	13	2003-06-01 00:00:00.000
10	51112	36350	978	13	2003-06-01 00:00:00.000
11	51112	36351	970	1	2001-05-02 00:00:00.000
12	51112	36352	969	1	2001-05-02 00:00:00.000

Figure 4-7. The partial results of joining on two columns

Joining Three or More Tables

Sometimes you will need to join only two tables together in a query, but more frequently, you will need to join three or more tables. You will often join three tables when there is a *many-to-many* relationship between two of the tables. For example, suppose you have a table listing college courses and a table listing students. You would need a third table that records which students take which courses. To join courses to students, your query will join all three tables.

In the AdventureWorks2008 database, you will find many reasons to join more than two tables in one query. For example, suppose you want to see a list of the product names for each order, along with the OrderDate column. This query requires the Sales.SalesOrderHeader, Sales.SalesOrderDetail, and Production.Product tables. Figure 4-8 shows how to connect these three tables.

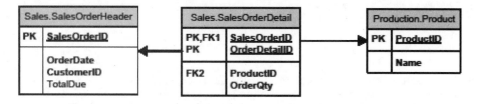

Figure 4-8. How to join Sales.SalesOrderHeader to Production.Product

To add a third or more tables, just continue the FROM clause. Take a look at the syntax:

```
SELECT <SELECT list> FROM <table1>
[INNER] JOIN <table2> ON <table1>.<col1> = <table2>.<col2>
[INNER] JOIN <table3> ON <table2>.<col2> = <table3>.<col3>
```

Type in and execute the query in Listing 4-5 to learn how to join more than two tables in one query.

Listing 4-5. Joining Three Tables

```
USE AdventureWorks2008;
GO

SELECT soh.SalesOrderID,soh.OrderDate,p.ProductID, p.Name
FROM Sales.SalesOrderHeader as soh
INNER JOIN Sales.SalesOrderDetail AS sod ON soh.SalesOrderID = sod.SalesOrderID
INNER JOIN Production.Product AS p ON sod.ProductID = p.ProductID
ORDER BY soh.SalesOrderID;
```

Figure 4-9 shows the results. Notice that even though the query joins three tables, the query displays columns from only two of the tables. To get from Sales.SalesOrderHeader to the names of the products ordered in the Production.Product table, the query must include the Sales.SalesOrderDetail table to connect the other two tables. Depending on the goal of the query, you may want to include columns from all tables involved in the query.

	SalesOrderID	OrderDate	ProductID	Name
1	43659	2001-07-01 00:00:00.000	711	Sport-100 Helmet, Blue
2	43659	2001-07-01 00:00:00.000	712	AWC Logo Cap
3	43659	2001-07-01 00:00:00.000	714	Long-Sleeve Logo Jersey, M
4	43659	2001-07-01 00:00:00.000	716	Long-Sleeve Logo Jersey, XL
5	43659	2001-07-01 00:00:00.000	709	Mountain Bike Socks, M
6	43659	2001-07-01 00:00:00.000	771	Mountain-100 Silver, 38
7	43659	2001-07-01 00:00:00.000	772	Mountain-100 Silver, 42
8	43659	2001-07-01 00:00:00.000	773	Mountain-100 Silver, 44
9	43659	2001-07-01 00:00:00.000	774	Mountain-100 Silver, 48
10	43659	2001-07-01 00:00:00.000	778	Mountain-100 Black, 48
11	43659	2001-07-01 00:00:00.000	776	Mountain-100 Black, 42
12	43659	2001-07-01 00:00:00.000	777	Mountain-100 Black, 44
13	43660	2001-07-01 00:00:00.000	758	Road-450 Red, 52

Figure 4-9. The partial results of joining three tables

Take another look at the FROM clause. The Sales.SalesOrderHeader table joins to the Sales. SalesOrderDetail table on the SalesOrderID column. Then the Sales.SalesOrderDetail table joins the Production.Product table on the ProductID column. If you have trouble figuring out how to join the tables, take it a step at a time. Join two tables first, and then add the third table.

Joining tables is a very important skill for T-SQL developers. Before you move on to the next section, make sure you are comfortable with what the chapter has covered so far by completing Exercise 4-1.

Exercise 4-1

Use the AdventureWorks2008 database to complete this exercise. You can find the solutions in the appendix.

1. The HumanResources.Employee table does not contain the employee names. Join that table to the Person.Person table on the BusinessEntityID column. Display the job title, birth date, first name, and last name.
2. The customer names also appear in the Person.Person table. Join the Sales.Customer table to the Person.Person table. The BusinessEntityID column in the Person.Person table matches the PersonID column in the Sales.Customer table. Display the CustomerID, StoreID, and TerritoryID columns along with the name columns.
3. Extend the query written in question 2 to include the Sales.SalesOrderHeader table. Display the SalesOrderID column along with the columns already specified. The Sales.SalesOrderHeader table joins the Sales.Customer table on CustomerID.
4. Write a query that joins the Sales.SalesOrderHeader table to the Sales.SalesPerson table. Join the BusinessEntityID column from the Sales.SalesPerson table to the SalesPersonID column in the Sales.SalesOrderHeader table. Display the SalesOrderID along with the SalesQuota and Bonus.
5. Add the name columns to the query written in step 4 by joining on the Person.Person table. See whether you can figure out which columns will be used to write the join.

6. The catalog description for each product is stored in the `Production.ProductModel` table. Display the columns that describe the product such as the color and size, along with the catalog description for each product.

7. Write a query that displays the names of the customers along with the product names that they have purchased. Hint: Five tables will be required to write this query!

Writing Outer Joins

When joining two tables with `INNER JOIN`, there must be an exact match between the two tables for a row to show up in the results. Occasionally, you'll need to retrieve all the rows from one of the tables even if the other table doesn't contain a match for every row. For example, you may want to display all the customers along with their orders, including the customers who have not placed orders yet. By using `OUTER JOIN`, you can retrieve all the rows from one table along with any rows that match from the other table.

Using LEFT OUTER JOIN

When writing `OUTER JOIN`, you must specify either `LEFT` or `RIGHT`. If the main table, the table that you want to see all the rows even if there is not a match, is on the left side of the join, you will specify `LEFT`. Figure 4-10 shows how the `Sales.Customer` and `Sales.SalesOrderHeader` tables connect when using `LEFT OUTER JOIN` so that all customers show up in the results even if they have not placed any orders.

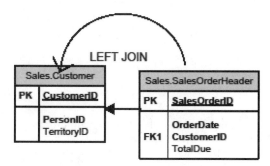

Figure 4-10. *How to perform* `LEFT JOIN`

Here is the syntax for `LEFT OUTER JOIN`:

```
SELECT <SELECT list>
FROM <table1>
LEFT [OUTER] JOIN <table2> ON <table1>.<col1> = <table2>.<col2>
```

Type in and execute the code in Listing 4-6 to learn how to write a `LEFT OUTER JOIN` query. Note that the word `OUTER` is optional.

Listing 4-6. Using LEFT OUTER JOIN

```
USE AdventureWorks2008;
GO
SELECT c.CustomerID, s.SalesOrderID, s.OrderDate
FROM Sales.Customer AS c
LEFT OUTER JOIN Sales.SalesOrderHeader AS s ON c.CustomerID = s.CustomerID
WHERE c.CustomerID IN (11028,11029,1,2,3,4);
```

Figure 4-11 displays the results. Just like **INNER JOIN**, you must determine which column or columns from one table join the column or columns from the other table. All the rows from the table on the left side of the join, the **Sales.Customer** table, that meet the criteria in the **WHERE** clause, show up in the results. The query returns rows from the right side of the join, the **Sales.SalesOrderHeader** table, only if they match on **CustomerID**. All of the columns from the **Sales.SalesOrderHeader** rows that don't match return **NULL** values. The query returns the customers along with the orders even for customers with no orders, customers 1–4.

	CustomerID	SalesOrderID	OrderDate
1	1	NULL	NULL
2	2	NULL	NULL
3	3	NULL	NULL
4	4	NULL	NULL
5	11028	43831	2001-07-29 00:00:00.000
6	11028	57943	2003-11-14 00:00:00.000
7	11028	67961	2004-04-09 00:00:00.000
8	11029	43794	2001-07-22 00:00:00.000
9	11029	57294	2003-11-02 00:00:00.000
10	11029	70593	2004-05-14 00:00:00.000

Figure 4-11 The results of using LEFT OUTER JOIN

Using **OUTER JOIN** is not difficult, but it seems to be confusing to people when they first try to use it. If the tables have the primary and foreign keys defined, the table joining with the primary key will usually be the table on the left side in a **LEFT OUTER JOIN**. Figure out which table must have rows returned even if there is not a match. That table must show up on the left side of a **LEFT OUTER JOIN**.

Using RIGHT OUTER JOIN

RIGHT OUTER JOIN differs from **LEFT OUTER JOIN** in just the location of the tables. If the main table, the table in which you want to see all the rows even if there is not a match, is on the right side of the join, you will specify **RIGHT**. Here is the syntax:

```
SELECT <SELECT list>
FROM <table2>
RIGHT [OUTER] JOIN <table1> ON <table1>.<col1> = <table2>.<col2>
```

Type in and execute the code in Listing 4-7 to learn how to write a query using **RIGHT OUTER JOIN**.

Listing 4-7. Using RIGHT OUTER JOIN

```
USE AdventureWorks2008;
GO
SELECT c.CustomerID, s.SalesOrderID, s.OrderDate
FROM Sales.SalesOrderHeader AS s
RIGHT OUTER JOIN Sales.Customer AS c ON c.CustomerID = s.CustomerID
WHERE c.CustomerID IN (11028,11029,1,2,3,4);
```

Figure 4-12 shows the results; they are identical to the results in Figure 4-11. The only difference between this query and the one from Listing 4-6 is the order of the tables within the **FROM** clause and the direction keyword. Again, all of the customers who meet the criteria display along with any orders that were placed. For customers with no orders, **NULL** values are returned in the **Sales.SalesOrderHeader** columns.

	CustomerID	SalesOrderID	OrderDate
1	1	NULL	NULL
2	2	NULL	NULL
3	3	NULL	NULL
4	4	NULL	NULL
5	11028	43831	2001-07-29 00:00:00.000
6	11028	57943	2003-11-14 00:00:00.000
7	11028	67961	2004-04-09 00:00:00.000
8	11029	43794	2001-07-22 00:00:00.000
9	11029	57294	2003-11-02 00:00:00.000
10	11029	70593	2004-05-14 00:00:00.000

Figure 4-12. Result of using RIGHT OUTER JOIN

Using OUTER JOIN to Find Rows with No Match

Sometimes it may be useful to find all the rows in one table that do not have corresponding rows in another table. For example, you may want to find all the customers who have never placed an order. Since the columns from the nonmatching rows contain **NULL** values, you can use **OUTER JOIN** to find rows with no match by checking for **NULL**. The syntax is as follows:

```
SELECT <SELECT list>
FROM <table1>
LEFT [OUTER] JOIN <table2> ON <table1>.<col1> = <table2>.<col2>
WHERE <col2> IS NULL
```

Type in and execute the code in Listing 4-8 to see how this works.

Listing 4-8. Using LEFT OUTER JOIN to Find the Rows with No Matches

```
USE AdventureWorks2008;
GO

SELECT c.CustomerID, s.SalesOrderID, s.OrderDate
FROM Sales.Customer AS c
LEFT OUTER JOIN Sales.SalesOrderHeader AS s ON c.CustomerID = s.CustomerID
WHERE s.SalesOrderID IS NULL;
```

Figure 4-13 shows the partial results. The query in Listing 4-8 returns a list of all customers who have not placed an order. After you run the query, scroll down to see that every row in the results contains NULL in the SalesOrderID column.

The LEFT JOIN returns all rows from Sales.Customer even if the customer has no orders. The customer rows with no orders contain NULL in the Sales.SalesOrderHeader columns. By checking for NULL, the customers with no orders show up in the results. Again, this might be complicated to understand at first. Just take it a step at a time when writing your own queries.

	CustomerID	SalesOrderID	OrderDate
1	215	NULL	NULL
2	46	NULL	NULL
3	169	NULL	NULL
4	507	NULL	NULL
5	630	NULL	NULL
6	338	NULL	NULL
7	229	NULL	NULL
8	567	NULL	NULL
9	461	NULL	NULL
10	398	NULL	NULL
11	292	NULL	NULL

Figure 4-13. The partial results of finding rows with no match

Adding a Table to the Right Side of a Left Join

The next step in learning how to use outer joins is understanding what to do when additional tables are added to the query. For example, you might want to display all the customers and their orders even if an order has not been placed, along with the ProductID from those orders that were placed. To keep the customers with no orders from dropping out of the results, you must continue to use LEFT JOIN. Figure 4-14 shows how these three tables can be joined to produce the correct results.

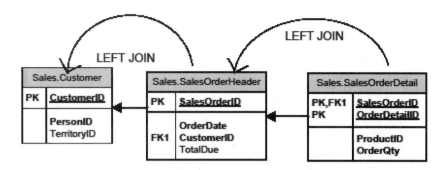

Figure 4-14. *How to connect the tables with two* LEFT OUTER JOINs

Take a look at the syntax:

```
SELECT <SELECT list>
FROM <table1> LEFT [OUTER]JOIN <table2> ON <table1>.<col1> = <table2>.<col2>
LEFT [OUTER] JOIN <table3> ON <table2>.<col3> = <table3>.<col4>
```

Listing 4-9 contains an example query. Type in and execute the code to learn how to write this type of join.

Listing 4-9. *Joining Three Tables with* LEFT JOIN

```
USE AdventureWorks2008;
GO

SELECT C.CustomerID, SOH.SalesOrderID, SOD.SalesOrderDetailID, SOD.ProductID
FROM Sales.Customer AS C
LEFT OUTER JOIN Sales.SalesOrderHeader AS SOH ON C.CustomerID = SOH.CustomerID
LEFT OUTER JOIN Sales.SalesOrderDetail AS SOD ON SOH.SalesOrderID = SOD.SalesOrderID
WHERE c.CustomerID IN (11028,11029,1,2,3,4);
```

Figure 4-15 shows the results. Because the columns from the nonmatching rows from
Sales.SalesOrderHeader contain **NULL**, they cannot join to the **Sales.SalesOrderDetail** table. If you must
join another table to the **Sales.SalesOrderHeader** table, you must use **LEFT OUTER JOIN** because you can't
join on the **NULL** values. On your own, change the query by removing the words **LEFT OUTER** in the join
between **Sales.SalesOrderHeader** and **Sales.SalesOrderDetail**. The customers with no orders will drop
out of the results.

	CustomerID	SalesOrderID	SalesOrderDetailID	ProductID
1	1	NULL	NULL	NULL
2	2	NULL	NULL	NULL
3	3	NULL	NULL	NULL
4	4	NULL	NULL	NULL
5	11028	43831	487	776
6	11028	57943	65072	779
7	11028	57943	65073	930
8	11028	57943	65074	873
9	11028	67961	98619	962
10	11029	43794	450	774
11	11029	57294	63489	779
12	11029	57294	63490	711
13	11029	57294	63491	882
14	11029	70593	107626	962
15	11029	70593	107627	872
16	11029	70593	107628	870

Figure 4-15. *The results of a querying multiple tables with* LEFT JOIN

I prefer listing the main table first and using left joins over right joins. If you list the main table first and you start down the LEFT OUTER JOIN path, you can continue to use LEFT. If you start out with RIGHT, you may have to switch to LEFT when you add more tables, which can be confusing.

Adding a Table to the Left Side of a Left Join

You may be wondering what kind of join you must use if you join another table to the left side of the join, in other words, to your main table. To be on the safe side, use LEFT OUTER JOIN to ensure that you will not lose any rows from the main table.

Figure 4-16 shows how to add the **Sales.Territory** table to the example started in the previous section. The **Sales.Territory** table joins to the main table, the **Sales.Customer** table. Since you want to make sure that all customers show up in the results, use LEFT OUTER JOIN to join this new table.

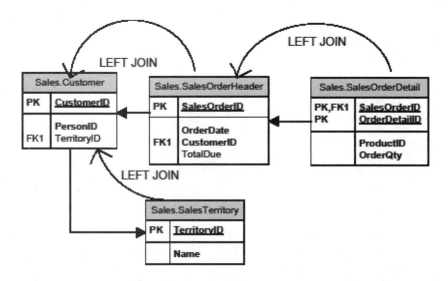

Figure 4-16. *How to add another table to the left side of the join*

Listing 4-10 shows two example queries that add another table to the main table. Type in and execute the code.

Listing 4-10. Adding Another Table to the Left Side of the Join

```
USE AdventureWorks2008;
GO

SELECT C.CustomerID, SOH.SalesOrderID, SOD.SalesOrderDetailID,
    SOD.ProductID, T.Name
FROM Sales.Customer AS C
LEFT OUTER JOIN Sales.SalesOrderHeader AS SOH ON C.CustomerID = SOH.CustomerID
LEFT OUTER JOIN Sales.SalesOrderDetail AS SOD ON SOH.SalesOrderID = SOD.SalesOrderID
LEFT OUTER JOIN Sales.SalesTerritory AS T ON C.TerritoryID = T.TerritoryID
WHERE c.CustomerID IN (11028,11029,1,2,3,4);
```

Figure 4-17 shows the results. The **Sales.SalesTerritory** table joins the **Sales.Customer** table on **TerritoryID**. Because you do not want to lose any rows from the **Sales.Customer** table, use **LEFT OUTER JOIN**.

	CustomerID	SalesOrderID	SalesOrderDetailID	ProductID	Name
1	1	NULL	NULL	NULL	Northwest
2	2	NULL	NULL	NULL	Northwest
3	3	NULL	NULL	NULL	Southwest
4	4	NULL	NULL	NULL	Southwest
5	11028	43831	487	776	Australia
6	11028	57943	65072	779	Australia
7	11028	57943	65073	930	Australia
8	11028	57943	65074	873	Australia

Figure 4-17. The partial results of joining to the left side of LEFT OUTER JOIN

FULL OUTER JOIN

FULL OUTER JOIN is similar to LEFT OUTER JOIN and RIGHT OUTER JOIN, but in this case, all the rows from each side of the join are returned. In other words, all rows from the left side of the join, even if there is not a match, and all rows from the right side, even if there is not a match, show up in the results. This type of join is rare and could indicate some problems with the database design or the data. For example, this type of join might be necessary if the **Sales.SalesOrderHeader** table contains orders with invalid **CustomerID** values. Here is the syntax:

```
SELECT <column list>
FROM <table1>
FULL [OUTER] JOIN <table2> ON <table1>.<col1>  = <table2>.<col2>
```

Because no good example exists in the AdventureWorks2008 database, Listing 4-11 includes a script that creates and populates a table of colors that can be used in the **Production.Product** table. After populating the table, it contains colors that do not appear in the **Production.Product** table, and it is missing a color that should be there. Don't worry about understanding the table creation and population part of the script at this point.

Listing 4-11. FULL OUTER JOIN Demonstration

```
USE AdventureWorks2008;
GO
IF OBJECT_ID('Production.ProductColor') IS NOT NULL BEGIN
    DROP TABLE Production.ProductColor;
END
CREATE table Production.ProductColor
    (Color nvarchar(15) NOT NULL PRIMARY KEY)
GO
--Insert most of the existing colors
INSERT INTO Production.ProductColor
SELECT DISTINCT COLOR
FROM Production.Product
WHERE Color IS NOT NULL and Color <> 'Silver'
```

```
--Insert some additional colors
INSERT INTO Production.ProductColor
VALUES ('Green'),('Orange'),('Purple');

--Here is the query:
SELECT c.Color AS "Color from list", p.Color, p.ProductID
FROM Production.Product AS p
FULL OUTER JOIN Production.ProductColor AS c ON p.Color = c.Color
ORDER BY p.ProductID;
```

Figure 4-18 displays the results. When colors from the **Production.ProductColor** table have no matches in the **Production.Product** table, the query returns **NULL** values in the second and third columns, which are from **Production.Product** (rows 1–3). When colors from the **Production.Product** table do not match the **Production.ProductColor** table (in this case silver) or no color for a product is specified, the query returns **NULL** values in the first column, which is from **Production.ProductColor** (rows 12–13). Finally, when a product has a color that matches one found in the **Production.ProductColor** table, the query returns all non-**NULL** values (rows 9–11). A query like this might be used to find problems in data so that it can be cleaned up before loading it into a production system or data warehouse.

	Color from list	Color	ProductID
1	Purple	NULL	NULL
2	Green	NULL	NULL
3	Orange	NULL	NULL
4	NULL	NULL	1
5	NULL	NULL	2
6	NULL	NULL	3
7	NULL	NULL	4
8	NULL	NULL	316
9	Black	Black	317
10	Black	Black	318
11	Black	Black	319
12	NULL	Silver	320
13	NULL	Silver	321

Figure 4-18. The results of using FULL OUTER JOIN

CROSS JOIN

Another type of rarely used join is **CROSS JOIN**. This is actually the same as the Cartesian product mentioned in the "Avoiding an Incorrect Join Condition" section. In this case, use **CROSS JOIN** when you intend to multiply two tables together—every row from one table matched to every row from another table. You might write a **CROSS JOIN** query to populate a table for a special purpose such as an inventory. You may need a list of every product in every possible location to create forms for the inventory crew. Here is the syntax:

```
SELECT <SELECT list> FROM <table1> CROSS JOIN <table2>
```

Notice that the **FROM** clause does not contain a join condition. Every possible row from one table joins every possible row from another table, so you do not have to specify a join condition. Listing 4-12 demonstrates how to write this type of query. Type in and execute the code.

Listing 4-12. A CROSS JOIN

```
USE AdventureWorks2008;
GO
--1
SELECT p.ProductID, l.LocationID
FROM Production.Product AS p
CROSS JOIN Production.Location AS l
ORDER BY ProductID;
--2
SELECT p.ProductID, l.LocationID
FROM Production.Product AS p
CROSS JOIN Production.Location AS l
ORDER BY LocationID;
```

Figure 4-19 shows the partial results. These queries, just sorted differently, each produce a row for every possible product and every possible location. Query 1 shows that product 1 displays along with every location. Query 2 shows that location 1 displays along with every product.

	ProductID	LocationID
1	1	1
2	1	2
3	1	3
4	1	4
5	1	5
6	1	6
7	1	7
8	1	10
9	1	20
10	1	30

	ProductID	LocationID
1	980	1
2	365	1
3	771	1
4	404	1
5	977	1
6	818	1
7	474	1
8	748	1
9	975	1
10	884	1

Figure 4-19. The partial results of a CROSS JOIN

Self-Joins

A *self-join* is a special type of query that joins a table back to itself. You can find an example of this in the AdventureWorks database from SQL Server 2005. The primary key in the `HumanResources.Employee` table is `EmployeeID`. The `ManagerID` is a foreign key pointing back to the same table. Every employee, except for one, has a manager, another employee appearing in the same table. The one employee with no manager is the CEO of AdventureWorks. The designers of AdventureWorks chose to eliminate the self-join when creating AdventureWorks2008 in favor of a new feature introduced with SQL Server 2008, the `HIERARCHYID` data type. You will learn about `HIERARCHYID` in Chapter 9.

You can actually join any table to itself even if it doesn't have a foreign key pointing back to the primary key as defined as the old `HumanResources.Employee` table. This relationship is called a *unary relationship*. Here is the syntax for a self-join:

```
SELECT <a.col1>, <b.col1>
FROM <table1> AS a
LEFT [OUTER] JOIN <table1> AS b ON a.<col1> = b.<col2>
```

Listing 4-13 demonstrates how to write a self-join. Be sure to type in and execute the code.

Listing 4-13. Using Self-Join

```
USE AdventureWorks;
GO
SELECT a.EmployeeID AS Employee,
    a.Title AS EmployeeTitle,
    b.EmployeeID AS ManagerID,
    b.Title AS ManagerTitle
FROM HumanResources.Employee AS a
LEFT OUTER JOIN HumanResources.Employee AS b ON a.ManagerID = b.EmployeeID;
```

Take a look at the results shown in Figure 4-20. Each employee, except for one, has a manager who is also an employee in the same table. The table has `ManagerID`, which is a foreign key pointing back to the `EmployeeID`. Since employee 109 does not have a manager, the query uses `LEFT OUTER JOIN`. Be sure to keep track of which table each column is supposed to come from. Even though the query uses the same table twice, it has two separate roles.

	Employee	EmployeeTitle	ManagerID	ManagerTitle
1	109	Chief Executive Officer	NULL	NULL
2	4	Senior Tool Designer	3	Engineering Manager
3	9	Design Engineer	3	Engineering Manager
4	11	Design Engineer	3	Engineering Manager
5	158	Research and Development Manager	3	Engineering Manager
6	263	Senior Tool Designer	3	Engineering Manager
7	267	Senior Design Engineer	3	Engineering Manager
8	270	Design Engineer	3	Engineering Manager
9	271	Marketing Specialist	6	Marketing Manager
10	272	Marketing Assistant	6	Marketing Manager
11	269	Marketing Assistant	6	Marketing Manager
12	203	Marketing Specialist	6	Marketing Manager

Figure 4-20. *The results of using a self-join*

The important thing to remember is that one table is used twice in the query. At least one of the table names must be aliased; it is not an option because you cannot have two tables with the same name in the query. You will have to qualify all the column names, so you may want to alias both table names to save typing.

This section covered several advanced joining techniques. Understanding how the techniques work and when to use them are very important skills. Practice what you have learned by completing Exercise 4-2.

Exercise 4-2

Use the AdventureWorks2008 and AdventureWorks (question 7) databases to complete this exercise. You can find the solutions in the appendix.

1. Write a query that displays all the products along with the `SalesOrderID` even if an order has never been placed for that product. Join to the `Sales.SalesOrderDetail` table using the `ProductID` column.
2. Change the query written in step 1 so that only products that have not been ordered show up in the query.
3. Write a query that returns all the rows from the `Sales.SalesPerson` table joined to the `Sales.SalesOrderHeader` table along with the `SalesOrderID` column even if no orders match. Include the `SalesPersonID` and `SalesYTD` columns in the results.
4. Change the query written in question 3 so that the salesperson's name also displays from the `Person.Person` table.

136

5. The `Sales.SalesOrderHeader` table contains foreign keys to the `Sales.CurrencyRate` and `Purchasing.ShipMethod` tables. Write a query joining all three tables, and make sure it contains all rows from `Sales.SalesOrderHeader`. Include the `CurrencyRateID`, `AverageRate`, `SalesOrderID`, and `ShipBase` columns.

6. Write a query that returns the `BusinesssEntityID` column from the `Sales.SalesPerson` table along with every `ProductID` from the `Production.Product` table.

7. Starting with the query written in Listing 4-13, join the table `a` to the `Person.Contact` table to display the employee's name. The `EmployeeID` column joins the `ContactID` column.

Writing Subqueries

The previous examples in this chapter demonstrated how to write queries using `JOIN`. This section demonstrates using subqueries in the `WHERE` clause. A *subquery* is a nested query—a query within a query. One reason to use a subquery is to find the rows in one table that match another table without actually joining the second table. For example, without actually joining the order table, you could use a subquery to display a list of the customers who have placed an order. Another technique, correlated subqueries, will be shown in Chapter 5.

Using a Subquery in an IN List

Using a subquery in an `IN` list is similar to the hard-coded `IN` list you learned to use in a `WHERE` clause in Chapter 2. Here is the syntax:

```
SELECT <select list> FROM <table1>
WHERE <col1> IN (SELECT <col2> FROM <table2>)
```

Listing 4-14 demonstrates this technique. Type in and execute the code.

Listing 4-14. Using a Subquery in the IN List

```
USE AdventureWorks2008;
GO
SELECT CustomerID, AccountNumber
FROM Sales.Customer
WHERE CustomerID IN (SELECT CustomerID FROM Sales.SalesOrderHeader);
```

This query returns a list of the customers who have placed an order (see Figure 4-21). The difference between this example and other examples in this chapter that join these tables is that the columns from the `Sales.SalesOrderHeader` table do not show up in the results. Each customer displays only once in the results, not once for each order placed. The subquery produces a list of possible values from one, and only one, column. The outer query compares a column to that list.

	CustomerID	AccountNumber
1	11000	AW00011000
2	11001	AW00011001
3	11002	AW00011002
4	11003	AW00011003
5	11004	AW00011004
6	11005	AW00011005
7	11006	AW00011006
8	11007	AW00011007
9	11008	AW00011008
10	11009	AW00011009

Figure 4-21. *The results of using a subquery in an IN list*

Using a Subquery and NOT IN

A subquery in the WHERE clause can also be used to find rows that do not match the values from another table by adding the NOT operator. You can find the customers who have not placed an order by adding the word NOT to the previous query. Type in and execute the code in Listing 4-15, which demonstrates using NOT IN.

Listing 4-15. *A Subquery with NOT IN*

```
USE AdventureWorks2008;
GO


SELECT CustomerID, AccountNumber
FROM Sales.Customer
WHERE CustomerID NOT IN
    (SELECT CustomerID FROM Sales.SalesOrderHeader);
```

This query returns the opposite results of Listing 4-14 (see Figure 4-22). The subquery returns a list of all the CustomerID values found in Sales.SalesOrderHeader. By using NOT IN, the query returns all the rows from Sales.Customer that do not match.

	CustomerID	AccountNumber
1	1	AW00000001
2	2	AW00000002
3	3	AW00000003
4	4	AW00000004
5	5	AW00000005
6	6	AW00000006
7	7	AW00000007
8	8	AW00000008
9	9	AW00000009
10	10	AW00000010
11	11	AW00000011

Figure 4-22. *The partial results of using a subquery with NOT IN*

Using a Subquery Containing NULL with NOT IN

Recall that you will often get incorrect results if you do not take **NULL** values into account. If the subquery contains any **NULL** values, using **NOT IN** will incorrectly produce no rows. For example, the values returned by a subquery are **NULL**, 1, 2, and 3. The values from the outer query (1, 2, and 10) must each be compared to that list. The database engine can tell that 10 is not 1, 2, or 3, but it cannot tell whether it is the same as **NULL**. The intended result is 10 since it doesn't match any of the values from the subquery, but because of the **NULL**, the comparison returns no results at all. Type in and execute the code in Listing 4-16, which shows incorrect results and how to correct the problem.

Listing 4-16. A Subquery with NOT IN

```
USE AdventureWorks2008;
GO


--1
SELECT CurrencyRateID, FromCurrencyCode, ToCurrencycode
FROM Sales.CurrencyRate
WHERE CurrencyRateID NOT IN
    (SELECT CurrencyRateID
     FROM Sales.SalesOrderHeader);


--2
SELECT CurrencyRateID, FromCurrencyCode, ToCurrencycode
FROM Sales.CurrencyRate
WHERE CurrencyRateID NOT IN
    (SELECT CurrencyRateID
     FROM Sales.SalesOrderHeader
     WHERE CurrencyRateID IS NOT NULL);
```

Figure 4-23 shows the results. Query 1 does not return any results because **NULL** values exist in the values returned by the subquery. Since any value from **CurrencyRateID** compared to **NULL** returns **UNKNOWN**, it is impossible to know whether any of the values meet the criteria. Query 2 corrects the problem by adding a **WHERE** clause to the subquery that eliminates **NULL** values.

Using a subquery in the **WHERE** clause is a very popular technique. Just make sure that you always eliminate the possibility of **NULL** values in the subquery.

	CurrencyRateID	FromCurrencyCode	ToCurrencycode

	CurrencyRateID	FromCurrencyCode	ToCurrencycode
1	1	USD	ARS
2	3	USD	BRL
3	5	USD	CNY
4	6	USD	DEM
5	7	USD	EUR
6	9	USD	GBP
7	10	USD	JPY

Figure 4-23. The results of code that corrects the NULL problem with NOT IN

Writing UNION Queries

A **UNION** query is not really a join, but it is a way to merge the results of two or more queries together. I like to think of it as "folding" one table onto another table. One reason for using a **UNION** query is to view data with one query that combines data from a production table along with data that has been archived into another table. A **UNION** query combines two or more queries, and the results are returned in one result set. Here is the syntax:

```
SELECT <col1>, <col2>,<col3>
FROM <table1>
UNION [ALL]
SELECT <col4>,<col5>,<col6>FROM <table2>
```

Figure 4-24 shows a diagram of how a **UNION** query might look. Each individual query must contain the same number of columns and be of compatible data types. For example, you could have an **INT** column and a **VARCHAR** column line up as long as the **VARCHAR** column contains only numbers.

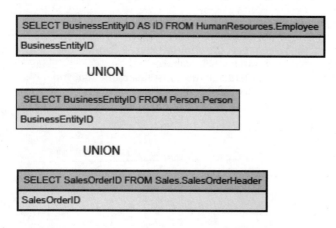

Figure 4-24. The diagram of a UNION query

Type in and execute the code in Listing 4-17 to learn how to use **UNION**.

Listing 4-17. Using UNION

```
USE AdventureWorks2008;
GO

--1
SELECT BusinessEntityID AS ID
FROM HumanResources.Employee
UNION
SELECT BusinessEntityID
FROM Person.Person
UNION
SELECT SalesOrderID
FROM Sales.SalesOrderHeader
ORDER BY ID;

--2
SELECT BusinessEntityID AS ID
FROM HumanResources.Employee
UNION ALL
SELECT BusinessEntityID
FROM Person.Person
UNION ALL
SELECT SalesOrderID
FROM Sales.SalesOrderHeader
ORDER BY ID;
```

Notice the difference in the two queries in Listing 4-17. Figure 4-25 shows the results. Query 2 uses **UNION ALL**, which returns all rows, even if they are duplicates. Leaving out the keyword **ALL** eliminates the duplicates. The first query in the **UNION** query determines the number of columns and the name of each column. When using a **UNION** query, only one **ORDER BY** clause can be used, and it will be located at the end of the statement.

Figure 4-25. The results of UNION queries

A **UNION** query is often used to combine the results of two tables so that they look the same. For example, a database has separate customer tables for each division of the company. By using a **UNION** query, the customers can be displayed together as if they were in the same table. It is also possible to write **UNION** queries using the same table.

When writing a **UNION** query, you must make sure that both queries contain the same number of columns in the results and that the data types are compatible. The first query sets the number of columns and the name of each column. The second and later queries must match up to the first query. The data type of each column follows precedence rules, so you cannot allow one query to return an integer where the other query returns a string. Run these practice queries to see what happens when a **UNION** query does not follow these rules:

```
--Incompatible types
select 1
Union all
select 'a'
--Number of columns don't match up
select 1
Union all
select 1,2
```

This section covered some alternate ways to utilize more than one table within a query. Practice these techniques by completing Exercise 4-3.

Use the AdventureWorks2008 database to complete this exercise. You can find the solutions in the appendix.

1. Using a subquery, display the product names and product ID numbers from the `Production.Product` table that have been ordered.
2. Change the query written in question 1 to display the products that have not been ordered.
3. If the `Production.ProductColor` table is not part of the AdventureWorks2008 database, run the code in Listing 4-11 to create it. Write a query using a subquery that returns the rows from the `Production.ProductColor` table that are not being used in the `Production.Product` table.
4. Write a query that displays the colors used in the `Production.Product` table that are not listed in the `Production.ProductColor` table using a subquery. Use the keyword `DISTINCT` before the column name to return each color only once.
5. Write a `UNION` query that combines the `ModifiedDate` from `Person.Person` and the `HireDate` from `HumanResources.Employee`.

Exploring Derived Tables and Common Table Expressions

Using derived tables and common table expressions allows T-SQL developers to solve some complicated query problems. You will find these techniques useful as you learn about aggregate queries (Chapter 5) and updating data (Chapter 6). With only the skills you have learned so far, using these techniques does not actually make writing queries any easier, but you will appreciate learning about them before you progress to more advanced skills.

Using Derived Tables

If you still work with some SQL Server 2000 systems, you may work with derived tables. A *derived table* is a subquery that appears in the `FROM` clause. Actually, you may see derived tables with SQL Server 2005 and 2008 code, but starting with 2005, another option, common table expressions, is available. You will learn about common table expressions in the next section.

Derived tables allow developers to join to queries instead of tables so that the logic of the query is isolated. At this point, I just want you to learn how to write a query using a derived table. This technique will be very useful as you learn to write more advanced queries. Here is the syntax:

```
SELECT <select list> FROM <table1>
[INNER] JOIN (SELECT <select list>
            FROM <table2>) AS B ON <table1>.<col1> = B.<col2>
```

The syntax shows `INNER JOIN`, but this could also be done with `OUTER JOIN` as well. Figure 4-26 shows a diagram representing a `LEFT OUTER JOIN` query joining the `Sales.Customer` table to a *query* of the `Sales.SalesOrderHeader` table as a derived table.

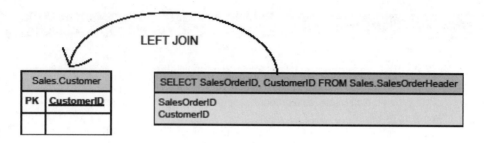

Figure 4-26. *The diagram of a derived query*

Listing 4-18 demonstrates how to use a derived table. Type in and execute the code. Make sure you take the time to understand how this works with these simple examples even though a regular join makes more sense at this point.

Listing 4-18. Using a Derived Table

```
USE AdventureWorks2008;
GO


SELECT c.CustomerID, s.SalesOrderID
FROM Sales.Customer AS c
INNER JOIN (SELECT SalesOrderID, CustomerID
            FROM Sales.SalesOrderHeader) AS s ON c.CustomerID = s.CustomerID;
```

Obviously, you could write this query using a regular **INNER JOIN**. Figure 4-27 shows the results. Keep in mind three rules when using derived tables. First, any columns that will be needed outside the derived table must be included in its **SELECT** list. Even though only **SalesOrderID** appears in the main **SELECT** list, **CustomerID** is required for joining. Second, the derived table requires an alias. Use the alias to refer to columns from the derived table in the outer query. Finally, the derived table may contain multiple tables, a **WHERE** clause, and even another derived table, but it may not contain an **ORDER BY** clause.

	CustomerID	SalesOrderID
1	11000	43793
2	11000	51522
3	11000	57418
4	11001	43767
5	11001	51493
6	11001	72773
7	11002	43736
8	11002	51238
9	11002	53237
10	11003	43701
11	11003	51315
12	11003	57783
13	11004	43810

Figure 4-27. *The results of a query with a virtual table*

Using Common Table Expressions

Microsoft introduced the common table expression (CTE) feature with SQL Server 2005. This gives developers another way to separate out the logic of one part of the query. When writing a CTE, you define one or more queries up front, which you can then immediately use. This technique will come in handy when learning more advanced skills. For simple problems, there is no advantage over derived tables, but CTEs have several advanced features covered in Chapter 10 that are not available with derived tables. Here is the simplest syntax:

```
WITH <CTE Name> AS (SELECT <select list> FROM <table1>)
SELECT <select list> FROM <table2>
[INNER] JOIN <CTE Name> ON <table2>.<col1> = <CTE Name>.<col2>
```

Type in and execute the code in Listing 4-19. Again, the example is very simple but should help you learn the technique.

Listing 4-19. Using a Common Table Expression

```
USE AdventureWorks2008;
GO

WITH orders AS (
    SELECT SalesOrderID, CustomerID
    FROM Sales.SalesOrderHeader
    )
SELECT c.CustomerID, orders.SalesOrderID
FROM Sales.Customer AS c
INNER JOIN orders ON c.CustomerID = orders.CustomerID;
```

You can see the results in Figure 4-28. The CTE begins with the word **WITH**. Because **WITH** is a keyword in several T-SQL commands, it must be either the first word in the batch, as in this example, or proceeded by a semicolon. The word **GO** begins a new batch. Supply the CTE name followed by the definition. The main query immediately follows the CTE definition. Treat the CTE as a regular table in the main query. Once the query completes executing, the CTE goes out of scope and can no longer be used.

	CustomerID	SalesOrderID
1	11000	43793
2	11000	51522
3	11000	57418
4	11001	43767
5	11001	51493
6	11001	72773
7	11002	43736
8	11002	51238
9	11002	53237
10	11003	43701

Figure 4-28. The results of a query using a CTE

Using a CTE to Solve a Complicated Join Problem

The examples in the previous sections on joining tables demonstrated very simple join conditions, one or two columns from one table equal to the same number of columns in another table. Join conditions may be much more complicated. For example, suppose you wanted to produce a list of all customers along with the orders, if any, placed on a certain date. Figure 4-29 shows a diagram of this query.

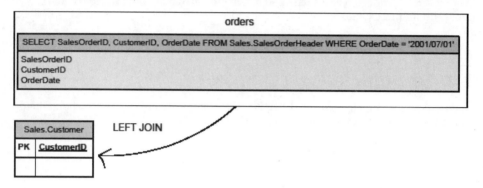

Figure 4-29. *A diagram of a CTE query*

Listing 4-20 demonstrates the problem and how to solve it with a CTE.

Listing 4-20. Using a CTE to Solve a Problem

```
USE AdventureWorks2008;
GO


--1
SELECT c.CustomerID, s.SalesOrderID, s.OrderDate
FROM Sales.Customer AS c
LEFT OUTER JOIN Sales.SalesOrderHeader AS s ON c.CustomerID = s.CustomerID
WHERE s.OrderDate = '2001/07/01';


--2
WITH orders AS (
    SELECT SalesOrderID, CustomerID, OrderDate
    FROM Sales.SalesOrderHeader
    WHERE OrderDate = '2001/07/01'
    )
SELECT c.CustomerID, orders.SalesOrderID, orders.OrderDate
FROM Sales.Customer AS c
LEFT OUTER JOIN orders ON c.CustomerID = orders.CustomerID
ORDER BY orders.OrderDate DESC;
```

Take a look at the results in Figure 4-30. Query 1 returns only the 43 rows with the specified order date. The nonmatching rows dropped out of the query because of the **NULL**s and values other than **2001/07/01** in the **OrderDate** column. If you want to show all customers even if there is not an order placed on the specified date, then by adding the **WHERE** clause to the CTE instead, the **NULL** values and other **OrderDate** values do not cause any problems, and the correct results are returned.

	CustomerID	SalesOrderID	OrderDate
34	29992	43692	2001-07-01 00:00:00.000
35	29491	43693	2001-07-01 00:00:00.000
36	29549	43694	2001-07-01 00:00:00.000
37	29958	43695	2001-07-01 00:00:00.000
38	29849	43696	2001-07-01 00:00:00.000
39	21768	43697	2001-07-01 00:00:00.000
40	28389	43698	2001-07-01 00:00:00.000
41	25863	43699	2001-07-01 00:00:00.000
42	14501	43700	2001-07-01 00:00:00.000
43	11003	43701	2001-07-01 00:00:00.000

	CustomerID	SalesOrderID	OrderDate
36	29614	43668	2001-07-01 00:00:00.000
37	29849	43696	2001-07-01 00:00:00.000
38	29596	43674	2001-07-01 00:00:00.000
39	29761	43679	2001-07-01 00:00:00.000
40	29824	43677	2001-07-01 00:00:00.000
41	29994	43662	2001-07-01 00:00:00.000
42	29734	43661	2001-07-01 00:00:00.000
43	29912	43684	2001-07-01 00:00:00.000
44	29945	NULL	NULL
45	29740	NULL	NULL

Figure 4-30. *The results of using a CTE to solve a tricky query*

This section demonstrated how to use derived tables and common table expressions. The examples, except for the last one, covered queries that you could have easily written using joins. In Chapter 5, you will learn more examples of how to use these techniques when regular joins will not work. Practice writing queries with derived tables and common table expressions by completing Exercise 4-4.

Exercise 4-4

Use the AdventureWorks2008 database to complete this exercise. You can find the solutions in the appendix.

1. Using a derived table, join the `Sales.SalesOrderHeader` table to the `Sales.SalesOrderDetail` table. Display the `SalesOrderID`, `OrderDate`, and `ProductID` columns in the results. The `Sales.SalesOrderDetail` table should be inside the derived table query.
2. Rewrite the query in question 1 with a common table expression.
3. Write a query that displays all customers along with the orders placed in 2001. Use a common table expression to write the query and include the `CustomerID`, `SalesOrderID`, and `OrderDate` columns in the results.

Thinking About Performance

Often, using different query techniques can produce the same execution plan, or at least similar performance. To see an example of this, toggle on the Include Actual Execution Plan setting, and run Listing 4-21, which shows two techniques to get the same results.

Listing 4-21. Comparing the Performance of Two Techniques

```
USE AdventureWorks2008;
GO


--1
SELECT DISTINCT c.CustomerID
FROM Sales.Customer AS c
INNER JOIN Sales.SalesOrderHeader AS o ON c.CustomerID = o.CustomerID;


--2
SELECT CustomerID
FROM Sales.Customer
WHERE CustomerID IN (SELECT CustomerID FROM Sales.SalesOrderHeader);
```

Figure 4-31 shows the identical execution plans. These queries produce identical results but with very different techniques.

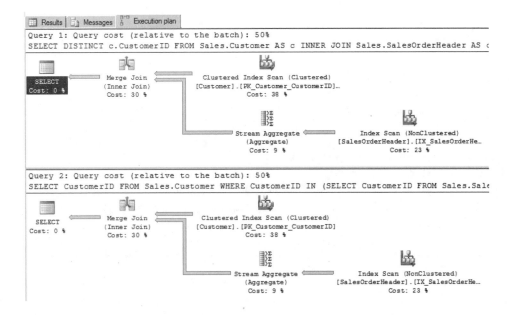

Results	Messages	Execution plan

```
Query 1: Query cost (relative to the batch): 50%
SELECT DISTINCT c.CustomerID FROM Sales.Customer AS c INNER JOIN Sales.SalesOrderHeader AS c
```

SELECT
Cost: 0 %

Merge Join
(Inner Join)
Cost: 30 %

Clustered Index Scan (Clustered)
[Customer].[PK_Customer_CustomerID]...
Cost: 38 %

Stream Aggregate
(Aggregate)
Cost: 9 %

Index Scan (NonClustered)
[SalesOrderHeader].[IX_SalesOrderHe...
Cost: 23 %

```
Query 2: Query cost (relative to the batch): 50%
SELECT CustomerID FROM Sales.Customer WHERE CustomerID IN (SELECT CustomerID FROM Sales.Sale
```

SELECT
Cost: 0 %

Merge Join
(Inner Join)
Cost: 30 %

Clustered Index Scan (Clustered)
[Customer].[PK_Customer_CustomerID]
Cost: 38 %

Stream Aggregate
(Aggregate)
Cost: 9 %

Index Scan (NonClustered)
[SalesOrderHeader].[IX_SalesOrderHe...
Cost: 23 %

Figure 4-31. *The identical execution plans*

As you learn to write more complicated queries, especially using aggregate functions in Chapter 5, you will learn that how you join the tables can make a big difference in performance. To experiment a bit more with performance, complete Exercise 4-5.

Exercise 4-5

Use the AdventureWorks2008 database to complete this exercise. You can find the solutions in the appendix.

Run the following code to add and populate a new column, OrderID, to the Sales.SalesOrderDetail table. After running the code, the new column will contain the same data as the SalesOrderID column.

```
USE AdventureWorks2008;
GO
ALTER TABLE Sales.SalesOrderDetail ADD OrderID INT NULL;
GO
UPDATE Sales.SalesOrderDetail SET OrderID = SalesOrderID;
```

1. Make sure that the Include Actual Execution Plan is turned on before running the code below. View the execution plan, and explain why one query performs better than the other.

```
--1
SELECT o.SalesOrderID,d.SalesOrderDetailID
FROM Sales.SalesOrderHeader AS o
INNER JOIN Sales.SalesOrderDetail AS d ON o.SalesOrderID = d.SalesOrderID;


--2
SELECT o.SalesOrderID,d.SalesOrderDetailID
FROM Sales.SalesOrderHeader AS o
INNER JOIN Sales.SalesOrderDetail AS d ON o.SalesOrderID = d.OrderID;
```

2. Compare the execution plans of the derived table example (Listing 4-18) and the CTE example (Listing 4-19). Explain why the query performance is the same or why one query performs better than the other.

Summary

For the data to make sense in reports and applications, tables must be joined together. As you can see from the number of topics in this chapter, there are many ways to do it. Most queries will use the **INNER JOIN** syntax, but for returning all the rows even if there is not a match, you will use an **OUTER JOIN**. After learning about joins, you learned about subqueries in the **WHERE** clause using **IN** and **UNION** queries. Finally, the chapter covered derived tables and common table expressions, which will help you solve more intriguing query puzzles as you learn more advanced techniques.

CHAPTER 5
■■■

Grouping and Summarizing Data

So far, you have learned to write simple queries that include filtering and ordering. You can also work with expressions built with operators and functions. The previous chapter taught you how to write queries with multiple tables so that the data makes sense in applications and reports. Now it is time to learn about a special type of query, *aggregate queries*, used to group and summarize data. You may find that writing aggregate queries is more challenging than the other queries you have learned so far, but by taking a step-by-step approach, you will realize that they are not difficult to write at all. Be sure to take the time to understand the examples and complete all the exercises before moving on to the next section.

Aggregate Functions

You use aggregate functions to summarize data in queries. The functions that you worked with in Chapter 3 operate on one value at a time. These functions operate on sets of values from multiple rows all at once. For example, you may need to supply information about how many orders were placed and the total amount ordered for a report. Here are the most commonly used aggregate functions:

- **COUNT**: Counts the number of rows or the number of non-**NULL** values in a column.
- **SUM**: Adds up the values in numeric or money data.
- **AVG**: Calculates the average in numeric or money data.
- **MIN**: Finds the lowest value in the set of values. This can be used on string data as well as numeric, money, or date data.
- **MAX**: Finds the highest value in the set of values. This can be used on string data as well as numeric, money, or date data.

    Keep the following in mind when working with these aggregate functions:

- The functions **AVG** and **SUM** will operate only on numeric and money data columns.
- The functions **MIN**, **MAX**, and **COUNT** will work on numeric, money, string, and temporal data columns.
- The aggregate functions will not operate on **TEXT**, **NTEXT**, and **IMAGE** columns. These data types are deprecated, meaning that they may not be supported in future versions of SQL Server.
- The aggregate functions ignore **NULL** values.
- **COUNT** can be used with an asterisk (*****) to give the count of the rows even if all the columns are **NULL**.
- Once an aggregate function is used in a query, the query becomes an aggregate query.

Here is the syntax for the simplest type of aggregate query where the aggregate function is used in the **SELECT** list:

```
SELECT <aggregate function>(<col1>)
FROM <table>
```

Listing 5-1 shows an example of using aggregate functions. Type in and execute the code to learn how these functions are used over the entire result set.

Listing 5-1. Using Aggregate Functions

```
USE AdventureWorks2008;
GO

--1
SELECT COUNT(*) AS CountOfRows,
    MAX(TotalDue) AS MaxTotal,
    MIN(TotalDue) AS MinTotal,
    SUM(TotalDue) AS SumOfTotal,
    AVG(TotalDue) AS AvgTotal
FROM Sales.SalesOrderHeader;

--2
SELECT MIN(Name) AS MinName,
    MAX(Name) AS MaxName,
    MIN(SellStartDate) AS MinSellStartDate
FROM Production.Product;
```

Take a look at the results in Figure 5-1. The aggregate functions operate on all the rows in the **Sales.SalesOrderHeader** table in query 1 and return just one row of results. The first expression, **CountOfRows**, uses an asterisk (*) to count all the rows in the table. The other expressions perform calculations on the **TotalDue** column. Query 2 demonstrates using the **MIN** and **MAX** functions on string and date columns. In these examples, the **SELECT** clause lists only aggregate expressions. You will learn how to add columns that are not part of aggregate expressions in the next section.

	CountOfRows	MaxTotal	MinTotal	SumOfTotal	AvgTotal
1	31465	187487.825	1.5183	123216786.1159	3915.9951

	MinName	MaxName		MinSellStartDate
1	Adjustable Race	Women's Tights, S		1998-06-01 00:00:00.000

Figure 5-1. The results of using aggregate functions

Now that you know how to use aggregate functions to summarize a result set, practice what you have learned by completing Exercise 5-1.

Exercise 5-1

Use the AdventureWorks2008 database to complete this exercise. You can find the solutions in the appendix.

1. Write a query to determine the number of customers in the `Sales.Customer` table.
2. Write a query that lists the total number of products ordered. Use the `OrderQty` column of the `Sales.SalesOrderDetail` table and the `SUM` function.
3. Write a query to determine the price of the most expensive product ordered. Use the `UnitPrice` column of the `Sales.SalesOrderDetail` table.
4. Write a query to determine the average freight amount in the `Sales.SalesOrderHeader` table.
5. Write a query using the `Production.Product` table that displays the minimum, maximum, and average `ListPrice`.

The GROUP BY Clause

The previous example query and exercise questions listed only aggregate expressions in the **SELECT** list. The aggregate functions operated on the entire result set in each query. By adding more nonaggregated columns to the **SELECT** list, you add grouping levels to the query, which requires the use of the **GROUP BY** clause. The aggregate functions then operate on the grouping levels instead of on the entire set of results. This section covers grouping on columns and grouping on expressions.

Grouping on Columns

You can use the **GROUP BY** clause to group data so that the aggregate functions apply to groups of values instead of the entire result set. For example, you may want to calculate the count and sum of the orders placed, grouped by order date or grouped by customer. Here is the syntax for the **GROUP BY** clause:

```
SELECT <aggregate function>(<col1>), <col2>
FROM <table>
GROUP BY <col2>
```

One big difference you will notice once the query contains a **GROUP BY** clause is that additional nonaggregated columns may be included in the **SELECT** list. Once nonaggregated columns are in the **SELECT** list, you must add the **GROUP BY** clause and include all the nonaggregated columns. Run this code example, and view the error message:

```
USE AdventureWorks2008;
GO
SELECT CustomerID,SUM(TotalDue) AS TotalPerCustomer
FROM Sales.SalesOrderHeader;
```

Figure 5-2 shows the error message. To get around this error, you will add the **GROUP BY** clause and include nonaggregated columns in that clause. Make sure that the **SELECT** list includes only those columns that you really need in the results, because the **SELECT** list directly affects which columns will be required in the **GROUP BY** clause.

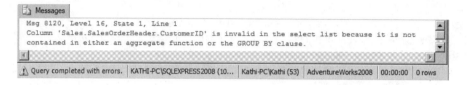

Figure 5-2. *The error message that results when the required* GROUP BY *clause is missing*

Type in and execute the code in Listing 5-2, which demonstrates how to use **GROUP BY**.

Listing 5-2. *Using the* GROUP BY *Clause*

```
USE AdventureWorks2008;
GO


--1
SELECT CustomerID,SUM(TotalDue) AS TotalPerCustomer
FROM Sales.SalesOrderHeader
GROUP BY CustomerID;

--2
SELECT TerritoryID,AVG(TotalDue) AS AveragePerTerritory
FROM Sales.SalesOrderHeader
GROUP BY TerritoryID;
```

Take a look at the results in Figure 5-3. Query 1 displays every customer with orders along with the sum of the **TotalDue** for each customer. The results are grouped by the **CustomerID**, and the sum is applied over each group of rows. Query 2 returns the average of the **TotalDue** values grouped by the **TerritoryID**. In each case, the nonaggregated column in the **SELECT** list must appear in the **GROUP BY** clause.

Figure 5-3. *The results of using the GROUP BY clause*

Any columns listed that are not part of an aggregate expression must be used to group the results. Those columns must be included in the **GROUP BY** clause. If you don't want to group on a column, don't list it in the **SELECT** list. This is where developers struggle when writing aggregate queries, so I cannot stress it enough.

Grouping on Expressions

The previous examples demonstrated how to group on columns, but it is possible to also group on expressions. You must include the exact expression from the **SELECT** list in the **GROUP BY** clause. Listing 5-3 demonstrates how to avoid incorrect results caused by adding a column instead of the expression to the **GROUP BY** clause.

Listing 5-3. How to Group on an Expression

```
Use AdventureWorks2008;
GO


--1
SELECT COUNT(*) AS CountOfOrders, YEAR(OrderDate) AS OrderYear
FROM Sales.SalesOrderHeader
GROUP BY OrderDate;


--2
SELECT COUNT(*) AS CountOfOrders, YEAR(OrderDate) AS OrderYear
FROM Sales.SalesOrderHeader
GROUP BY YEAR(OrderDate);
```

You can find the results in Figure 5-4. Notice that query 1 will run, but instead of returning one row per year, the query returns multiple rows with unexpected values. Because the **GROUP BY** clause contains **OrderDate**, the grouping is on **OrderDate**. The **CountOfOrders** expression is the count by **OrderDate**, not **OrderYear**. The expression in the **SELECT** list just changes how the data displays; it doesn't affect the calculations.

Query 2 fixes this problem by including the exact expression from the **SELECT** list in the **GROUP BY** clause. Query 2 returns only one row per year, and **CountOfOrders** is correctly calculated.

Results

	CountOfOrders	OrderYear
1	7	2001
2	9	2002
3	14	2003
4	65	2004
5	1	2001
6	11	2002
7	15	2003
8	91	2004

	CountOfOrders	OrderYear
1	13951	2004
2	1379	2001
3	3692	2002
4	12443	2003

Figure 5-4. *Using an expression in the GROUP BY clause*

You use aggregate functions along with the **GROUP BY** clause to summarize data over groups of rows. Be sure to practice what you have learned by completing Exercise 5-2.

Exercise 5-2

Use the AdventureWorks2008 database to complete the exercise. You can find the solutions in the appendix.

1. Write a query that shows the total number of items ordered for each product. Use the `Sales.SalesOrderDetail` table to write the query.
2. Write a query using the `Sales.SalesOrderDetail` table that displays a count of the detail lines for each `SalesOrderID`.
3. Write a query using the `Production.Product` table that lists a count of the products in each product line.
4. Write a query that displays the count of orders placed by year for each customer using the `Sales.SalesOrderHeader` table.

The ORDER BY Clause

You already know how to use the **ORDER BY** clause, but special rules exist for using the **ORDER BY** clause in aggregate queries. If a nonaggregate column appears in the **ORDER BY** clause, it must also appear in the **GROUP BY** clause, just like the **SELECT** list. Here is the syntax:

```
SELECT <aggregate function>(<col1>),<col2>
FROM <table1>
GROUP BY <col2>
ORDER BY <col2>
```

Type in the following code to see the error that results when a column included in the **ORDER BY** clause is missing from the **GROUP BY** clause:

```
USE AdventureWorks2008;
GO

SELECT CustomerID,SUM(TotalDue) AS TotalPerCustomer
FROM Sales.SalesOrderHeader
GROUP BY CustomerID
ORDER BY TerritoryID;
```

Figure 5-5 shows the error message that results from running the code. To avoid this error, make sure that you add only those columns to the **ORDER BY** clause that you intend to be grouping levels.

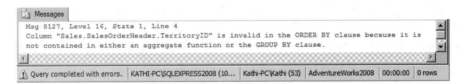

Figure 5-5. *The error message resulting from including a column in the* ORDER BY *clause that is not a grouping level*

Listing 5-4 demonstrates how to use the **ORDER BY** clause within an aggregate query. Be sure to type in and execute the code.

Listing 5-4. Using an ORDER BY

```
USE AdventureWorks2008;
GO


--1
SELECT CustomerID,SUM(TotalDue) AS TotalPerCustomer
FROM Sales.SalesOrderHeader
GROUP BY CustomerID
ORDER BY CustomerID;

--2
SELECT TerritoryID,AVG(TotalDue) AS AveragePerTerritory
FROM Sales.SalesOrderHeader
GROUP BY TerritoryID
ORDER BY TerritoryID;

--3
SELECT CustomerID,SUM(TotalDue) AS TotalPerCustomer
FROM Sales.SalesOrderHeader
GROUP BY CustomerID
ORDER BY SUM(TotalDue) DESC;
```

View the results of Listing 5-4 in Figure 5-6. As you can see, the **ORDER BY** clause follows the same rules as the **SELECT** list. Queries 1 and 2 return the results in the order of the nonaggregated column that is listed in the **GROUP BY** clause. Query 3 displays the results in the order of the sum of **TotalDue** in descending order.

	CustomerID	TotalPerCustomer
1	11000	9115.1341
2	11001	7054.1875
3	11002	8966.0143
4	11003	8993.9155
5	11004	9056.5911
6	11005	8974.0698
7	11006	8971.5283
8	11007	9073.1551

	TerritoryID	AveragePerTerritory
1	1	4528.2108
2	2	26334.4923
3	3	27451.842
4	4	5015.0159
5	5	21750.1654
6	6	5286.8975
7	7	3419.4253
8	8	2264.4923

	CustomerID	TotalPerCustomer
1	29722	1179857.4657
2	29818	1179475.8399
3	29715	1134747.4413
4	30117	1084439.0265
5	29614	1074154.3035
6	29639	1045197.0498
7	29701	1005539.7181
8	29994	984324.0473

Figure 5-6. Using ORDER BY

The WHERE Clause

The WHERE clause in an aggregate query may contain anything allowed in the WHERE clause in any other query type. It may not, however, contain an aggregate expression. You use the WHERE clause to eliminate rows before the groupings and aggregates are applied. To filter after the groupings are applied, you will use the HAVING clause. You'll learn about HAVING in the next section. Type in and execute the code in Listing 5-5, which demonstrates using the WHERE clause in an aggregate query.

Listing 5-5. Using the WHERE Clause

```
USE AdventureWorks2008;
GO
SELECT CustomerID,SUM(TotalDue) AS TotalPerCustomer
FROM Sales.SalesOrderHeader
WHERE TerritoryID in (5,6)
GROUP BY CustomerID;
```

The results in Figure 5-7 contain only those rows where the **TerritoryID** is either 5 or 6. The query eliminates the rows before the grouping is applied. Notice that **TerritoryID** doesn't appear anywhere in the query except for the **WHERE** clause. The **WHERE** clause may contain any of the columns in the table as long as it doesn't contain an aggregate expression.

	CustomerID	TotalPerCustomer
1	28648	3953.9884
2	29976	22723.508
3	15913	787.0584
4	13660	5248.7611
5	29999	2166.664
6	18546	32.5754
7	23716	29.8019
8	29761	80385.0824
9	17026	288.836
10	18523	177.8388

Figure 5-7. *The results of using the WHERE clause in an aggregate query*

The HAVING Clause

To eliminate rows based on an aggregate expression, use the **HAVING** clause. The **HAVING** clause may contain aggregate expressions that do or do not appear in the **SELECT** list. For example, you could write a query that returns the sum of the total due for customers who have placed at least ten orders. The count of the orders does not have to appear in the **SELECT** list. Alternately, you could include only those customers who have spent at least $10,000 (sum of total due), which does appear in the list.

You can also include nonaggregate columns in the **HAVING** clause as long as the columns appear in the **GROUP BY** clause. In other words, you can eliminate some of the groups with the **HAVING** clause. Behind the scenes, however, the database engine may move that criteria to the **WHERE** clause because it is more efficient to eliminate those rows first. Criteria involving nonaggregate columns actually belongs in the **WHERE** clause, but the query will still work with the criteria appearing in the **HAVING** clause.

Most of the operators such as equal to (=), less than (<), and between that are used in the **WHERE** clause will work. Here is the syntax:

```
SELECT <aggregate function1>(<col1>),<col2>
FROM <table1>
GROUP BY <col2>
HAVING <aggregate function2>(<col3>) = <value>
```

Like the **GROUP BY** clause, the **HAVING** clause will be in aggregate queries only. Listing 5-6 demonstrates the **HAVING** clause. Be sure to type in and execute the code.

Listing 5-6. Using the HAVING Clause

```
USE AdventureWorks2008;
GO


--1
SELECT CustomerID,SUM(TotalDue) AS TotalPerCustomer
FROM Sales.SalesOrderHeader
GROUP BY CustomerID
HAVING SUM(TotalDue) > 5000;


--2
SELECT CustomerID,SUM(TotalDue) AS TotalPerCustomer
FROM Sales.SalesOrderHeader
GROUP BY CustomerID
HAVING COUNT(*) = 10 AND SUM(TotalDue) > 5000;


--3
SELECT CustomerID,SUM(TotalDue) AS TotalPerCustomer
FROM Sales.SalesOrderHeader
GROUP BY CustomerID
HAVING CustomerID > 27858;
```

You can find the results in Figure 5-8. Query 1 shows only the rows where the sum of the TotalDue exceeds 5,000. The TotalDue column appears within an aggregate expression in the SELECT list. Query 2 demonstrates how an aggregate expression not included in the SELECT list may be used, in this case the count of the rows, in the HAVING clause. Query 3 contains a nonaggregated column, CustomerID, in the HAVING clause, but it is a column in the GROUP BY clause. In this case, you could have moved the criteria to the WHERE clause instead and received the same results.

Results

	CustomerID	TotalPerCustomer
1	14324	5659.1783
2	15675	7963.05
3	11453	9035.563
4	14155	6622.5524
5	12804	6572.7942
6	30030	68644.5658
7	13050	6244.6309
8	28264	6627.0497

	CustomerID	TotalPerCustomer
1	29830	38452.4651
2	29842	156413.2374
3	29622	262408.3464
4	29588	17361.1884
5	29508	10227.5269
6	29569	24082.9023
7	29961	79847.8229
8	29606	16030.152

	CustomerID	TotalPerCustomer
1	28648	3953.9884
2	29976	19322.199
3	29312	77.3169
4	28387	645.2869
5	27984	620.4354
6	28671	4774.2852
7	29335	3953.9884
8	29999	1821.0996

Figure 5-8. *The partial results of using the* `HAVING` *clause*

Developers often struggle when trying to figure out whether the filter criteria belongs in the `WHERE` clause or in the `HAVING` clause. It may help you remember if you understand the order in which the database engine processes the clauses. First review the order in which you write the clauses in an aggregate query:

- `SELECT`
- `FROM`
- `WHERE`
- `GROUP BY`
- `HAVING`
- `ORDER BY`

The database engine processes the **WHERE** clause before the groupings and aggregates are applied. Here is the order that the database engine actually processes the query:

- FROM
- WHERE
- GROUP BY
- HAVING
- SELECT
- ORDER BY

The database engine processes the **WHERE** clause before it processes the groupings and aggregates. Use the **WHERE** clause to completely eliminate rows from the query. For example, your query might eliminate all the orders except those placed in 2008. The database engine processes the **HAVING** clause after it processes the groupings and aggregates. Use the **HAVING** clause to eliminate rows based on aggregate expressions or groupings. For example, use the **HAVING** clause to remove the customers who have placed fewer than ten orders. Practice what you have learned about the **HAVING** clause by completing Exercise 5-3.

Exercise 5-3

Use the AdventureWorks2008 to complete this exercise. You can find the solutions in the appendix.

1. Write a query that returns a count of detail lines in the `Sales.SalesOrderDetail` table by `SalesOrderID`. Include only those sales that have more than three detail lines.
2. Write a query that creates a sum of the `LineTotal` in the `Sales.SalesOrderDetail` table grouped by the `SalesOrderID`. Include only those rows where the sum exceeds 1,000.
3. Write a query that groups the products by `ProductModelID` along with a count. Display the rows that have a count that equals 1.
4. Change the query in question 3 so that only the products with the color blue or red are included.

DISTINCT

You can use the keyword **DISTINCT** in any **SELECT** list. For example, you can use **DISTINCT** to eliminate duplicate rows in a regular query. This section discusses using **DISTINCT** and aggregate queries.

Using DISTINCT vs. GROUP BY

Developers often use the **DISTINCT** keyword to eliminate duplicate rows from a regular query. Be careful when tempted to do this; using **DISTINCT** to eliminate duplicate rows may be a sign that there is a problem with the query. Assuming that the duplicate results are valid, you will get the same results by using **GROUP BY** instead. Type in and execute the code in Listing 5-7 to see how this works.

Listing 5-7. Using DISTINCT and GROUP BY

```
Use AdventureWorks2008;
GO

--1
SELECT DISTINCT SalesOrderID
FROM Sales.SalesOrderDetail;

--2
SELECT SalesOrderID
FROM Sales.SalesOrderDetail
GROUP BY SalesOrderID;
```

Queries 1 and 2 return identical results (see Figure 5-9). Even though query 2 contains no aggregate expressions, it is still an aggregate query because **GROUP BY** has been added. By grouping on SalesOrderID, only the unique values show up in the returned rows.

Figure 5-9. The results of DISTINCT vs. GROUP BY

DISTINCT Within an Aggregate Expression

You may also use **DISTINCT** within an aggregate query to cause the aggregate functions to operate on unique values. For example, instead of the count of rows, you could write a query that counts the number of unique values in a column. Type in and execute the code in Listing 5-8 to see how this works.

Listing 5-8. UsingDISTINCT in an Aggregate Expression

```
USE AdventureWorks2008;
GO


--1
SELECT COUNT(*) AS CountOfRows,
    COUNT(SalesPersonID) AS CountOfSalesPeople,
    COUNT(DISTINCT SalesPersonID) AS CountOfUniqueSalesPeople
FROM Sales.SalesOrderHeader;

--2
SELECT SUM(TotalDue) AS TotalOfAllOrders,
    SUM(Distinct TotalDue) AS TotalOfDistinctTotalDue
FROM Sales.SalesOrderHeader;
```

Take a look at the results in Figure 5-10. Query 1 contains three aggregate expressions all using COUNT. The first one counts all rows in the table. The second expression counts the values in SalesPersonID. The expression returns a much smaller value because the data contains many NULL values, which are ignored by the aggregate function. Finally, the third expression returns the count of unique SalesPersonID values by using the DISTINCT keyword.

Query 2 demonstrates that DISTINCT works with other aggregate functions, not just COUNT. The first expression returns the sum of TotalDue for all rows in the table. The second expression returns the sum of unique TotalDue values.

Results		
CountOfRows	CountOfSalesPeople	CountOfUniqueSalesPeople
31465	3806	17

TotalOfAllOrders	TotalOfDistinctTotalDue
123216786.1159	91735344.3814

Figure 5-10. Using DISTINCT in an aggregate expression

You can use DISTINCT either to return unique rows from your query or to make your aggregate expression operate on unique values in your data. Practice what you have learned by completing Exercise 5-4.

Exercise 5-4

Use the AdventureWorks2008 database to complete this exercise. You can find the solutions in the appendix.

1. Write a query using the `Sales.SalesOrderDetail` table to come up with a count of unique `ProductID` values that have been ordered.
2. Write a query using the `Sales.SalesOrderHeader` table that returns the count of unique `TerritoryID` values per customer.

Aggregate Queries with More Than One Table

So far, the examples have demonstrated how to write aggregate queries involving just one table. You may use aggregate expressions and the **GROUP BY** and **HAVING** clauses when joining tables as well; the same rules apply. Type in and execute the code in Listing 5-9 to learn how to do this.

Listing 5-9. Writing Aggregate Queries with Two Tables

```
USE AdventureWorks2008;
GO


--1
SELECT c.CustomerID, c.AccountNumber, COUNT(*) AS CountOfOrders,
    SUM(TotalDue) AS SumOfTotalDue
FROM Sales.Customer AS c
INNER JOIN Sales.SalesOrderHeader AS s ON c.CustomerID = s.CustomerID
GROUP BY c.CustomerID, c.AccountNumber
ORDER BY c.CustomerID;


--2
SELECT c.CustomerID, c.AccountNumber, COUNT(*) AS CountOfOrders,
    SUM(TotalDue) AS SumOfTotalDue
FROM Sales.Customer AS c
LEFT OUTER JOIN Sales.SalesOrderHeader AS s ON c.CustomerID = s.CustomerID
GROUP BY c.CustomerID, c.AccountNumber
ORDER BY c.CustomerID;
```

```
--3
SELECT c.CustomerID, c.AccountNumber,COUNT(s.SalesOrderID) AS CountOfOrders,
    SUM(COALESCE(TotalDue,0)) AS SumOfTotalDue
FROM Sales.Customer AS c
LEFT OUTER JOIN Sales.SalesOrderHeader AS s ON c.CustomerID = s.CustomerID
GROUP BY c.CustomerID, c.AccountNumber
ORDER BY c.CustomerID;
```

You can see the results of Listing 5-9 in Figure 5-11. All three queries join the **Sales.Customer** and **Sales.SalesOrderHeader** tables together and attempt to count the orders placed and calculate the sum of the total due for each customer.

	CustomerID	AccountNumber	CountOfOrders	SumOfTotalDue
1	11000	AW00011000	3	9115.1341
2	11001	AW00011001	3	7054.1875
3	11002	AW00011002	3	8966.0143
4	11003	AW00011003	3	8993.9155
5	11004	AW00011004	3	9056.5911

	CustomerID	AccountNumber	CountOfOrders	SumOfTotalDue
1	1	AW00000001	1	NULL
2	2	AW00000002	1	NULL
3	3	AW00000003	1	NULL
4	4	AW00000004	1	NULL
5	5	AW00000005	1	NULL

	CustomerID	AccountNumber	CountOfOrders	SumOfTotalDue
1	1	AW00000001	0	0.00
2	2	AW00000002	0	0.00
3	3	AW00000003	0	0.00
4	4	AW00000004	0	0.00
5	5	AW00000005	0	0.00

Figure 5-11. *The partial results of using aggregates with multiple tables*

Using an **INNER JOIN**, query 1 includes only the customers who have placed an order. By changing to an **LEFT OUTER JOIN**, query 2 includes all customers but incorrectly returns a count of 1 for customers with no orders and returns a **NULL** for the **SumOfTotalDue** when you probably want to see 0. Query 3 solves the first problem by changing **COUNT(*)** to **COUNT(s.SalesOrderID)**, which eliminates the **NULL** values and correctly returns 0 for those customers who have not placed an order. Query 3 solves the second problem by using **COALESCE** to change the **NULL** value to 0.

Remember that writing aggregate queries with multiple tables is really not different from with just one table; the same rules apply.

You can use your knowledge from the previous chapters, such as how to write a **WHERE** clause and how to join tables to write aggregate queries. Practice what you have learned by completing Exercise 5-5.

Exercise 5-5

Use the AdventureWorks2008 database to complete this exercise. You can find the solutions in the appendix.

1. Write a query joining the `Person.Person`, `Sales.Customer`, and `Sales.SalesOrderHeader` tables to return a list of the customer names along with a count of the orders placed.
2. Write a query using the `Sales.SalesOrderHeader`, `Sales.SalesOrderDetail`, and `Production.Product` tables to display the total sum of products by `ProductID` and `OrderDate`.

Isolating Aggregate Query Logic

Several techniques exist that allow you to separate an aggregate query from the rest of the statement. Sometimes this is necessary because the grouping levels and the columns that must be displayed are not compatible. This section will demonstrate these techniques.

Using a Correlated Subquery in the WHERE Clause

In Chapter 4 you learned how to add subqueries to the `WHERE` clause. Developers often use another type of subquery, the *correlated subquery*, to isolate an aggregate query. In a correlated subquery, the subquery refers to the outer query within the subquery's `WHERE` clause.

You will likely see this query type used, so I want you to be familiar with it, but other options shown later in the section will be better choices for your own code. Here is the syntax:

```
SELECT <select list>
FROM <table1>
WHERE <value or column> = (SELECT <aggregate function>(<col1>)
    FROM <table2>
    WHERE <col2> = <table1>.<col3>)
```

Notice that the predicate in the `WHERE` clause contains an equal to (=) operator instead of the `IN` operator. Recall that the subqueries described in the "Using a Subquery in an IN List" section in Chapter 4 require the `IN` operator because the subquery returns multiple rows. The query compares the value from a column in the outer query to a list of values in the subquery when using the `IN` operator. When using a correlated subquery, the subquery returns only one value for each row of the outer query, and you can use the other operators, such as equal to. In this case, the query compares a value or column from one row to one value returned by the subquery. Take a look at Listing 5-10, which demonstrates this technique.

Listing 5-10. Using a Correlated Subquery in the WHERE Clause

```
Use AdventureWorks2008;
GO

--1
SELECT CustomerID, SalesOrderID, TotalDue
FROM Sales.SalesOrderHeader AS soh
WHERE 10 =
    (SELECT COUNT(*)
     FROM Sales.SalesOrderDetail
     WHERE SalesOrderID = soh.SalesOrderID);

--2
SELECT CustomerID, SalesOrderID, TotalDue
FROM Sales.SalesOrderHeader AS soh
WHERE 10000 <
    (SELECT SUM(TotalDue)
     FROM Sales.SalesOrderHeader
     WHERE CustomerID = soh.CustomerID);

--3
SELECT CustomerID
FROM Sales.Customer AS c
WHERE CustomerID > (
    SELECT SUM(TotalDue)
    FROM Sales.SalesOrderHeader
    WHERE CustomerID = c.CustomerID);
```

You can see the partial results in Figure 5-12. Query 1 displays the **Sales.SalesOrderHeader** rows where there are ten matching detail rows. Inside the subquery's **WHERE** clause, the **SalesOrderID** from the subquery must match the **SalesOrderID** from the outer query. Usually when the same column name is used, both must be qualified with the table name or alias. In this case, if the column is not qualified, it refers to the tables in the subquery. Of course, if the subquery contains more than one table, you may have to qualify the column name.

	CustomerID	SalesOrderID	TotalDue
1	29580	43665	16158.6961
2	29491	43693	23126.45
3	29955	43843	37106.2915
4	29888	43845	9661.1367
5	30107	43869	55408.1581
6	29925	43877	23223.5397
7	29901	43901	25575.00
8	29487	44131	23095.3463

	CustomerID	SalesOrderID	TotalDue
1	29825	43659	23153.2339
2	29734	43661	36865.8012
3	29994	43662	32474.9324
4	29898	43664	27510.4109
5	29580	43665	16158.6961
6	30052	43666	5694.8564
7	29974	43667	6876.3649
8	29614	43668	40487.7233

	CustomerID
1	11012
2	11013
3	11014
4	11021
5	11022
6	11040
7	11062
8	11063

Figure 5-12. *A correlated subquery in the* WHERE *clause*

Query 2 displays rows from the **Sales.SalesOrderHeader** table but only for customers who have the sum of **TotalDue** greater than 10,000. In this case, the **CustomerID** from the outer query must equal the **CustomerID** from the subquery. Query 3 demonstrates how you can compare a column to the results of the aggregate expression in the subquery. The query compares the **CustomerID** to the sum of the orders and displays the customers who have ordered less than the **CustomerID**. Of course, this particular example may not make sense from a business rules perspective, but it shows that you can compare a column to the value of an aggregate function using a correlated subquery.

Inline Correlated Subqueries

You may also see correlated subqueries used within the **SELECT** list. I really do not recommend this technique because if the query contains more than one correlated subquery, performance deteriorates quickly. You will learn about better options later in this section. Here is the syntax for the inline correlated subquery:

```
SELECT <select list>,
    (SELECT <aggregate function>(<col1>)
     FROM <table2> WHERE <col2> = <table1>.<col3>) AS <alias name>
FROM <table1>
```

The subquery must produce only one row for each row of the outer query, and only one expression may be returned from the subquery. Listing 5-11 shows two examples of this query type.

Listing 5-11. Using an Inline Correlated Subquery

```
USE AdventureWorks2008;
GO

--1
SELECT CustomerID,
    (SELECT COUNT(*)
     FROM Sales.SalesOrderHeader
     WHERE CustomerID = c.CustomerID) AS CountOfSales
FROM Sales.Customer AS C
ORDER BY CountOfSales DESC;

--2
SELECT CustomerID,
    (SELECT COUNT(*) AS CountOfSales
     FROM Sales.SalesOrderHeader
     WHERE CustomerID = c.CustomerID) AS CountOfSales,
    (SELECT SUM(TotalDue)
     FROM Sales.SalesOrderHeader
     WHERE CustomerID = c.CustomerID) AS SumOfTotalDue,
    (SELECT AVG(TotalDue)
     FROM Sales.SalesOrderHeader
     WHERE CustomerID = c.customerID) AS AvgOfTotalDue
FROM Sales.Customer AS c
ORDER BY CountOfSales DESC;
```

You can see the results in Figure 5-13. Query 1 demonstrates how an inline correlated subquery returns one value per row. Notice the **WHERE** clause in the subquery. The **CustomerID** column must be equal to the **CustomerID** in the outer query. The alias for the column must be added right after the subquery definition, not the column definition.

Results

	CustomerID	CountOfSales
1	11091	28
2	11176	28
3	11185	27
4	11200	27
5	11223	27

	CustomerID	CountOfSales	SumOfTotalDue	AvgOfTotalDue
1	11176	28	1458.6118	52.0932
2	11091	28	1314.2103	46.936
3	11277	27	1585.6648	58.7283
4	11200	27	1617.0356	59.8902
5	11223	27	1331.9455	49.3313

Figure 5-13. *Using an inline correlated subquery*

Normally, when working with the same column name from two tables, both must be qualified. Within the subquery, if the column is not qualified, the column is assumed to be from the table within the subquery. If the subquery involves multiple tables, well, then you will probably have to qualify the columns.

Notice that Query 2 contains three correlated subqueries because three values are required. Although one correlated subquery doesn't usually cause a problem, performance quickly deteriorates as additional correlated subqueries are added to the query. Luckily, other techniques exist to get the same results with better performance.

Using Derived Tables

In Chapter 4 you learned about derived tables. You can use derived tables to isolate the aggregate query from the rest of the query, especially when working with SQL Server 2000, without a performance hit. Here is the syntax:

```
SELECT <col1>,<col4>,<col3> FROM <table1> AS a
INNER JOIN
    (SELECT <aggregate function>(<col2>) AS <col4>,<col3>
     FROM <table2> GROUP BY <col3>) AS b ON a.<col1> = b.<col3>
```

Listing 5-12 shows how to use this technique. Type in and execute the code.

Listing 5-12. *Using a Derived Table*

```
USE AdventureWorks2008;
GO

SELECT c.CustomerID,CountOfSales,
    SumOfTotalDue, AvgOfTotalDue
```

```
FROM Sales.Customer AS c INNER JOIN
    (SELECT CustomerID, COUNT(*) AS CountOfSales,
        SUM(TotalDue) AS SumOfTotalDue,
        AVG(TotalDue) AS AvgOfTotalDUE
    FROM Sales.SalesOrderHeader
    GROUP BY CustomerID) AS s
ON c.CustomerID = s.CustomerID;
```

You can see the results in Figure 5-14. This query has much better performance than the second query in Listing 5-11, but it produces the same results. Remember that any column required in the outer query must be listed in the derived table. You must also supply an alias for the derived table.

	CustomerID	CountOfSales	SumOfTotalDue	AvgOfTotalDue
1	11012	2	89.7923	44.8961
2	11013	2	125.9258	62.9629
3	11014	2	152.9873	76.4936
4	11021	1	2621.0158	2621.0158
5	11022	1	2566.1194	2566.1194
6	11040	1	2597.8108	2597.8108
7	11062	1	2598.9158	2598.9158
8	11063	1	2622.1098	2622.1098

Figure 5-14. *The partial results of using a derived table*

Besides the increase in performance, the derived table may return more than one row for each row of the outer query, and multiple aggregates may be included. If you are working with some legacy SQL Server 2000 systems, keep derived tables in mind for solving complicated T-SQL problems.

Common Table Expressions

You learned about common table expressions (CTEs) in Chapter 4. A CTE also allows you to isolate the aggregate query from the rest of the statement. The CTE is not stored as an object; it just makes the data available during the query. Here is the syntax:

```
WITH <cteName> AS (SELECT <aggregate function>(<col2>) AS <col4>, <col3>
    FROM <table2> GROUP BY <col3>)
SELECT <col1>,<col4>,<col3>
FROM <table1> INNER JOIN b ON <cteName>.<col1> = <table1>.<col3>
```

Type in and execute the code in Listing 5-13 to learn how to use a CTE with an aggregate query.

Listing 5-13. Using a Common Table Expression

```
USE AdventureWorks2008;
GO

WITH s AS
    (SELECT CustomerID, COUNT(*) AS CountOfSales,
        SUM(TotalDue) AS SumOfTotalDue,
        AVG(TotalDue) AS AvgOfTotalDUE
     FROM Sales.SalesOrderHeader
     GROUP BY CustomerID)
SELECT c.CustomerID,CountOfSales,
    SumOfTotalDue, AvgOfTotalDue
FROM Sales.Customer AS c INNER JOIN s
ON c.CustomerID = s.CustomerID;
```

Figure 5-15 displays the results. This query looks a lot like the one in Listing 5-12, just rearranged a bit. At this point, there is no real advantage to the CTE over the derived table, but it is easier to read in my opinion. CTEs have several extra features that you will learn about in Chapter 10.

	CustomerID	CountOfSales	SumOfTotalDue	AvgOfTotalDue
1	11012	2	89.7923	44.8961
2	11013	2	125.9258	62.9629
3	11014	2	152.9873	76.4936
4	11021	1	2621.0158	2621.0158
5	11022	1	2566.1194	2566.1194
6	11040	1	2597.8108	2597.8108
7	11062	1	2598.9158	2598.9158
8	11063	1	2622.1098	2622.1098

Figure 5-15. Using a common table expression

Using Derived Tables and CTEs to Display Details

Suppose you want to display several nonaggregated columns along with some aggregate expressions that apply to the entire result set or to a larger grouping lever. For example, you may need to display several columns from the **Sales.SalesOrderHeader** table and calculate the percent of the **TotalDue** for each sale compared to the **TotalDue** for all the customer's sales. If you group by **CustomerID**, you cannot include other nonaggregated columns from **Sales.SalesOrderHeader** unless you group by those columns. To get around this, you can use a derived table or a CTE. Type in and execute the code in Listing 5-14 to learn this technique.

Listing 5-14. Displaying Details

```
USE AdventureWorks2008;
GO

--1
SELECT c.CustomerID, SalesOrderID, TotalDue, AvgOfTotalDue,
    TotalDue/SumOfTotalDue * 100 AS SalePercent
FROM Sales.SalesOrderHeader AS soh
INNER JOIN
    (SELECT CustomerID, SUM(TotalDue) AS SumOfTotalDue,
     AVG(TotalDue) AS AvgOfTotalDue
     FROM Sales.SalesOrderHeader
     GROUP BY CustomerID) AS c ON soh.CustomerID = c.CustomerID
ORDER BY c.CustomerID;

--2
WITH c AS
    (SELECT CustomerID, SUM(TotalDue) AS SumOfTotalDue,
        AVG(TotalDue) AS AvgOfTotalDue
     FROM Sales.SalesOrderHeader
     GROUP BY CustomerID)
SELECT c.CustomerID, SalesOrderID, TotalDue,AvgOfTotalDue,
    TotalDue/SumOfTotalDue * 100 AS SalePercent
FROM Sales.SalesOrderHeader AS soh
INNER JOIN c ON soh.CustomerID = c.CustomerID
ORDER BY c.CustomerID;
```

Take a look at the results in Figure 5-16. The queries return the same results and just use different techniques. Inside the derived table or CTE, the data is grouped by CustomerID. The outer query contains no grouping at all, and any columns can be used. Either of these techniques performs much better than the equivalent query written with correlated subqueries.

Results

	CustomerID	SalesOrderID	TotalDue	AvgOfTotalDue	SalePercent
1	11000	43793	3756.989	3038.378	41.21
2	11000	51522	2587.8769	3038.378	28.39
3	11000	57418	2770.2682	3038.378	30.39
4	11001	51493	2674.0227	2351.3958	37.90
5	11001	43767	3729.364	2351.3958	52.86
6	11001	72773	650.8008	2351.3958	9.22
7	11002	43736	3756.989	2988.6714	41.90
8	11002	51238	2535.964	2988.6714	28.28

	CustomerID	SalesOrderID	TotalDue	AvgOfTotalDue	SalePercent
1	11000	43793	3756.989	3038.378	41.21
2	11000	51522	2587.8769	3038.378	28.39
3	11000	57418	2770.2682	3038.378	30.39
4	11001	51493	2674.0227	2351.3958	37.90
5	11001	43767	3729.364	2351.3958	52.86
6	11001	72773	650.8008	2351.3958	9.22
7	11002	43736	3756.989	2988.6714	41.90
8	11002	51238	2535.964	2988.6714	28.28

Figure 5-16. *The results of displaying details with a derived table and a CTE*

The OVER Clause

The **OVER** clause provides a way to add aggregate values to a nonaggregate query. For example, you may need to write a report that compares the total due of each order to the total due of the average order. The query is not really an aggregate query, but one aggregate value from the entire results set or a grouping level is required to perform the calculation. Here is the syntax:

```
SELECT <col1>,<aggregate function>(<col2>) OVER([PARTITION BY <col3>])
FROM <table1>
```

Type in and execute the code in Listing 5-15 to learn how to use **OVER**.

Listing 5-15. *Using the OVER Clause*

```
USE AdventureWorks2008;
GO

SELECT CustomerID, SalesOrderID, TotalDue,
    AVG(TotalDue) OVER(PARTITION BY CustomerID) AS AvgOfTotalDue,
    SUM(TotalDue) OVER(PARTITION BY CustomerID) AS SumOfTOtalDue,
    TotalDue/(SUM(TotalDue) OVER(PARTITION BY CustomerID)) * 100
        AS SalePercentPerCustomer,
    SUM(TotalDue) OVER() AS SalesOverAll
FROM Sales.SalesOrderHeader
ORDER BY CustomerID;
```

Figure 5-17 displays the results. The **PARTITION BY** part of the expressions specifies the grouping over which the aggregate is calculated. In this example, when partitioned by **CustomerID**, the function calculates the value grouped over **CustomerID**. When no **PARTITION BY** is specified as in the **SalesOverAll** column, the aggregate is calculated over the entire result set.

	CustomerID	SalesOrderID	TotalDue	AvgOfTotalDue	SumOfTOtalDue	SalePercentPerCustomer	SalesOverAll
1	11000	43793	3756.989	3038.378	9115.1341	41.21	140707584.8246
2	11000	51522	2587.8769	3038.378	9115.1341	28.39	140707584.8246
3	11000	57418	2770.2682	3038.378	9115.1341	30.39	140707584.8246
4	11001	51493	2674.0227	2351.3958	7054.1875	37.90	140707584.8246
5	11001	43767	3729.364	2351.3958	7054.1875	52.86	140707584.8246
6	11001	72773	650.8008	2351.3958	7054.1875	9.22	140707584.8246
7	11002	43736	3756.989	2988.6714	8966.0143	41.90	140707584.8246
8	11002	51238	2535.964	2988.6714	8966.0143	28.28	140707584.8246

Figure 5-17. Using the OVER clause

This feature would be much more useful if you could include a **GROUP BY** in the query and partition over a different level, but it doesn't work that way. If you need to do this, you are probably better off solving the problem with a CTE.

The **OVER** clause allows you to add an aggregate function to an otherwise nonaggregate query. Practice using the **OVER** clause by completing Exercise 5-65.

Exercise 5-6

Use the AdventureWorks2008 database to complete this exercise. You can find the solutions in the appendix.

1. Write a query that joins the **HumanResources.Employee** table to the **Person.Person** table so that you can display the **FirstName**, **LastName**, and **HireDate** columns for each employee. Display the **JobTitle** along with a count of employees for the title. Use a derived table to solve this query.

2. Rewrite the query from question 1 using a CTE.

3. Rewrite the query from question 1 using the **OVER** clause.

4. Display the **CustomerID**, **SalesOrderID**, and **OrderDate** for each **Sales.SalesOrderHeader** row as long as the customer has placed at least five orders. Use any of the techniques from this section to come up with the query.

Thinking About Performance

Inline correlated subqueries are very popular among developers. Unfortunately, the performance is poor compared to other techniques, such as derived tables and CTEs. Toggle on the Include Actual Execution Plan setting before typing and executing the code in Listing 5-16.

Listing 5-16. Comparing a Correlated Subquery to a Common Table Expression

```
USE AdventureWorks2008;
GO


--1
SELECT CustomerID,
    (SELECT COUNT(*) AS CountOfSales
     FROM Sales.SalesOrderHeader
     WHERE CustomerID = c.CustomerID) AS CountOfSales,
    (SELECT SUM(TotalDue)
     FROM Sales.SalesOrderHeader
     WHERE CustomerID = c.CustomerID) AS SumOfTotalDue,
    (SELECT AVG(TotalDue)
     FROM Sales.SalesOrderHeader
     WHERE CustomerID = c.customerID) AS AvgOfTotalDue
FROM Sales.Customer AS c
ORDER BY CountOfSales DESC;


--2
WITH Totals AS
    (SELECT COUNT(*) AS CountOfSales,
           SUM(TotalDue) AS SumOfTotalDue,
           AVG(TotalDue) AS AvgOfTotalDue,
           CustomerID
     FROM Sales.SalesOrderHeader
     GROUP BY CustomerID)
SELECT c.CustomerID, CountOfSales,SumOfTotalDue, AvgOfTotalDue
FROM Totals
INNER JOIN Sales.Customer AS c ON Totals.CustomerID = c.CustomerID
ORDER BY CountOfSales DESC;
```

Figure 5-18 displays a portion of the execution plan windows. These plans are pretty complex, but the important thing to note is that query 1, with the correlated subqueries, takes up 61 percent of the resources. Query 2, with the CTE, produces the same results but requires only 39 percent of the resources.

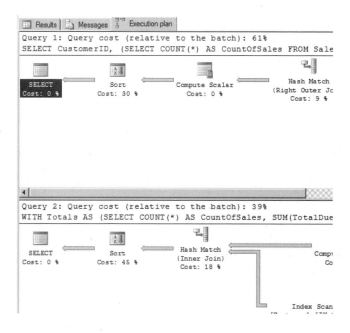

Figure 5-18. *The execution plans when comparing a derived table to a CTE*

As you can see, the way you write a query can often have a big impact on the performance. Complete Exercise 5-7 to learn more about the performance of aggregate queries.

Exercise 5-7

Use the AdventureWorks2008 database to complete this exercise. You can find the solutions in the appendix.

1. Make sure that the Include Actual Execution Plan setting is turned on before typing and executing the following code. Compare the execution plans to see whether the CTE query performs better than the OVER clause query.

```
USE AdventureWorks2008;
GO


--1
WITH SumSale AS
    (SELECT SUM(TotalDue) AS SumTotalDue,
        CustomerID
    FROM Sales.SalesOrderHeader
    GROUP BY CustomerID)
```

```
SELECT o.CustomerID, TotalDue,
    TotalDue / SumTotalDue * 100 AS PercentOfSales
FROM SumSale INNER JOIN Sales.SalesOrderHeader AS o
ON SumSale.CustomerID = o.CustomerID
ORDER BY CustomerID;


--2
SELECT CustomerID, TotalDue,
    TotalDue / SUM(TotalDue) OVER(PARTITION BY CustomerID) * 100
     AS PercentOfSales
FROM Sales.SalesOrderHeader
ORDER BY CustomerID;
```

2. The following queries each contain two calculations: percent of sales by customer and percent of sales by territory. Type in and execute the code to see the difference in performance. Make sure the Include Actual Execution Plan setting is turned on before running the code.

```
USE AdventureWorks2008;
GO


--1
WITH SumSale AS
   (SELECT SUM(TotalDue) AS SumTotalDue,
        CustomerID
    FROM Sales.SalesOrderHeader
    GROUP BY CustomerID),
 TerrSales AS
    (SELECT SUM(TotalDue) AS SumTerritoryTotalDue, TerritoryID
     FROM Sales.SalesOrderHeader
     GROUP BY TerritoryID )
SELECT o.CustomerID, TotalDue,
    TotalDue / SumTotalDue * 100 AS PercentOfCustSales,
    TotalDue / SumTerritoryTotalDue * 100 AS PercentOfTerrSales
FROM SumSale
INNER JOIN Sales.SalesOrderHeader AS o ON SumSale.CustomerID = o.CustomerID
INNER JOIN TerrSales ON TerrSales.TerritoryID = o.TerritoryID
ORDER BY CustomerID;
```

```
--2
SELECT CustomerID, TotalDue,
    TotalDue / SUM(TotalDue) OVER(PARTITION BY CustomerID) * 100
    AS PercentOfCustSales,
    TotalDue / SUM(TotalDue) OVER(PARTITION BY TerritoryID) * 100
    AS PercentOfTerrSales
FROM Sales.SalesOrderHeader
ORDER BY CustomerID;
```

Summary

If you follow the steps outlined in the preceding sections, you will be able to write aggregate queries. With practice, you will become proficient.

Keep the following rules in mind when writing an aggregate query:

- Any column not contained in an aggregate function in the **SELECT** list or **ORDER BY** clause must be part of the **GROUP BY** clause.
- Once an aggregate function, the **GROUP BY** clause, or the **HAVING** clause appears in a query, it is an aggregate query.
- Use the **WHERE** clause to filter out rows before the grouping and aggregates are applied. The **WHERE** clause does not allow aggregate functions.
- Use the **HAVING** clause to filter out rows using aggregate functions.
- Don't include anything in the **SELECT** list or **ORDER BY** clause that you don't want as a grouping level.
- Use common table expressions or derived tables instead of correlated subqueries to solve tricky aggregate query problems.
- Remember that aggregate functions ignore **NULL** values except for **COUNT(*)**

■ ■ ■

Manipulating Data

The data stored in most databases is not static. The application users constantly add data to tables as customers place orders, the company hires employees, and the payroll department writes checks. Automated processes periodically load new data into reporting databases, such as data warehouses, and into production systems. Users and processes also update existing rows or delete rows from tables.

In Chapters 1 through 5, you learned how to retrieve data from SQL Server. These skills are important for generating reports and displaying data. Those skills will come in handy as you learn to insert new rows, update the values in existing rows, and delete rows from tables. This chapter covers how to manipulate data in many different scenarios, such as by using one table, joins, and subqueries.

Inserting New Rows

Many ways exist to add new rows to tables in SQL Server databases. Be aware that there are other tools such as SQL Server Integration Services (SSIS) that you can use to load data into SQL Server, but because this book is about T-SQL, this section covers the
T-SQL statements to insert data. To learn more about SSIS, see the book *Pro SQL Server 2005 Integration Services* by Jim Wightman (Apress, 2007).

Run the following code to create a table that you will populate with data in this section:

```
USE AdventureWorksLT2008;
GO
IF OBJECT_ID('demoCustomer') IS NOT NULL BEGIN
    DROP TABLE demoCustomer;
END;
CREATE TABLE demoCustomer(CustomerID INT NOT NULL PRIMARY KEY,
    FirstName NVARCHAR(50) NOT NULL, MiddleName NVARCHAR(50) NULL,
    LastName NVARCHAR(50) NOT NULL);
```

■ **Note** You may notice that I have used two different techniques to check for the existence of a table before dropping it. When using SQL Server Management Studio to create the script, the code checks for the table in the `sys.objects` table. When I write the code myself, I check the results of the `OBJECT_ID` function. Either technique works.

Adding One Row with Literal Values

Adding one row with literal values is the simplest way to add data to an existing table. For example, a user may fill out a Windows or web form in an application and click Save. At that point, the application builds and sends a single **INSERT** statement to SQL Server containing the values that the user entered on the form. To insert new rows, you will use the **INSERT** statement. The syntax of the **INSERT** statement, which has two variations, is simple:

```
INSERT [INTO] <table1> [(<col1>,<col2>)] SELECT <value1>,<value2>;
INSERT [INTO] <table1> [(<col1>,<col2>)] VALUES (<value1>,<value2>);
```

The **INTO** keyword is optional, but I like to include it. Type in and execute the code in Listing 6-1 to learn this technique. The last statement displays the inserted data.

Listing 6-1. Adding One Row at a Time with Literal Values

```
USE AdventureWorksLT2008;
GO

--1
INSERT INTO dbo.demoCustomer (CustomerID, FirstName, MiddleName, LastName)
VALUES (1,'Orlando','N.','Gee');

--2
INSERT INTO dbo.demoCustomer (CustomerID, FirstName, MiddleName, LastName)
SELECT 3, 'Donna','F.','Cameras';

--3
INSERT INTO dbo.demoCustomer
VALUES (4,'Janet','M.','Gates');

--4
INSERT INTO dbo.demoCustomer
SELECT 6,'Rosmarie','J.','Carroll';

--5
INSERT INTO dbo.demoCustomer (CustomerID, FirstName, MiddleName, LastName)
VALUES (2,'Keith',NULL,'Harris');

--6
INSERT INTO dbo.demoCustomer (CustomerID, FirstName, LastName)
VALUES (5,'Lucy','Harrington');
```

```
--7
SELECT CustomerID, FirstName, MiddleName, LastName
FROM dbo.demoCustomer;
```

Figure 6-1 shows the results of query 7. The **INSERT INTO** clause specifies the table name and optionally the column names. Statement 1 inserts the row using the **VALUES** clause. Notice that parentheses surround the literal values in the statement. Statement 2 uses a slightly different syntax with the keyword **SELECT**. In this case, you could successfully run the **SELECT** part of the statement because it is a valid statement by itself.

	CustomerID	FirstName	MiddleName	LastName
1	1	Orlando	N.	Gee
2	2	Keith	NULL	Harris
3	3	Donna	F.	Cameras
4	4	Janet	M.	Gates
5	5	Lucy	NULL	Harrington
6	6	Rosmarie	J.	Carroll

Figure 6-1. The results after inserting six rows

■ **Note** This book uses the word *query* for T-SQL commands that return data. It uses the word *statement* for other T-SQL commands.

Both statements 1 and 2 specify the column names in parentheses. The order of the values must match the order of the column names. Statements 3 and 4 look very similar to the first two statements, but these statements do not specify the column names. Although not specifying the column names does work some of the time, the best practice is to specify the columns. Not only does this help clarify the code, it often, but not always, keeps the code from breaking if new nonrequired columns are added to the table later.

Notice that statement 5 inserts **NULL** into the **MiddleName** column. Statement 6 just leaves **MiddleName** out of the statement altogether. Both of these statements work because the **MiddleName** column is optional.

Avoiding Common Insert Errors

The statements in the previous section successfully added six rows to the **dbo.demoCustomer** table because they were carefully written to avoid breaking any of the constraints and column requirements. Listing 6-2 demonstrates several invalid statements. Type in and execute the code to learn about some of the things that can go wrong when inserting data into tables.

Listing 6-2. Attempting to Insert Rows with Invalid INSERT Statements

```
USE AdventureWorksLT2008;
GO


PRINT '1';
--1
INSERT INTO dbo.demoCustomer (CustomerID, FirstName, MiddleName, LastName)
VALUES (1, 'Dominic','P.','Gash');

PRINT '2';
--2
INSERT INTO dbo.demoCustomer (CustomerID, MiddleName, LastName)
VALUES (10,'M.','Garza');

GO
PRINT '3';
GO


--3
INSERT INTO dbo.demoCustomer
VALUES (11,'Katherine','Harding');

GO
PRINT '4';
GO


--4
INSERT INTO dbo.demoCustomer (CustomerID, FirstName, LastName)
VALUES (11, 'Katherine', NULL,'Harding');

GO
PRINT '5';
GO


--5
INSERT INTO dbo.demoCustomer (CustomerID, FirstName, LastName)
VALUES ('A','Katherine','Harding');
```

Figure 6-2 shows the error messages that result from running Listing 6-2. Statement 1 attempts to add another row with the **CustomerID** value 1. Since a row with **CustomerID** 1 already exists in the table, the **INSERT** statement violates the primary key constraint. Because the primary key of a table uniquely identifies a row, you may not insert duplicate values. If the primary key is a composite key, however, you can have duplicate values in any of the columns but not duplicates of the entire key. A primary key may not contain any **NULL** values in the key columns.

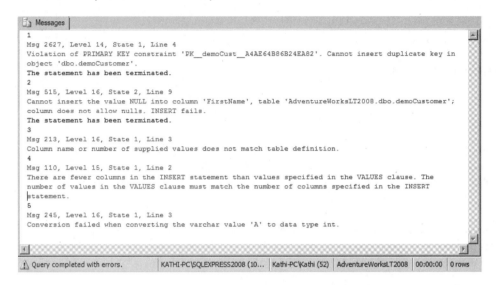

Figure 6-2. *The results of attempting to insert rows with invalid INSERT statements*

Statement 2 violates the **NOT NULL** constraint on the **FirstName** column. Every row must contain a non-**NULL** value in the **FirstName** and **LastName** columns.

The database engine does not discover problems with statements 1 and 2 until the code runs. The problems with statements 3 and 4 are compile errors that cause the entire batch to fail. To show all the error messages for the listing, the word **GO** separates statements 3 and 4 into their own batches. In fact, even the **PRINT** statement will not run if it is contained in the same batch as these statements. The intent of statements 3 and 4 is to insert a row with a **NULL MiddleName**. Because statement 3 does not specify the column names, the database engine expects a value for each of the four columns in the table definition. Since the statement supplies only three values, the statement fails. Statement 4 does supply the column names, but the **VALUES** clause does not supply the same number of values. Once again, the statement fails.

Statement 5 also contains a compile error. It attempts to insert a string value when the column, **CustomerID**, accepts only an integer.

Inserting Multiple Rows with One Statement

Beginning with SQL Server 2008, you can write one statement using a new feature called *row constructors* to insert multiple rows. With previous versions of SQL Server, you could write an **INSERT** statement with a **UNION** query to avoid writing multiple **INSERT** statements. Type in and execute Listing 6-3 to learn how to use both techniques.

Listing 6-3. *Inserting Multiple Rows with One INSERT*

```
USE AdventureWorksLT2008;
GO


--1
INSERT INTO dbo.demoCustomer (CustomerID, FirstName, MiddleName, LastName)
SELECT 7,'Dominic','P.','Gash'
UNION
SELECT 10,'Kathleen','M.','Garza'
UNION
SELECT 11, 'Katherine',NULL,'Harding';

--2
INSERT INTO dbo.demoCustomer (CustomerID, FirstName, MiddleName, LastName)
VALUES (12,'Johnny','A.','Capino'),(16,'Christopher','R.','Beck'),
    (18,'David','J.','Liu');

--3
SELECT CustomerID,FirstName, MiddleName, LastName
FROM dbo.demoCustomer
WHERE CustomerID >= 7;
```

Figure 6-3 displays the rows inserted by Listing 6-3. Statement 1 uses the **UNION** query technique. You can successfully select just the five lines that make up the **UNION** query part of the **INSERT** statement and run it by itself. Statement 2 demonstrates how to use the new row constructor technique. By using row constructors, you can specify multiple lists of values, separated by commas, in one **VALUES** clause.

	CustomerID	FirstName	MiddleName	LastName
1	7	Dominic	P.	Gash
2	10	Kathleen	M.	Garza
3	11	Katherine	NULL	Harding
4	12	Johnny	A.	Capino
5	16	Christopher	R.	Beck
6	18	David	J.	Liu

Figure 6-3. *Inserting multiple rows with one INSERT statement*

Inserting Rows from Another Table

So far, you have learned how to insert literal values into a table. Often you will need to insert data from one table or query into another table. For example, you may need to load production data into a data warehouse. Often application programmers think about data in terms of individual rows and insert data one row at a time when it is possible, and almost always more efficient, to insert more rows at once. They will often loop through one table, saving the values in variables, and then insert the values in the second table.

My favorite analogy involves 2 boxes and 100 car keys. How would you move the keys from one box to the other most efficiently without picking up either of the boxes? Would you pick up one key at a time and move it? No, you would probably grab up all the keys if you could and just move them all at once. If you could not pick up all the keys in one trip, you could at least move them in two or three batches. Listing 6-4 shows how to import rows from one table into another all within one statement.

This example demonstrates "moving all the car keys at once." Type in and execute the code to see how this works.

Listing 6-4. Inserting Rows from Another Table

```
USE AdventureWorksLT2008;
GO


--1
INSERT INTO dbo.demoCustomer (CustomerID, FirstName, MiddleName, LastName)
SELECT CustomerID, FirstName, MiddleName, LastName
FROM SalesLT.Customer
WHERE CustomerID BETWEEN 19 AND 35;


--2
INSERT INTO dbo.demoCustomer (CustomerID, FirstName, MiddleName, LastName)
SELECT s.CustomerID, c.FirstName, c.MiddleName, c.LastName
FROM SalesLT.Customer AS c
INNER JOIN SalesLT.SalesOrderHeader AS s ON c.CustomerID = s.CustomerID;


--3
SELECT CustomerID, FirstName, MiddleName, LastName
FROM dbo.demoCustomer
WHERE CustomerID > 18;
```

Figure 6-4 shows some of the rows added to the **dbo.demoCustomer** table by Listing 6-4. Statement 1 inserts the rows from the **SalesLT.Customer** table where the **CustomerID** is between 19 and 35. Statement 2 inserts the rows from a query that joins the **SalesLT.Customer** and **SalesLT.SalesOrderHeader** tables. The **SELECT** parts of the statements are valid queries that you can run without the **INSERT** clauses. You can use any of the techniques you have learned so far to write **SELECT** statements to insert data into a table as long as the data selected meets the constraints and requirements of the target table.

	CustomerID	First Name	Middle Name	Last Name
1	19	John	A.	Beaver
2	20	Jean	P.	Handley
3	21	Jinghao	NULL	Liu
4	22	Linda	E.	Burnett
5	23	Kerim	NULL	Hanif
6	24	Kevin	NULL	Liu
7	25	Donald	L.	Blanton
8	28	Jackie	E.	Blackwell
9	29	Bryan	NULL	Hamilton
10	30	Todd	R.	Logan
11	34	Barbara	J.	German
12	29485	Catherine	R.	Abel
13	29531	Cory	K.	Booth
14	29546	Christop...	R.	Beck
15	29568	Donald	L.	Blanton
16	29584	Walter	J.	Brian
17	29612	Richard	A.	Byham
18	29638	Rosmarie	J.	Carroll
19	29644	Brigid	F.	Cavendi...

Figure 6-4. The partial results of adding rows from another table

Inserting Missing Rows

You have seen what can happen when you attempt to insert a new row that violates the primary key. You can use the technique in the "Using OUTER JOIN to Find Rows with No Match" section of Chapter 4 to insert rows into one table that don't exist in the source table. Type in and execute the code in Listing 6-5 to learn how this works.

Listing 6-5. Inserting Missing Rows

```
USE AdventureWorksLT2008;
GO


--1
INSERT INTO dbo.demoCustomer (CustomerID, FirstName, MiddleName, LastName)
SELECT c.CustomerID, c.FirstName, c.MiddleName, c.LastName
FROM SalesLT.Customer AS c
LEFT OUTER JOIN dbo.demoCustomer AS d ON c.CustomerID = d.CustomerID
WHERE d.CustomerID IS NULL;


--2
SELECT COUNT(CustomerID) AS CustomerCount
FROM dbo.demoCustomer;
```

Figure 6-5 shows the customer count after adding the missing rows. By using the **LEFT OUTER JOIN** and checking for **NULL** values in the target table, the **SELECT** part of the **INSERT** statement finds the missing rows and inserts those rows into the table. As mentioned in the "Inserting Rows from Another Table" section, any valid **SELECT** statement may be used to insert rows into a table. If you run the same code a second or third time, you will find that the row count doesn't change. Since the code inserted all the missing rows, there are no new rows to insert after the first time.

Figure 6-5. The results of checking the row count after adding the missing rows

Creating and Populating a Table in One Statement

The **SELECT INTO** statement allows you to create a table and populate it with one statement. Developers often use this technique to create temporary tables, or *work tables.*

```
SELECT <col1>,<col2>
INTO <table2>
FROM <table1>;
```

Type in and execute the code in Listing 6-6 to learn how to use this technique. The first part of the code drops the **dbo.demoCustomer** table because the **SELECT INTO** statement will fail if the table already exists.

Listing 6-6. Using SELECT INTO to Create and Populate a Table

```
USE AdventureWorksLT2008;
GO

IF EXISTS (SELECT * FROM sys.objects
            WHERE object_id = OBJECT_ID(N'[dbo].[demoCustomer]')
                AND type in (N'U'))
DROP TABLE dbo.demoCustomer;

GO

--1
SELECT CustomerID, FirstName, MiddleName, LastName,
    FirstName + ISNULL(' ' + MiddleName,'') + ' ' +  LastName AS FullName
INTO dbo.demoCustomer
FROM SalesLT.Customer;
```

```
--2
SELECT CustomerID, FirstName, MiddleName, LastName, FullName
FROM dbo.demoCustomer;
```

Figure 6-6 displays the partial results. Statement 1 lists the columns and an expression along with the word **INTO** and the name of the table to create. The resulting table contains a column, **FullName**, which the statement created with the expression. Even though you could write a query that does not specify an alias for the expression, you must specify the alias for the expression when writing **SELECT INTO** statements. The database engine uses the column and alias names when creating the new table.

	CustomerID	FirstName	MiddleName	LastName	FullName
1	1	Orlando	N.	Gee	Orlando N. Gee
2	2	Keith	NULL	Harris	Keith Harris
3	3	Donna	F.	Carreras	Donna F. Carreras
4	4	Janet	M.	Gates	Janet M. Gates
5	5	Lucy	NULL	Harrington	Lucy Harrington
6	6	Rosmarie	J.	Carroll	Rosmarie J. Carroll
7	7	Dominic	P.	Gash	Dominic P. Gash
8	10	Kathleen	M.	Garza	Kathleen M. Garza
9	11	Katherine	NULL	Harding	Katherine Harding
10	12	Johnny	A.	Caprio	Johnny A. Caprio
11	16	Christopher	R.	Beck	Christopher R. Beck
12	18	David	J.	Liu	David J. Liu

Figure 6-6. The partial results of creating and populating a table with SELECT INTO

Figure 6-7 shows the table definition of the **dbo.demoCustomer** table found by navigating to the table in the Object Explorer window of SQL Server Management Studio. You may have to right-click Tables and select Refresh to see the new table. Except for the missing primary key, the column definitions match the columns from the **SalesLT.Customer** table, which was the source of the data. The data in the **FullName** column can be 152 characters—the three name columns plus the two spaces.

- AdventureWorksLT2008
  - Database Diagrams
  - Tables
    - System Tables
    - dbo.BuildVersion
    - dbo.demoCustomer
      - Columns
        - CustomerID (int, not null)
        - FirstName (Name(nvarchar(50)), not null)
        - MiddleName (Name(nvarchar(50)), null)
        - LastName (Name(nvarchar(50)), not null)
        - FullName (nvarchar(152), not null)

Figure 6-7. The dbo.demoCustomer table definition

Developers often use the **SELECT INTO** statement to create an empty table by adding **1 = 2** to the **WHERE** clause. Because one never equals two, the statement creates the table but does not add any rows. Even if you want to create and populate a work table, the performance of the entire system is often better by creating the empty table first and then populating it with a regular **INSERT** statement when you are working with a large number of rows. This is because the **SELECT INTO** statement locks system tables that can cause problems for other connections. Using a **CREATE TABLE** first and then populating it locks the system tables only momentarily. Using the **SELECT INTO** syntax locks the tables until the entire statement completes.

Inserting Rows into Tables with Default Column Values

Column definitions often specify a default value, called a *default constraint*, if the **INSERT** statement does not supply a value for the column. This is different from inserting **NULL**. When inserting **NULL**, you specify **NULL** in the **INSERT** statement, or the **NULL** value is a result of the **SELECT** statement used to insert the data. You might also omit the column from the **INSERT** statement to insert **NULL**. If the column definition specifies a default constraint, you can just leave that column out of the **INSERT** statement to automatically insert the default value. Run the code in Listing 6-7 to learn how to insert data into tables when one or more of the columns have a default value. The first part of the code creates the table and adds the default constraints.

Listing 6-7. Inserting Data with a Column Default Constraint

```
USE AdventureWorksLT2008;
GO
IF  EXISTS (SELECT * FROM sys.objects
            WHERE object_id = OBJECT_ID(N'[dbo].[demoDefault]')
                AND type in (N'U'))
DROP TABLE [dbo].[demoDefault]
GO

CREATE TABLE [dbo].[demoDefault](
    [KeyColumn] [int] NOT NULL PRIMARY KEY,
        [HasADefault1] [DATETIME2](1) NOT NULL,
        [HasADefault2] [NVARCHAR](50) NULL,
)
GO
ALTER TABLE [dbo].[demoDefault] ADD  CONSTRAINT [DF_demoDefault_HasADefault]
    DEFAULT (GETDATE()) FOR [HasADefault1]
GO
ALTER TABLE [dbo].[demoDefault] ADD  CONSTRAINT [DF_demoDefault_HasADefault2]
    DEFAULT ('the default') FOR [HasADefault2]
GO

--1
INSERT INTO dbo.demoDefault(HasADefault1,HasADefault2,KeyColumn)
VALUES ('2009-04-24','Test 1',1),('2009-10-1',NULL,2);
```

```
--2
INSERT INTO dbo.demoDefault (HasADefault1,HasADefault2,KeyColumn)
VALUES (DEFAULT,DEFAULT,3),(DEFAULT,DEFAULT,4);

--3
INSERT INTO dbo.demoDefault (KeyColumn)
VALUES (5),(6);

--4
SELECT HasADefault1,HasADefault2,KeyColumn
FROM dbo.demoDefault;
```

Figure 6-8 shows the results. Statement 1 inserts literal values into the **HasADefault1** and **HasADefault2** columns. Even though the two columns have default constraints, you can still override them and insert your own values. Notice that the row inserted with **KeyColumn** value 2 contains a **NULL** value in the **HasADefault2** column. The statement specified and inserted **NULL**, not the default value.

	HasADefault1	HasADefault2	KeyColumn
1	2009-04-24 00:00:00.0	Test 1	1
2	2009-10-01 00:00:00.0	NULL	2
3	2009-04-25 21:14:00.8	the default	3
4	2009-04-25 21:14:00.8	the default	4
5	2009-04-25 21:14:00.8	the default	5
6	2009-04-25 21:14:00.8	the default	6

Figure 6-8. *The results of inserting rows into a table with column default constraints*

Statements 2 and 3 take advantage of the default constraints. Statement 2 specifies the keyword **DEFAULT** instead of a value. Statement 3 just omits the two columns. Whenever using the keyword **DEFAULT** or omitting the columns, the default definition determines the values to be inserted. The **GETDATE** function provides default values for the **HasDefault1** column. The literal value "the default" is filled in for **HasADefault2**.

Inserting Rows into Tables with Automatically Populating Columns

In addition to default constraints, three types of columns exist that are always autopopulated. In other words, you should not specify values for these columns. The columns types are as follows:

- **ROWVERSION**: Formerly called **TIMESTAMP**, this contains a binary number that is unique within a database. Developers generally use **ROWVERSION** to determine whether changes have been made to a row.
- **IDENTITY**: This contains an autoincrementing numeric value. Developers often use **INDENTIY** columns when an ID number is needed for a table.

- *Computed columns*: These have a definition that is usually based on the values of other columns in the same row. The values in a computed column can be stored in the table by specifying the keyword PERSISTED in the column definition. If the table definition does not contain PERSISTED, it will be calculated each time it is accessed.

Be sure to always specify the column names, avoiding the automatically populated columns when you write an INSERT statement to avoid causing an error.

■ **Note** There is an exception to the rule about inserting data into IDENTITY columns. You can change a session-specific setting called IDENTITY_INSERT that will allow you to insert a value into an IDENTITY column. Developers and database administrators often do this when loading data and the IDENTITY values must be preserved. After loading the data, the IDENTITY column will work as before after you turn off IDENTITY_INSERT in that session or insert into the table from a different session.

Type in and execute the code in Listing 6-8. The first part of the code creates a table with the special column types.

Listing 6-8. Inserting Rows into Tables with Autopopulated Columns

```
USE [AdventureWorksLT2008]
GO


IF  EXISTS (SELECT * FROM sys.objects
            WHERE object_id = OBJECT_ID(N'[dbo].[demoAutoPopulate]')
                AND type in (N'U'))
DROP TABLE [dbo].[demoAutoPopulate]

CREATE TABLE [dbo].[demoAutoPopulate](
    [RegularColumn] [NVARCHAR](50) NOT NULL PRIMARY KEY,
    [IdentityColumn] [INT] IDENTITY(1,1) NOT NULL,
    [RowversionColumn] [ROWVERSION] NOT NULL,
    [ComputedColumn] AS ([RegularColumn]+CONVERT([NVARCHAR],
        [IdentityColumn],(0))) PERSISTED)
GO


--1
INSERT INTO dbo.demoAutoPopulate (RegularColumn)
VALUES ('a'),('b'),('c');
```

```
--2
SELECT RegularColumn, IdentityColumn, RowversionColumn,ComputedColumn
FROM demoAutoPopulate;
```

Figure 6-9 shows the results. Statement 1 specified values for **RegularColumn** only. The database engine automatically determined the values for the other columns. Notice that the **IdentityColumn** contains an incrementing value. The **ComputedColumn** contains the result of the expression **RegularColumn + CAST(IdentityColumn AS NVARCHAR)**.

	RegularColumn	IdentityColumn	RowversionColumn	ComputedColumn
1	a	1	0x00000000000007D8	a1
2	b	2	0x00000000000007D9	b2
3	c	3	0x00000000000007DA	c3

Figure 6-9. The results of inserting rows into a table with autopopulating columns

You have learned how to insert new rows into tables by using literal values or data from a query. Before moving on to the next section, where you will learn how to delete data, practice inserting new rows into a table by completing Exercise 6-1.

Exercise 6-1

Use the AdventureWorksLT2008 database to complete this exercise. You can find the solutions in the appendix.

Run the following code to create required tables. You can also download the code from this book's page at http://www.apress.com to save typing time.

```
USE AdventureWorksLT2008;
GO
IF  EXISTS (SELECT * FROM sys.objects
            WHERE object_id = OBJECT_ID(N'[dbo].[demoProduct]')
                AND type in (N'U'))
DROP TABLE [dbo].[demoProduct]
GO

CREATE TABLE [dbo].[demoProduct](
    [ProductID] [INT] NOT NULL PRIMARY KEY,
    [Name] [dbo].[Name] NOT NULL,
    [Color] [NVARCHAR](15) NULL,
    [StandardCost] [MONEY] NOT NULL,
    [ListPrice] [MONEY] NOT NULL,
```

```sql
    [Size] [NVARCHAR](5) NULL,
    [Weight] [DECIMAL](8, 2) NULL,
);
IF  EXISTS (SELECT * FROM sys.objects
            WHERE object_id = OBJECT_ID(N'[dbo].[demoSalesOrderHeader]')
                AND type in (N'U'))
DROP TABLE [dbo].[demoSalesOrderHeader]
GO

CREATE TABLE [dbo].[demoSalesOrderHeader](
    [SalesOrderID] [INT] NOT NULL PRIMARY KEY,
    [SalesID] [INT] NOT NULL IDENTITY,
    [OrderDate] [DATETIME] NOT NULL,
    [CustomerID] [INT] NOT NULL,
    [SubTotal] [MONEY] NOT NULL,
    [TaxAmt] [MONEY] NOT NULL,
    [Freight] [MONEY] NOT NULL,
    [DateEntered] [DATETIME],
    [TotalDue]  AS (ISNULL((([SubTotal]+[TaxAmt])+[Freight],(0))),
    [RV] ROWVERSION NOT NULL);
GO

ALTER TABLE [dbo].[demoSalesOrderHeader] ADD  CONSTRAINT
    [DF_demoSalesOrderHeader_DateEntered]
DEFAULT (getdate()) FOR [DateEntered];

GO
IF  EXISTS (SELECT * FROM sys.objects
    WHERE object_id = OBJECT_ID(N'[dbo].[demoAddress]')
    AND type in (N'U'))
DROP TABLE [dbo].[demoAddress]
GO

CREATE TABLE [dbo].[demoAddress](
    [AddressID] [INT] NOT NULL IDENTITY PRIMARY KEY,
    [AddressLine1] [NVARCHAR](60) NOT NULL,
    [AddressLine2] [NVARCHAR](60) NULL,
    [City] [NVARCHAR](30) NOT NULL,
    [StateProvince] [dbo].[Name] NOT NULL,
    [CountryRegion] [dbo].[Name] NOT NULL,
    [PostalCode] [NVARCHAR](15) NOT NULL
);
```

1. Write a SELECT statement to retrieve data from the SalesLT.Product table. Use these values to insert five rows into the dbo.demoProduct table using literal values. Write five individual INSERT statements.

2. Insert five more rows into the dbo.demoProduct table. This time write one INSERT statement.

3. Write an INSERT statement that inserts all the rows into the dbo.demoSalesOrderHeader table from the SalesLT.SalesOrderHeader table. Hint: Pay close attention to the properties of the columns in the dbo.demoSalesOrderHeader table.

4. Write a SELECT INTO statement that creates a table, dbo.tempCustomerSales, showing every CustomerID from the SalesLT.Customer along with a count of the orders placed and the total amount due for each customer.

5. Write an INSERT statement that inserts all the products into the dbo.demoProduct table from the SalesLT.Product table that have not already been inserted. Do not specify literal ProductID values in the statement.

6. Write an INSERT statement that inserts all the addresses into the dbo.demoAddress table from the SalesLT.Address table. Before running the INSERT statement, type in and run the following command so that you can insert values into the AddressID column:

```
SET IDENTITY_INSERT dbo.demoAddress ON;
```

Deleting Rows

You now know how to add new rows to tables. This section covers deleting existing rows, which is an important but dangerous task. Many developers and database administrators have accidentally removed the data from an entire table when intending to remove just one row. Care must be taken whenever deleting rows, especially when writing ad hoc queries.

Using DELETE

The DELETE statement is very simple. At a minimum, you need the word DELETE and the table name. This will remove all rows from the table. Most of the time, you will intend to just remove a portion of the rows. Here is the syntax:

```
DELETE [FROM] <table1>
[WHERE <condition>]
```

If you omit the WHERE clause, the statement removes every row from the table. The table still exists, just without any rows. When writing ad hoc DELETE statements, always test your WHERE clause with a SELECT statement first to make sure you know exactly which rows you are deleting. Type in and execute the code in Listing 6-9. The listing creates several copies of the main tables from the AdventureWorksLT2008 database. To avoid typing the table creation portion, you can download the code from the book's page at http://www.apress.com.

Listing 6-9. Creating Demo Tables

```
USE AdventureWorksLT2008;
GO

IF  EXISTS (SELECT * FROM sys.objects
            WHERE object_id = OBJECT_ID(N'[dbo].[demoProduct]')
              AND type in (N'U'))
DROP TABLE [dbo].[demoProduct];
GO

SELECT * INTO dbo.demoProduct FROM SalesLT.Product;

IF  EXISTS (SELECT * FROM sys.objects
            WHERE object_id = OBJECT_ID(N'[dbo].[demoCustomer]')
              AND type in (N'U'))
DROP TABLE [dbo].[demoCustomer];
GO

SELECT * INTO dbo.demoCustomer FROM SalesLT.Customer;
IF  EXISTS (SELECT * FROM sys.objects
            WHERE object_id = OBJECT_ID(N'[dbo].[demoAddress]')
              AND type in (N'U'))
DROP TABLE [dbo].[demoAddress];
GO

SELECT * INTO dbo.demoAddress FROM SalesLT.Address;
IF  EXISTS (SELECT * FROM sys.objects
            WHERE object_id = OBJECT_ID(N'[dbo].[demoSalesOrderHeader]')
              AND type in (N'U'))
DROP TABLE [dbo].[demoSalesOrderHeader];
GO

SELECT * INTO dbo.demoSalesOrderHeader FROM SalesLT.SalesOrderHeader;

IF  EXISTS (SELECT * FROM sys.objects
            WHERE object_id = OBJECT_ID(N'[dbo].[demoSalesOrderDetail]')
              AND type in (N'U'))
DROP TABLE [dbo].[demoSalesOrderDetail];
GO

SELECT * INTO dbo.demoSalesOrderDetail FROM SalesLT.SalesOrderDetail;
```

You should now have several tables that you can use to practice deleting data. Type in and execute the code in Listing 6-10 to learn how to delete rows from tables.

Listing 6-10. Deleting Rows from Tables

```
USE AdventureWorksLT2008;
GO
--1
SELECT CustomerID
FROM dbo.demoCustomer;

--2
DELETE dbo.demoCustomer;

--3
SELECT CustomerID
FROM dbo.demoCustomer;

--4
SELECT ProductID
FROM dbo.demoProduct
WHERE ProductID > 900;

--5
DELETE dbo.demoProduct
WHERE ProductID > 900;

--6
SELECT ProductID
FROM dbo.demoProduct
WHERE ProductID > 900;
```

Figure 6-10 shows the rows before and after running the DELETE statements affecting the dbo.demoCustomer and dbo.demoProduct tables. Running a SELECT statement before deleting data is a good idea and enables you to test your WHERE clause. Make sure you know which rows will be deleted before you delete them. Statement 2 removes every row from dbo.demoCustomer. Statement 5 removes the rows from dbo.demoProduct where the ProductID was greater than 900. The word FROM is optional.

Figure 6-10. *The partial results before and after rows deleted*

Deleting from a Table Using a Join or a Subquery

Listing 6-10 demonstrated how to remove rows from a table when the statement contains just one table. You can also remove rows from a table that is involved in a join to restrict which rows the statement deletes. You may delete rows from only one of the tables. Often developers will use a subquery instead of a join to accomplish the same thing. Here is the syntax:

```
DELETE <alias>
FROM <table1> AS <alias>
INNER JOIN <table2> ON <alias>.<col1> = <table2>.<col2>
[WHERE <condition>]

DELETE [FROM] <table1>
WHERE <col1> IN (SELECT <col2> FROM <table2>)
```

The syntax shows `INNER JOIN`, but you could use an `OUTER JOIN` if that makes sense for the particular deletion. Type in and execute the code in Listing 6-11 to learn how to use both of these techniques. If you did not run the code in Listing 6-9 that creates the tables used in these examples and the code in Listing 6-10 that deletes some of the data, do that first.

Listing 6-11. Deleting When Joining or Using a Subquery

```
USE AdventureWorksLT2008;
GO


--1
SELECT d.SalesOrderID, SalesOrderNumber
FROM dbo.demoSalesOrderDetail AS d
```

```
INNER JOIN dbo.demoSalesOrderHeader AS h ON d.SalesOrderID = h.SalesOrderID
WHERE h.SalesOrderNumber = 'SO71797'

--2
DELETE d
FROM dbo.demoSalesOrderDetail AS d
INNER JOIN dbo.demoSalesOrderHeader AS h ON d.SalesOrderID = h.SalesOrderID
WHERE h.SalesOrderNumber = 'SO71797'

--3
SELECT d.SalesOrderID, SalesOrderNumber
FROM dbo.demoSalesOrderDetail AS d
INNER JOIN dbo.demoSalesOrderHeader AS h ON d.SalesOrderID = h.SalesOrderID
WHERE h.SalesOrderNumber = 'SO71797'

--4
SELECT SalesOrderID, ProductID
FROM dbo.demoSalesOrderDetail
WHERE ProductID NOT IN
    (SELECT ProductID FROM dbo.demoProduct WHERE ProductID IS NOT NULL);

--5
DELETE FROM dbo.demoSalesOrderDetail
WHERE ProductID NOT IN
    (SELECT ProductID FROM dbo.demoProduct WHERE ProductID IS NOT NULL);

--6
SELECT SalesOrderID, ProductID
FROM dbo.demoSalesOrderDetail
WHERE ProductID NOT IN
    (SELECT ProductID FROM dbo.demoProduct WHERE ProductID IS NOT NULL);
```

Figure 6-11 shows the results before and after deleting. Again, write SELECT statements first to test your WHERE clause and to make sure you will delete the correct rows. Statement 2 joins the dbo.demoSalesOrderDetail table to the dbo.demoSalesOrderHeader table. The statement deletes the rows from the dbo.demoSalesOrderDetail table that have a SalesOrderNumber of SO71797 in the dbo.demoSalesOrderHeader table. The value in one table determines which rows in another table to be deleted. Notice that statements 1 and 2 are identical except for the first line in each. Statement 1 is a query to determine which rows that statement 2 will delete. The syntax and this example used an INNER JOIN, but you can also use an OUTER JOIN.

Results

	SalesOrderID	SalesOrderNumber
1	71797	SO71797
2	71797	SO71797
3	71797	SO71797
4	71797	SO71797

	SalesOrderID	SalesOrderNumber

	SalesOrderID	ProductID
1	71776	907
2	71780	905
3	71780	983
4	71780	988

	SalesOrderID	ProductID

Figure 6-11. *The partial results before and after deleting rows with a join and a subquery*

Statement 5 uses a subquery in the `WHERE` clause to determine which rows to delete. Again, the code tests the `WHERE` clause first with a `SELECT` statement to make sure the correct rows will be deleted.

Another way to delete the rows using a join specifies the table name after the `DELETE` keyword instead of specifying the alias. Using the alias ensures that the `DELETE` part of the statement is tied to the `SELECT` part of the statement. I have seen developers write `DELETE` statements that inadvertently deleted all rows from a production table because the `DELETE` part of the statement was not really connected to the rest of the statement. I recommend that you always use the technique shown in Listing 6-11 to avoid deleting all the rows in a table by mistake. Here is an example that is really a `DELETE` statement and a `SELECT` statement when the intention is just a `DELETE` statement:

```
DELETE dbo.demoSalesOrderDetail
SELECT d.SalesOrderID
FROM dbo.demoSalesOrderDetail AS d
INNER JOIN dbo.demoSalesOrderHeader AS h ON d.SalesOrderID = h.SalesOrderID
WHERE h.SalesOrderNumber = 'SO71797';
```

Truncating

A way to quickly delete all the rows from a table is to use the `TRUNCATE TABLE` statement. This is a very fast way to empty a large table. Although deleting rows requires that the user account have `DELETE` permission on the table, truncating a table requires the user be in the dbo or db_ddladmin database roles or the sysadmin server role. Generally, users running an application will not be members of these powerful roles. Here is the syntax:

```
TRUNCATE TABLE <table1>
```

Listing 6-12 demonstrates how to use `TRUNCATE`. If you did not run Listing 6-9 that created the tables, do that first before typing and running the code in Listing 6-12.

Listing 6-12. Truncating Tables

```
USE AdventureWorksLT2008;
GO


--1
SELECT SalesOrderID, OrderDate
FROM dbo.demoSalesOrderHeader;


--2
TRUNCATE TABLE dbo.demoSalesOrderHeader;


--3
SELECT SalesOrderID, OrderDate
FROM dbo.demoSalesOrderHeader;
```

Figure 6-12 shows the results before and after truncating the table. One of the reasons that TRUNCATE is so much more powerful than DELETE is that it actually drops and re-creates the table behind the scenes. That is much quicker than deleting all the rows, but no WHERE clause is allowed with TRUNCATE. The TRUNCATE statement can be used only when you intend to empty the table.

	SalesOrderID	OrderDate
1	71774	2004-06-01 00:00:00.000
2	71776	2004-06-01 00:00:00.000
3	71780	2004-06-01 00:00:00.000
4	71782	2004-06-01 00:00:00.000
5	71783	2004-06-01 00:00:00.000
6	71784	2004-06-01 00:00:00.000
7	71796	2004-06-01 00:00:00.000
8	71797	2004-06-01 00:00:00.000
9	71815	2004-06-01 00:00:00.000
	SalesOrderID	OrderDate

Figure 6-12. The results before and after truncating

Deleting data is a very risky operation. That is why database administrators consider a good backup strategy an important part of their jobs. Practice what you have learned about deleting data by completing Exercise 6-2.

Exercise 6-2

Use the AdventureWorksLT2008 database to complete this exercise. Before starting the exercise, run Listing 6-9 to re-create the demo tables. You can find the solutions in the appendix.

1. Write a query that deletes the rows from the `dbo.demoCustomer` table where the `LastName` values begin with the letter *S*.
2. Delete the rows from the `dbo.demoCustomer` table if the customer has not placed an order or if the sum of the `TotalDue` from the `dbo.demoSalesOrderHeader` table for the customer is less than $1,000.
3. Delete the rows from the `dbo.demoProduct` table that have never been ordered.

Updating Existing Rows

Updating data is a very important part to T-SQL but requires extreme caution. Only deleting rows, which was discussed in the previous section, requires more care. Well, maybe that is not true; you could actually drop tables or entire databases accidentally. Most of the time within applications, the user will be working with one row at a time. For example, they may be viewing a screen that displays and allows editing of one employee, one department, or one order. Often automated processes update data in entire tables or many rows at one time. In this section, you will learn how to use the UPDATE statement to update existing rows in several scenarios, including single tables, joins, and aggregates. Run the code in Listing 6-9 to repopulate some tables you will use for the examples in this section.

Using the UPDATE Statement

To update existing rows in a table, use the UPDATE statement. Most of the time you will add a WHERE clause to make sure that you update only the appropriate rows. Often database administrators have to restore backups of databases to get back data that has been accidentally updated because the WHERE clause was incorrect or missing. Here is the syntax of the UPDATE statement:

```
UPDATE <table1>
SET <col1> = <new value1>,<col2> = <new value2>
[WHERE <condition>]
```

You can use expressions, literal values, or other columns to update existing data. Developers often think that updating data must be done one row at a time. I have talked to many developers who would argue with me that they must update one row at a time because some of the rows must be updated with one value and some with another. In those cases, maybe they can write an UPDATE statement for each business rule or use the CASE function but not perform one update for each row. Type in and execute the code in Listing 6-13 to learn how to update data.

Listing 6-13. Updating Data in a Table

```
USE AdventureWorksLT2008;
GO

--1
SELECT CustomerID, NameStyle, Title
FROM dbo.demoCustomer
ORDER BY CustomerID;

--2
UPDATE dbo.demoCustomer
SET NameStyle = 1;

--3
SELECT CustomerID, NameStyle, Title
FROM dbo.demoCustomer
ORDER BY CustomerID;

--4
UPDATE dbo.demoCustomer
SET NameStyle = 0
WHERE Title = 'Ms.';

--5
SELECT CustomerID, NameStyle, Title
FROM dbo.demoCustomer
ORDER BY CustomerID;
```

Figure 6-13 shows the results before and after the updates. Query 1 just displays a few rows from the table. Statement 2 updates all the rows in the table changing the **NameStyle**, a bit column, from 0 to 1. Query 3 shows the result of that change. Statement 4 changes the **NameStyle** value to 0 for the rows where the **Title** is *Ms.* Query 5 displays the final changes.

Results

	CustomerID	NameStyle	Title
1	1	0	Mr.
2	2	0	Mr.
3	3	0	Ms.
4	4	0	Ms.

	CustomerID	NameStyle	Title
1	1	1	Mr.
2	2	1	Mr.
3	3	1	Ms.
4	4	1	Ms.

	CustomerID	NameStyle	Title
1	1	1	Mr.
2	2	1	Mr.
3	3	0	Ms.
4	4	0	Ms.

Figure 6-13. *The partial results before and after updating*

Updating Data with Expressions and Columns

The statements in the previous section updated the **dbo.demoCustomer** table with literal values. You can also perform updates using expressions or other columns. Developers and database administrators often must perform large updates to data, sometimes on a periodic basis or to fulfill one-time requests. Here is the syntax for this technique:

```
UPDATE <table1>
SET <col1> = <expression>
[WHERE <condition>]
```

Again, you can use expressions, hard-coded values, or other columns in your **UPDATE** statement. When multiple rows must be updated, such as batch processing that happens after business hours, perform updates in sets, not one row at a time. Type in and execute the code in Listing 6-14 to learn how to perform these updates.

Listing 6-14. Update with Expressions, Columns, or Data from Another Table

```
USE AdventureWorksLT2008;
GO

--1
SELECT FirstName,LastName, CompanyName,
   LEFT(FirstName,3) + '.' + LEFT(LastName,3) AS NewCompany
FROM dbo.demoCustomer;
```

```
--2
UPDATE dbo.demoCustomer
SET CompanyName = LEFT(FirstName,3) + '.' + LEFT(LastName,3);

--3
SELECT FirstName,LastName, CompanyName,
    LEFT(FirstName,3) + '.' + LEFT(LastName,3) AS NewCompany
FROM dbo.demoCustomer;
```

Figure 6-14 shows the results before and after the update. Query 1 displays the data before the update. The **NewCompany** column contains the expression that will be used in the **UPDATE** statement. You will find it is useful to display the expression, especially if it is complicated, to make sure that your update will do exactly what you expect. Statement 2 updates the data, changing **CompanyName** in the **dbo.demoCustomer** table to the new value derived from the **FirstName** and **LastName** columns. Finally, Query 3 displays the updated data. At this point, the **CompanyName** should be equivalent to the **NewCompany** expression.

	First Name	Last Name	CompanyName	NewCompany
1	Orlando	Gee	A Bike Store	Orl.Gee
2	Keith	Harris	Progressive Sports	Kei.Har
3	Donna	Carreras	Advanced Bike Components	Don.Car
4	Janet	Gates	Modular Cycle Systems	Jan.Gat

	First Name	Last Name	CompanyName	NewCompany
1	Orlando	Gee	Orl.Gee	Orl.Gee
2	Keith	Harris	Kei.Har	Kei.Har
3	Donna	Carreras	Don.Car	Don.Car
4	Janet	Gates	Jan.Gat	Jan.Gat

Figure 6-14. *The results before and after updating with an expression*

Updating with a JOIN

So far, you have seen how to write **UPDATE** statements with a single table. When joining, you can update only a single table, but by joining with another table, you can limit the rows to be updated or use the second table to provide the value. Here is the syntax:

```
UPDATE <alias>
SET <col1> = <expression>
FROM <table1> AS <alias>
INNER JOIN <table2> on <alias>.<col2>  = <table2>.<col3>
```

The syntax shows an **INNER JOIN**, but you could perform an **OUTER JOIN** if that makes sense for the particular update. Type in and execute the code in Listing 6-15 to learn how to perform an update using this technique.

Listing 6-15. Updating with a Join

```
USE AdventureWorksLT2008;
GO
--1
SELECT AddressLine1, AddressLine2
FROM dbo.demoAddress;

--2
UPDATE a
SET AddressLine1 = FirstName + ' ' + LastName,
    AddressLine2 = AddressLine1 + ISNULL(' ' + AddressLine2,'')
FROM dbo.demoAddress AS a
INNER JOIN SalesLT.CustomerAddress AS ca ON a.AddressID = ca.AddressID
INNER JOIN dbo.demoCustomer AS c ON ca.CustomerID = c.CustomerID;

--3
SELECT AddressLine1, AddressLine2
FROM dbo.demoAddress;
```

Figure 6-15 shows the results before and after the update. In this case, Statement 2 uses columns from the second table, the **dbo.demoCustomer** table, to build an expression to update **AddressLine1**. The statement uses another expression to move the original **AddressLine1** and **AddressLine2**, if any, to **AddressLine2**. The **dbo.demoAddress** table does not join directly to the **dbo.demoCustomer** table but must join through an intermediary table, **SalesLT.CustomerAddress**.

	AddressLine1	AddressLine2
1	8713 Yosemite Ct.	NULL
2	1318 Lasalle Street	NULL
3	9178 Jumping St.	NULL
4	9228 Via Del Sol	NULL
5	26910 Indela Road	NULL
6	2681 Eagle Peak	NULL
7	7943 Walnut Ave	NULL
8	6388 Lake City Way	NULL

	AddressLine1	AddressLine2
1	Virginia Miller	8713 Yosemite Ct.
2	John Beaver	1318 Lasalle Street
3	Paulo Lisboa	9178 Jumping St.
4	Kay Krane	9228 Via Del Sol
5	Gregory Alderson	26910 Indela Road
6	Robert Bernacchi	2681 Eagle Peak
7	Keith Harris	7943 Walnut Ave
8	Kathleen Garza	6388 Lake City ...

Figure 6-15. The results before and after updating with a join

Updating with Aggregate Functions

The examples in the previous two sections demonstrated how you can update data using expressions involving literal values, columns, and functions. None of the examples included aggregate functions, however. You may not use expressions containing aggregate functions to update data directly. Type this code to see what happens when you try to use an aggregate function to perform an update:

```
USE AdventureWorksLT2008;
GO


UPDATE o
SET SubTotal = SUM(LineTotal)
FROM SalesLT.SalesOrderHeader AS o INNER JOIN SalesLT.SalesOrderDetail AS d
ON o.SalesOrderID = o.SalesOrderID;
```

You can isolate an aggregate query into a common table expression and then use the aggregated values to make the updates. Listing 6-16 shows how to use this technique. The first part of the code creates and partially populates a summary table that will be used in the example.

Listing 6-16. Updates with Aggregate Expressions

```
USE AdventureWorksLT2008;
GO


IF  EXISTS (SELECT * FROM sys.objects
            WHERE object_id = OBJECT_ID(N'[dbo].[demoCustomerSummary]')
                AND type in (N'U'))
DROP TABLE [dbo].[demoCustomerSummary];
GO


CREATE TABLE dbo.demoCustomerSummary (CustomerID INT NOT NULL PRIMARY KEY,
    SaleCount INTEGER NULL,
    TotalAmount MONEY NULL);


GO


INSERT INTO dbo.demoCustomerSummary (CustomerID, SaleCount,TotalAmount)
SELECT CustomerID, 0, 0
FROM dbo.demoCustomer;


GO
```

```
--1
SELECT CustomerID, SaleCount, TotalAmount
FROM dbo.demoCustomerSummary
WHERE CustomerID in (29485,29531,29568,92584,29612);


--2
WITH Totals AS (
    SELECT COUNT(*) AS SaleCount,SUM(TotalDue) AS TotalAmount,
        CustomerID
    FROM dbo.demoSalesOrderHeader
    GROUP BY CustomerID)
UPDATE c SET TotalAmount = Totals.TotalAmount,
    SaleCount = Totals.SaleCount
FROM dbo.demoCustomerSummary AS c
INNER JOIN Totals ON c.CustomerID = Totals.CustomerID;


--3
SELECT CustomerID, SaleCount, TotalAmount
FROM dbo.demoCustomerSummary
WHERE CustomerID in (29485,29531,29568,92584,29612);
```

Figure 6-16 shows the results before and after the update. This code first creates a table called `dbo.demoCustomerSummary`. Then the code populates the new table with all the `CustomerID` values from the `dbo.demoCustomer` table and zeros in the summary columns. Finally, statement 2 uses a common table expression containing an aggregate query summarizing the sales for each customer. The statement uses the values calculated in the common table expression to update the table. See the "Exploring Derived Tables and Common Table Expressions" section in Chapter 4 to review common table expression. See Chapter 5 to review aggregate queries.

	CustomerID	SaleCount	TotalAmount
1	29485	0	0.00
2	29531	0	0.00
3	29568	0	0.00
4	29612	0	0.00

	CustomerID	SaleCount	TotalAmount
1	29485	1	43962.7901
2	29531	1	7330.8972
3	29568	1	2669.3183
4	29612	1	608.1766

Figure 6-16. The results before and after updating with a common table expression

You now know how to update data in existing tables with literal values, expressions, and other columns. Now practice what you have learned by completing Exercise 6-3.

Exercise 6-3

Use the AdventureWorksLT2008 database to complete this exercise. Run the code in Listing 6-9 to re-create tables used in this exercise. You can find the solutions in the appendix.

1. Write an UPDATE statement that changes all NULL values of the AddressLine2 column in the dbo.demoAddress table to *N/A*.
2. Write an UPDATE statement that increases the ListPrice of every product in the dbo.demoProduct table by 10 percent.
3. Write an UPDATE statement that corrects the UnitPrice and LineTotal of each row of the dbo.demoSalesOrderDetail table by joining the table on the dbo.demoProduct table.
4. Write an UPDATE statement that updates the SubTotal column of each row of the dbo.demoSalesOrderHeader table with the sum of the LineTotal column of the dbo.demoSalesOrderDemo table.

Using Transactions

A *transaction* is a unit of work in SQL Server. Most of the time, a transaction is one statement that inserts, updates, or deletes data. It is possible, however, to define an explicit transaction that includes more than one statement. You can also include SELECT statements in a transaction. Every statement within a transaction must succeed, or the entire transaction fails.

The classic example involves a bank ATM where a customer can transfer money from a savings account to a checking account. Imagine the problems created if an error occurred after the system subtracted the money from the savings account but before the money showed up in the checking account! By using an explicit transaction, any error between the two updates will roll back both of them. If an error occurred, the money would just go back to the savings account like nothing was ever done. This section covers writing multiple statements within explicit transactions, how to commit or roll back transactions, and what happens when transactions last longer than needed.

Writing an Explicit Transaction

The important thing to remember when working with SQL Server is to keep transactions as short as they can be and still do the work. Once a transaction starts, the database engine puts locks on tables involved within the transaction so that the tables usually may not be accessed by another query. For example, don't write an application that begins a transaction and then waits for user input before completing the transaction. The tables could be locked while the user leaves the computer for a lunch break! Here is the syntax for a simple transaction:

```
BEGIN TRAN|TRANSACTION
    <statement 1>
    <statement 2>
COMMIT [TRAN|TRANSACTION]
```

Listing 6-17 demonstrates what happens when a transaction fails. Type in and execute the code.

Listing 6-17. Explicit Transactions

```
IF  EXISTS (SELECT * FROM sys.objects
            WHERE object_id = OBJECT_ID(N'[dbo].[demoTransaction]')
               AND type in (N'U'))
DROP TABLE [dbo].[demoTransaction];
GO

CREATE TABLE dbo.demoTRANSACTION (col1 INT NOT NULL);
GO

--1
BEGIN TRAN
    INSERT INTO dbo.demoTRANSACTION (col1) VALUES (1);
    INSERT INTO dbo.demoTRANSACTION (col1) VALUES (2);
COMMIT TRAN

--2
BEGIN TRAN
    INSERT INTO dbo.demoTRANSACTION (col1) VALUES (3);
    INSERT INTO dbo.demoTRANSACTION (col1) VALUES ('a');
COMMIT TRAN

GO
--3
SELECT col1
FROM dbo.demoTRANSACTION;
```

Figure 6-17 shows the results. After running the batch, the query window will display the Messages tab first with an error message. You will have to click the Results tab to see the inserted rows. Transaction block 1 successfully inserts two rows with integer values into the table. Transaction block 2 inserts the value 3 and the value **a**. Because you cannot insert the string value **a** into a column of type INT, the statement fails. Because the two statements are within the same transaction, the entire transaction rolls back. Query 3 returns the inserted rows, which are only the rows inserted in the first transaction.

Figure 6-17. The results of using explicit transactions to insert data

Rolling Back a Transaction

You can purposely roll a transaction back before it is committed by issuing a **ROLLBACK** command even without an error condition. For example, what if the bank ATM added the money to the checking account before removing it from the savings account and didn't check the savings account balance first? The transaction could roll back the transaction once the balance was checked but before the transaction was committed. Here is the syntax for rolling back a transaction:

```
BEGIN TRAN|TRANSACTION
    <statement 1>
    <statement 2>
ROLLBACK [TRAN|TRANSACTION]
```

In Chapter 7 you will learn how to trap errors and use conditional logic that will allow your code to **COMMIT** or **ROLLBACK** based on certain conditions. For now, type in and execute Listing 6-18 to learn how to use the **ROLLBACK** command.

Listing 6-18. Using a ROLLBACK Command

```
IF  EXISTS (SELECT * FROM sys.objects
            WHERE object_id = OBJECT_ID(N'[dbo].[demoTransaction]')
              AND type in (N'U'))
DROP TABLE [dbo].[demoTransaction];
GO


CREATE TABLE dbo.demoTRANSACTION (col1 INT NOT NULL);
GO


--1
BEGIN TRAN
    INSERT INTO dbo.demoTRANSACTION (col1) VALUES (1);
    INSERT INTO dbo.demoTRANSACTION (col1) VALUES (2);
COMMIT TRAN
```

```
--2
BEGIN TRAN
    INSERT INTO dbo.demoTRANSACTION (col1) VALUES (3);
    INSERT INTO dbo.demoTRANSACTION (col1) VALUES (4);
ROLLBACK TRAN

GO
--3
SELECT col1
FROM dbo.demoTRANSACTION;
```

Figure 6-18 shows the results. Transaction block 1 completes successfully and inserts the two rows in the table. Transaction block 2 contains two valid statements, but because it contains the **ROLLBACK** command instead of the **COMMIT** command, the transaction does not complete. Query 3 shows that the batch inserts only values 1 and 2 into the table.

Figure 6-18. *The results of a rolled-back transaction*

Locking Tables

SQL Server has different "isolation levels" to control how transactions from one connection affect **SELECT** statements from another connection. Learning about isolation levels is beyond the scope of this book, but this section will demonstrate the default behavior. For this example, you will use two query windows, so follow the instructions carefully.

1. From query window 1, run this code:

```
USE AdventureWorksLT2008;
GO
IF  EXISTS (SELECT * FROM sys.objects
            WHERE object_id = OBJECT_ID(N'[dbo].[demoTransaction]')
                AND type in (N'U'))
DROP TABLE [dbo].[demoTransaction];
GO

CREATE TABLE dbo.demoTRANSACTION (col1 INT NOT NULL);
GO

BEGIN TRAN
    INSERT INTO dbo.demoTRANSACTION (col1) VALUES (1);
```

```
        INSERT INTO dbo.demoTRANSACTION (col1) VALUES (2);
```

2. Switch to window 2, and run this code:

```
USE AdventureWorksLT2008;
GO
SELECT col1 FROM dbo.demoTransaction;
```

3. At this point, you will see nothing returned from the code from step 2 as it continues to execute. Switch to window 1, and run this code:

```
COMMIT TRAN
```

4. Switch back to window 2 to view the results.

Once you committed the transaction in step 3, the **SELECT** statement in window 2 could complete. To learn more about locks, transactions, and isolation levels, read the book *SQL Server 2008 Transact-SQL Recipes* by Joseph Sack (Apress, 2008). You will learn how to add conditional logic to your transactions in Chapter 7. For now, practice what you have learned by completing Exercise 6-4.

Exercise 6-4

Use the AdventureWorksLT2008 database to complete this exercise. Run the following script to create a table for this exercise. You can find the solutions in the appendix.

```
IF OBJECT_ID('dbo.Demo') IS NOT NULL BEGIN
    DROP TABLE dbo.Demo;
END;
GO
CREATE TABLE dbo.Demo(ID INT PRIMARY KEY, Name VARCHAR(25));
```

1. Write a transaction that includes two **INSERT** statements to add two rows to the **dbo.Demo** table.
2. Write a transaction that includes two **INSERT** statements to add two more rows to the **dbo.Demo** table. Attempt to insert a letter instead of a number into the **ID** column in one of the statements. Select the data from the **dbo.Demo** table to see which rows made it to the table.

Thinking About Performance

SQL Server performs best when working on sets of data instead of one row at a time. Often developers write code that loops through a record set and performs an update or insert for each pass through the loop. The example code in Listing 6-19 demonstrates the difference in performance between the two techniques. Download and run the code from this book's page on http://www.apress.com. You may need to stop the code execution after a few minutes.

Listing 6-19. The Difference Between the Set-Based and Iterative Approaches

```sql
USE AdventureWorks2008;
GO
--Create a work table
IF  EXISTS (SELECT * FROM sys.objects
             WHERE object_id = OBJECT_ID(N'[dbo].[demoPerformance]')
                AND type in (N'U'))
DROP TABLE [dbo].[demoPerformance];
GO

CREATE TABLE [dbo].[demoPerformance](
    [SalesOrderID] [int] NOT NULL,
    [SalesOrderDetailID] [int] NOT NULL,
 CONSTRAINT [PK_demoPerformance] PRIMARY KEY CLUSTERED
(
    [SalesOrderID] ASC,
    [SalesOrderDetailID] ASC
)WITH (PAD_INDEX  = OFF, STATISTICS_NORECOMPUTE  = OFF, IGNORE_DUP_KEY = OFF,
    ALLOW_ROW_LOCKS  = ON, ALLOW_PAGE_LOCKS  = ON) ON [PRIMARY]
) ON [PRIMARY]


GO

PRINT 'Insert all rows start';
PRINT getdate();

--Insert all rows from the Sales.SalesOrderDetail table at once
INSERT INTO dbo.demoPerformance(SalesOrderID, SalesOrderDetailID)
SELECT SalesOrderID, SalesOrderDetailID
FROM Sales.SalesOrderDetail;

PRINT 'Insert all rows end';
PRINT getdate();

--Remove all rows from the first insert
TRUNCATE TABLE [dbo].[demoPerformance];

PRINT 'Insert rows one at a time begin';
PRINT getdate();
```

```
--Set up a loop to insert one row at a time
WHILE EXISTS(

    SELECT *
    FROM Sales.SalesOrderDetail AS d LEFT JOIN dbo.demoPerformance AS p
    ON d.SalesOrderID = p.SalesOrderID
        AND d.SalesOrderDetailID = p.SalesOrderDetailID
    WHERE p.SalesOrderID IS NULL) BEGIN


    INSERT INTO dbo.demoPerformance (SalesOrderID,SalesOrderDetailID)
    SELECT TOP 1 d.SalesOrderID, d.SalesOrderDetailID
    FROM Sales.SalesOrderDetail AS d LEFT JOIN dbo.demoPerformance AS p
    ON d.SalesOrderID = p.SalesOrderID
        AND d.SalesOrderDetailID = p.SalesOrderDetailID
    WHERE p.SalesOrderID IS NULL;

END
PRINT 'Insert rows one at a time end';
PRINT getdate();
```

After the code executes or you stop execution after a few minutes, click the Messages tab to see the results (Figure 6-19). Run this statement to see how many rows were actually inserted from the loop:

```
USE AdventureWorks2008;
GO
SELECT COUNT(*) FROM dbo.demoPerformance;
```

The loop inserted only 10,000 rows for me in almost 4 minutes! The first **INSERT** statement, inserting more than a million rows, took less than a second to run.

Figure 6-19. *The results of comparing one insert vs. a loop with multiple inserts*

Database Cleanup

Run the script in Listing 6-20 to clean up the tables used in this chapter. You can download the script from this book's page at http://www.apress.com. Alternately, you can reinstall the sample databases by following the instructions in the "Installing the Sample Databases" section in Chapter 1.

Listing 6-20. Deleting Demo Tables

```
USE [AdventureWorksLT2008];
GO

IF  EXISTS (SELECT * FROM sys.objects
            WHERE object_id = OBJECT_ID(N'[dbo].[demoProduct]')
                AND type in (N'U'))
DROP TABLE [dbo].[demoProduct];
GO

IF  EXISTS (SELECT * FROM sys.objects
            WHERE object_id = OBJECT_ID(N'[dbo].[demoCustomer]')
                AND type in (N'U'))
DROP TABLE [dbo].[demoCustomer];
GO

IF  EXISTS (SELECT * FROM sys.objects
            WHERE object_id = OBJECT_ID(N'[dbo].[demoAddress]')
                AND type in (N'U'))
DROP TABLE [dbo].[demoAddress];
GO

IF  EXISTS (SELECT * FROM sys.objects
            WHERE object_id = OBJECT_ID(N'[dbo].[demoSalesOrderHeader]')
                AND type in (N'U'))
DROP TABLE [dbo].[demoSalesOrderHeader];
GO

IF  EXISTS (SELECT * FROM sys.objects
            WHERE object_id = OBJECT_ID(N'[dbo].[demoSalesOrderDetail]')
                AND type in (N'U'))
DROP TABLE [dbo].[demoSalesOrderDetail];
GO
```

```
IF  EXISTS (SELECT * FROM sys.objects
            WHERE object_id = OBJECT_ID(N'[dbo].[demoTransaction]')
              AND type in (N'U'))
DROP TABLE [dbo].[demoTransaction];
GO


IF  EXISTS (SELECT * FROM sys.objects
            WHERE object_id = OBJECT_ID(N'[dbo].[demoCustomerSummary]')
              AND type in (N'U'))
DROP TABLE [dbo].[demoCustomerSummary];
GO


IF  EXISTS (SELECT * FROM sys.objects
            WHERE object_id = OBJECT_ID(N'[dbo].[demoDefault]')
              AND type in (N'U'))
DROP TABLE [dbo].[demoDefault];
GO


IF  EXISTS (SELECT * FROM sys.objects
            WHERE object_id = OBJECT_ID(N'[dbo].[demoAutoPopulate]')
              AND type in (N'U'))
DROP TABLE [dbo].[demoAutoPopulate];


USE AdventureWorks2008;
GO


IF  EXISTS (SELECT * FROM sys.objects
            WHERE object_id = OBJECT_ID(N'[dbo].[demoPerformance]')
              AND type in (N'U'))
DROP TABLE [dbo].[demoPerformance];
```

Summary

How to write data modification statements is not difficult to learn once you've mastered the basics of selecting data. These tasks do, however, require much more care because it is possible to unintentionally modify and delete rows or even empty entire tables. Always check the WHERE clause with a SELECT statement first when writing ad hoc statements.

Whenever possible, do modifications on sets of data, not one row at a time. You will often see amazing differences in performance. Many developers learn to operate on one row at a time, but this is not the best way for SQL Server to work.

CHAPTER 7

■ ■ ■

Understanding T-SQL Programming Logic

Even though the primary purpose of T-SQL is to retrieve and manipulate data, like other programming languages, it also contains logic elements. Most of the time you will write T-SQL statements that retrieve or update data, but you can also set up loops and write code with conditional flow. Often database administrators write scripts in T-SQL to perform maintenance tasks that require more than just retrieving or updating data. For example, you might need to write a script that checks the last backup date of all databases on the server or write a script that checks the free space of all the databases. Although most administrative tasks are beyond the scope of this book, you may find many uses in your environment for the techniques you learn in this chapter.

Variables

If you have programmed in any other language, you have probably used *variables* in your programs. Variables hold temporary values in memory. For example, you might use a variable to hold the results of a calculation, or the results of a string concatenation, or to control the number of times a loop executes.

Declaring and Initializing a Variable

To use a variable, you must first *declare* it. Beginning with SQL Server 2008, you can *initialize*, that is, assign a value, to the variable at the same time that you declare it. Earlier versions of SQL Server required that you assign a value on a separate line. Here
is the syntax for declaring a variable and assigning a value both at the same and later
in the code:

```
DECLARE @variableName <type>[(size)] = <value1>
SET @variableName = <value2>
SELECT @variableName = <value3>
SELECT @variableName = <col1> FROM <table1>
```

You assign a value to a variable after you declare it by using the **SET** statement or by using the **SELECT** statement. The **SET** statement allows working with only one variable at a time. The **SELECT** statement allows multiple variables to be modified in the same statement. Using a **SELECT** statement to assign values to multiple variables is more efficient than individual **SET** statements. In most cases, the difference is so small that you should just write your code using whichever technique you prefer. You can also assign a value to a variable from a column within a query. When doing so, that is the only thing the query can do; the query cannot return a result set. Type in and execute Listing 7-1 to learn how to declare and assign variables.

Listing 7-1. Declaring and Using Variables

```
USE AdventureWorks2008;
GO


--1
DECLARE @myNumber INT = 10;
PRINT 'The value of @myNumber';
PRINT @myNumber;
SET @myNumber = 20;
PRINT 'The value of @myNumber';
PRINT @myNumber;
GO


--2
DECLARE @myString VARCHAR(100), @myBit BIT;
SELECT @myString = 'Hello, World', @myBit = 1;
PRINT 'The value of @myString';
PRINT @myString;
PRINT 'The value of @myBit';
PRINT @myBit;
GO


--3
DECLARE @myUnicodeString NVARCHAR(100);
SET @myUnicodeString = N'This is a Unicode String';
PRINT 'The value of @myUnicodeString';
PRINT @myUnicodeString;
GO
```

```
--4
DECLARE @FirstName NVARCHAR(50), @LastName NVARCHAR(50);
SELECT @FirstName  = FirstName, @LastName = LastName
FROM Person.Person
WHERE BusinessEntityID = 1;

PRINT 'The value of @FirstName';
PRINT @FirstName;
PRINT 'The value of @LastName';
PRINT @LastName;
GO

--5
PRINT 'The value of @myString';
PRINT @myString;
```

Figure 7-1 shows the results of the script. The script in Listing 7-1 consists of five batches after setting the database context. Batch 1 declares and initializes the local variable **@myNumber** in one line to the value 10. Local variables in T-SQL begin with the **@** symbol and are in scope within the current connection and the current batch. Another line in the batch sets the value of the variable to 20 using the **SET** command. The **SET** command will set the value of only one variable at a time. Using the **PRINT** command, you can print the value of a variable.

```
Messages
The value of @myNumber
10
The value of @myNumber
20
The value of @myString
Hello, World
The value of @myBit
1
The value of @myUnicodeString
This is a Unicode String
The value of @FirstName
Ken
The value of @LastName
Sánchez
Msg 137, Level 15, State 2, Line 4
Must declare the scalar variable "@myString".
```

Figure 7-1. *The results of declaring and initializing a variable*

Batch 2 demonstrates how you can declare more than one variable on the same line. The batch uses a **SELECT** statement to assign values to both the variables in the same statement. Batch 3 demonstrates that you set the value of an **NVARCHAR** string a bit differently. You must begin the string with the uppercase letter *N*. By doing so, SQL Server converts the string to Unicode. If you do not begin the string with *N*, the string will remain as a non-Unicode string, and you may lose any special characters.

In batch 4, the SELECT statement assigns the value of the FirstName and LastName columns to two variables from one row of the Person.Person table. In this case, the WHERE clause restricts the SELECT statement to just one row. If the statement did not have a WHERE clause or a less restrictive one, the statement would assign the last value returned to the variable.

Batch 5 demonstrates that the variable declared in batch 2 is no longer in scope. Variables go out of scope when the batch completes. Even if there is only one batch in the script, once the code completes, the variable goes out of scope and is no longer in memory.

Using Expressions and Functions with Variables

The previous example demonstrated how to declare and assign a literal value or a value from a query. You can also use any expression and function to assign a value to a variable. For example, you may need to save the count of the rows of a query for later in the script, or you may need to save the value of a file name concatenated to a file path for a maintenance script. Type in and execute the code in Listing 7-2 to learn more about variables.

Listing 7-2. Using Expressions and Functions to Assign Variable Values

```
USE AdventureWorks2008;
GO


--1
DECLARE @myINT1 INT = 10, @myINT2 INT = 20, @myINT3 INT;
SET @myINT3 = @myINT1 * @myINT2;
PRINT 'Value of @myINT3: ' + CONVERT(VARCHAR,@myINT3);
GO


--2
DECLARE @myString VARCHAR(100);
SET @myString = 'Hello, ';
SET @myString += 'World';
PRINT 'Value of @myString: ' + @myString;
GO


--3
DECLARE @CustomerCount INT;
SELECT @CustomerCount = COUNT(*)
FROM Sales.Customer;
PRINT 'Customer Count: ' + CAST(@CustomerCount AS VARCHAR);
```

```
--4
DECLARE @FullName NVARCHAR(152);
SELECT @FullName = FirstName + ISNULL(' ' + MiddleName,'') + ' ' + LastName
FROM Person.Person
WHERE BusinessEntityID = 1;
PRINT 'FullName: ' + @FullName;
```

Figure 7-2 shows the results. Batch 1 declares three integer variables and assigns a value to two of them. The next line uses the **SET** statement to assign the sum of the two variables to the third one. Finally, to print the label explaining the value and the value on the same line, the code converts the **@myINT3** variable to a string.

Figure 7-2. *The results of using variables with expressions*

Batch 2 assigns the value **Hello** (with a space after it) to the **@myString** variable. The next line uses the += operator, new to SQL Server 2008, to concatenate another string, *World*, to the variable. The += operator is available in many programming languages as a shorter way to write an assignment. Without the shortcut, the code would look like this:

```
SET @myString = @myString + 'World';
```

Batch 3 assigns the result of the aggregate expression **COUNT(*)** to the variable **@CustomerCount**. When assigning a value to a variable from a query, you will assign only one value to a variable. In this case, the query returns only one value, the count of all the rows from the table. The query in Batch 4 also returns one row because of the criteria in the **WHERE** clause. The query assigns a value to the **@FullName** variable for one row only.

Using Variables in WHERE and HAVING Clauses

So far, the examples in this book have used literal values in the expressions, also known as *predicates*, in **WHERE** and **HAVING** clauses. You will often not know ahead of time what values will be needed, so it makes sense to use variables. Type in and execute the code in Listing 7-3 to learn more about using a variable instead of a literal value in a **WHERE** or **HAVING** clause.

Listing 7-3. Using a Variable in a WHERE or HAVING Clause Predicate

```
USE AdventureWorks2008;
GO

--1
DECLARE @ID INT;
SET @ID = 1;

SELECT BusinessEntityID, FirstName, LastName
FROM Person.Person
WHERE BusinessEntityID = @ID;
GO

--2
DECLARE @FirstName NVARCHAR(50);
SET @FirstName = N'Ke%';

SELECT BusinessEntityID, FirstName, LastName
FROM Person.Person
WHERE FirstName LIKE @FirstName
ORDER BY BusinessEntityID;
GO

--3
DECLARE @ID INT = 1;
--3.1
SELECT BusinessEntityID, FirstName, LastName
FROM Person.Person
WHERE @ID = CASE @ID WHEN 0 THEN 0 ELSE BusinessEntityID END;

SET @ID = 0;

--3.2
SELECT BusinessEntityID, FirstName, LastName
FROM Person.Person
WHERE @ID = CASE @ID WHEN 0 THEN 0 ELSE BusinessEntityID END;

GO
```

```
--4
DECLARE @Amount INT = 10000;

SELECT SUM(TotalDue) AS TotalSales, CustomerID
FROM Sales.SalesOrderHeader
GROUP BY CustomerID
HAVING SUM(TotalDue) > @Amount;
```

Figure 7-3 shows the results. Batch 1 declares a variable **@ID** and assigns the value 1. The query uses the variable in the **WHERE** clause to restrict the results to just the row from the **Person.Person** table where the **BusinessEntityID** is 1. Batch 2 demonstrates how pattern matching with **LIKE** can be used. The variable contains the wildcard **%**. The query returns all rows where the **FirstName** begins with *Ke*.

Results

	BusinessEntityID	FirstName	LastName
1	1	Ken	Sánchez

	BusinessEntityID	FirstName	LastName
1	1	Ken	Sánchez
2	17	Kevin	Brown
3	58	Kendall	Keil
4	105	Kevin	Homer
5	195	Kevin	Liu

	BusinessEntityID	FirstName	LastName
1	1	Ken	Sánchez

	BusinessEntityID	FirstName	LastName
1	285	Syed	Abbas
2	293	Catherine	Abel
3	295	Kim	Abercrombie
4	2170	Kim	Abercrombie
5	38	Kim	Abercrombie

	TotalSales	CustomerID
1	68644.5658	30030
2	93888.441	29784
3	302061.1054	30076
4	76266.9402	29538
5	340396.3242	29615

Figure 7-3. *The partial results of using a variable in the WHERE and HAVING clauses*

Batch 3 uses the variable **@ID** within a **CASE** expression in the **WHERE** clause. The variable starts out with the value 1. Query 3.1 returns only the row in which **BusinessEntityID** equals 1. Take a closer look at the **CASE** expression. The variable does not equal 0, so the **CASE** expression returns the column **BusinessEntityID**. The variable **@ID** equals the **BusinessEntityID** in only one row. In query 3.2, the value of **@ID** is 0. The **CASE** expression returns 0 because **@ID** is equal to 0. Since **@ID** is equal to 0 and the **CASE** expression returns 0, the query returns every row. Zero is always equal to zero.

Batch 4 demonstrates that the variables can also be used in the **HAVING** clause of an aggregate query. Recall from Chapter 5 that you use the **HAVING** clause to filter the rows after the database engine processes the **GROUP BY** clause. The query returns only the rows from the **Sales.SalesOrderHeader** table where the **TotalSales** value by **CustomerID** exceeds the value stored in **@Amount**.

Now that you understand some of the things you can do with variables, practice working with them by completing Exercise 7-1.

Exercise 7-1

Use the AdventureWorks2008 database to complete this exercise. You can find the solutions in the appendix.

1. Write a script that declares an integer variable called **@myInt**. Assign 10 to the variable, and then print it.
2. Write a script that declares a **VARCHAR(20)** variable called **@myString**. Assign **This is a test** to the variable, and print it.
3. Write a script that declares two integer variables called **@MaxID** and **@MinID**. Use the variables to print the highest and lowest **SalesOrderID** values from the **Sales.SalesOrderHeader** table.
4. Write a script that declares an integer variable called **@ID**. Assign the value **70000** to the variable. Use the variable in a **SELECT** statement that returns all the rows from the **Sales.SalesOrderHeader** table that have a **SalesOrderID** greater than the value of the variable.
5. Write a script that declares three variables, one integer variable called **@ID**, an **NVARHCAR(50)** variable called **@FirstName**, and a **VARCHAR(50)** variable called **@LastName**. Use a **SELECT** statement to set the value of the variables with the row from the **Person.Person** table with **BusinessEntityID = 1**. Print a statement in the "BusinessEntityID: FirstName LastName" format.
6. Write a script that declares an integer variable called **@SalesCount**. Set the value of the variable to the total count of sales in the **Sales.SalesOrderHeader** table. Use the variable in a **SELECT** statement that shows the difference between the **@SalesCount** and the count of sales by customer.

The IF... ELSE Construct

Use **IF** along with the optional **ELSE** keyword to control code flow in your T-SQL scripts. Use **IF** just as you would in any other programming language to execute a statement or group of statements based on an expression that must evaluate to **TRUE** or **FALSE**. For example, you might need to display an error message if the count of the rows in a table is too low. If the count exceeds a given value, your code repopulates a production table.

Using IF

Always follow the keyword **IF** with a condition that evaluates to **TRUE** or **FALSE**. You can follow the condition with the next statement to run on the same line or on the next line. If the condition applies to a group of statements, you will use **BEGIN** and **END** to designate which statements are within the **IF** block. Here is the syntax:

```
IF <condition> <statement>

IF <condition>
    <statement>

IF <condition> BEGIN
    <statement1>
    [<statement2>]
END
```

To make my code more readable and avoid mistakes, I use the first and third methods but avoid the second. For example, I might decide later to add a **PRINT** statement before the line to execute when the condition is true. In that case, I might accidentally cause the **IF** to apply just to the **PRINT** statement by forgetting to go back and add **BEGIN** and **END**. Type in and execute the code in Listing 7-4 to learn how to use **IF**.

Listing 7-4. Using IF to Control Code Execution

```
USE AdventureWorks2008;
GO

--1
DECLARE @Count INT;

SELECT @Count = COUNT(*)
FROM Sales.Customer;

IF @Count > 500 BEGIN
    PRINT 'The customer count is over 500.';
END;
GO

--2
DECLARE @Name VARCHAR(50);

SELECT @Name = FirstName + ' ' + LastName
FROM Person.Person
WHERE BusinessEntityID = 1;

--2.1
IF CHARINDEX('Ken',@Name) > 0 BEGIN
    PRINT 'The name for BusinessEntityID = 1 contains "Ken"';
END;
```

```
--2.2
IF CHARINDEX('Kathi',@Name) > 0 BEGIN
    PRINT 'The name for BusinessEntityID = 1 contains "Kathi"';
END;
```

Figure 7-4 shows the results. Batch 1 retrieves the count of the rows in the **Sales.Customer** table. If the count exceeds 500, then the **PRINT** statement executes. You can use any valid statements within the **IF** block. These code examples use **PRINT** statements so that you can easily see the results. Batch 2 assigns the value returned by the expression **FirstName + ' ' + LastName** to the variable. The 2.1 **IF** block executes the **PRINT** statement if the value contains *Ken*. The 2.2 **IF** block executes the **PRINT** statement if the value contains *Kathi*. Since the value does not contain *Kathi*, nothing prints.

Figure 7-4. The results of using IF

Using ELSE

Often you will need to perform an alternate option if the condition you are checking is false. If you are using the **BEGIN** and **END** keywords in the **IF** block, you must close the block first before adding **ELSE**. Just like **IF**, you can use **BEGIN** and **END** to designate the **ELSE** block. You can also type the statement on the same line or the next line if you choose. Here is the syntax for many of the ways you can use **ELSE**:

```
IF <condition> <statement>
ELSE <statement>

IF <condition> BEGIN
    <statement1>
    [<statement2>]
END
ELSE <statement>

IF <condition> BEGIN
    <statement1>
    [<statement2>]
END
ELSE BEGIN
    <statement1>
    [<statement2>]
END
```

The syntax examples show some of the ways you can use **ELSE** along with **IF**. You can use **BEGIN** and **END** with both or either parts of the construct. Type in and execute Listing 7-5 to learn how to use ELSE.

Listing 7-5. Using ELSE

```
USE AdventureWorks2008;
GO


--1
DECLARE @Count INT;

SELECT @Count = COUNT(*)
FROM Sales.Customer;

IF @Count < 500 PRINT 'The customer count is less than 500.';
ELSE PRINT 'The customer count is 500 or more.';
GO


--2
DECLARE @Name NVARCHAR(101);

SELECT @Name = FirstName + ' ' + LastName
FROM Person.Person
WHERE BusinessEntityID = 1;


--2.1
IF CHARINDEX('Ken', @Name) > 0 BEGIN
    PRINT 'The name for BusinessEntityID = 1 contains "Ken"';
END;
ELSE BEGIN
    PRINT 'The name for BusinessEntityID = 1 does not contain "Ken"';
    PRINT 'The name is ' + @Name;
END;
--2.2
IF CHARINDEX('Kathi', @Name) > 0 BEGIN
    PRINT 'The name for BusinessEntityID = 1 contains "Kathi"';
END;
ELSE BEGIN
    PRINT 'The name for BusinessEntityID = 1 does not contain "Kathi"';
    PRINT 'The name is ' + @Name;
END;
```

Figure 7-5 shows the results. This listing looks almost like Listing 7-4 except that it contains the **ELSE** blocks. Batch 1 saves the count of the customers in a variable. This time, if the count is less than 500, the **PRINT** statement in the **IF** block executes. In this case, the count exceeds 500, so the **PRINT** statement in the **ELSE** block executes. Batch 2 executes the **PRINT** statement in the **IF** block of the 2.1 section of code because the value of the variable contains *Ken*. The 2.2 section of code executes the **PRINT** statement in the **ELSE** block because the value of the variable does not contain *Kathi*.

```
The customer count is 500 or more.
The name for BusinessEntityID = 1 contains "Ken"
The name for BusinessEntityID = 1 does not contain "Kathi"
The name is Ken Sánchez
```

Figure 7-5. *The results of using ELSE*

Using Multiple Conditions

So far, the examples have shown only one condition along with each **IF** or **ELSE**. You can include multiple conditions along with **AND** and **OR** just like within a **WHERE** clause. You can also control the logic with parentheses. For example, you may need to execute a statement only if the current day is Monday and the count of the rows in a table exceeds a certain value. Type in and execute the code in Listing 7-6.

Listing 7-6. *Using Multiple Conditions with IF and ELSE*

```
USE AdventureWorks2008;
GO

--1
DECLARE @Count INT;

SELECT @Count = COUNT(*)
FROM Sales.Customer;

IF @Count > 500 AND DATEPART(dw,getdate()) = 2 BEGIN
    PRINT 'The count is over 500.';
    PRINT 'Today is Monday.';
END
ELSE BEGIN
    PRINT 'Either the count is too low or today is not Monday.';
END;
```

```
--2
IF @Count > 500 AND (DATEPART(dw,getdate()) = 2 OR DATEPART(m,getdate())= 5) BEGIN
    PRINT 'The count is over 500.'
    PRINT 'It is either Monday or the month is May.'
END
```

Figure 7-6 shows the results. This listing contains just one batch after setting the database context. IF block 1 checks to see whether the count exceeds 500 and whether the current day of the week is Monday. You may get different results depending on the day of the week you run the code. IF block 2 checks first to see whether the day of the week is Monday or whether the current month is May. The block then checks the count, which must exceed 500. Since both the count exceeds 500 and I executed the code in May, the statements print. Again, you may get different results depending on when you run the code example.

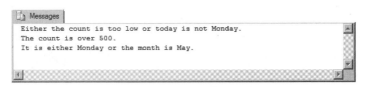

Figure 7-6. The results of using multiple conditions with IF

Nesting IF…ELSE

You can nest IF and ELSE blocks inside other IF and ELSE blocks to create even more complex logic. For example, you may need to check to make sure the current date is not a Sunday and execute a statement. Then within the IF block, check to make sure the table has at least a certain number of rows before executing another statement. The BEGIN and END keywords are sometimes optional, but I suggest you include them to make sure that the code is correct and readable. Here are two of the possible syntax examples:

```
IF <condition> BEGIN
    [<statement1>]
    IF <condition> BEGIN
        <statement2>
    END
END

IF <condition> BEGIN
    <statement1>
END
```

```
ELSE BEGIN
    [statment2]
    IF <condition> BEGIN
        <statement3>
        [<statement4>]
    END
    ELSE <statement5>
END
```

As you can probably tell, nesting **IF** blocks can cause your code to become complicated. Be sure to use comments and consistent formatting to make sure you will understand what the code does a few months or years after you write it. Type in and execute the code in Listing 7-7 to learn how to nest **IF** blocks.

Listing 7-7. Using a Nested IF Block

```
USE AdventureWorks2008;
GO

DECLARE @Count INT;

SELECT @Count = COUNT(*)
FROM Sales.Customer;

IF @Count > 500 BEGIN
    PRINT 'The count is over 500.';
    IF DATEPART(dw,getdate())= 2 BEGIN
        PRINT 'Today is Monday.';
    END;
    ELSE BEGIN
        PRINT 'Today is not Monday.';
    END;
END;
```

Figure 7-7 shows the results. Since the count exceeds 500, the code executes the first **PRINT** statement. Then depending on the day that you execute the code, one of the statements inside the nested **IF…ELSE** block will print. Be careful when writing nested **IF** blocks to make sure that the logic ends up what you intend it to be.

Figure 7-7. *The results of using a nested IF block*

Using IF EXISTS

You can use IF EXISTS to check for the results of a SELECT statement before executing the statements within the IF block. For example, you could check to see whether a certain part number is listed in the parts table. If it is, then perform an update. If not, then insert the row. You may have noticed IF EXISTS being used in Chapter 6 to check the system tables to make sure a table exists before dropping it. Here is the syntax:

```
IF [NOT] EXISTS(SELECT * FROM <TABLE1> [WHERE <condition>]) BEGIN
    <statement1>
    [<statement2>]
END
```

This is one of the cases where using the asterisk (*) is perfectly acceptable. The database engine just checks to see whether the query will return even one row but does not return any rows at all. The EXISTS function returns only TRUE or FALSE. Type in and execute Listing 7-8 to learn how to use IF EXISTS.

Listing 7-8. *Using IF EXISTS*

```
USE AdventureWorks2008;
GO

--1
IF EXISTS(SELECT * FROM Person.Person WHERE BusinessEntityID = 1) BEGIN
   PRINT 'There is a row with BusinessEntityID = 1';
END
ELSE BEGIN
   PRINT 'There is not a row with BusEntityID = 1';
END;

--2
IF NOT EXISTS(SELECT * FROM Person.Person WHERE FirstName = 'Kathi') BEGIN
   PRINT 'There is not a person with the first name "Kathi".';
END;
```

Figure 7-8 shows the results. Listing 7-8 contains one batch after setting the database context. **IF** block 1 checks to see whether there is a row in the **Person.Person** table with **BusinessEntityID = 1**. You can also use **ELSE** along with **IF EXISTS**. **IF** block 2 uses the **NOT** keyword to make sure that there is not a row with the **FirstName** *Kathi* and executes the **PRINT** statements since there is not a row with that name.

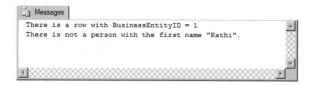

Figure 7-8. *The results of using* IF EXISTS

You should now know how to use **IF** and **ELSE** in a number of situations. Practice what you have learned by completing Exercise 7-2.

Exercise 7-2

Use the AdventureWorks2008 database to complete this exercise. You can find the solutions in the appendix.

1. Write a batch that declares an integer variable called @Count to save the count of all the Sales.SalesOrderDetail records. Add an IF block that that prints "Over 100,000" if the value exceeds 100,000. Otherwise, print "100,000 or less."
2. Write a batch that contains nested IF blocks. The outer block should check to see whether the month is October or November. If that is the case, print "The month is " and the month name. The inner block should check to see whether the year is even or odd and print the result. You can modify the month to check to make sure the inner block fires.
3. Write a batch that uses IF EXISTS to check to see whether there is a row in the Sales. SalesOrderHeader table that has SalesOrderID = 1. Print "There is a SalesOrderID = 1" or "There is not a SalesOrderID = 1" depending on the result.

WHILE

Use the **WHILE** construct to set up *loops*, or code that executes a number of times, in T-SQL. For example, you might have a script that updates 10,000 rows each time within the loop because updating 10,000 rows at a time is more efficient than updating millions of rows at once.

Using a WHILE Loop

The WHILE loop requires a condition, in other words, an expression that evaluates to true or false, to determine when the looping should stop. If you do not specify a condition, the loop will run until you stop it or some error condition causes it to stop. Here is the syntax:

```
WHILE <condition> BEGIN
    <statement1>
    [<statement2>]
END
```

You can use several different techniques to create the condition that the database engine checks to determine when to exit the loop. One technique is to declare a variable, usually an integer, to be used as a counter. At the beginning of the loop, the code compares the variable to a value. Inside the loop, the code increments the variable. Another common way to control the loop is by using the EXISTS keyword. This might be used if a statement within the loop modifies data in the table used in the EXISTS condition. Type in and execute Listing 7-9 to learn how to use WHILE.

Listing 7-9. Using WHILE

```
USE AdventureWorks2008;
GO


--1
DECLARE @Count INT = 1;

WHILE @Count < 5 BEGIN
    PRINT @Count;
    SET @Count += 1;
END;
GO


--2
IF  EXISTS (SELECT * FROM sys.objects
            WHERE object_id = OBJECT_ID(N'dbo.demoContactType')
                AND type in (N'U'))
DROP TABLE dbo.demoContactType;
GO
CREATE TABLE dbo.demoContactType(ContactTypeID INT NOT NULL PRIMARY KEY,
    Processed BIT NOT NULL);
GO
INSERT INTO dbo.demoContactType(ContactTypeID,Processed)
SELECT ContactTypeID, 0
FROM Person.ContactType;
```

```
DECLARE @Count INT = 1;
WHILE EXISTS(SELECT * From dbo.demoContactType  WHERE Processed = 0) BEGIN
    UPDATE dbo.demoContactType SET Processed = 1
    WHERE ContactTypeID = @Count;
    SET @Count += 1;
END;
PRINT 'Done!';
```

Figure 7-9 shows the partial results. Batch 1 declares a variable and sets the value to 1 to use as a counter. Once the value of **@Count** reached 5, the execution exited the loop. It is very important that you set the value of the counter before the **WHILE** statement. If the value is **NULL**, then the statement incrementing the value of the counter will not actually do anything since adding one to **NULL** returns **NULL**. In this case, the loop will run indefinitely. The other option is to check for a **NULL** counter variable inside the loop and set the value at that point. The code prints the value of the counter each time through the loop.

Figure 7-9. The results of using a WHILE loop

The next example contains more than one batch because it creates and populates a table to be updated within the loop. This example also contains a variable called **@Count**, but the value of **@Count** does not control the execution. This **WHILE** loop checks to see whether any rows in the table **dbo.demoContactType** have a zero value in the **Processed** column. Each time through the loop, the code updates any rows with a **ContactTypeID** equal to the current value of **@Count**. (I removed all but two of the statements reporting that one row has been updated to save space in Figure 7-9.) When no more rows exist with **Processed = 0**, the code completes, and the **PRINT** statement executes. I purposely chose a small table for this example because processing a table row by row is very inefficient.

Using ROWCOUNT

When you run a T-SQL statement, your statement will return, update, insert, or delete all rows meeting the criteria or join condition. By turning on the **ROWCOUNT** setting, you can specify the number of rows affected by each execution of the statements. The setting stays in effect for the current connection until it is turned off. This technique may be used in a **WHILE** loop to process a smaller portion of the rows at a time. Recall the car key analogy in Chapter 6 where you should move all the keys at once instead of one at a time. If the pile of keys is too large to transfer at once, you might make two or three transfers but would not resort to moving one key at a time. Here is the syntax:

```
SET ROWCOUNT <number|@variable>
SET ROWCOUNT 0
```

To turn off ROWCOUNT, set the value to 0. Type in and execute the code in Listing 7-10 to learn how to use ROWCOUNT.

Listing 7-10. Using SET ROW COUNT to Limit the Number of Rows Affected

```
USE AdventureWorks2008;
GO

IF  EXISTS (SELECT * FROM sys.objects
            WHERE object_id = OBJECT_ID(N'dbo.demoSalesOrderDetail')
               AND type in (N'U'))
DROP TABLE dbo.demoSalesOrderDetail;
GO
CREATE TABLE dbo.demoSalesOrderDetail(SalesOrderID INT NOT NULL,
    SalesOrderDetailID INT NOT NULL, Processed BIT NOT NULL);
GO
SET ROWCOUNT 0;

INSERT INTO dbo.demoSalesOrderDetail(SalesOrderID,SalesOrderDetailID,Processed)
SELECT SalesOrderID, SalesOrderDetailID, 0
FROM Sales.SalesOrderDetail;
PRINT 'Populated work table';

SET ROWCOUNT 50000;
WHILE EXISTS(SELECT * From dbo.demoSalesOrderDetail  WHERE Processed = 0) BEGIN

    UPDATE dbo.demoSalesOrderDetail SET Processed = 1
    WHERE Processed = 0;
    PRINT 'Updated 50,000 rows';
END;
PRINT 'Done!';
```

Figure 7-10 shows the results. The code first creates and populates a copy of the Sales.SalesOrderDetail table. A statement changes the ROWCOUNT to 50,000 so the UPDATE statement inside the loop will update only 50,000 rows at a time. Once there are no rows left with the value zero in the Processed column, the loop completes. Be careful when writing a loop like this. If the WHERE clause that makes sure that the statement includes only the rows that need to be updated is missing, the loop will continue indefinitely. That's because it will otherwise keep updating the same rows over and over. Notice that I include the SET ROWCOUNT 0 line before the code to create the table. By default, ROWCOUNT is turned off, so the insert works as expected the first time. Without turning off **ROWCOUNT**, the **INSERT** statement inserts only 50,000 rows the second time you run it.

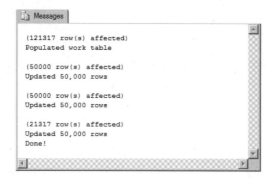

Figure 7-10. The results of using the ROWCOUNT setting

Nesting WHILE Loops

Just as you can nest **IF** blocks, you can create **WHILE** loops within **WHILE** loops. You can also nest **IF** blocks within **WHILE** loops and **WHILE** loops within **IF** blocks. The important thing to remember when your T-SQL scripts become more complex is to keep your formatting consistent and add comments to your code. You may understand what your code does when you write it, but you may have a hard time figuring it out months or years later when you need to troubleshoot a problem or make a change. Type in and execute Listing 7-11 to learn how to nest **WHILE** loops.

Listing 7-11. Using a Nested WHILE Loop

```
DECLARE @OuterCount INT = 1;
DECLARE @InnerCount INT;

WHILE @OuterCount < 10 BEGIN
    PRINT 'Outer Loop';
    SET @InnerCount = 1;
    WHILE @InnerCount < 5 BEGIN
        PRINT '   Inner Loop';
        SET @InnerCount += 1;
    END;
    SET @OuterCount += 1;
END;
```

Figure 7-11 shows the results. The **PRINT** statements show which loop is executing at the time. Make sure that you reset the value of the inner loop counter in the outer loop right before the inner loop. Otherwise, the inner loop will not run after the first time because the counter is already too high.

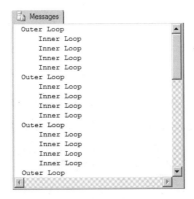

Figure 7-11. The results of running a nested WHILE loop

Exiting a Loop Early

Most of the time a **WHILE** loop continues until the controlling condition returns false. You can also cause code execution to exit early by using the **BREAK** statement. Usually you will include a nested **IF** statement that controls when the **BREAK** statement will execute. One reason you might want to use **BREAK** is if you decide not to include a controlling condition at the top of the loop and include the condition in an **IF** block instead. The condition may be a query checking to see whether any rows remain to be updated. Type in and execute the code in Listing 7-12 to learn how to use **BREAK**.

Listing 7-12. Using BREAK

```
DECLARE @Count INT = 1;

WHILE @Count < 50  BEGIN
    PRINT @Count;
    IF @Count = 10 BEGIN
        PRINT 'Exiting the WHILE loop';
        BREAK;
    END;
    SET @Count += 1;
END;
```

Figure 7-12 shows the results. If the code did not include the **BREAK** statement, the loop would print the numbers from 1 to 49. Instead, the loop exits when it reaches 10.

Figure 7-12. *The results of using the* BREAK *command*

Using CONTINUE

The CONTINUE command causes the loop to continue at the top. In other words, the code following the CONTINUE statement does not execute. Generally, you will find the CONTINUE within an IF block nested inside the WHILE loop. Type in and execute Listing 7-13 to learn how to use CONTINUE.

Listing 7-13. Using CONTINUE *in a* WHILE *Loop*

```
DECLARE @Count INT = 1;

WHILE @Count < 10 BEGIN
    PRINT @Count;
    SET @Count += 1;
    IF @Count = 3 BEGIN
        PRINT 'CONTINUE';
        CONTINUE;
    END;
    PRINT 'Bottom of loop';
END;
```

Figure 7-13 shows the results. Each time though the loop, the print statement at the bottom of the loop executes except for the time when the counter equals 3. Notice that the counter increments before the IF block. If the counter incremented at the bottom of the loop, then the loop would execute indefinitely.

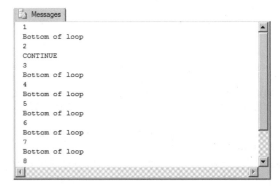

Figure 7-13. *The results of using CONTINUE in a WHILE loop*

Now that you know how to write code with a **WHILE** loop, practice what you have learned by completing Exercise 7-3.

Exercise 7-3

Use the AdventureWorks2008 database to complete this exercise. You can find the solutions in the appendix.

1. Write a script that contains a **WHILE** loop that prints out the letters *A* to *Z*. Use the function **CHAR** to change a number to a letter. Start the loop with the value 65. Here is an example that uses the **CHAR** function:

   ```
   DECLARE @Letter CHAR(1);
   SET @Letter = CHAR(65);
   PRINT @Letter;
   ```

2. Write a script that contains a **WHILE** loop nested inside another **WHILE** loop. The counter for the outer loop should count up from 1 to 100. The counter for the inner loop should count up from 1 to 5. Print the product of the two counters inside the inner loop.

3. Change the script in question 2 so the inner loop exits instead of printing when the counter for the outer loop is evenly divisible by 5.

4. Write a script that contains a **WHILE** loop that counts up from 1 to 100. Print "Odd" or "Even" depending on the value of the counter.

Error Handling

No matter what language you are programming in, there is always the possibility of error conditions that your code must handle. T-SQL has two ways to deal with errors, both of which you will learn about in this section. If you are writing T-SQL code within an application, for example, with a .NET language, your program will probably deal with the errors. If, however, you are writing a T-SQL script, you will handle errors at the T-SQL level. You can do both; you can handle errors within T-SQL and decide what you want sent back to the calling application.

Often the source of errors in T-SQL is problems with updates or inserts. For example, you might try to insert a row into a table that violates the primary key constraint by inserting a row with a duplicate key value. Other errors occur because of nondata reasons, such as divide-by-zero errors, for example.

Using @@ERROR

The traditional way to trap errors in T-SQL is to check the value of the **@@ERROR** function, formerly called a *global variable*. The **@@ERROR** function returns a number greater than zero if an error exists. Type in and execute the code in Listing 7-14 to learn how to use this method of error handling.

Listing 7-14. Using @@ERROR to Handle Errors

```
USE AdventureWorks2008;
GO


--1
DECLARE @errorNo INT;
PRINT 1/0;
SET @errorNo = @@ERROR;
IF @errorNo > 0 BEGIN
    PRINT 'An error has occurred.'
    PRINT @errorNo;
    PRINT @@ERROR;
END;


GO


--2
DECLARE @errorNo INT;
DROP TABLE testTable;
SET @errorNo = @@ERROR;
```

```
IF @errorNo > O BEGIN
    PRINT 'An error has occurred.'
    PRINT @errorNo;
    PRINT @@ERROR;
END;
GO


--3
DECLARE @errorNo INT;
SET IDENTITY_INSERT Person.ContactType ON;
INSERT INTO Person.ContactType(ContactTypeID,Name,ModifiedDate)
VALUES (1,'Accounting Manager',GETDATE());
SET @errorNo = @@ERROR;
IF @errorNo > O BEGIN
    PRINT 'An error has occurred.';
    PRINT @errorNo;
END;
```

Figure 7-14 shows the results. Even if you do not use the error trapping, the error prints on the screen in red, and the database engine returns an error message to the client. Notice that the code saves the value of the **@@ERROR** function before doing anything else. That is because, once another statement runs, the value of **@@ERROR** changes. Just by accessing it, the value goes back to zero. By saving the value in a local variable, you can check to see whether the value exceeds zero and deal with the error, in this case, just printing the value. You could roll back a transaction or halt execution of the batch.

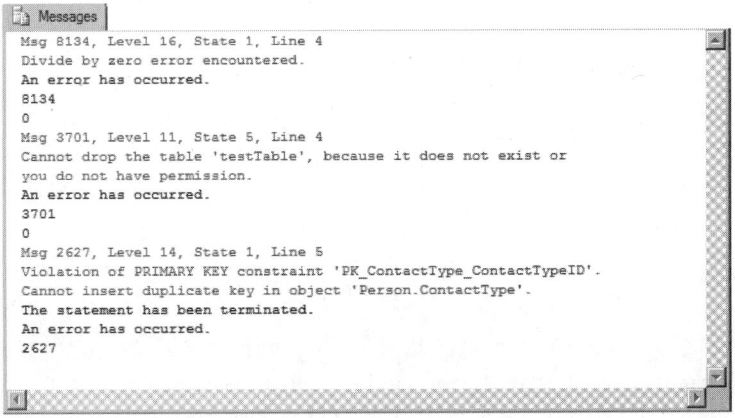

Figure 7-14. The results of using @@ERROR to trap errors

Batch 1 attempts to divide by zero. Batch 2 tries to drop a table that doesn't exist. Batch 3 inserts a row into the **Person.ContactType** table but violates the primary key so the row cannot be inserted.

Using GOTO

T-SQL allows you to use **GOTO** statements to cause code execution to jump to a label in another part of the code where processing continues after the label. I recommend that you reserve **GOTO** for handling errors and do not turn your T-SQL batches into "spaghetti code" with **GOTO**. Type in and execute the code in Listing 7-15 to learn how to use **GOTO**.

Listing 7-15. Using GOTO

```
DECLARE @errorNo INT;

PRINT 'Beginning of code.'
PRINT 1/0;
SET @errorNo = @@ERROR;
IF @errorNo > 0 GOTO ERR_LABEL;
PRINT 'No error';

ERR_LABEL:
PRINT 'At ERR_LABEL';
```

Figure 7-15 shows the results. Because of the divide-by-zero error, the code skips over one of the **PRINT** statements and jumps to the label. T-SQL does not have a "return" statement, so at that point, you could include other **GOTO** statements and labels to control handling errors.

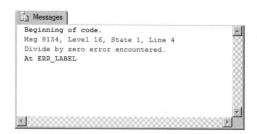

```
Messages
Beginning of code.
Msg 8134, Level 16, State 1, Line 4
Divide by zero error encountered.
At ERR_LABEL
```

Figure 7-15. The results of using GOTO

Using TRY ... CATCH

Beginning with SQL Server 2005, you can use the **TRY...CATCH** error handling construct, which I recommend over the older method of error handling, checking the value of **@@ERROR** described earlier. **TRY...CATCH** error handling is similar to the error handling in other programming languages such as C# and VB .NET. Along with this new method, you use several new functions that provide information about the error. You can also avoid sending an error message to the client if you choose. Here is the syntax:

```
BEGIN TRY
    <statements that might cause an error>
END TRY
BEGIN CATCH
    <statements to access error information and deal with the error>
END CATCH
```

Table 7-1 lists the new functions you use along with **TRY...CATCH**. One benefit is that the functions retain their values while in the **CATCH** block. You can access the values as many times as needed. Once outside of the **CATCH** block, the values of the error functions revert to **NULL**.

Table 7-1. *The Error Functions*

Function	Purpose
ERROR_NUMBER()	Provides the error number. This was the only information you could get in previous releases.
ERROR_SEVERITY()	Provides the severity of the error. The severity must exceed 10 in order to be trapped.
ERROR_STATE()	Provides the state code of the error. This refers to the cause of the error.
ERROR_PROCEDURE()	Returns the name of a stored procedure or trigger that caused the error.
ERROR_LINE()	Returns the line number that caused the error.
ERROR_MESSAGE()	Returns the actual text message describing the error.

Listing 7-16 demonstrates how to use **TRY...CATCH**. Type in and execute the code to learn how to use it.

Listing 7-16. *Using TRY...CATCH*

```
USE AdventureWorks2008;
GO

--1
BEGIN TRY
    PRINT 1/0;
END TRY
```

```
BEGIN CATCH
    PRINT 'Inside the Catch block';
    PRINT ERROR_NUMBER();
    PRINT ERROR_MESSAGE();
    PRINT ERROR_NUMBER();
END CATCH
PRINT 'Outside the catch block';
PRINT ERROR_NUMBER()
GO

--2
BEGIN TRY
    DROP TABLE testTable;
END TRY
BEGIN CATCH
    PRINT 'An error has occurred.'
    PRINT ERROR_NUMBER();
    PRINT ERROR_MESSAGE();
END CATCH;
```

Figure 7-16 shows the results. One difference between **TRY...CATCH** and **@@ERROR** is that you can print the error numbers and messages multiple times within the **CATCH** block. The values reset to **NULL** once execution leaves the **CATCH** block. When using **TRY...CATCH**, the error will not print at all unless you purposely print it. It is possible to just ignore the error.

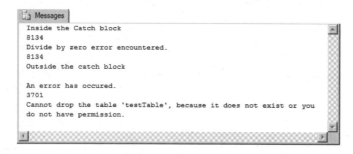

Figure 7-16. The results of using TRY...CATCH

Viewing Untrappable Errors

TRY...CATCH cannot trap some errors. For example, if the code contains an incorrect table or column name or a database server is not available, the entire batch of statements will fail, and the error will not be trapped. One interesting way to work around this problem is to encapsulate calls within stored procedures and then call the stored procedure inside the **TRY** block. You will learn about stored procedures in Chapter 8. Database administrators might use the stored procedure technique for management jobs, for example, checking the job history on each server. If one server is down, the database administrator would want the code to continue to check the other servers. Type in and execute Listing 7-17 to see some examples.

Listing 7-17. Untrappable Errors

```
USE AdventureWorks2008;
GO


--1
PRINT 'Syntax error.';
GO
BEGIN TRY
    SELECT FROM Sales.SalesOrderDetail;
END TRY
BEGIN CATCH
    PRINT ERROR_NUMBER();
END CATCH;
GO


--2
PRINT 'Invalid column.';
GO
BEGIN TRY
    SELECT ABC FROM Sales.SalesOrderDetail;
END TRY
BEGIN CATCH
    PRINT ERROR_NUMBER();
END CATCH;
```

Figure 7-17 shows the results. I put the **PRINT** statements before each **TRY...CATCH** block in separate batches because they would not print along with these incorrect statements. Example 1 is a syntax error; the **SELECT** list is empty. Example 2 contains an invalid column name.

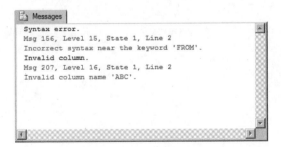

Figure 7-17. The results of running untrappable errors

Using RAISERROR

By using **TRY...CATCH**, you can avoid having an error message return to the client application, basically "trapping" the error. Sometimes you might want to return a different error or return an error to the client when one doesn't exist. For example, you might want to return an error message to a client when the code tries to update a nonexistent row. This would not cause a database error, but you might want to cause an error to fire anyway from SQL Server to the client application. You can use the **RAISERROR** function to raise an error back to the client. Here is the syntax:

```
RAISERROR(<message>,<severity>,<state>)
```

The **RAISERROR** function has several other optional parameters that provide additional functionality, but for a first look, these three parameters may be all you need. You can create reusable custom error messages by using the **sp_addmessage** stored procedure or just use a variable or hard-coded string with **RAISERROR**. Type in and execute Listing 7-18 to learn how to use **RAISERROR**.

Listing 7-18. Using RAISERROR

```
USE master;
GO


--1 This code section creates a custom error message
IF EXISTS(SELECT * FROM sys.messages where message_id = 50002) BEGIN
    EXEC sp_dropmessage 50002;
END
GO
PRINT 'Creating a custom error message.'
EXEC sp_addmessage 50002, 16,
   N'Customer missing.';
GO


USE AdventureWorks2008;
GO
--2
IF NOT EXISTS(SELECT * FROM Sales.Customer
         WHERE CustomerID = -1) BEGIN
   RAISERROR(50002,16,1);
END
GO
```

```
--3
BEGIN TRY
    PRINT 1/0;
END TRY
BEGIN CATCH
    IF ERROR_NUMBER() = 8134 BEGIN
        RAISERROR('A bad math error!',16,1);
    END;
END CATCH;
```

Figure 7-18 shows the results. You can provide either a message number or a message string for the message parameter. Batch 1 sets up a custom error message that you can use later when raising an error as in Batch 2. Batch 3 returns a different error to the client than the one that actually happened. Since the code returned an ad hoc error message, the database engine supplied the default number, 50000. The second parameter, severity, ranges from 1 to 25. When under 11, the message is a warning or information. You might want to build a dynamic error based on what happened in your code. If you would like to do this, make sure you save the message in a variable. You cannot build the message dynamically inside the **RAISERROR** function. See the Books Online article "Database Engine Error Severities" to learn more about error severities, but you will generally use 16 for errors correctable by the user. The state parameter is an integer between 1 and 255. You can use state to define where in the code the error occurred.

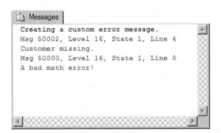

Figure 7-18. *The results of using RAISERROR*

Using TRY...CATCH with Transactions

You can use **TRY...CATCH** to make sure that transactions complete successfully so that the transaction may be rolled back if necessary. Include the transaction in the **TRY** block. Type in and execute Listing 7-19, which shows a simple example.

Listing 7-19. Using TRY...CATCH with a Transaction

```
--1
CREATE TABLE #Test (ID INT NOT NULL PRIMARY KEY);
GO

--2
BEGIN TRY
    --2.1
    BEGIN TRAN
        --2.1.1
        INSERT INTO #Test (ID)
        VALUES (1),(2),(3);
        --2.1.2
        UPDATE #Test SET ID = 2 WHERE ID = 1;
    --2.2
    COMMIT
END TRY

--3
BEGIN CATCH
    --3.1
    PRINT ERROR_MESSAGE();
    --3.2
    PRINT 'Rolling back transaction';
    ROLLBACK;
END CATCH;
```

Figure 7-19 shows the error message and the transaction rolled back. Statement 2.1.2 attempts to set the value ID to 2 in the row where it equals 1. This violates the primary key; you cannot have two rows with the value 2. If the entire transaction had been successful, the **COMMIT** statement would have committed the transaction. Instead, the **CATCH** block fired, giving you the chance to handle the error.

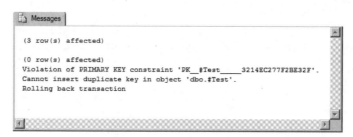

Figure 7-19. The results of using TRY...CATCH with a transaction

Trapping and handling errors is a very important part of T-SQL. If anything can go wrong, it often will. Practice what you have learned by completing Exercise 7-4.

Exercise 7-4

Use AdventureWorks2008 to complete this exercise. You can find the solutions in the appendix.

1. Write a statement that attempts to insert a duplicate row into the `HumanResources.Department` table. Use the `@@ERROR` function to display the error.
2. Change the code you wrote in question 1 to use `TRY…CATCH`. Display the error number, message, and severity.
3. Change the code you wrote in question 2 to raise a custom error message instead of the actual error message.

Temporary Tables and Table Variables

Temporary, or *temp*, tables and table variables allow you to save data in short-lived table structures that you can use in your scripts. For example, you may need to save the results of complicated calculations for further processing. The use of temp tables and table variables is controversial. You can find many articles and newsgroup discussions stating that no one should ever use these structures. In my opinion, temp tables and table variables are just more tools that you can use if you need them. I have found that they often allow me to break extremely complicated queries into smaller, more manageable pieces, sometimes with better performance.

Creating Local Temp Tables

Temp tables look and behave just like regular tables except that they live in the tempdb database instead of a user database like AdventureWorks2008. The tempdb database is one of the system databases required for SQL Server. SQL Server also uses tempdb as a work area for sorting and other behind-the-scene tasks.

To create a local temp table, preface the table name with the number sign (#). Only the connection in which the table was created can see a local temp table. Chapter 8 covers creating tables with the `CREATE TABLE` command, but you have learned how to use the `SELECT INTO` syntax to create a table. You have also typed in numerous `CREATE TABLE` statements to create work tables for examples and exercises in Chapter 6. Here is the minimum syntax to create a local temp table using the `CREATE TABLE` command:

```
CREATE TABLE #tableName (<col1> <data type>,<col2> <data type>)
```

Temp tables can have anything that a regular table has such as primary keys, defaults, and indexes. Type in and execute the code from Listing 7-20 to learn how to create a temp table.

Listing 7-20. Creating and Populating Local Temp Table

```
USE AdventureWorks2008;
GO
CREATE TABLE #myCustomers(CustomerID INT, FirstName VARCHAR(25),
    LastName VARCHAR(25));
GO

INSERT INTO #myCustomers(CustomerID,FirstName,LastName)
SELECT C.CustomerID, FirstName,LastName
FROM Person.Person AS P INNER JOIN Sales.Customer AS C
ON P.BusinessEntityID = C.PersonID;

SELECT CustomerID, FirstName, LastName
FROM #myCustomers;

DROP TABLE #myCustomers;
```

Figure 7-20 shows the results. The code first uses the **CREATE TABLE** command to create the table, **#myCustomers**. This example is very simple. The command could define a primary key, **CustomerID**, and define that the **FirstName** and **LastName** columns should not contain **NULL** values. The script could include an **ALTER TABLE** command to add an index. The script populates the table with a regular insert statement, inserting the rows from a join on two tables. The **SELECT** statement looks like any other **SELECT** statement. Finally, the **DROP TABLE** command destroys the table. Even though the table will drop automatically when the connection closes, it is a good practice to drop temp tables when you are done using them.

	CustomerID	FirstName	LastName
1	29485	Catherine	Abel
2	29486	Kim	Abercrombie
3	29487	Humberto	Acevedo
4	29484	Gustavo	Achong
5	29488	Pilar	Ackerman
6	28866	Aaron	Adams
7	13323	Adam	Adams
8	21139	Alex	Adams

Figure 7-20. The partial results of creating and populating a temp table

Creating Global Temp Tables

You can create two kinds of temp tables: local and global. When creating a local temp table, you can access the table only within the connection where it was created. When the connection closes, the database engine destroys the temp table. When creating a global temp table, any connection can see the table. When the last connection to the temp table closes, the database engine destroys the temp table.

Global temp tables begin with two number signs. Type in and execute the code from Listing 7-21 to learn how to create a global temp table. Do not close the query window once you are done.

Listing 7-21. Creating and Populating a Global Temp Table

```
USE AdventureWorks2008;
GO
CREATE TABLE ##myCustomers(CustomerID INT, FirstName VARCHAR(25),
    LastName VARCHAR(25));
GO

INSERT INTO ##myCustomers(CustomerID,FirstName,LastName)
SELECT C.CustomerID, FirstName,LastName
FROM Person.Person AS P INNER JOIN Sales.Customer AS C
ON P.BusinessEntityID = C.PersonID;

SELECT CustomerID, FirstName, LastName
FROM ##myCustomers;

--Run the drop statement when you are done
--DROP TABLE ##myCustomers;
```

By using two number signs (##) in the name, you create a global temp table. Open another query window, and type the same **SELECT** statement to see that you can access the table from another connection. The results will look the same as Figure 7-20. Be sure to drop temp tables, especially global temp tables, when you no longer need them.

You will not find many reasons to use global temp tables. For example, suppose that an application creates a global temp table. If another user runs the same code to create the global temp table with the same name while the first temp table exists, an error will occur. I have actually seen this error happen in a commercially available application!

Creating Table Variables

Table variables became available in SQL Server 2000. At that time, many T-SQL developers decided they should always use table variables instead of temp tables because of a myth about them. Many developers believe that table variables exist in memory instead of tempdb, but that is not the case. Table variables do live in tempdb. Here is the syntax for creating a table variable:

```
DECLARE @tableName TABLE (<col1> <data type>,<col2> <data type>)
```

Because a table variable is a variable, it follows the same scoping rules as other variables. Table variables go out of scope at the end of the batch, not when the connection closes, and you cannot perform an **ALTER TABLE** command to give the table variable nonclustered indexes or make any changes to the definition of a table variable once it is declared. Table variables are fine for small tables that you will not need after running the batch. Temp tables are the better choice for tables with large numbers of rows that could benefit from nonclustered indexes or when you need to use the table after the batch is done. Type in and execute Listing 7-22 to learn how to use a table variable.

Listing 7-22. Creating and Populating Table Variable

```
USE AdventureWorks2008;

DECLARE @myCustomers TABLE (CustomerID INT, FirstName VARCHAR(25),
    LastName VARCHAR(25))

INSERT INTO @myCustomers(CustomerID,FirstName,LastName)
SELECT C.CustomerID, FirstName,LastName
FROM Person.Person AS P INNER JOIN Sales.Customer AS C
ON P.BusinessEntityID = C.PersonID;

SELECT CustomerID, FirstName, LastName
FROM @myCustomers;
```

The results are identical to those in Figure 7-20. Again, if you need to save a very large number of rows temporarily, you may find that a temporary table is a better choice. Another reason you might want to use a temp table is that you can create it with a **SELECT INTO** statement, which is not possible with a table variable. The advantage of a **SELECT INTO** is that you do not need to know the column names and data types up front. See the "Creating and Populating a Table in One Statement" section in Chapter 6 for more information.

Using a Temp Table or Table Variable

You may be wondering why you might need to use a temporary table. For example, in the human resources system database where I work, most of the tables have history and future rows. The tables have effective dates and effective sequences. The effective sequences determine the valid row for a given date for a given employee. Instead of figuring out the effective date and effective sequence for each employee over and over in my scripts, I create a temporary table to hold that information.

Another way I use temp tables is to store a list of values for filtering queries. For example, suppose a user can select one value or more values to filter a report. The reporting application sends a comma-delimited list of values to a stored procedure. You can add each value from the comma-delimited list to a temp table or table variable and then use that table to filter the report results. You will learn about stored procedures in Chapter 8. Listing 7-23 shows how to use a table variable populated from a list of values. Type in and execute the code.

Listing 7-23. Using a Temp Table to Solve a Query Problem

```
USE AdventureWorks2008;
GO
```

```
--1
DECLARE @IDTable TABLE (ID INT);
DECLARE @IDList VARCHAR(2000);
DECLARE @ID INT;
DECLARE @Loc INT;

--2
SET @IDList = '16496,12506,11390,10798,2191,11235,10879,15040,3086';

--3
SET @Loc = CHARINDEX(',',@IDList);
--4
WHILE @Loc > 0 BEGIN
    --4.1
    SET @ID = LEFT(@IDList,@Loc-1);
    --4.2
    SET @IDList = SUBSTRING(@IDList,@Loc +1,2000);
    --4.3
    INSERT INTO @IDTable(ID)
    VALUES (@ID);
    --4.4
    SET @Loc = CHARINDEX(',',@IDList);
END;
--5
IF LEN(@IDList) > 0 BEGIN
    SET @ID = @IDList;
    INSERT INTO @IDTable(ID)
    VALUES (@ID);
END;

--6
SELECT BusinessEntityID, FirstName, LastName
FROM Person.Person AS p
INNER JOIN @IDTable ON p.BusinessEntityID = ID;
```

Figure 7-21 shows the results. Code section 1 declares four variables: **@IDTable**, which is a table variable; **@IDList** to hold the comma-delimited list sent from the application; **@ID** to hold one individual value from the list; and **@Loc** to hold the location of the comma. Statement 2 sets the value of **@IDList**, which represents the list of values sent by the application.

	BusinessEntityID	FirstName	LastName
1	16496	Gabriel	Mitchell
2	12506	Alejandro	Liang
3	11390	Christy	Tang
4	10798	Katherine	Smith
5	2191	Alfredo	Fuentes Espinosa
6	11235	Isabella	Martin
7	10879	Jenna	Hall
8	15040	Eduardo	Bell
9	3086	Stephanie	Ward

Figure 7-21. *The results of using a table variable*

The code finds each ID value from the comma-delimited string and stores the value in the table variable. Statement 3 finds the location of the first comma in the list and stores the location in **@Loc**. Code section 4 is a **WHILE** loop. Inside the **WHILE** loop, statement 4.1 stores the first value in the **@ID** variable, and statement 4.2 removes that value along with the comma from **@IDList** based on the value of **@Loc**. Statement 4.3 inserts the value stored in **@ID** into the table variable, **@IDTable**. Finally, at the bottom of the loop, statement 4.4 locates the next comma, resetting the value of **@Loc**. The loop continues as long as the code continues to find a comma in **@IDList**. Once the loop completes, the last value is most likely still in **@IDList**. Code section 5 checks the length of **@IDList** and inserts the last value into the table variable. Query 6 joins the **@IDTable** to the **Person.Person** table, effectively using **@IDTable** as a filter.

Using a Temp Table or Table Variable as an Array

An *array* is a collection of values used in many programming languages. T-SQL does not have an array structure, but programmers sometimes use temp tables or table variables as arrays. I often use this method in my administrative scripts to perform a backup or check the space used on each database on a server, for example. Listing 7-24 demonstrates how you might use a table variable as an array. Type in and execute the code to learn how to use this technique.

Listing 7-24. *Using an "Array"*

```
--1
SET NOCOUNT ON;
GO
```

```
--2
DECLARE @IDTable TABLE(ArrayIndex INT NOT NULL IDENTITY,
    ID INT);
DECLARE @RowCount INT;
DECLARE @ID INT;
DECLARE @Count INT = 1;

--3
INSERT INTO @IDTable(ID)
VALUES(500),(333),(200),(999);

--4
SELECT @RowCount = COUNT(*)
FROM @IDTable;

--5
WHILE @Count <= @RowCount BEGIN
    --5.1
    SELECT @ID = ID
    FROM @IDTable
    WHERE ArrayIndex = @Count;
    --5.2
    PRINT CAST(@COUNT AS VARCHAR) + ': ' + CAST(@ID AS VARCHAR);
    --5.3
    SET @Count += 1;
END;
```

Figure 7-22 shows the results. Statement 1 sets the **NOCOUNT** property to **ON**. This will remove the messages showing how many each statement affects. In this case, the messages just get in the way. Code section 2 declares the variables used in this example. The table variable, **@IDTable**, contains an identity column called **ArrayIndex**. See Chapter 6 for more information about identity columns. Statement 3 populates **@IDTable** with several values. Since the database engine populates the **INDEX** column automatically, you now have a two-dimensional "array." Statement 4 populates the **@RowCount** variable with the number of rows in **@IDTable**. Code section 5 is a **WHILE** loop that runs once for each row in **@IDTable**. During each iteration of the loop, statement 5.1 sets the value of **@ID** with the **ID** column from **@IDTable** corresponding to the **ArrayIndex** column matching **@Count**. Statement 5.2 prints the **@Count** and **@ID** values, but you could do whatever you need to do instead of just printing the values. Statement 5.3 increments the **@Count**.

Figure 7-22. The results of using an "array"

Temp tables and table variables are just more tools in your T-SQL tool belt, but use them wisely.

Using a Cursor

Another way to loop through a result set is by using a cursor. This is a very controversial topic, especially for beginners. Developers frequently overuse cursors and end up writing poorly performing code. I'll cover cursors so that you are familiar with them and so that you understand the example in the "Thinking About Performance" section. Type in and execute the code from Listing 7-25, which shows a simple example.

Listing 7-25. Using a Cursor

```
USE AdventureWorks2008;
GO


--1
DECLARE @ProductID INT;
DECLARE @Name NVARCHAR(25);


--2
DECLARE products CURSOR FAST_FORWARD FOR
    SELECT ProductID, Name
    FROM Production.Product;


--3
OPEN products;


--4
FETCH NEXT FROM products INTO @ProductID, @Name;
```

```
--5
WHILE @@FETCH_STATUS = 0 BEGIN
    --5.1
    PRINT @ProductID;
    PRINT @Name;
    --5.2
    FETCH NEXT FROM products INTO @ProductID, @Name;
END

--6
CLOSE products;
DEALLOCATE products;
```

Figure 7-23 shows the results. Code section 1 declares variables that will be used later in the code. Statement 2 declares the cursor. The cursor must have a name and a **SELECT** statement. I included the option **FAST_FORWARD** to improve the performance. See Books Online if you are interested in learning more about cursor options. Statement 3 opens the cursor so that it is ready for access. Statement 4 reads the first row from the cursor into the variables. There must be one variable for each column selected in the cursor definition. The **WHILE** loop checks the status of the last read of the cursor. As long as the value is zero, the loop continues. Section 5.1 prints out the variables, but you could do anything you need to do at this point. Statement 5.2 is very important; it reads the next row. Without statement 5.2, the **WHILE** loop would continue indefinitely. Finally, section 6 cleans up the cursor. Cursors are another tool at your disposal, but use them only when another better-performing option is not available. Developers often use cursors to update one row at a time, which is usually a very bad idea.

Figure 7-23. *The partial results of using a cursor*

Complete Exercise 7-5 to practice what you have learned about temporary tables and table variables.

Exercise 7-5

Use the AdventureWorks2008 database to complete this exercise. You can find the solutions in the appendix.

1. Create a temp table called `#CustomerInfo` that contains `CustomerID`, `FirstName`, and `LastName` columns. Include `CountOfSales` and `SumOfTotalDue` columns. Populate the table with a query using the `Sales.Customer`, `Person.Person`, and `Sales.SalesOrderHeader` tables.
2. Change the code written in question 1 to use a table variable instead of a temp table.
3. Create a table variable with two integer columns, one of them an `IDENTITY` column. Use a `WHILE` loop to populate the table with 1,000 random integers using the following formula. Use a second `WHILE` loop to print the values from the table variable one by one.

```
CAST(RAND() * 10000 AS INT) + 1
```

Thinking About Performance

This chapter focuses on the logic features available T-SQL instead of retrieving or updating data. Depending on the task at hand, you may or may not need to use this functionality. In my job, I often write or support very complex T-SQL scripts that run once each night. The performance of these scripts is not as critical as that of the performance of T-SQL code in an application or a report, but over time I have rewritten several to perform better. For example, a programmer from one of our software vendors wrote a custom program for us that created a denormalized table of information from our financial system. That table is needed by many other systems in the enterprise. The program as originally written took more than an hour to run. Luckily, I had the original source code and found that the program populated this table one row and one column at a time. I was able to rewrite the program with a T-SQL script that ran in less than five minutes by using a set-based approach and inserting or updating all the rows at once from each source table instead of one row at a time.

The following example compares two ways to solve a typical problem. The first uses a cursor solution and the second a set-based approach. The requirements are to calculate sales totals by order year, order month, and `TerritoryID`. The report must also show the total sales for the previous month in the same row. Every territory, year, and month possible must appear on the report even if there are no sales for a particular combination. To save typing, you might want to download the code from this book's page at `http://www.apress.com`. Listing 7-26 uses a cursor and two nested `WHILE` loops to create a temp table with the totals. On my laptop, the code took 19 seconds to run.

Listing 7-26. Using a Cursor to Populate a Report

```
USE AdventureWorks2008;
GO

DECLARE @Year INT;
DECLARE @Month INT;
DECLARE @TerritoryID INT;
DECLARE @Total MONEY;
```

```
DECLARE @PreviousTotal MONEY;
DECLARE @FirstYear INT;
DECLARE @LastYear INT;
DECLARE @BeginDate DATETIME;
DECLARE @EndDate DATETIME;

CREATE TABLE #Totals(OrderYear INT, OrderMonth INT,
    TerritoryID INT, TotalSales MONEY,
    PreviousSales MONEY);

SELECT @FirstYear = MIN(YEAR(OrderDate)),
    @LastYear = MAX(YEAR(OrderDate))
FROM Sales.SalesOrderHeader;

DECLARE Territory CURSOR FAST_FORWARD FOR
    SELECT TerritoryID
    FROM Sales.SalesTerritory;

OPEN Territory;
FETCH NEXT FROM Territory INTO @TerritoryID;
WHILE @@FETCH_STATUS = 0 BEGIN
    SET @Year = @FirstYear;

    WHILE @Year <= @LastYear BEGIN
        SET @Month = 1;
        WHILE @Month <= 12 BEGIN
            SET @BeginDate = CAST(@Year AS VARCHAR) + '/' +
                CAST(@Month AS VARCHAR) + '/1';
            SET @EndDate = DATEADD(M,1,@BeginDate);
            SET @Total = 0;
            SELECT @Total = SUM(LineTotal)
            FROM Sales.SalesOrderDetail AS SOD
            INNER JOIN Sales.SalesOrderHeader AS SOH
            ON SOD.SalesOrderID = SOH.SalesOrderID
            WHERE TerritoryID = @TerritoryID
                AND OrderDate >= @BeginDate AND OrderDate < @EndDate;

            SET @PreviousTotal = 0;
            SET @EndDate = @BeginDate;
            SET @BeginDate = DATEADD(M,-1,@BeginDate);
```

```
SELECT @PreviousTotal = SUM(LineTotal)
            FROM Sales.SalesOrderDetail AS SOD
            INNER JOIN Sales.SalesOrderHeader AS SOH
            ON SOD.SalesOrderID = SOH.SalesOrderID
            WHERE TerritoryID = @TerritoryID
                AND OrderDate >= @BeginDate AND OrderDate < @EndDate;

            INSERT INTO #Totals(TerritoryID, OrderYear,
            OrderMonth,TotalSales, PreviousSales)
            SELECT @TerritoryID, @Year, @Month,
            ISNULL(@Total,0), ISNULL(@PreviousTotal,0);

            SET @Month +=1;
        END; -- Month loop
        SET @Year += 1;
    END; -- Year Loop
    FETCH NEXT FROM Territory INTO @TerritoryID;
END; -- Territory cursor
CLOSE Territory;
DEALLOCATE Territory;

SELECT OrderYear, OrderMonth, TerritoryID,
    TotalSales, PreviousSales
FROM #Totals
ORDER BY OrderYear, OrderMonth, TerritoryID;

SELECT OrderYear, OrderMonth, TerritoryID,
    TotalSales, PreviousSales
FROM #Totals
WHERE TerritoryID = 1 AND TotalSales <> 0 AND PreviousSales <> 0
ORDER BY OrderYear, OrderMonth;

DROP TABLE #Totals;
```

The code in Listing 7-26 uses a cursor-based approach to populate a temp table for the report. The code creates a cursor that loops through the **TerritoryID** values. Inside the cursor loop, a **WHILE** loop of months is nested inside a **WHILE** loop of possible years. The code performs the calculations and inserts a row within the innermost loop. Finally, after the loops complete, two **SELECT** statements display the results. This code actually performs better than other code I have seen. It is not unusual to see code that not only loops through the territories but also loops through all the sales. Now try the example in Listing 7-27, which produces the same results much faster, in about 1 second on my laptop.

Listing 7-27. Populating a Report with a Set-Based Approach

```
USE AdventureWorks2008;
GO


--1
CREATE TABLE #Totals(TerritoryID INT, OrderYear INT, OrderMonth INT,
    TotalSales MONEY, PreviousSales MONEY
    );


--2
CREATE TABLE #SalesMonths(MonthNo INT);


--3
INSERT INTO #SalesMonths(MonthNo)
VALUES (1),(2),(3),(4),(5),(6),(7),(8),(9),(10),(11),(12);


--4
WITH SalesYears AS (
    SELECT YEAR(OrderDate) AS OrderYear
    FROM Sales.SalesOrderHeader
    GROUP BY YEAR(OrderDate)
    )
INSERT INTO #Totals(OrderYear, OrderMonth, TerritoryID,
    TotalSales, PreviousSales)
SELECT OrderYear, MonthNo,TerritoryID, 0 AS TotalSales,0 AS PreviousSales
FROM SalesYears, Sales.SalesTerritory, #SalesMonths
ORDER BY OrderYear, MonthNo, TerritoryID;


--5
WITH Totals AS (
    SELECT SUM(LineTotal) AS TotalSales,
        YEAR(OrderDate) AS OrderYear,
        MONTH(OrderDate) AS OrderMonth, TerritoryID
    FROM Sales.SalesOrderDetail AS SOD
    INNER JOIN Sales.SalesOrderHeader AS SOH
        ON SOD.SalesOrderID = SOH.SalesOrderID
    GROUP BY YEAR(OrderDate), MONTH(OrderDate), TerritoryID
)
UPDATE #Totals SET TotalSales = Totals.TotalSales
FROM #Totals INNER JOIN Totals ON #Totals.OrderYear = Totals.OrderYear
   AND #Totals.OrderMonth = Totals.OrderMonth
   AND #Totals.TerritoryID = Totals.TerritoryID;
```

```
--6
WITH Totals AS (
    SELECT SUM(LineTotal) AS TotalSales,
        YEAR(DATEADD(M,1,OrderDate)) AS OrderYear,
        MONTH(DATEADD(M,1,OrderDate)) AS OrderMonth, TerritoryID
    FROM Sales.SalesOrderDetail AS SOD
    INNER JOIN Sales.SalesOrderHeader AS SOH
        ON SOD.SalesOrderID = SOH.SalesOrderID
    GROUP BY YEAR(DATEADD(M,1,OrderDate)),
            MONTH(DATEADD(M,1,OrderDate)), TerritoryID
)
UPDATE #Totals SET PreviousSales = Totals.TotalSales
FROM #Totals INNER JOIN Totals ON #Totals.OrderYear = Totals.OrderYear
    AND #Totals.OrderMonth = Totals.OrderMonth
    AND #Totals.TerritoryID = Totals.TerritoryID;


--7
SELECT OrderYear, OrderMonth, TerritoryID,
    TotalSales, PreviousSales
FROM #Totals
ORDER BY OrderYear, OrderMonth, TerritoryID;


--8
SELECT OrderYear, OrderMonth, TerritoryID,
    TotalSales, PreviousSales
FROM #Totals
WHERE TerritoryID = 1 AND TotalSales <> 0 AND PreviousSales <> 0
ORDER BY OrderYear, OrderMonth;
DROP TABLE #Totals;
DROP TABLE #SalesMonths;
```

Figure 7-24 shows the results of Listing 7-27. Statement 1 creates a temp table to hold the results. Statement 2 creates a temp table, **#SalesMonths**. Statement 3 populates the **#SalesMonths** table with the numbers 1 through 12. Statement 4 contains a CTE, **SalesYears**, listing all the unique years in the **Sales.SalesOrderHeader** table. The **SELECT** statement in statement 4 joins the **SalesYears**, **#SalesMonths**, and **Sales.SalesTerritory** tables in a Cartesian product that inserts every possible combination into a temp table, **#Totals**. It fills in zeros for the **TotalSales** and **PreviousSales** columns. Statement 5 updates the **TotalSales** column of the **#Totals** table with the sum of the **LineTotal** column. Statement 6 updates the **PreviousSales** column of the **#Totals** table. Statement 7 displays all the rows in the **#Totals** table. Statement 8 displays a subset of the rows that actually have some sales.

	ProductID	OrderYear	OrderMonth	TerritoryID	TotalSales	PreviousSales
1	1	2001	1	1	0.00	0.00
2	1	2001	1	2	0.00	0.00
3	1	2001	1	3	0.00	0.00
4	1	2001	1	4	0.00	0.00
5	1	2001	1	5	0.00	0.00
6	1	2001	1	6	0.00	0.00
7	1	2001	1	7	0.00	0.00
8	1	2001	1	8	0.00	0.00

	ProductID	OrderYear	OrderMonth	TerritoryID	TotalSales	PreviousSales
1	707	2001	8	1	141.3055	80.746
2	707	2001	9	1	100.9325	141.3055
3	707	2001	10	1	100.9325	100.9325
4	707	2001	11	1	322.984	100.9325
5	707	2001	12	1	262.4245	322.984
6	707	2002	3	1	80.746	60.5595
7	707	2002	4	1	60.5595	80.746
8	707	2002	5	1	282.611	60.5595

Figure 7-24. *The partial results of the set-based approach*

The point of this example is to show that most of the time a set-based approach can be found and is more efficient. It may take more practice and experience before you can come up with this solution, but the more you work with T-SQL, the better you will get.

Summary

If you learn how to write programs in any programming language, you will probably find the second or third language even easier to learn because the logic is the same. You will generally have ways to execute or avoid executing lines of code based on certain criteria. You will have ways to repeatedly execute lines code of code by looping. Whether or not you decide to implement this logic in T-SQL scripts will depend on the design of your application, the standards in your shop, or your personal preferences.

This chapter covered using variables, conditional logic, looping, and temporary table structures. In Chapter 8, you will use what you have learned in this chapter as you create stored procedures, user-defined functions, and more.

CHAPTER 8

■ ■ ■

Moving Logic to the Database

So far, you have worked exclusively with tables by using Data Manipulation Language (DML) statements. You have learned to manipulate data by inserting new rows and updating or deleting existing rows. You can use many other objects in a SQL Server database to make your database applications more efficient and secure. This chapter teaches you how add restrictions to tables and to create these other objects by using In this chapter, you will Data Definition Language (DDL) statements. learn about constraints on tables, views, stored procedures, user-defined functions, and user-defined types. You will also learn about triggers, special objects that fire when data is modified. Because SQL Server provides so many options for creating these objects, this chapter does not explore every possible one. The chapter does, however, provide enough detail to teach you most of what you will encounter as you become an expert T-SQL developer.

Tables

SQL Server and other database systems store data in tables. You have learned how to retrieve data from tables as well as insert, update, and delete data. Specifically, you learned how to create temporary tables in Chapter 7 and saw how to create tables using the **SELECT INTO** and **CREATE TABLE** syntax in Chapter 6. You might think of a table as just a way to store data, but you can also enforce some business rules based on constraints built into the table definition.

As a beginning T-SQL developer, you will most likely write T-SQL code against a database already in place, possibly from a software vendor or one created by a design team using data-modeling software to create the tables. Although your job description may not include writing scripts to create tables, you do need to understand how the table definition controls what data you can insert into a table and how you can update the data. This section covers many options available when creating or altering tables such as calculated columns, primary keys, foreign keys, and other constraints. The point of this section is not to get you to memorize how to add keys and constraints but to understand the implications of having them in place.

■ **Tip** By using SQL Server Management Studio, you can script the commands to create existing tables and other objects in the database. This is a great way to help you write scripts or to help you learn the syntax. To script the definition, right-click the object, and select the "Script table as" menu.

Adding Check Constraints to a Table

As you know, each column in a table must have a specific data type and usually a maximum size that controls what data can be inserted or updated and whether a column may contain NULL values. For example, you cannot add a non-numeric string to an INT column. It is also possible to further control what data you can add by defining check constraints. For example, you may want to restrict the values of a column to a particular range of values.

■ **Note** The NULL and NOT NULL options are also called *constraints*.

Here is the syntax to add a check constraint to a table when creating the table and later with an ALTER TABLE command:

```
--Adding during CREATE TABLE
CREATE TABLE <table name> (<col1> <data type>,<col2> <data type>,
    CONSTRAINT <constraint name> CHECK (<condition>))

--Adding during ALTER TABLE
CREATE TABLE <table name> (<col1> <data type>, <col2> <data type>)
ALTER TABLE <table name> ADD CONSTRAINT <constraint name> CHECK (<condition>)
```

The condition looks much like the criteria in a WHERE clause. Type in and execute the code in Listing 8-1 to learn how to add a constraint.

Listing 8-1. Adding a Check Constraint

```
USE tempdb;
GO
--1
IF OBJECT_ID('table1') IS NOT NULL BEGIN
    DROP TABLE table1;
END;

--2
CREATE TABLE table1 (col1 SMALLINT, col2 VARCHAR(20),
    CONSTRAINT ch_table1_col2_months
    CHECK (col2 IN ('January','February','March','April','May',
        'June','July','August','September','October',
        'November','December')
    )
);
```

```
--3
ALTER TABLE table1 ADD CONSTRAINT ch_table1_col1
    CHECK (col1 BETWEEN 1 and 12);

PRINT 'Janary';
--4
INSERT INTO table1 (col1,col2)
VALUES (1,'Janary');

PRINT 'February';
--5
INSERT INTO table1 (col1,col2)
VALUES (2,'February');

PRINT 'March';
--6
INSERT INTO table1 (col1,col2)
VALUES (13,'March');

PRINT 'Change 2 to 20';
--7
UPDATE table1 SET col1 = 20;
```

Figure 8-1 shows the results. Code section 1 drops the table in case it already exists. Statement 2 creates **table1** along with a constraint specifying that the exact months of the year may be entered into **col2**. Statement 3 adds another constraint to the table, specifying values for **col1**. Statements 4 to 6 insert new rows into **table1**. Only statement 5 succeeds because the values in 4 and 6 each violate one of the constraints. If the constraints had not been added to the table, these inserts would have worked. Statement 7 attempts to update the one successful row with an invalid **col1**. You can see all the error messages in Figure 8-1.

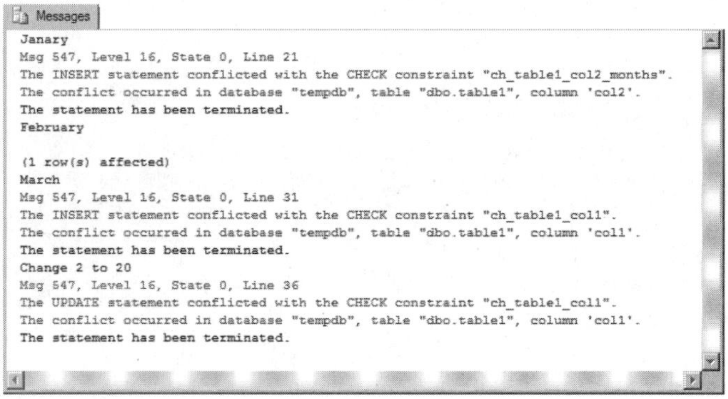

Figure 8-1. The results of attempting to violate check constraints

Adding UNIQUE Constraints

You can specify that a column or columns in a table contain unique values. Unlike primary keys, which you will learn more about in the next section, unique columns may contain one **NULL** value. In the case of multiple columns, you must decide whether to have a constraint on each column or a constraint that covers several columns. In the first case, each column value must be unique; in the second case, the combination of the column values must be unique. You can add **UNIQUE** constraints to tables when you create them or later with an **ALTER TABLE** statement. Here is the syntax:

```
--Adding individual constraints
CREATE TABLE <table name> (<col1> <data type> UNIQUE, <col2> <data type> UNIQUE)

--Adding a combination constraint
CREATE TABLE <table name> (<col1> <data type>, <col2> <data type>,
    CONSTRAINT <constraint name> UNIQUE (<col1>,<col2>))

--Add a constraint with ALTER TABLE
CREATE TABLE <table name> (<col1> <data type>, <col2> <data type>)
ALTER TABLE ADD CONSTRAINT <constraint name> UNIQUE (<col1>,<col2>)
```

The first syntax example creates a separate constraint on each column within the **CREATE TABLE** statement. The other two examples each create one constraint on a combination of the columns. If you do not specify a constraint name as in the first syntax example, SQL Server will come up with a name for you. Listing 8-2 contains example code showing how to create **UNIQUE** constraints. Type in and execute the code to learn more.

Listing 8-2. Creating Tables with UNIQUE Constraints

```
USE tempdb;
GO
--1
IF OBJECT_ID('table1') IS NOT NULL BEGIN
    DROP TABLE table1;
END;

--2
CREATE TABLE table1 (col1 INT UNIQUE,
    col2 VARCHAR(20), col3 DATETIME);
GO

--3
ALTER TABLE table1 ADD CONSTRAINT
    unq_table1_col2_col3 UNIQUE (col2,col3);
```

```
--4
PRINT 'Statement 4'
INSERT INTO table1(col1,col2,col3)
VALUES (1,2,'1/1/2009'),(2,2,'1/2/2009');

--5
PRINT 'Statement 5'
INSERT INTO table1(col1,col2,col3)
VALUES (3,2,'1/1/2009');

--6
PRINT 'Statement 6'
INSERT INTO table1(col1,col2,col3)
VALUES (1,2,'1/2/2009');

--7
PRINT 'Statement 7'
UPDATE table1 SET col3 = '1/2/2009'
WHERE col1 = 1;
```

Figure 8-2 shows the results. Code section 1 drops the table in case it already exists. Statement 2 creates **table1** with three columns. It creates a **UNIQUE** constraint on **col1**. Statement 3 adds another **UNIQUE** constraint on the combination of columns **col2** and **col3**. Statement 4 adds two rows to the table successfully. Statement 5 violates the constraint on **col2** and **col3**. Statement 6 violates the constraint on **col1**. Statement 7 violates the constraint on **col2** and **col3** with an **UPDATE** to the table.

```
Messages
 Statement 4

 (2 row(s) affected)
 Statement 5
 Msg 2627, Level 14, State 1, Line 21
 Violation of UNIQUE KEY constraint 'unq_table1_col2_col3'.
 Cannot insert duplicate key in object 'dbo.table1'.
 The statement has been terminated.
 Statement 6
 Msg 2627, Level 14, State 1, Line 26
 Violation of UNIQUE KEY constraint 'UQ__table1__357D0D3F6DCC4D03'.
 Cannot insert duplicate key in object 'dbo.table1'.
 The statement has been terminated.
 Statement 7
 Msg 2627, Level 14, State 1, Line 31
 Violation of UNIQUE KEY constraint 'unq_table1_col2_col3'.
 Cannot insert duplicate key in object 'dbo.table1'.
 The statement has been terminated.
```

Figure 8-2. *The results of adding UNIQUE constraints*

Another interesting thing about **UNIQUE** constraints is that you will not see them in the Constraints section in SQL Server Management Studio. Instead, you will find them in the Indexes

273

section. When creating a unique constraint, you are actually creating a unique index. Figure 8-3 shows the constraints, as indexes, added to **table1**.

```
☐ ▦ dbo.table1
   ⊞ 📁 Columns
   ⊞ 📁 Keys
      📁 Constraints
   ⊞ 📁 Triggers
   ☐ 📁 Indexes
        🔑 unq_table1_col2_col3 (Unique, Non-Clustered)
        🔑 UQ__table1__357D0D3F6DCC4D03 (Unique, Non-Clustered)
   ⊞ 📁 Statistics
```

Figure 8-3. *The unique constraints defined on* **table1** *are indexes.*

Adding a Primary Key to a Table

Throughout this book, you have read about primary keys. You can use a primary key to uniquely define a row in a table. A primary key must have these characteristics:

- A primary key may be made of one column or multiple columns, called a *composite key*.
- A table can have only one primary key.
- The values of a primary key must be unique.
- If the primary key is a composite key, the combination of the values must be unique.
- None of the columns making up a primary key can contain **NULL** values.

I once received a call from a developer asking me to remove the primary key from a table because it was preventing him from inserting rows into a table in one of our enterprise systems. He insisted that the table definition must be wrong. I spent ten minutes explaining that the primary key was preventing him from making a mistake and helped him figure out the correct statements. After this developer moved on to another company, I received almost the identical phone call from his replacement. Primary keys and other constraints are there to ensure data consistency, not to make your job harder.

You can add a primary key to a table when you create the table using the **CREATE TABLE** statement or later by using the **ALTER TABLE** statement. Here is the syntax:

```
--Single column key
CREATE TABLE <table name> (<column1> <data type> NOT NULL PRIMARY KEY
    [CLUSTERED|NONCLUSTERED] <column2> <data type>)


--Composit key
CREATE TABLE <table name>(<column1> <data type> NOT NULL,
    <column2> <data type> NOT NULL, <column3> <data type>,
    CONSTRAINT <constraint name> PRIMARY KEY [CLUSTERED|NONCLUSTERED]
    (<column1>,<column2>)
)
```

```
--Using Alter table
CREATE TABLE <table name>(<column1> <data type> NOT NULL,
    <column2> <data type>)

ALTER TABLE <table name> ADD CONSTRAINT <primary key name>
    PRIMARY KEY [CLUSTERED|NONCLUSTERED] (<column1>)
```

Take a look at the keys and indexes of the `HumanResources.Department` table in the AdventureWorks2008 database (see Figure 8-4). When you create a primary key, the database engine automatically creates an index composed of that key. One of the indexes, `PK_Department_DepartmentID`, is also the primary key composed of the `DepartmentID` column.

```
□ □ HumanResources.Department
   ⊞ □ Columns
   □ □ Keys
        ⚷ PK_Department_DepartmentID
   ⊞ □ Constraints
   ⊞ □ Triggers
   □ □ Indexes
        ⋔ AK_Department_Name (Unique, Non-Clustered)
        ⋔ PK_Department_DepartmentID (Clustered)
   ⊞ □ Statistics
```

Figure 8-4. *The indexes of the* `HumanResources.Department` *table*

Listing 8-3 contains some examples that create tables with primary keys, either during the `CREATE` command or later with the `ALTER` command. Type in and execute the code to learn more.

Listing 8-3. *Creating Primary Keys*

```
USE tempdb;
GO

--1
IF OBJECT_ID('table1') IS NOT NULL BEGIN
    DROP TABLE table1;
END;

IF OBJECT_ID('table2') IS NOT NULL BEGIN
    DROP TABLE table2;
END;

IF OBJECT_ID('table3') IS NOT NULL BEGIN
    DROP TABLE table3;
END;
```

```
--2
CREATE TABLE table1 (col1 INT NOT NULL PRIMARY KEY,
    col2 VARCHAR(10));

--3
CREATE TABLE table2 (col1 INT NOT NULL,
    col2 VARCHAR(10) NOT NULL, col3 INT NULL,
    CONSTRAINT PK_table2_col1col2 PRIMARY KEY
    (col1, col2)
);

--4
CREATE TABLE table3 (col1 INT NOT NULL,
    col2 VARCHAR(10) NOT NULL, col3 INT NULL);

--5
ALTER TABLE table3 ADD CONSTRAINT PK_table3_col1col2
    PRIMARY KEY NONCLUSTERED (col1,col2);
```

Figure 8-5 shows the resulting tables. Code section 1 drops the tables if they already exist in the database. Statement 2 creates **table1** with a primary key made of **col1**. The code does not contain the optional keyword **CLUSTERED**. The keyword **CLUSTERED** specifies that the primary key is also a clustered index. (See Chapter 1 for more information about clustered and nonclustered indexes.) By default, if no clustered index already exists on the table, as in this case, the primary key will become a clustered index. Because the code in statement 2 did not specify the primary key constraint name, the database engine named the primary key for you.

Statement 3 creates a composite primary key composed of **col1** and **col2**. You actually do not have to specify **NOT NULL** when defining the primary key, because SQL Server will change the primary key columns to **NOT NULL** for you. I prefer to specify the **NOT NULL** constraint in the **CREATE TABLE** statement for clarity, especially if I am saving the script. Again, since there is no other clustered index, the primary key will also be a clustered index on **table2**.

Statement 4 creates **table3** without specifying a primary key. Statement 5, an **ALTER TABLE** statement, adds the primary key, in this case a nonclustered index. The primary key is often a clustered index, but that is not a requirement. You will often see the clustered index composed of a smaller column, such as an **INT** column, if the primary key contains several large columns. The reason is that the clustered index is automatically part of every other index, so having a "narrow" clustered index saves space in the database.

Figure 8-5. The tables created with primary keys

Creating Foreign Keys

You have seen how to join tables on the primary key of one table to the foreign key of another table beginning with Chapter 4. Having foreign keys defined on tables is not a requirement to join tables together, but explicitly defined foreign keys can help enforce what is called *referential integrity*. Referential integrity means that data consistency between tables is maintained. For example, no orders may exist without a valid customer for that order.

Just like primary keys, you can define a foreign key within the **CREATE TABLE** command or later in an **ALTER TABLE** statement. Here is the syntax for creating simple foreign keys:

```
--On one column in the CREATE TABLE
CREATE TABLE <table1> (<col1> <data type> FOREIGN KEY REFERENCES <table2> (<col3>))


--On two columns in the CREATE TABLE
CREATE TABLE <table1> (<col1> <data type>, <col2> <data type>,
    CONSTRAINT <foreign key name> FOREIGN KEY (<col1>,<col2>)
    REFERENCES <table2> (<col3>,<col4>))


--Adding with ALTER table
CREATE TABLE <table1> (<col1> <data type>, <col2> <data type>)
ALTER TABLE <table1> ADD CONSTRAINT <foreign key name> FOREIGN KEY (<col1>)
    REFERENCES <table2> (<col3>))
```

The table specified after **REFERENCES** is the table that the foreign key refers to. For example, if you were defining the foreign key on the orders table, **table2** would be the **customers** table. The column or columns specified after the **REFERENCES** keyword generally will be the primary key of that table. If the column or columns referred to are not the primary key, they at least have to be defined as **UNIQUE**. Type in and execute Listing 8-4, which shows a simple example.

Listing 8-4. Adding a Foreign Key

```
USE tempdb;
GO
--1
IF OBJECT_ID('table2') IS NOT NULL BEGIN
    DROP TABLE table2;
END;

IF OBJECT_ID('table1') IS NOT NULL BEGIN
    DROP TABLE table1;
END;

--2
CREATE TABLE table1 (col1 INT NOT NULL PRIMARY KEY,
    col2 VARCHAR(20), col3 DATETIME);

--3
CREATE TABLE table2 (col4 INT NULL,
    col5 VARCHAR(20) NOT NULL,
    CONSTRAINT pk_table2 PRIMARY KEY (col5),
    CONSTRAINT fk_table2_table1 FOREIGN KEY (col4) REFERENCES table1(col1)
    );
GO

--4
PRINT 'Adding to table1';
INSERT INTO table1(col1,col2,col3)
VALUES(1,'a','1/1/2009'),(2,'b','1/2/2009'),(3,'c','1/3/2009');

--5
PRINT 'Adding to table2';
INSERT INTO table2(col4,col5)
VALUES(1,'abc'),(2,'def');
```

```
--6
PRINT 'Violating foreign key with insert';
INSERT INTO table2(col4,col5)
VALUES (7,'abc');


--7
PRINT 'Violating foreign key with update';
UPDATE table2 SET col4 = 6
WHERE col4 = 1;
```

Figure 8-6 shows the results of adding the foreign key and then violating it. Code section 1 drops **table1** and **table2** if they exist. Notice that the code drops **table2** first. If the drop statements are reversed and you run the code multiple times, it will fail. **table1** may not be dropped while the foreign key pointing to it exists. To eliminate this problem, drop **table2** first.

Statement 2 creates **table1**. Statement 3 creates **table2** with the foreign key. Statement 4 adds three rows to **table1**. Statement 5 inserts two valid rows to **table2**. Any value for col4 must already exist in **col1** of **table1**. Statement 6 attempts to insert a row with the value 7. Since the value 7 does not exist in **col1** of **table1**, the statement fails. Statement 7 attempts to update an existing row with an invalid value. The statement fails because the value, 6, does not exist in **col1** of **table1**.

```
Messages

Adding to table1

(3 row(s) affected)
Adding to table2

(2 row(s) affected)
Violating foreign key with insert
Msg 547, Level 16, State 0, Line 33
The INSERT statement conflicted with the FOREIGN KEY constraint "fk_table2_table1".
The conflict occurred in database "tempdb", table "dbo.table1", column 'col1'.
The statement has been terminated.
Violating foreign key with update
Msg 547, Level 16, State 0, Line 38
The UPDATE statement conflicted with the FOREIGN KEY constraint "fk_table2_table1".
The conflict occurred in database "tempdb", table "dbo.table1", column 'col1'.
The statement has been terminated.
```

Figure 8-6. *The results of adding a foreign key*

Creating Foreign Keys with Delete and Update Rules

You saw in the previous section that foreign keys ensure that only valid values from the referenced table are used. For example, if you have an order table, only valid **CustomerID** values from the customer table may be used. You can also define what should happen if a customer with orders is deleted from the database. Will all orders also be deleted at the same time? Should SQL Server prevent the customer from being deleted? What about changing the **CustomerID** in the customer table? Will that change also change the **CustomerID** in the order table or prevent the change? You can define all that behavior within the foreign key definition. A rule may be set up for deletions and for updates. Here are the possible values:

- **CASCADE**: Applies the same action to the foreign key table
- **NO ACTION**: Prevents the deletion or update and rolls back the transaction
- **SET NULL**: Sets the value of the foreign key columns to **NULL**
- **SET DEFAULT**: Sets the value of the foreign key columns to the default values

Here is the syntax for creating foreign keys with update and delete rules:

```
CREATE TABLE <table1> (<col1> <data type>,<col2> <data type>,
    CONSTRAINT <foreign key name> FOREIGN KEY (<col1>) REFERENCES <table2> (<col3>)
    [ON DELETE [NO ACTION|CASCADE|SET NULL|SET DEFAULT]]
    [ON UPDATE [NO ACTION|CASCADE|SET NULL|SET DEFAULT]])
```

By default, the **NO ACTION** option applies if no rule is defined. In this case, if you attempt to delete a customer who has placed one or more orders, SQL Server will return an error message and roll back the transaction. To use **SET NULL**, the columns making up the foreign key must allow **NULL** values. To use **SET DEFAULT**, the columns making up the foreign key must have defaults defined. The other requirement is that the default values must be a valid value that satisfies the foreign key. Type in and execute the code in Listing 8-5 to learn how these rules work.

Listing 8-5. Using Update and Delete Rules

```
USE tempdb;
GO
--1
IF OBJECT_ID('table2') IS NOT NULL BEGIN
    DROP TABLE table2;
END;

IF OBJECT_ID('table1') IS NOT NULL BEGIN
    DROP TABLE table1;
END;

--2
CREATE TABLE table1 (col1 INT NOT NULL PRIMARY KEY,
    col2 VARCHAR(20), col3 DATETIME);

--3 default rules
PRINT 'No action by default';
CREATE TABLE table2 (col4 INT NULL DEFAULT 7,
    col5 VARCHAR(20) NOT NULL,
    CONSTRAINT pk_table2 PRIMARY KEY (col5),
    CONSTRAINT fk_table2_table1 FOREIGN KEY (col4) REFERENCES table1(col1)
    );
```

```
--4
PRINT 'Adding to table1';
INSERT INTO table1(col1,col2,col3)
VALUES(1,'a','1/1/2009'),(2,'b','1/2/2009'),(3,'c','1/3/2009'),
    (4,'d','1/4/2009'),(5,'e','1/6/2009'),(6,'g','1/7/2009'),
    (7,'g','1/8/2009');

--5
PRINT 'Adding to table2';
INSERT INTO table2(col4,col5)
VALUES(1,'abc'),(2,'def'),(3,'ghi'),
    (4,'jkl');

--6
SELECT col4, col5 FROM table2;

--7
PRINT 'Delete from table1'
DELETE FROM table1 WHERE col1 = 1;

--8
ALTER TABLE table2 DROP CONSTRAINT fk_table2_table1;

--9
PRINT 'Add CASCADE';
ALTER TABLE table2 ADD CONSTRAINT fk_table2_table1
    FOREIGN KEY (col4) REFERENCES table1(col1)
    ON DELETE CASCADE
    ON UPDATE CASCADE;

--10
PRINT 'Delete from table1';
DELETE FROM table1 WHERE col1 = 1;

--11
PRINT 'Update table1';
UPDATE table1 SET col1 = 10 WHERE col1 = 4;
```

```
--12
ALTER TABLE table2 DROP CONSTRAINT fk_table2_table1;

--13
PRINT 'Add SET NULL';
ALTER TABLE table2 ADD CONSTRAINT fk_table2_table1
    FOREIGN KEY (col4) REFERENCES table1(col1)
    ON DELETE SET NULL
    ON UPDATE SET NULL;

--14
DELETE FROM table1 WHERE col1 = 2;

--15
ALTER TABLE table2 DROP CONSTRAINT fk_table2_table1;

--16
PRINT 'Add SET DEFAULT';
ALTER TABLE table2 ADD CONSTRAINT fk_table2_table1
    FOREIGN KEY (col4) REFERENCES table1(col1)
    ON DELETE SET DEFAULT
    ON UPDATE SET DEFAULT;

--17
PRINT 'Delete from table1';
DELETE FROM table1 WHERE col1 = 3;

--18
SELECT col4, col5 FROM table2;
```

Figure 8-7 shows the information and error messages that result from running the script. Code section 1 drops **table1** and **table2** if they exist. Statement 2 creates **table1**. Statement 3 creates **table2** with a foreign key referencing **table1** with the default **NO ACTION** rules. In my experience, most of the time the default **NO ACTION** is in effect preventing updates and deletions from the referenced table, as in statement 3. Statements 4 and 5 add a few rows to the tables. Statement 7 deletes a row from table1. Since that deletion violates the foreign key rules, the statement rolls back and produces an error.

```
    Messages

No action by default
Adding to table1

(7 row(s) affected)
Adding to table2

(4 row(s) affected)
Delete from table1
Msg 547, Level 16, State 0, Line 37
The DELETE statement conflicted with the REFERENCE constraint "fk_table2_table1".
The conflict occurred in database "tempdb", table "dbo.table2", column 'col4'.
The statement has been terminated.
Add CASCADE
Delete from table1

(1 row(s) affected)
Update table1

(1 row(s) affected)
Add SET NULL

(1 row(s) affected)
Add SET DEFAULT
Delete from table1

(1 row(s) affected)
```

Figure 8-7. *The results of applying foreign key rules*

Statement 8 drops the foreign key constraint so that statement 9 can re-create the foreign key with the **CASCADE** options. Statement 10, which deletes the row from **table1** with **col1** equal to 1, succeeds. The **CASCADE** rule also automatically deletes the matching row from **table2**. (Figure 8-8 shows how **table2** looks after population and at the end of the script.) Statement 11 changes the value of **col1** in **table1** to 10 where the value is equal to 4. The **CASCADE** rule automatically updates the matching row in **table2**.

Statement 12 drops the foreign key constraint so that statement 13 can re-create the foreign key with the **SET NULL** option. Statement 14 deletes a row from table1. The **SET NULL** rule automatically changes the matching value in **table2** to **NULL**.

Statement 15 drops the foreign key constraint so that statement 16 can re-create the foreign key with the **SET DEFAULT** option. Statement 17 deletes a row from table1. The **SET DEFAULT** rule automatically changes the matching value in **table2** to the default value 7. Finally, statement 18 displays the rows after all the automatic changes. Review the script again. Except for the **INSERT** statement, the script contains no other explicit changes to the data in **table2**. The rule in effect at the time of each data change to **table1** automatically made changes to the data in **table2**.

	col4	col5
1	1	abc
2	2	def
3	3	ghi
4	4	jkl

	col4	col5
1	NULL	def
2	7	ghi
3	10	jkl

Figure 8-8. *The results of changes based on foreign key options*

Defining Automatically Populated Columns

You have seen automatically populated columns used in the "Inserting Rows into Tables with Automatically Populating Columns" section in Chapter 6. This section will show you how to define IDENTITY columns, ROWVERSION columns, COMPUTED columns, and columns with DEFAULT values. Here are the syntax examples:

```
--IDENTITY
CREATE TABLE <table name> (<col1> INT NOT NULL IDENTITY[(<seed>,<increment>)],
    <col1> <data type>)


--ROWVERSION
CREATE TABLE <table name> (<col1> <data type>,<col2> ROWVERSION)


--Calculated column
CREATE TABLE <table name> (<col1> <data type>,<col2> AS <computed column definition>
    [PERSISTED])


--Default column
CREATE TABLE <table name> (<col1> <data type> DEFAULT <default value or function>)
```

Several rules apply to using these column types:

- A table may contain only one IDENTITY column
- By default, IDENTITY columns begin with the value 1 and increment by 1. You can specify different values by specifying seed and increment values.
- You may not insert values into IDENTITY columns unless the IDENTITY_INSERT setting is turned on for the table and session.
- A table may contain only one ROWVERSION column.
- The ROWVERSION value will be unique within the database.
- You may not insert values into ROWVERSION columns.
- Each time you update the row, the ROWVERSION value changes.
- A table may contain multiple COMPUTED columns.
- Do not specify a data type for COMPUTED columns.
- You may not insert values into COMPUTED columns.
- By specifying the option PERSISTED, the database engine stores the value in the table.
- You can define indexes on PERSISTED COMPUTED columns.
- You can specify other non-COMPUTED columns, literal values, and scalar functions in the COMPUTED column definition.
- You do not need to specify a value for a column with a DEFAULT value defined.
- You can use expressions with literal values and scalar functions, but not other column names with DEFAULT value columns.

- If a value is specified for a column with a DEFAULT, the specified value applies.
- If a column with a DEFAULT value specified allows NULL values, you can still specify NULL for the column.

Listing 8-6 demonstrates creating and populating tables with these automatically populating columns. Type in and execute the code to learn more.

Listing 8-6. Defining Tables with Automatically Populating Columns

```
USE tempdb;
GO


--1
IF OBJECT_ID('table3') IS NOT NULL BEGIN
    DROP TABLE table3;
END;


--2
CREATE TABLE table3 (col1 VARCHAR(10),
    idCol INT NOT NULL IDENTITY,
    rvCol ROWVERSION,
    defCol DATETIME2 DEFAULT GETDATE(),
    calcCol1 AS DATEADD(m,1,defCol),
    calcCol2 AS col1 + ':' + col1 PERSISTED);
GO


--3
INSERT INTO table3 (col1)
VALUES ('a'), ('b'), ('c'), ('d'), ('e'), ('g');


--4
INSERT INTO table3 (col1, defCol)
VALUES ('h', NULL),('i','1/1/2009');


--5
SELECT col1, idCol, rvCol, defCol, calcCol1, calcCol2
FROM table3;
```

Figure 8-9 shows the results. Statement 1 drops **table3** if it exists. Statement 2 creates **table3** with one regular column, **col1**, and several other columns that may be automatically populated. Statement 3 inserts several rows into **table3**, specifying values only for **col1**. Statement 4 inserts two more rows, specifying values for **col1** and the column with a DEFAULT value, **defCol**. Notice that the first row inserted in statement 4 specifies NULL for **defCol**. Statement 5 just returns the results.

If you run the script more than once, you will see that the ROWVERSION column, rvCol, contains different values each time. Notice, also, that in the row where col1 equals h, both devCol and calcCol1 also contain NULL. That is because statement 4 explicitly inserted a NULL value into defCol. Since the value for calcCol1 is based on defCol and any operation on NULL returns NULL, calcCol1 also contains a NULL in that row. Statement 4 inserts a row with another explicit value for defCol, and calcCol1 reflects that as well.

	col1	idCol	rvCol	defCol	calcCol1	calcCol2
1	a	1	0x00000000000009D6	2009-05-26 11:38:16.5670000	2009-06-26 11:38:16.5670000	a:a
2	b	2	0x00000000000009D7	2009-05-26 11:38:16.5670000	2009-06-26 11:38:16.5670000	b:b
3	c	3	0x00000000000009D8	2009-05-26 11:38:16.5670000	2009-06-26 11:38:16.5670000	c:c
4	d	4	0x00000000000009D9	2009-05-26 11:38:16.5670000	2009-06-26 11:38:16.5670000	d:d
5	e	5	0x00000000000009DA	2009-05-26 11:38:16.5670000	2009-06-26 11:38:16.5670000	e:e
6	g	6	0x00000000000009DB	2009-05-26 11:38:16.5670000	2009-06-26 11:38:16.5670000	g:g
7	h	7	0x00000000000009DC	NULL	NULL	h:h
8	i	8	0x00000000000009DD	2009-01-01 00:00:00.0000000	2009-02-01 00:00:00.0000000	i:i

Figure 8-9. The results of populating a table with automatically populating columns

Even though the main purpose of database tables is to store data, you can enforce many business rules by the table definition. Practice what you have learned by completing Exercise 8-1.

Exercise 8-1

Use the AdventureWorks2008 database to complete this exercise. You can find the solutions in the appendix.

1. Create a table called dbo.testCustomer. Include a CustomerID that is an identity column primary key. Include FirstName and LastName columns. Include an Age column with a check constraint specifying that the value must be less than 120. Include an Active column that is one character with a default of Y and allows only Y or N. Add some rows to the table.

2. Create a table called dbo.testOrder. Include a CustomerID column that is a foreign key pointing to dbo.testCustomer. Include an OrderID column that is an identity column primary key. Include an OrderDate column that defaults to the current date and time. Include a ROWVERSION column. Add some rows to the table.

3. Create a table called dbo.testOrderDetail. Include an OrderID column that is a foreign key pointing to dbo.testOrder. Include an integer ItemID column, a Price column, and a Qty column. The primary key should be a composite key composed of OrderID and ItemID. Create a computed column called LineItemTotal that multiplies Price times Qty. Add some rows to the table.

Views

SQL Server stores data in tables, but you can create objects, called *views*, that you query just like tables. Views do not store data; they are just saved query definitions. Developers can use views to simplify coding. For example, in the AdventureWorks2008 database, the **Person.Person** table contains name columns for several other tables, such as the **HumanResources.Employee** table. You could create views to join the **Person.Person** table to the other tables so that you would always have the name columns available, therefore simplifying queries for reports.

You can also simplify security by using views. You can give a user permission to select data from a view when the user does not have permission to select data from the tables comprising the view. This keeps users from seeing or modifying data that they should not access.

■ **Note** An indexed view, also known as a *materialized view*, actually does contain data. SQL Server Express does not support indexed views, so this section does not cover them. See Books Online for more information about creating and using indexed views.

Creating Views

Creating views is easy. You can create views using most **SELECT** statements, including those made with common table expressions. For example, you might want to create a view that lists all the customers in the **Sales.Customer** table from the AdventureWorks2008 database along with their names from the **Person.Person** table. You could use that view instead of the **Sales.Customer** table in other queries. Here is the syntax to create, alter, and drop views:

```
CREATE VIEW <view name> AS SELECT <col1>, <col2> FROM <table>
ALTER VIEW <view name> AS SELECT <col1>, <col2> FROM <table>
DROP VIEW <view name>
```

Type in and execute the code in Listing 8-7 to learn how to create and use views.

Listing 8-7. Creating and Using a View

```
USE AdventureWorks2008;
GO


--1
IF OBJECT_ID('dbo.vw_Customer') IS NOT NULL BEGIN
    DROP VIEW dbo.vw_Customer;
END;
GO
```

```
--2
CREATE VIEW dbo.vw_Customer AS
    SELECT c.CustomerID, c.AccountNumber, c.StoreID,
        c.TerritoryID, p.FirstName, p.MiddleName,
        p.LastName
    FROM Sales.Customer AS c
    INNER JOIN Person.Person AS p ON c.PersonID = p.BusinessEntityID
GO


--3
SELECT CustomerID,AccountNumber,FirstName,
    MiddleName, LastName
FROM dbo.vw_Customer;

GO


--4
ALTER VIEW dbo.vw_Customer AS
    SELECT c.CustomerID,c.AccountNumber,c.StoreID,
        c.TerritoryID, p.FirstName,p.MiddleName,
        p.LastName, p.Title
    FROM Sales.Customer AS c
    INNER JOIN Person.Person AS p ON c.PersonID = p.BusinessEntityID

GO


--5
SELECT CustomerID,AccountNumber,FirstName,
    MiddleName, LastName, Title
FROM dbo.vw_Customer
ORDER BY CustomerID;
```

Figure 8-10 shows the results. Code section 1 drops the view if it already exists. Code section 2 creates the view. Notice that the GO statements surround the CREATE VIEW code so that it has its own batch. Any time you create or alter a view, the code must be contained within a batch that has no other code except for comments. Notice that the view begins with the characters vw_ designating that it is a view, not a table. Often companies will have naming conventions such as this; be sure to find out whether your shop requires special naming for views. Statement 3 selects several of the columns from the view. At this point, you could include a WHERE clause, include an ORDER BY clause, or involve the view in an aggregate query if you wanted. Basically, you can treat the view like a table in a SELECT statement. Statement 4 alters the view, adding a column. Statement 5 is another SELECT statement, which includes the new column and an ORDER BY clause.

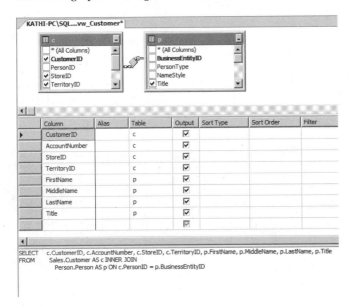

	CustomerID	Account Number	First Name	Middle Name	Last Name
1	29485	AW00029485	Catherine	R.	Abel
2	29486	AW00029486	Kim	NULL	Abercrombie
3	29487	AW00029487	Humberto	NULL	Acevedo
4	29484	AW00029484	Gustavo	NULL	Achong
5	29488	AW00029488	Pilar	NULL	Ackerman
6	28866	AW00028866	Aaron	B	Adams
7	13323	AW00013323	Adam	NULL	Adams
8	21139	AW00021139	Alex	C	Adams
9	29170	AW00029170	Alexandra	J	Adams
10	19419	AW00019419	Allison	I	Adams

	CustomerID	Account Number	First Name	Middle Name	Last Name	Title
1	11000	AW00011000	Jon	V	Yang	NULL
2	11001	AW00011001	Eugene	L	Huang	NULL
3	11002	AW00011002	Ruben	NULL	Torres	NULL
4	11003	AW00011003	Christy	NULL	Zhu	NULL
5	11004	AW00011004	Elizabeth	NULL	Johnson	NULL
6	11005	AW00011005	Julio	NULL	Ruiz	NULL
7	11006	AW00011006	Janet	G	Alvarez	NULL
8	11007	AW00011007	Marco	NULL	Mehta	NULL

Figure 8-10. *The results of creating and using a view*

To see the view in SQL Server Management Studio, navigate to the Views section of the AdventureWorks2008 database. You will see the newly created view along with several views that ship with the database. Notice that each of the preexisting views belongs to one of the schemas in the database. Just like tables, you can script out the definition or bring up a graphical designer. Figure 8-11 shows the graphical designer for the view.

Figure 8-11. *The graphical designer for views*

Avoiding Common Problems with Views

You may decide that you should set up views joining all the tables in the database and just write queries against those views, but there are often problems associated with using views as the main strategy for database development. One problem is the confusion that can result from views created on top of other views. Tracking down logic errors becomes difficult when they are buried in layers of views. If the underlying table structure changes, the view may produce strange results, as shown in Listing 8-8. Make sure that you do not use views in a way that will negatively impact performance. For example, suppose you created a view containing the customers, customer addresses, sales, and sales details tables. If you just wanted a list of customers, you could query the view but would be also accessing tables you did not need to view at that time.

Developers often want to add an **ORDER BY** clause to a view definition. This is actually disallowed except under specific conditions and does not make sense because you can always add the **ORDER BY** clause to the outer query. (To add an **ORDER BY** to a view definition, you must add the **TOP** specifier to the view. You will learn about **TOP** in Chapter 10.) In fact, the database engine does not guarantee that the data will be returned in the order specified in the view definition according to the **CREATE VIEW** topic in SQL Server Books Online. Type in and execute the code in Listing 8-8 to learn more about two common problems with views.

Listing 8-8. Common Problems Using Views

```
USE AdventureWorks2008;
GO


--1
IF OBJECT_ID('vw_Dept') IS NOT NULL BEGIN
    DROP VIEW dbo.vw_Dept;
END;
IF OBJECT_ID('demoDept') IS NOT NULL BEGIN
    DROP TABLE dbo.demoDept;
END;


--2
SELECT DepartmentID,Name,GroupName,ModifiedDate
INTO dbo.demoDept
FROM HumanResources.Department;

GO
--3
CREATE VIEW dbo.vw_Dept AS
    SELECT *
    FROM dbo.demoDept;
GO
```

```
--4
SELECT DepartmentID, Name, GroupName, ModifiedDate
FROM dbo.vw_dept;


--5
DROP TABLE dbo.demoDept;
GO


--6
SELECT DepartmentID, GroupName, Name, ModifiedDate
INTO dbo.demoDept
FROM HumanResources.Department;
GO


--7
SELECT DepartmentID, NAME, GroupName, ModifiedDate
FROM dbo.vw_dept;
GO


--8
DROP VIEW dbo.vw_dept;
GO


--9
CREATE VIEW dbo.vw_dept AS
    SELECT TOP(100) PERCENT DepartmentID,
        Name, GroupName, ModifiedDate
    FROM dbo.demoDept
    ORDER BY Name;
GO


--10
SELECT DepartmentID, Name, GroupName, ModifiedDate
FROM dbo.vw_dept;
```

Figure 8-12 shows the results. Code section 1 drops the view and a work table in case they already exist. Statement 2 creates the table **dbo.demoDept** from the **HumanResources.Department** table. Statement 3 creates a view, **dbo.vw_dept**, using the asterisk (*) syntax against the **dbo.demoDept** table. Statement 4 selects all the rows from the view, and the results look as expected in the first result set.

Statement 5 drops the **dbo.demoDept** table, and Statement 6 creates and populates the table again but with the columns in a different order. Statement 7 selects the rows from the view, but this time with surprising results. Because the table was dropped and re-created differently, the columns in the view are now mismatched, as shown in the second result set. The **Name** and **GroupName** columns are reversed.

Statement 8 drops the view, and statement 9 creates it while attempting to enforce a specific order in the view definition. Statement 10 shows within the final set of results that the **ORDER BY** clause within the view definition did not make any difference.

	DepartmentID	Name	GroupName	ModifiedDate
1	1	Engineering	Research and Development	1998-06-01 00:00:00.000
2	2	Tool Design	Research and Development	1998-06-01 00:00:00.000
3	3	Sales	Sales and Marketing	1998-06-01 00:00:00.000
4	4	Marketing	Sales and Marketing	1998-06-01 00:00:00.000
5	5	Purchasing	Inventory Management	1998-06-01 00:00:00.000

	DepartmentID	NAME	GroupName	ModifiedDate
1	1	Research and Development	Engineering	1998-06-01 00:00:00.000
2	2	Research and Development	Tool Design	1998-06-01 00:00:00.000
3	3	Sales and Marketing	Sales	1998-06-01 00:00:00.000
4	4	Sales and Marketing	Marketing	1998-06-01 00:00:00.000
5	5	Inventory Management	Purchasing	1998-06-01 00:00:00.000

	DepartmentID	Name	GroupName	ModifiedDate
1	1	Engineering	Research and Development	1998-06-01 00:00:00.000
2	2	Tool Design	Research and Development	1998-06-01 00:00:00.000
3	3	Sales	Sales and Marketing	1998-06-01 00:00:00.000
4	4	Marketing	Sales and Marketing	1998-06-01 00:00:00.000
5	5	Purchasing	Inventory Management	1998-06-01 00:00:00.000
6	6	Research and Development	Research and Development	1998-06-01 00:00:00.000

Figure 8-12. *The results of demonstrating some common problems with views*

Manipulating Data with Views

So far, you have seen how you can use views to select data. You can also modify the data of a table by updating a view as long as the view meets several requirements:

- Modifying the data of a view by inserting or updating may affect only one base table.
- You may not delete data from a view that consists of more than one table.
- The columns updated must be directly linked to updateable table columns; in other words, you cannot update a view column based on an expression or an otherwise non-updatable column.
- Inserts into views are possible only if all columns that require a value are exposed through the view.

As you can see, modifying data through views can be much more complicated than through tables, especially if the view is made of more than one table. Type in and execute the code in Listing 8-9 to learn how to update data using views.

Listing 8-9. Modifying Data Through Views

```
USE AdventureWorks2008;
GO


--1
IF OBJECT_ID('dbo.demoCustomer') IS NOT NULL BEGIN
    DROP TABLE dbo.demoCustomer;
END;
IF OBJECT_ID('dbo.demoPerson') IS NOT NULL BEGIN
    DROP TABLE dbo.demoPerson;
END;
IF OBJECT_ID('dbo.vw_Customer') IS NOT NULL BEGIN
    DROP VIEW dbo.vw_Customer;
END;


--2
SELECT CustomerID, TerritoryID, StoreID, PersonID
INTO dbo.demoCustomer
FROM Sales.Customer;

SELECT BusinessEntityID, Title, FirstName, MiddleName, LastName
INTO dbo.DemoPerson
From Person.Person;
GO


--3
CREATE VIEW vw_Customer AS
    SELECT CustomerID, TerritoryID, PersonID, StoreID,
        Title, FirstName, MiddleName, LastName
    FROM dbo.demoCustomer
    INNER JOIN dbo.demoPerson ON PersonID = BusinessEntityID;
GO


--4
SELECT CustomerID, FirstName, MiddleName, LastName
FROM dbo.vw_Customer
WHERE CustomerID IN (29484,29486,29489,100000);


--5
PRINT 'Update one row';
UPDATE dbo.vw_Customer SET FirstName = 'Kathi'
WHERE CustomerID = 29486;
```

```
--6
GO
PRINT 'Attempt to update both sides of the join'
GO
UPDATE dbo.vw_Customer SET FirstName = 'Franie',TerritoryID = 5
WHERE CustomerID = 29489;

--7
GO
PRINT 'Attempt to delete a row';
GO
DELETE FROM dbo.vw_Customer
WHERE CustomerID = 29484;

--8
GO
PRINT 'Insert into dbo.demoCustomer';
INSERT INTO dbo.vw_Customer(TerritoryID,
    StoreID, PersonID)
VALUES (5,5,100000);

--9
GO
PRINT 'Attempt to insert a row into demoPerson';
GO
INSERT INTO dbo.vw_Customer(Title, FirstName, LastName)
VALUES ('Mrs.','Lady','Samoyed');

--10
SELECT CustomerID, FirstName, MiddleName, LastName
FROM dbo.vw_Customer
WHERE CustomerID IN (29484,29486,29489,100000);

--11
SELECT CustomerID, TerritoryID, StoreID, PersonID
FROM dbo.demoCustomer
WHERE PersonID = 100000;
```

Since this code will produce some errors, view the error messages, and then click the Results tab (see Figure 8-13). Code section 1 drops the two tables and the view involved in this script if they exist. Code section 2 creates the two tables **dbo.demoPerson** and **dbo.demoCustomer** using **SELECT INTO** statements. Since the two tables must be in place before the view is created, the code to create **dbo.vw_Customer** is in a separate batch. Statement 4 shows how three of the rows look before the data is manipulated and is the first result set in Figure 8-13. Statement 5 changes the first name of one row from *Kim* to *Kathi*. This statement succeeds because the update affects only one of the tables.

Statement 6 attempts to update two of the columns. Because the **FirstName** column is from one base table and **TerritoryID** is from a different base table, the update fails. Statement 7 attempts to delete a row from the view but fails. Deletions will work only if the view consists of one base table.

Statement 8 successfully inserts one row into the **dbo.demoCustomer** table through the view. Statement 9 attempts to insert a row into **dbo.demoPerson** but fails because the view does not expose the non-**NULL** column, **BusinessEntityID**, and there is no way to add a valid value. Statements 10 and 11 show the results of the script. The script updated only one row and added one row to **dbo.demoCustomer** through the view.

Results

	CustomerID	FirstName	MiddleName	LastName
1	29484	Gustavo	NULL	Achong
2	29486	Kim	NULL	Abercrombie
3	29489	Frances	B.	Adams

	CustomerID	FirstName	MiddleName	LastName
1	29484	Gustavo	NULL	Achong
2	29486	Kathi	NULL	Abercrombie
3	29489	Frances	B.	Adams

	CustomerID	TerritoryID	StoreID	PersonID
1	30119	5	5	100000

Figure 8-13. *The results of manipulating data through a view*

Developers can use views to simplify database programming, but care must be taken to avoid performance and logic problems. Practice what you have learned by completing Exercise 8-2.

Exercise 8-2

Use the AdventureWorks2008 database to complete this exercise. You can find the solutions in the appendix.

1. Create a view called **dbo.vw_Products** that displays a list of the products from the **Production.Product** table joined to the **Production.ProductCostHistory** table. Include columns that describe the product and show the cost history for each product. Test the view by creating a query that retrieves data from the view.
2. Create a view called **dbo.vw_CustomerTotals** that displays the total sales from the **TotalDue** column per year and month for each customer. Test the view by creating a query that retrieves data from the view.

User-Defined Functions

You learned about the built-in functions available in SQL Server in Chapter 3. You can also create your own T-SQL user-defined functions (UDFs) that you can use in the same ways as the built-in functions. You will learn about two types of user-defined functions in this chapter: *scalar valued*, which return one value, and *table-valued*, which return record sets. By using UDFs, you can reuse code to simplify development and hide complex logic.

Creating User-Defined Scalar Functions

A scalar function returns one value and may take one or more parameters. You can create your own scalar functions to simplify your code. For example, your application may have a complex calculation that appears in many queries. Instead of including the formula in every query, you can create and include the function in your queries instead. Keep these facts about scalar UDFs in mind:

- UDFs can be used almost anywhere in a T-SQL statement.
- UDFs can accept one or more parameters.
- UDFs return one value.
- UDFs can use logic such as **IF** blocks and **WHILE** loops.
- UDFs can access data, though this is not a good idea.
- UDFs cannot update data.
- UDFs can call other functions.
- The UDF definition must include a return value.

You may have noticed that scalar-valued UDFs can access data, but this is not a good use of UDFs. UDFs should generally not be dependent on the tables in a particular database. They should be reusable as possible. Another problem with UDFs that access data is that the performance can be very poor, especially when used inline in a T-SQL query. The queries within the function run for each row in the outer query. Here is the syntax for creating, altering, and deleting user-defined scalar functions:

```
CREATE FUNCTION <scalar function Name> (<@param1> <data type1>,
    <@param2> <data type2>)
RETURNS <data type> AS
BEGIN
    <statements>
    RETURN <value>
END


ALTER FUNCTION <scalar function Name> ([<@param1> <data type>,
    <@param2> <data type>])
RETURNS <data type> AS
```

```
BEGIN
    <statements>
    RETURN <value>
END

DROP FUNCTION <scalar function name>
```

Listing 8-10 demonstrates how to create and use user-defined functions. Type in and execute the code to learn more.

Listing 8-10. *Creating and Using User-Defined Scalar Functions*

```
USE AdventureWorks2008;
GO


--1
IF OBJECT_ID('dbo.udf_Product') IS NOT NULL BEGIN
    DROP FUNCTION dbo.udf_Product;
END;
IF OBJECT_ID('dbo.udf_Delim') IS NOT NULL BEGIN
    DROP FUNCTION dbo.udf_Delim;
END;
GO


--2
CREATE FUNCTION dbo.udf_Product(@num1 INT, @num2 INT) RETURNS INT AS
BEGIN

    DECLARE @Product INT;
    SET @Product = ISNULL(@num1,0) * ISNULL(@num2,0);
    RETURN @Product;

END;
GO


--3
CREATE FUNCTION dbo.udf_Delim(@String VARCHAR(100),@Delimiter CHAR(1))
    RETURNS VARCHAR(200) AS
BEGIN
    DECLARE @NewString VARCHAR(200) = '';
    DECLARE @Count INT = 1;
```

```
    WHILE @Count <= LEN(@String) BEGIN
        SET @NewString += SUBSTRING(@String,@Count,1) + @Delimiter;
        SET @Count += 1;
    END

    RETURN @NewString;
END
GO


--3
SELECT StoreID, TerritoryID,
    dbo.udf_Product(StoreID, TerritoryID) AS TheProduct,
    dbo.udf_Delim(FirstName,',') AS FirstNameWithCommas
FROM Sales.Customer AS c
INNER JOIN Person.Person AS p ON c.PersonID= p.BusinessEntityID ;
```

Figure 8-14 shows the results. Code section 1 drops the UDFs in case they already exist. Code section 2 creates the UDFs **dbo.udf_Product** and **dbo.udf_Delim**. The **dbo.udf_Product** UDF takes two **INT** parameters. Inside the UDF, the two parameters are multiplied together after correcting for **NULL** values. The code saves the product in a variable, **@Product**, which is returned.

The second UDF, **dbo.udf_Delim**, takes two parameters: **@String**, which is a **VARCHAR(100)**, and **@Delimiter**, which is a one-character string. Inside the definition, a loop builds a new string inserting the delimiter after each character in the original string. The function returns the new string. Query 3 uses the new functions in the **SELECT** list, multiplying the **StoreID** by the **TerritoryID** and adding commas to the **FirstName** column. Each of these function are database agnostic; you could add them to any database.

	StoreID	TerritoryID	TheProduct	FirstNameWithCommas
1	294	4	1176	C,a,t,h,e,r,i,n,e,
2	296	3	888	K,i,m,
3	298	2	596	H,u,m,b,e,r,t,o,
4	292	5	1460	G,u,s,t,a,v,o,
5	300	9	2700	P,i,l,a,r,
6	NULL	4	0	A,a,r,o,n,
7	NULL	4	0	A,d,a,m,
8	NULL	1	0	A,l,e,x,

Figure 8-14. The results of using two user-defined scalar functions

Using Table-Valued User-Defined Functions

The second type of UDF returns a record set instead of one value. You cannot use this type of UDF inline within a query, but you can use it in place of a table or save the results into a temp table or table variable for use later in your script.

The AdventureWorks2008 database contains one example of a table-valued UDF. This function accepts a **@PersonID** value and returns information about the contact. Using SSMS, navigate to the AdventureWorks2008 database, and drill down to the **dbo.ufnGetContactInformation** function via

Programmability ➤ Functions ➤ Table-valued Functions. Once you reach the function, right-click and choose Script Function as ➤ Create to ➤ New Query Editor Window. You will see why this is a function instead of a view. Because the **Person.Person** table contains information about contacts from many different tables, the function uses logic to figure out which query to run to pull the information. You cannot define logic like that in a view, so that is why the AdventureWorks2008 developers chose to create the table-valued UDF.

To work with a table-valued UDF, you can select from it like a table or use the **CROSS APPLY** operator to join the function to another table. Here is the syntax:

```
SELECT <col1>,<col2> FROM <schema>.<udf name>(<@param>)
SELECT <col1>,<col2> FROM <table1> CROSS APPLY <udf name>(<table1>.<col3>)
```

Listing 8-11 demonstrates using the **dbo.ufnGetContactInformation** function. Type in and execute to learn more.

Listing 8-11. Using a Table-Valued UDF

```
USE AdventureWorks2008;
GO


--1
SELECT PersonID,FirstName,LastName,JobTitle,BusinessEntityType
FROM dbo.ufnGetContactInformation(1);

--2
SELECT PersonID,FirstName,LastName,JobTitle,BusinessEntityType
FROM dbo.ufnGetContactInformation(7822);

--3
SELECT e.BirthDate, e.Gender, c.FirstName,c.LastName,c.JobTitle
FROM HumanResources.Employee as e
CROSS APPLY dbo.ufnGetContactInformation(e.BusinessEntityID ) AS c;

--4
SELECT sc.CustomerID,sc.TerritoryID,c.FirstName,c.LastName
FROM Sales.Customer AS sc
CROSS APPLY dbo.ufnGetContactInformation(sc.PersonID) AS c;
```

Figure 8-15 shows the partial results. Query 1 calls the UDF with the parameter 1. The logic inside the UDF determines that **BusinessEntityID** 1 belongs to an employee and returns that information. Query 2 calls the UDF with parameter 7822. The logic inside the UDF determines that this **BusinessEntityID** belongs to a customer and returns the appropriate information. Query 3 uses the **CROSS APPLY** operator to join the **HumanResources.Employee** table to the UDF. Instead of supplying an individual value to find one name, the query supplies the **BusinessEntityID** column of the **HumanResources.Employee** table to the function. Columns from the UDF and the table appear in the

SELECT list. Query 4 uses **CROSS APPLY** to join the UDF on the **Sales.Customer** table. Another option, **OUTER APPLY**, returns rows even if a **NULL** value is passed to the UDF, similar to an **OUTER JOIN**.

	PersonID	First Name	Last Name	Job Title		Business Entity Type
1	1	Ken	Sánchez	Chief Executive Officer		Employee

	PersonID	First Name	Last Name	Job Title		Business Entity Type
1	7822	Faith	Hughes	NULL		Consumer

	Birth Date	Gender	First Name	Last Name		Job Title
1	1959-03-02	M	Ken	Sánchez		Chief Executive Officer
2	1961-09-01	F	Terri	Duffy		Vice President of Engineering
3	1964-12-13	M	Roberto	Tamburello		Engineering Manager
4	1965-01-23	M	Rob	Walters		Senior Tool Designer
5	1942-10-29	F	Gail	Erickson		Design Engineer

	CustomerID	TerritoryID	First Name	Last Name
1	11000	9	Jon	Yang
2	11001	9	Eugene	Huang
3	11002	9	Ruben	Torres
4	11003	9	Christy	Zhu
5	11004	9	Elizabeth	Johnson

Figure 8-15. *The partial results of using a table-valued UDF*

You will probably find many reasons to write scalar-valued user-defined functions. Table-valued UDFs are not as common. Beginning with SQL Server 2005, you can also create user-defined functions with a .NET language. Creating functions with a .NET language is beyond the scope of this book. Practice what you have learned about UDFs by completing Exercise 8-3.

Exercise 8-3

Use the AdventureWorks2008 database to complete this exercise. You can find the solutions in the appendix.

1. Create a user-defined function called **dbo.fn_AddTwoNumbers** that accepts two integer parameters. Return the value that is the sum of the two numbers. Test the function.
2. Create a user-defined function called **dbo.Trim** that takes a **VARCHAR(250)** parameter. This function should trim off the spaces from both the beginning and the end of the string. Test the function.
3. Create a function **dbo.fn_RemoveNumbers** that removes any numeric characters from a **VARCHAR(250)** string. Test the function. Hint: The **ISNUMERIC** function checks to see whether a string is numeric. Check Books Online to see how to use it.
4. Write a function called **dbo.fn_FormatPhone** that takes a string of ten numbers. The function will format the string into this phone number format: "(###) ###-####." Test the function.

Stored Procedures

Stored procedures are the "workhorses" of T-SQL. Developers and database administrators use them to increase security as well as encapsulate logic. Stored procedures can contain programming logic, update data, create other objects, and more. Essentially, stored procs are just saved scripts, and they can do anything that the stored procedure owner can do. Like views, the user of the stored procedure doesn't usually need to have permissions on the tables used within the stored procedure.

▪ **Tip** Stored procedures are often used to prevent SQL injection attacks. Hackers employing SQL injection techniques insert SQL commands into web forms that build SQL statements dynamically. Eventually the hacker takes over databases, servers, and networks. This problem is not unique to SQL Server; other database systems have been attacked as well.

Stored procedures and UDFs have many similarities but have some distinct differences. One interesting difference is that they both take parameters, but stored procedures can accept special parameters called OUTPUT parameters. These parameters can be used to get modified values from the stored procedures. UDFs can accept parameters but can return only a single return value. A stored procedure can also return an integer value, usually reporting the success of the stored procedure or some other informational code. Table 8-1 shows some of the differences between stored procedures and UDFs as well as views.

Table 8-1. *The Differences Between Stored Procedures and User-Defined Functions*

Feature	SP	Scalar UDF	Table UDF	View
Return tabular data	Yes	No	Yes	Yes
Update data	Yes	No	No	No
Create other objects	Yes	No	No	No
Call from a proc	Yes	Yes	Yes	Yes
Can call a proc	Yes	No	No	No
Can call a function	Yes	Yes	Yes	Yes
Can call inline	No	Yes	No	No
Use to populate a table	Yes	No	Yes	Yes
Return value required	No	Yes	Yes (table)	N/A
Return value optional	Yes	No	No	N/A
Takes parameters	Yes	Yes	Yes	No

Output parameters	Yes	No	No	No

You will find that creating stored procedures is easy. Here's the syntax to create, alter, drop, and execute a stored procedure:

```
CREATE PROC[EDURE] <proc name> [<@param1> <data type>,<@param2> <data type>] AS
    <statements>
    [RETURN <INT>]


ALTER PROC[EDURE] <proc name> [<@param1> <data type>,<@param2> <data type>] AS
    <statements>
    [RETURN <INT>]


EXEC <proc name> <param values>


DROP PROC[EDURE] <proc name>
```

Some shops require that developers use stored procedures for all database calls from their applications. I have also heard of shops that did not allow stored procedures at all. Chances are you will work with stored procedures at some point in your career. Listing 8-12 shows how to create a stored proc. Type in and execute the code to learn more.

Listing 8-12. Creating and Using a Stored Procedure

```
USE AdventureWorks2008;
GO


--1
IF OBJECT_ID('dbo.usp_CustomerName') IS NOT NULL BEGIN
    DROP PROC dbo.usp_CustomerName;
END;
GO


--2
CREATE PROC dbo.usp_CustomerName AS
    SELECT c.CustomerID,p.FirstName,p.MiddleName,p.LastName
    FROM Sales.Customer AS c
    INNER JOIN Person.Person AS p on c.PersonID = p.BusinessEntityID
    ORDER BY p.LastName, p.FirstName,p.MiddleName ;

    RETURN 0;
GO
```

```
--3
EXEC dbo.usp_CustomerName
GO
--4
ALTER PROC dbo.usp_CustomerName @CustomerID INT AS
    SELECT c.CustomerID,p.FirstName,p.MiddleName,p.LastName
    FROM Sales.Customer AS c
    INNER JOIN Person.Person AS p on c.PersonID = p.BusinessEntityID
    WHERE c.CustomerID = @CustomerID;

    RETURN 0;
GO


--5
EXEC dbo.usp_CustomerName @CustomerID = 15128;
```

Figure 8-16 shows the results. Code section 1 drops the stored procedure if it already exists. Code section 2 creates the stored procedure, **dbo.usp_CustomerName**. The proc simply joins the **Sales.Customer** table to the **Person.Person** table and returns several columns from those tables. Notice that the query includes the **ORDER BY** clause. Unlike views, the **ORDER BY** clause will actually return the rows in the order specified. Statement 3 calls the proc with the **EXEC** command. Code section 4 changes the stored proc by adding a parameter and using that parameter in a **WHERE** clause. Statement 5 calls the modified proc supplying a value for the **@CustomerID** parameter. You could have left out the name of the parameter when you called the stored procedure in this case. Supplying the name of the parameter makes the code easier to read and understand.

	CustomerID	FirstName	MiddleName	LastName
1	29485	Catherine	R.	Abel
2	29486	Kim	NULL	Abercrombie
3	29487	Humberto	NULL	Acevedo
4	29484	Gustavo	NULL	Achong
5	29488	Pilar	NULL	Ackerman

	CustomerID	FirstName	MiddleName	LastName
1	15128	Angelica	NULL	Barnes

Figure 8-16. *The partial results of using a stored procedure*

Using Default Values with Parameters

SQL Server requires that you supply a value for each parameter unless you define a default value for the parameter. When a parameter has a default value, you can skip the parameter when you call the stored procedure. In that case, you will have to name the other parameters, not just rely on the position in the list. Once you use a named parameter when calling the stored procedure, you must continue naming parameters. You may want to get in the habit of naming the parameters anyway, because it makes your code easier to understand. Here is the syntax for creating a stored procedure with default value parameters:

303

```
CREATE PROC[EDURE] <proc name> <@param1> <data type> = <default value> AS
    <statements>
    [return <value>]
```

Listing 8-13 shows how to use default value parameters. Type in and execute the code to learn more.

Listing 8-13. Using Default Value Parameters

```
USE AdventureWorks2008;
GO


--1
IF OBJECT_ID('dbo.usp_CustomerName') IS NOT NULL BEGIN
    DROP PROC dbo.usp_CustomerName;
END;
GO


--2
CREATE PROC dbo.usp_CustomerName @CustomerID INT = -1 AS
    SELECT c.CustomerID,p.FirstName,p.MiddleName,p.LastName
    FROM Sales.Customer AS c
    INNER JOIN Person.Person AS p on c.PersonID = p.BusinessEntityID
    WHERE @CustomerID = CASE @CustomerID WHEN -1 THEN -1 ELSE c.CustomerID END;

    RETURN 0;
GO


--3
EXEC dbo.usp_CustomerName 15128;


--4
EXEC dbo.usp_CustomerName ;
```

Figure 8-17 shows the results. Code section 1 drops the stored proc if it exists. Code section 2 creates the stored proc along with the parameter **@CustomerID** and the default value –1. In this case, if the user calls the stored proc without a value for **@CustomerID**, the stored proc will return all the rows. Statement 3 calls the stored proc with a value, and the stored proc returns the one matching row. Statement 4 calls the stored proc without the parameter value, and the stored proc returns all the rows.

	CustomerID	FirstName	MiddleName	LastName
1	15128	Angelica	NULL	Barnes

	CustomerID	FirstName	MiddleName	LastName
1	29485	Catherine	R.	Abel
2	29486	Kim	NULL	Abercrombie
3	29487	Humberto	NULL	Acevedo
4	29484	Gustavo	NULL	Achong
5	29488	Pilar	NULL	Ackerman

Figure 8-17. The partial results of using a default value parameter

Using the OUTPUT Parameter

You can use an **OUTPUT** parameter to get back a value from a stored proc. This is one of those gray areas where you may decide to use a scalar-value UDF with a return value instead. In my opinion, if the logic is not portable to any database, use a stored procedure. Save scalar-valued UDFs for truly database-agnostic uses. Here is the syntax for creating and using an **OUTPUT** parameter with a stored proc:

```
CREATE PROC[EDURE] <proc name> <@param> <data type> OUTPUT AS
    <statements>
    [return <value>]
GO


DECLARE <@variable> <data type>
EXEC <proc name> [<@param> =] <@variable> OUTPUT
PRINT <@variable>
```

You can include as many parameters as you need, and your **OUTPUT** parameter can pass a value to the stored proc as well as return a value. Type in and execute Listing 8-14 to learn how to use an **OUTPUT** parameter.

Listing 8-14. Using an OUTPUT Parameter

```
USE AdventureWorks2008;
GO


--1
IF OBJECT_ID('dbo.usp_OrderDetailCount') IS NOT NULL BEGIN
    DROP PROC dbo.usp_OrderDetailCount;
END;
GO
```

```
--2
CREATE PROC dbo.usp_OrderDetailCount @OrderID INT,
    @Count INT OUTPUT AS

    SELECT @Count = COUNT(*)
    FROM Sales.SalesOrderDetail
    WHERE SalesOrderID = @OrderID;

    RETURN 0;
GO


--3
DECLARE @OrderCount INT;
--4
EXEC usp_OrderDetailCount 71774, @OrderCount OUTPUT;
--5
PRINT @OrderCount;
```

Code section 1 drops the stored proc if it exists. Code section 2 creates the stored proc, dbo.usp_OrderDetailCount, along with two parameters, @OrderID and @Count. The first parameter accepts a SalesOrderID value. The second parameter is the OUTPUT parameter, which returns the count of the orders for that SalesOrderID. Statement 3 creates a variable, @OrderCount, to be used as the OUTPUT parameter. Statement 4 calls the stored proc with the value for @OrderID and the variable for the @Count parameter. In statement 5, the final value of @Count from inside the stored procedure saved to the variable @OrderCount prints in the Message window. The call to the stored proc could also have looked like this:

```
EXEC dbo.usp_OrderDetailCount @OrderID = 71774, @Count = @OrderCount OUTPUT.
```

One mistake that developers often make is to forget to use the OUTPUT keyword when calling the stored proc. To get the modified parameter value back, you must use OUTPUT.

Saving the Results of a Stored Proc in a Table

One very popular use of a stored procedure is to save the results in a temp or work table for later processing. When saving the results of a stored proc in a table, define the table define ahead of time. All the columns must be in place and of compatible data types. Here is the syntax for inserting the rows returned from a stored procedure into a table:

```
INSERT [INTO] <table name> EXEC <stored proc> [<@param value>]
```

Listing 8-15 shows how to save the results of a proc into a table. Type in and execute the code to learn more.

Listing 8-15. Inserting the Rows from a Stored Proc into a Table

```
USE AdventureWorks2008;
GO


--1
IF OBJECT_ID('dbo.tempCustomer') IS NOT NULL BEGIN
    DROP TABLE dbo.tempCustomer;
END
IF OBJECT_ID('dbo.usp_CustomerName') IS NOT NULL BEGIN
    DROP PROC dbo.usp_CustomerName;
END;
GO


--2
CREATE TABLE dbo.tempCustomer(CustomerID INT, FirstName NVARCHAR(50),
    MiddleName NVARCHAR(50), LastName NVARCHAR(50))
GO


--3
CREATE PROC dbo.usp_CustomerName @CustomerID INT = -1 AS
    SELECT c.CustomerID,p.FirstName,p.MiddleName,p.LastName
    FROM Sales.Customer AS c
    INNER JOIN Person.Person AS p on c.PersonID = p.BusinessEntityID
    WHERE @CustomerID = CASE @CustomerID WHEN -1 THEN -1 ELSE c.CustomerID END;

    RETURN 0;
GO


--4
INSERT INTO dbo.tempCustomer EXEC dbo.usp_CustomerName;


--5
SELECT CustomerID, FirstName, MiddleName, LastName
FROM dbo.tempCustomer;
```

Figure 8-18 shows the results. Code section 1 drops the table and stored proc if they exist. Statement 2 creates the table **dbo.tempCustomer**, matching up columns and data types. They do not need to have the same names as the stored proc, but they should have the same number of columns, in the same order, and of compatible data types. Code section 3 creates the stored procedure. Statement 4 calls the stored proc while at the same time storing the results in **dbo.tempCustomer**. Query 5 returns the results.

	CustomerID	FirstName	MiddleName	LastName
1	29485	Catherine	R.	Abel
2	29486	Kim	NULL	Abercrombie
3	29487	Humberto	NULL	Acevedo
4	29484	Gustavo	NULL	Achong
5	29488	Pilar	NULL	Ackerman
6	28866	Aaron	B	Adams
7	13323	Adam	NULL	Adams
8	21139	Alex	C	Adams

Figure 8-18. *The results of saving the results of a stored proc into a table*

Using a Logic in Stored Procedures

So far, you have seen stored procs that do not do much more than run queries, but stored procedures are capable of so much more. You can include conditional code, loops, error trapping, object creation statements, and more within stored procedures. Listing 8-16 shows an example. Type in and execute the code to learn more.

Listing 8-16. *Using Logic in a Stored Procedure*

```
USE tempdb;
GO


--1
IF OBJECT_ID('usp_ProgrammingLogic') IS NOT NULL BEGIN
    DROP PROC usp_ProgrammingLogic;
END;
GO


--2
CREATE PROC usp_ProgrammingLogic AS
    --2.1
    CREATE TABLE #Numbers(number INT NOT NULL);
    --2.2
    DECLARE @count INT;
    SET @count = ASCII('!');

    --2.3
    WHILE @count < 200 BEGIN
        INSERT INTO #Numbers(number) VALUES (@count);
        SET @count = @count + 1;
    END;
```

```
    --2.4
    ALTER TABLE #Numbers ADD symbol NCHAR(1);
    --2.5
    UPDATE #Numbers SET symbol = CHAR(number);

    --2.6
    SELECT number, symbol FROM #Numbers
GO
--3
```

```
EXEC usp_ProgrammingLogic;
```

Figure 8-19 shows the results. This stored proc creates a table of numbers and the ASCII symbol for each number. This is a simple example just to give you an idea of what you can do. Anything you have learned in this book can be encapsulated within a stored procedure.

	number	symbol
1	33	!
2	34	"
3	35	#
4	36	$
5	37	%
6	38	&
7	39	'
8	40	(
9	41	)
10	42	*

Figure 8-19. *The partial results of using a stored procedure with programming logic*

Developers can use stored procedures for all database calls. Database administrators can set up stored procedures as scheduled jobs for batch processing or for reports. Beginning with SQL Server 2005, developers can also create stored procedures with a .NET language, called *CLR integration*. Creating stored procedures in this way is beyond the scope of this book. See SQL Server Books Online for more information about creating stored procedures with .NET. Now that you have seen many of the possibilities of using stored procedures, complete Exercise 8-4 to practice what you have learned.

Exercise 8-4

Use the AdventureWorks2008 database to complete this exercise. You can find the solutions in the appendix.

1. Create a stored procedure called `dbo.usp_CustomerTotals` instead of a view from question 2 in Exercise 8-2. Test the stored procedure.

2. Modify the stored procedure created in question 1 to include a parameter @CustomerID. Use the parameter in the WHERE clause of the query in the stored procedure. Test the stored procedure.

3. Create a stored procedure called dbo.usp_ProductSales that accepts a ProductID for a parameter and has an OUTPUT parameter that returns the total number sold for the product. Test the stored procedure.

User-Defined Data Types

Within a database, you can create user-defined data types. User-defined data types (UDTs) are nothing more than native data types that you have given a specific name. This enables you to make sure that a particular type of column is consistently defined throughout the database. For example, databases often contain ZIP code and phone number columns as UDTs.

Take a look at the UDTs defined for the AdventureWorks2008 database by navigating to Programmability ➤ Types ➤ User-Defined Data Types. If you double-click the **Phone** data type, you can see the graphical editor for the type (see Figure 8-20).

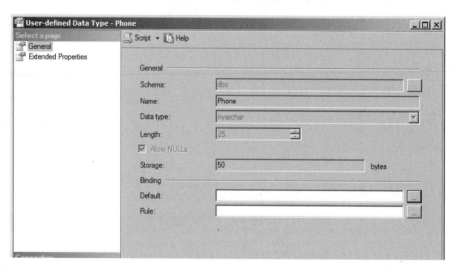

Figure 8-20. *The properties of the Phone data type*

The **Phone** data type is an **NVARCHAR(25)** that allows **NULL** values. The Binding section for Default and Rule are blank. In previous versions of SQL Server, you could create defaults and rules that were then applied to columns or UDTs. The binding features have been deprecated and should not be used. Once you have the data type defined, you can use it when defining columns in tables as any other data type. Here is the syntax for creating a UDT:

```
CREATE TYPE <type name> FROM <native type and size> [NULL|NOT NULL]
```

Listing 8-17 shows how to create a UDT. Type in and execute the code to learn more.

Listing 8-17. Creating a User-Defined Type

```
USE [AdventureWorks2008];
GO
IF  EXISTS (
    SELECT * FROM sys.types st
    JOIN sys.schemas ss ON st.schema_id = ss.schema_id
    WHERE st.name = N'CustomerID' AND ss.name = N'dbo') BEGIN

    DROP TYPE [dbo].[CustomerID];
END;
GO


CREATE TYPE dbo.CustomerID FROM INT NOT NULL;
```

Now that the new UDT exists, you can use it when defining new tables. Another type of object introduced with SQL Server 2005 has a very close name, *user-defined type*. This new type must be created with a .NET language called a Common Language Runtime (CLR) data type. The new CLR types can contain multiple properties and can contain methods. Creating CLR types is beyond the scope of this book, but three CLR data types ship with SQL Server 2008. These three types are covered in Chapter 9.

Triggers

Triggers are a very powerful feature of SQL Server. As with most powerful things, they can also cause many problems. Triggers are like a special type of stored procedure that runs whenever data is modified. You can define triggers on tables that fire when new rows are inserted or when existing rows are updated or deleted. Triggers can insert data into auditing tables, roll back the current update, or even modify the row that caused the trigger to fire in the first place. Obviously, they can have an impact on performance, and care must be taken so that triggers are not used in a way that causes them to fire repeatedly because of one update.

Any code within a trigger must be very efficient. The transaction that caused the trigger to fire cannot complete until the trigger is successfully completed. One common use of triggers is to enforce *referential integrity*, or the primary key/foreign key relationships between tables. For example, a trigger that fires when a customer is deleted from the customer table might delete all the orders for that customer. In actuality, this use of triggers is not necessary. Database designers can use foreign key constraints to take care of situations like this.

Traditionally, triggers were defined only on tables. A new type of trigger is available in SQL Server 2005 that you can define on a database or on the server. These are called Data Definition Language (DDL) triggers. These fire when operations such as creating a table or adding a login are performed. They can be used to prevent these operations or log them, for example.

Since this is a beginning book, it does not cover creating triggers. Just be aware that triggers often exist in databases and are frequently the cause of performance or logic problems that are difficult to track down.

Thinking About Performance

This chapter covers many ways that you can add logic to the database to enforce business rules or make development easier. One common problem is using UDFs that access data inline in a query. The database engine will have to execute the function for each row of the query. Listing 8-18 illustrates this point. Run the first part of the code to create the objects. Then run query 3 and see how long it takes. Run query 4, and see how long that query takes.

Listing 8-18. Performance Issues with UDFs

```
--RUN THIS FIRST
USE AdventureWorks2008;
GO

IF OBJECT_ID('dbo.udf_ProductTotal') IS NOT NULL BEGIN
    DROP FUNCTION dbo.udf_ProductTotal;
END;
GO

CREATE FUNCTION dbo.udf_ProductTotal(@ProductID INT,@Year INT) RETURNS MONEY AS
BEGIN

    DECLARE @Sum MONEY;

    SELECT @Sum = SUM(LineTotal)
    FROM Sales.SalesOrderDetail AS sod
    INNER JOIN Sales.SalesOrderHeader AS soh
            ON sod.SalesOrderID = soh.SalesOrderID
    WHERE ProductID = @ProductID AND YEAR(OrderDate) = @Year;

    RETURN ISNULL(@Sum,0);

END;
GO
--TO HERE

--3 Run this by itself to see how long it runs
SELECT ProductID, dbo.udf_ProductTotal(ProductID, 2004) AS SumOfSales
FROM Production.Product
ORDER BY SumOfSales DESC;
```

```
--4 Run this by itself to see how long it runs
WITH Sales AS (
    SELECT SUM(LineTotal) AS SumOfSales, ProductID,
        YEAR(OrderDate) AS OrderYear
    FROM Sales.SalesOrderDetail AS sod
    INNER JOIN Sales.SalesOrderHeader AS soh
        ON sod.SalesOrderID = soh.SalesOrderID
    GROUP BY ProductID, YEAR(OrderDate)
)
SELECT p.ProductID, ISNULL(SumOfSales,0) AS SumOfSales
FROM Production.Product AS p
LEFT OUTER JOIN Sales ON p.ProductID = Sales.ProductID
    AND OrderYear = 2004
ORDER BY SumOfSales DESC;
```

On my laptop, query 3 takes 6 or 7 seconds to run, and query 4 takes 1 second. Since the user-defined function must access the `Sales.SalesOrderDetail` table once for every product, it takes a lot of resources. Unfortunately, the execution plans, if you choose to compare them, do not accurately reflect the difference. On my computer, query 4 takes 100 percent of the resources in the execution plans, but I know that is not true since query 4 runs so much faster.

Database Cleanup

You have created quite a few objects during this chapter. You can either run the script in Listing 8-19 (also available on the catalog page for this book at `http://www.apress.com`) to clean up the objects from the examples or reinstall the sample databases according to the instructions in the "Installing the Sample Databases" section in Chapter 1.

Listing 8-19. Database Cleanup

```
USE AdventureWorks2008;
GO

IF OBJECT_ID('vwCustomer') IS NOT NULL BEGIN
    DROP VIEW vwCustomer;
END;

IF OBJECT_ID('vw_Dept') IS NOT NULL BEGIN
    DROP VIEW dbo.vw_Dept;
END;

IF OBJECT_ID('demoDept') IS NOT NULL BEGIN
    DROP TABLE dbo.demoDept;
END;
```

```
IF OBJECT_ID('dbo.demoCustomer') IS NOT NULL BEGIN
    DROP TABLE dbo.demoCustomer;
END;
IF OBJECT_ID('dbo.demoPerson') IS NOT NULL BEGIN
    DROP TABLE dbo.demoPerson;
END;

IF OBJECT_ID('dbo.vw_Customer') IS NOT NULL BEGIN
    DROP VIEW dbo.vw_Customer;
END;

IF OBJECT_ID('dbo.udf_Product') IS NOT NULL BEGIN
    DROP FUNCTION dbo.udf_Product;
END;

IF OBJECT_ID('dbo.udf_Delim') IS NOT NULL BEGIN
    DROP FUNCTION dbo.udf_Delim;
END;

IF OBJECT_ID('dbo.usp_CustomerName') IS NOT NULL BEGIN
    DROP PROC dbo.usp_CustomerName;
END;

IF OBJECT_ID('dbo.usp_OrderDetailCount') IS NOT NULL BEGIN
    DROP PROC dbo.usp_OrderDetailCount;
END;

IF OBJECT_ID('dbo.tempCustomer') IS NOT NULL BEGIN
    DROP TABLE dbo.tempCustomer;
END

IF OBJECT_ID('dbo.usp_CustomerName') IS NOT NULL BEGIN
    DROP PROC dbo.usp_CustomerName;
END;

IF OBJECT_ID('usp_ProgrammingLogic') IS NOT NULL BEGIN
    DROP PROC usp_ProgrammingLogic
END;

IF OBJECT_ID('dbo.CustomerID') IS NOT NULL BEGIN
    DROP TYPE dbo.CustomerID
END;
```

```
IF OBJECT_ID('dbo.udf_ProductTotal') IS NOT NULL BEGIN
    DROP FUNCTION dbo.udf_ProductTotal;
END;

IF OBJECT_ID ('dbo.testCustomer') IS NOT NULL BEGIN
    DROP TABLE dbo.testCustomer;
END;

IF OBJECT_ID('dbo.testOrder') IS NOT NULL BEGIN
    DROP TABLE dbo.testOrder;
END;

IF OBJECT_ID('dbo.testOrderDetail') IS NOT NULL BEGIN
    DROP TABLE dbo.testOrderDetail;
END;

IF OBJECT_ID('dbo.vw_Products') IS NOT NULL BEGIN
    DROP VIEW dbo.vw_Products;
END;

IF OBJECT_ID('dbo.vw_CustomerTotals') IS NOT NULL BEGIN
    DROP VIEW dbo.vw_CustomerTotals;
END;

IF OBJECT_ID('dbo.fn_AddTwoNumbers') IS NOT NULL BEGIN
    DROP FUNCTION dbo.fn_AddTwoNumbers;
END;

IF OBJECT_ID('dbo.Trim') IS NOT NULL BEGIN
    DROP FUNCTION dbo.Trim;
END

IF OBJECT_ID('dbo.fn_RemoveNumbers') IS NOT NULL BEGIN
     DROP FUNCTION dbo.fn_RemoveNumbers;
END;
IF OBJECT_ID('dbo.fn_FormatPhone') IS NOT NULL BEGIN
    DROP FUNCTION dbo.fn_FormatPhone;
END;

IF OBJECT_ID('dbo.usp_CustomerTotals') IS NOT NULL BEGIN
    DROP PROCEDURE dbo.usp_CustomerTotals;
END;
```

```
IF OBJECT_ID('dbo.usp_ProductSales') IS NOT NULL BEGIN
    DROP PROCEDURE dbo.usp_ProductSales;
END;

IF  EXISTS (
    SELECT * FROM sys.types st
    JOIN sys.schemas ss ON st.schema_id = ss.schema_id
    WHERE st.name = N'CustomerID' AND ss.name = N'dbo') BEGIN

    DROP TYPE [dbo].[CustomerID];
END;
```

Summary

SQL Server contains many ways to enforce business rules and ensure data integrity. You can set up primary and foreign keys, constraints, and defaults in table definitions. You can create user-defined functions, stored procedures, views, and user-defined data types to add other ways to enforce business rules. You have many options that you can use to make development simpler and encapsulate logic. Each new version of SQL Server adds new data types and functions. Chapter 9 covers some of the new data types added with SQL Server 2005 and 2008. The new CLR data types, HIERARCHYID and the spatial data types, are especially interesting.

CHAPTER 9

■ ■ ■

Working with New Data Types

You have learned how to retrieve data from SQL Server tables in a number of ways: through simple queries, through joins, with functions, and more. You have learned to manipulate data, write scripts, and create database objects. Essentially, you have learned the T-SQL basics. Not only have you learned these skills, but you have learned to think about the best way to solve a problem, not just the easy way.

This chapter introduces you to the data types supported in SQL Server 2005 and 2008. You will learn about XML data, sparse columns, the new CLR data types (**HIERARCHYID**, **GEOMETRY**, and **GEOGRAPHY**), enhanced date and time data types, large-value data types (**MAX**), and **FILESTREAM** data. Some of these, such as the CLR data types, are nothing like the traditional data types you have been using throughout this book. This chapter provides a glimpse of these interesting new data types.

Chapters 1 through 8 covered the important skills you need to become a proficient T-SQL developer. Since this chapter covers "bonus material," it does not contain exercises. I encourage you to practice working with any of the new data types that interest you or that you think will be beneficial in your job.

Large-Value String Data Types (MAX)

Microsoft has introduced new large-value string data types for storing character data with the release of SQL Server 2005. It has deprecated the old data types **TEXT** and **NTEXT**. This means that, in some future release of SQL Server, these data types will no longer work; for now, however, the deprecated data types still work in SQL Server 2008.

You have worked with **VARCHAR**, **NVARCHAR**, **CHAR**, and **NCHAR** columns. These data types contain string data, but there is a limit to the number of characters you can store in these types. For storing more data in previous versions of SQL Server, you could use the **TEXT** and **NTEXT** data types. Going forward, you should replace these data types with **VARCHAR(MAX)** and **NVARCHAR(MAX)**.

The **TEXT** and **NTEXT** data types have many limitations. For example, you cannot declare a variable of type **TEXT** or **NTEXT**, use it with most functions, or use it within most search criteria. The **MAX** data types represent the benefits of both the regular string data types and the **TEXT** and **NTEXT** data types when storing large strings. They allow you to store large amounts of data and have the same functionality of the traditional data types.

When creating string data types, you supply a number of characters. Instead of supplying a number, use the word **MAX** when the data is going to surpass the maximum normally allowed. Table 9-1 lists the differences between the string value data types.

Table 9-1. *The String Data Types*

Name	Type	Maximum Characters	Character Set
CHAR	Fixed width	8,000	ASCII
NCHAR	Fixed width	4,000	Unicode
VARCHAR	Variable width	8,000	ASCII
NVARCHAR	Variable width	4,000	Unicode
TEXT	Variable width	$2^{31} - 1$	ASCII
NTEXT	Variable width	$2^{30} - 1$	Unicode
VARCHAR(MAX)	Variable width	$2^{31} - 1$	ASCII
NVARCHAR(MAX)	Variable width	$2^{30} - 1$	Unicode

You work with the **MAX** string data types just like you do with the traditional types for the most part. Type in and execute Listing 9-1 to learn how to work with the **MAX** types.

Listing 9-1. *Using VARCHAR(MAX)*

```
--1
CREATE TABLE #maxExample (maxCol VARCHAR(MAX),
    line INT NOT NULL IDENTITY PRIMARY KEY);
GO

--2
INSERT INTO #maxExample(maxCol)
VALUES ('This is a varchar(max)');

--3
INSERT INTO #maxExample(maxCol)
VALUES (REPLICATE('aaaaaaaaaa',9000));

--4
INSERT INTO #maxExample(maxCol)
VALUES (REPLICATE(CONVERT(VARCHAR(MAX),'bbbbbbbbbb'),9000));
```

```
--5
SELECT LEFT(MaxCol,10) AS Left10,LEN(MaxCol) AS varLen
FROM #maxExample;

GO
DROP TABLE #maxExample;
```

Figure 9-1 shows the results. Statement 1 creates a temp table, **#maxExample**, with a **VARCHAR(MAX)** column. Statement 2 inserts a row into the table with a short string. Statement 3 inserts a row using the **REPLICATE** function to create a very large string. If you look at the results, the row inserted by statement 3 contains only 8,000 characters. Statement 4 also inserts a row using the **REPLICATE** function. This time the statement explicitly converts the string to be replicated to a **VARCHAR(MAX)**. That is because, without explicitly converting it, the string is just a **VARCHAR**. The **REPLICATE** function, like most string functions, returns the same data types as supplied to it. To return a **VARCHAR(MAX)**, the function must receive a **VARCHAR(MAX)**. Statement 5 uses the **LEFT** function to return the first ten characters of the value stored in the **maxCol** column, demonstrating that you can use string functions with **VARCHAR(MAX)**. Attempting to use **LEFT** on a **TEXT** column will just produce an error. It uses the **LEN** function to see how many characters the column stores in each row. Only 8,000 characters of the row inserted in statement 3 made it to the table since the value wasn't explicitly converted to **VARCHAR(MAX)** before the **REPLICATE** function was applied.

	Left10	varLen
1	This is a	22
2	aaaaaaaaaa	8000
3	bbbbbbbbbb	90000

Figure 9-1. *The results of using the VARCHAR(MAX) data type*

If you get a chance to design a database, you may be tempted to make all your string value columns into **MAX** columns. Microsoft recommends that you use the **MAX** data types only when it is likely that you will exceed the 8,000- or 4,000-character limits. To be most efficient, size your columns to the expected data.

Large-Value Binary Data Types

You probably have less experience with the data types that store binary data. You can use **BINARY**, **VARBINARY**, and **IMAGE** to store binary data including files such as images, movies, and Word documents. The **BINARY** and **VARBINARY** data types can hold up to 8,000 bytes. The **IMAGE** data type, also deprecated, holds data that exceeds 8,000 bytes, up to 2GB. Beginning with SQL Server 2005, use the **VARBINARY(MAX)** data type, which can store up to 2GB of binary data, instead of **IMAGE**.

Creating VARBINARY(MAX) Data

To store data into a **VARBINARY(MAX)** column, or any of the binary data columns, you can use the **CONVERT** or **CAST** function to change string data into binary. Using a program written in a .NET language or any language type that supports working with SQL Server 2008, you can save actual files into **VARBINARY(MAX)** columns. In this simple demonstration, you will add data by converting string data. Type in and execute Listing 9-2 to learn more.

Listing 9-2. Using VARBINARY(MAX) Data

```
USE AdventureWorks2008;
GO


--1
IF OBJECT_ID('dbo.BinaryTest') IS NOT NULL BEGIN
    DROP TABLE dbo.BinaryTest;
END;


--2
CREATE TABLE dbo.BinaryTest (DataDescription VARCHAR(50),
    BinaryData VARBINARY(MAX));

GO


--3
INSERT INTO dbo.BinaryTest (DataDescription,BinaryData)
VALUES ('Test 1', CONVERT(VARBINARY(MAX),'this is the test 1 row')),
    ('Test 2', CONVERT(VARBINARY(MAX),'this is the test 2 row'));


--4
SELECT DataDescription, BinaryData, CONVERT(VARCHAR(MAX), BinaryData)
FROM dbo.BinaryTest;
```

Figure 9-2 shows the results. Code section 1 drops the **dbo.BinaryTest** table if it already exists. Statement 2 creates the **dbo.BinaryTest** table containing the **BinaryData** column of type **VARBINARY(MAX)**. Statement 3 inserts two rows. To insert data into the **BinaryData** column, it must be converted into a binary type. Query 4 displays the data. To read the data, the statement converts it back into a string data type.

	DataDescription	BinaryData	(No column name)
1	Test 1	0x746869732069732074686520746573742031206F77	this is the test 1 row
2	Test 2	0x746869732069732074686520746573742032206F77	this is the test 2 row

Figure 9-2. The results of using a VARBINARY(MAX) column

Using FILESTREAM

Often database applications involving files, such as images or Word documents, store just the path to the file in the database and store the actual file on a share in the network. This is more efficient than storing large files within the database since the file system works more efficiently than SQL Server with streaming file data. This solution also poses some problems. Since the files live outside the database, you have to make sure that they are secure. You cannot automatically apply the security set up in the database to the files. Another issue is backups. When you back up a database, how do you make sure that the backups of the file shares are done at the same time so that the data is consistent in case of a restore?

The **FILESTREAM** object solves these issues by storing the files on the file system but making the files become part of the database. You do this by adding the word **FILESTREAM** to the **VARBINARY(MAX)** column.

The SQL Server instance must be configured to allow **FILESTREAM** data, and the database must have a file group defined. AdventureWorks2008 has the file group defined, and if you installed your SQL Server instance according to the instructions in Chapter 1, the configuration should be in place.

For this demonstration, you will need to find the folder on your computer that stores the file data. Inside the Object Explorer in SQL Server Management Studio, right-click the AdventureWorks2008 database, and choose Properties. Click the Files page, and scroll until you can see the file location of the FileStreamDocuments folder. Figure 9-3 shows the location on my system.

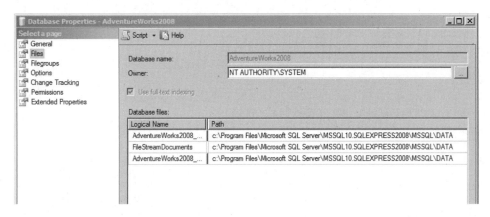

Figure 9-3. *The location of the FileStreamDocuments folder on my system*

Navigate to the appropriate folder on your system. You should see a Documents folder as well as the database files for all the databases hosted on the instance. Inside the Documents folder, there will be a folder with a unique identifier name. This folder corresponds to the **Production.Documents** table since it has a **FILESTREAM** column. Figure 9-4 shows the Documents folder on my system.

Figure 9-4. *The Documents folder*

Keep the Documents folder open as you run the code in Listing 9-3.

Listing 9-3. Working with a FILESTREAM Column

```
USE AdventureWorks2008;
GO


--1
IF OBJECT_ID('dbo.NotepadFiles') IS NOT NULL BEGIN
    DROP TABLE dbo.NotepadFiles;
END;


--2
CREATE table dbo.NotepadFiles(Name VARCHAR(25),
    FileData VARBINARY(MAX) FILESTREAM,
    RowID UNIQUEIDENTIFIER ROWGUIDCOL
        NOT NULL UNIQUE DEFAULT NEWSEQUENTIALID())


--3
INSERT INTO dbo.NotepadFiles(Name,FileData)
VALUES ('test1.txt', CONVERT(VARBINARY(MAX),'This is a test')),
    ('test2.txt', CONVERT(VARBINARY(MAX),'This is the second test'));


--4
SELECT Name,FileData,CONVERT(VARCHAR(MAX),FileData), RowID
FROM dbo.NotepadFiles;
```

Figure 9-5 shows the results. Code section 1 drops the **NotepadFiles** table in case it already exists. Statement 2 creates the **NotePadFiles** table. The **Name** column holds the file name. The **FileData** column is the **FILESTREAM** column. To create the **FILESTREAM** column, specify the **FILESTREAM** keyword when creating a **VARBINARY(MAX)** column. The **RowID** column is a special data type called **ROWGUIDID**. The **NEWSEQUENTIALID** function populates the **RowID** column. This function creates a unique value for each row, which is required when using **FILESTREAM** data.

	Name	FileData	(No column name)	RowID
1	test1.txt	0x54686973206973206120074657374	This is a test	802E5AA9-0B4E-DE11-A9BB-001E68C7DB6A
2	test2.txt	0x5468697320697320746865207365636F6E6420074657374	This is the second test	812E5AA9-0B4E-DE11-A9BB-001E68C7DB6A

Figure 9-5. The results of populating a FILESTREAM column

Statement 3 inserts two rows into the table. The data to be inserted into the **FileData** column must be of type **VARBINARY(MAX)** so the statement converts it. Statement 4 shows the results. The **FileData** column displays the binary data. By converting it to **VARCHAR(MAX)**, you can read the data.

Take a look at the Documents folder, which should now have another folder to hold the files for this table. If you navigate further down to the actual files, you will see two files that can be opened in Notepad. When working with a production database, the user would have an application that opens the file through calls to SQL Server with the appropriate program, not by navigating to the actual file.

When you delete a row from the **NotepadFiles** table, the corresponding file on disk will also disappear. If you drop the table, the entire folder will disappear. Run this code, and then check the Documents folder once again:

```
DROP TABLE NotepadFiles;
CHECKPOINT;
```

The database engine does not delete the folder until the database commits all transactions to disk, called a *checkpoint*. By running the **CHECKPOINT** command, you force the checkpoint.

XML Data

Beginning with SQL Server 2005, Microsoft added the **XML** data type, the XQuery language, and several new functions for working with XML data. XML stands for Extensible Markup Language, and it looks a lot like HTML except that it generally contains data. Companies often use XML to exchange data between incompatible systems or with their vendors and customers.

Fully covering XML support in SQL Server would take another complete book, so I'll just briefly discuss it here. In the past, to work with XML, databases stored the XML data in **TEXT** columns. The database was just a storage place for the XML data. There was nothing to validate the XML data or to query just part of the XML data. To learn about SQL Server support for XML in depth, check out the book *Pro SQL Server 2008 XML* by Michael Coles (Apress, 2008).

Retrieving Data As XML

Instead of retrieving data into rows and columns, essentially a grid, you can also retrieve the results of a query into XML using the **FOR XML** clause. This feature has been available since SQL Server 2000, but I thought it was interesting enough to include in this chapter. There are four possible modes: **RAW**, **AUTO**, **PATH**, and **EXPLICIT**. The first three are very easy to use, and each returns the data in a different format. Type in and execute the code in Listing 9-4 to learn more.

Listing 9-4. Using XML in SQL Server 2008

```
USE AdventureWorks2008;
GO


--1
SELECT CustomerID, LastName, FirstName, MiddleName
FROM Person.Person AS p
INNER JOIN Sales.Customer AS c ON p.BusinessEntityID = c.PersonID
FOR XML RAW;



--2
SELECT CustomerID, LastName, FirstName, MiddleName
FROM Person.Person AS p
INNER JOIN Sales.Customer AS c ON p.BusinessEntityID = c.PersonID
FOR XML AUTO;


--3
SELECT CustomerID, LastName, FirstName, MiddleName
FROM Person.Person AS p
INNER JOIN Sales.Customer AS c ON p.BusinessEntityID = c.PersonID
FOR XML PATH;
```

Figure 9-6 shows that the results display in one row from each query as a link. You can see that each row contains the same data, just formatted a bit differently in each case.

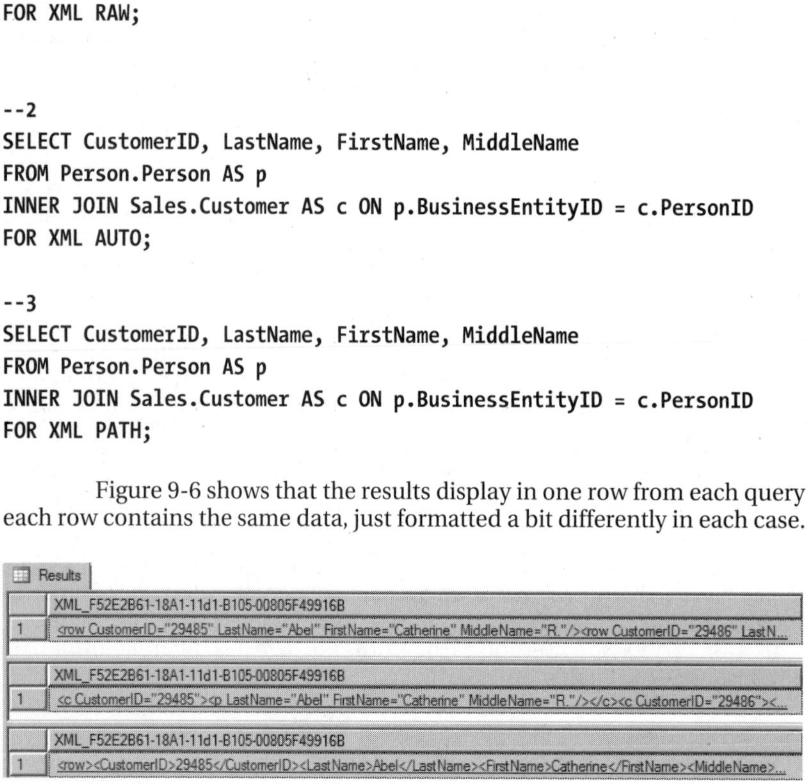

Figure 9-6. The results of using the FOR XML clause

When you click one of the links, you can see the full XML. Figure 9-7 shows the XML generated from the third statement.

```
<row>
    <CustomerID>29485</CustomerID>
    <LastName>Abel</LastName>
    <FirstName>Catherine</FirstName>
    <MiddleName>R.</MiddleName>
</row>
<row>
    <CustomerID>29486</CustomerID>
    <LastName>Abercrombie</LastName>
    <FirstName>Kim</FirstName>
</row>
<row>
    <CustomerID>29487</CustomerID>
    <LastName>Acevedo</LastName>
    <FirstName>Humberto</FirstName>
</row>
<row>
    <CustomerID>29484</CustomerID>
    <LastName>Achong</LastName>
    <FirstName>Gustavo</FirstName>
</row>
```

Figure 9-7. The XML generated with the FOR XML PATH clause

Using the XML Data Type

You can now store XML in an **XML** column instead of a **TEXT** column. As mentioned, this is not an extensive look at everything you can do with XML but just a short introduction. Type in and execute the code in Listing 9-5.

Listing 9-5. Using XML As a Data Type

```
USE AdventureWorks2008;
GO


--1
CREATE TABLE #CustomerList (CustomerInfo XML);


--2
DECLARE @XMLInfo XML;
```

```
--3
SET @XMLInfo = (SELECT CustomerID, LastName, FirstName, MiddleName
FROM Person.Person AS p
INNER JOIN Sales.Customer AS c ON p.BusinessEntityID = c.PersonID
FOR XML PATH);

--4
INSERT INTO #CustomerList(CustomerInfo)
VALUES(@XMLInfo);

--5
SELECT CustomerInfo FROM #CustomerList;

DROP TABLE #CustomerList;
```

Figure 9-8 shows the results. Statement 1 creates a table with an **XML** column. Statement 2 declares a variable with the **XML** data type. Statement 3 saves the information in XML format about each customer from the **Sales.Customer** and **Person.Person** tables into a variable. The data comes from the same query that you saw in the previous section. Statement 4 inserts a row into the **#CustomerList** table using the variable. Query 5 returns the **CustomerInfo** column from the table without using the **FOR XML** clause. Since the table stores the data in XML format, the statement looks just like a regular **SELECT** statement yet returns the data as XML.

Figure 9-8. *The results of using the XML data type*

Enhanced Date and Time

Previous versions of SQL Server have the **DATETIME** and **SMALLDATE** time data types for working with temporal data. One big complaint by developers has been that there was not an easy way to store just dates or just time. SQL Server 2008 contains several new temporal data types. You can now use the **DATE** and **TIME** data types as well as the new **DATETIME2** and **DATETIMEOFFSET** data types.

Using DATE, TIME, and DATETIME2

You can store just a date or time value by using the new **DATE** and **TIME** data types. The traditional **DATETIME** and **SMALLDATETIME** data types default to 12 a.m. when you do not specify the time. You can also specify a precision, from zero to seven decimal places, when using the **TIME** and **DATETIME2** data types. Type in and execute Listing 9-6 to learn how to use the new types.

Listing 9-6. Using DATE and TIME

```
USE tempdb;

--1
IF OBJECT_ID('dbo.DateDemo') IS NOT NULL BEGIN
    DROP TABLE dbo.DateDemo;
END
GO

--2
CREATE TABLE dbo.DateDemo(JustTheDate DATE, JustTheTime TIME(1),
    NewDateTime2 DATETIME2(3), UTCDate DATETIME2);
GO

--3
INSERT INTO dbo.DateDemo (JustTheDate, JustTheTime, NewDateTime2,
    UTCDate)
VALUES (SYSDATETIME(), SYSDATETIME(), SYSDATETIME(), SYSUTCDATETIME());

--4
SELECT JustTheDate, JustTheTime, NewDateTime2, UTCDate
FROM dbo.DateDemo;
```

Figure 9-9 shows the results. Code section 1 drops the **dbo.DateDemo** table if it already exists. Statement 2 creates the **dbo.DateDemo** table with a **DATE**, a **TIME**, and two **DATETIME2** columns. Notice that the **TIME** and **DATETIME2** columns have the precision specified. The default is seven places if a precision is not specified. Statement 3 inserts a row into the table using the new **SYSDATETIME** function. This function works like the **GETDATE** function except that it has greater precision than **GETDATE**. The statement populates the **UTCDate** column with the **SYSUTCDATETIME** function, which provides the Coordinated Universal Time (UTC). Statement 4 shows the results. The **JustTheDate** value shows that even though the **SYSDATETIME** function populated it, it stored only the date. The **JustTheTime** values stored only the time with one decimal place past the seconds. The **NewDateTime2** column stored both the date and time with three decimal places. The **UTCDate** column stored the UTC date along with seven decimal places. Since the computer running this demo is in Central time, the time is five hours different.

	JustTheDate	JustTheTime	NewDateTime2	UTCDate
1	2009-07-05	19:38:11.0	2009-07-05 19:38:10.993	2009-07-06 00:38:10.9925904

Figure 9-9. The results of using the new date and time data types

One issue I have seen with these new data types is that running SQL Server on Vista 64-bit does not record all the decimal places with the new data types and fills in with zeros after three places. You will see better results when running SQL Server on different operating systems.

Most business applications will not require the default precision of seven places found with the TIME and DATETIME2 types. Be sure to specify the required precision when creating tables with columns of these types to save space in your database.

Using DATETIMEOFFSET

The new DATETIMEOFFSET data type contains, in addition to the date and time, a time zone offset for working with dates and times in different time zones. This is the difference between the UTC date and time and the stored date. Along with the new data type, several new functions for working with DATETIMEOFFSET are available. Type in and execute Listing 9-7 to learn how to work with this new data type.

Listing 9-7. Using the DATETIMEOFFSET Data Type

```
USE tempdb;


--1
IF OBJECT_ID('dbo.OffsetDemo') IS NOT NULL BEGIN
    DROP TABLE dbo.OffsetDemo;
END;


--2
CREATE TABLE dbo.OffsetDemo(Date1 DATETIMEOFFSET);
GO


--3
INSERT INTO dbo.OffsetDemo(Date1)
VALUES (SYSDATETIMEOFFSET()),
    (SWITCHOFFSET(SYSDATETIMEOFFSET(),'+00:00')),
    (TODATETIMEOFFSET(SYSDATETIME(),'+05:00'))


--4
SELECT Date1
FROM dbo.OffsetDemo;
```

Figure 9-10 shows the results. Code section 1 drops the dbo.OffsetDemo table if it exists. Statement 2 creates the table with a DATETIMEOFFSET column, Date1. Statement 3 inserts three rows into the table using the new functions for working with the new data types. The SYSDATETIMEOFFSET function returns the date and time on the server along with the time zone offset. The computer I am using is five hours behind UTC, so the value –05:00 appears after the current date and time. Using the SWITCHOFFSET function, you can switch a DATETIMEOFFSET value to another time zone. Notice that by switching to

+00:00, the UTC time, the date and time values adjust. By using the **TODATETIMEOFFSET** function, you can add a time zone to a regular date and time.

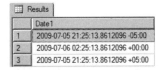

Figure 9-10. *The results of using DATETIMEOFFSET*

The new data type and functions may be useful to you if you work with data in different time zones. When time changes go into effect, such as daylight saving time, the offsets do not adjust. Keep that in mind if you choose to work with **DATETIMEOFFSET**.

HIERARCHYID

SQL Server 2008 ships with the **HIERARCHYID** data type used to represent hierarchical relationships in data, for example, family trees, organizational charts, or directory structures. This new data type is a CLR data type, which means that it can contain multiple properties, instead of just one value. The **HIERARCHYID** column also has methods, which means that columns and variables of this type can "do something" and not just contain a value. The **HIERARCHYID** data type ships with SQL Server 2008, and you can use it even if you do not want to create any custom types.

You learned about joining a table to itself in the "Self-Joins" section in Chapter 4. In older versions of AdventureWorks, the **ManagerID** column points back to the **EmployeeID** column in the **HumanResources.Employee** table. To follow the org chart from this table, you must recursively follow the chain of command from the CEO down each manager-employee path to the lowest employee, which is pretty difficult to do with T-SQL. Chapter 10 covers how to do this in the "Writing Recursive Queries" section. The AdventureWorks2008 database replaces the self-join with **OrganizationalNode**, a **HIERARCHYID** column, which is much easier to query.

Viewing HIERARCHYID

If you just write a query to view the **OrganizationalNode** in the **HumanResources.Employee** table, you will see binary data. That is because CLR data types are stored as binary values. To view the data in readable form, you must use the **ToString** method of the type. The **OrganizationalLevel** column in the table is a computed column based on **OrganizationalNode** using the **GetLevel** method. Type in and execute Listing 9-8 to view the data.

Listing 9-8. Viewing the OrganizationalNode

```
USE AdventureWorks2008;
GO

SELECT BusinessEntityID,
    SPACE((OrganizationLevel) * 3) + JobTitle AS Title,
    OrganizationNode, OrganizationLevel,
    OrganizationNode.ToString() AS Readable
FROM HumanResources.Employee
ORDER BY Readable;
```

Figure 9-11 shows the partial results. As mentioned, the **OrganizationalNode** data is meaningless unless you use the **ToString** method as in the **Readable** column. By using the **SPACE** function to indent the **JobTitle** column from the table to produce the **Title** column in the results and by sorting on the **Readable** column, you can see the relationships between the job titles in the data.

	BusinessEntityID	Title	OrganizationNode	OrganizationLevel	Readable
1	1	Chief Executive Officer	0x	0	/
2	2	Vice President of Engineering	0x58	1	/1/
3	3	Engineering Manager	0x5AC0	2	/1/1/
4	4	Senior Tool Designer	0x5AD6	3	/1/1/1/
5	5	Design Engineer	0x5ADA	3	/1/1/2/
6	6	Design Engineer	0x5ADE	3	/1/1/3/
7	7	Research and Development Manager	0x5AE1	3	/1/1/4/
8	8	Research and Development Engineer	0x5AE158	4	/1/1/4/1/
9	9	Research and Development Engineer	0x5AE168	4	/1/1/4/2/
10	10	Research and Development Manager	0x5AE178	4	/1/1/4/3/
11	11	Senior Tool Designer	0x5AE3	3	/1/1/5/
12	12	Tool Designer	0x5AE358	4	/1/1/5/1/
13	13	Tool Designer	0x5AE368	4	/1/1/5/2/
14	14	Senior Design Engineer	0x5AE5	3	/1/1/6/
15	15	Design Engineer	0x5AE7	3	/1/1/7/
16	16	Marketing Manager	0x68	1	/2/
17	17	Marketing Assistant	0x6AC0	2	/2/1/
18	18	Marketing Specialist	0x6B40	2	/2/2/

Figure 9-11. The partial results of querying the HumanResources.Employee table

The very first node in the hierarchy is the CEO, or chief executive officer, of the company, represented as a slash (/) in the **Readable** column. The level for the CEO is 0, which you can see in the computed column **OrganizationLevel**. Several employees have an **OrganizationLevel** of 1; these employees report directly to the CEO. If you scroll down through all the results, you will see that these have a value, 1 through 6, in between two slashes. The vice president of engineering is the first node in level 1. The marketing manager is the second node in level 1. Each of these employees has other employees reporting to them. Those employees have a level of 2. For example, the engineering manager reports to the vice president of engineering and has a **Readable** value of **/1/1/**. Four employees report to the engineering manager. These employees all have **Readable** values that begin with **/1/1/** along with an additional value, 1 through 4.

Creating a Hierarchy

As you can see from the previous example, querying hierarchical data using **HIERARCHYID** is not difficult. Maintaining the data, however, is much more challenging. To add a new value or update existing values, you must use the built-in methods of the data type. If you have worked with nodes and pointers in other programming languages, you will find this is very similar. To learn how to insert nodes using these methods to create hierarchical data, type in and execute the code in Listing 9-9.

Listing 9-9. Creating a Hierarchy with HIERARCHYID

```
Use tempdb;
GO


--1
IF OBJECT_ID('SportsOrg') IS NOT NULL BEGIN
    DROP TABLE SportsOrg;
END;
GO


--2
CREATE TABLE SportsOrg
    (DivNode HIERARCHYID NOT NULL PRIMARY KEY CLUSTERED,
    DivLevel AS DivNode.GetLevel(), --Calculated column
    DivisionID INT NOT NULL,
    Name VARCHAR(30) NOT NULL);
GO


--3
INSERT INTO SportsOrg(DivNode,DivisionID,Name)
VALUES(HIERARCHYID::GetRoot(),1,'State');
GO


--4
DECLARE @ParentNode HIERARCHYID, @LastChildNode HIERARCHYID;


--5
SELECT @ParentNode = DivNode
FROM SportsOrg
WHERE DivisionID = 1;


--6
SELECT @LastChildNode = max(DivNode)
FROM SportsOrg
WHERE DivNode.GetAncestor(1) = @ParentNode;
```

```
--7
INSERT INTO SportsOrg(DivNode,DivisionID,Name)
VALUES (@ParentNode.GetDescendant(@LastChildNode,NULL),
2,'Madison County');

--8
SELECT DivisionID,DivLevel,DivNode.ToString() AS Node,Name
FROM SportsOrg;
```

Figure 9-12 shows the results. You might be surprised how much code was required just to insert two rows! Code section 1 drops the **SportsOrg** table if it already exists. Statement 2 creates the **SportsOrg** table with the **DivisionID** and **Name** columns to identify each division or team. The **DivNode** column is a **HIERARCHYID** column, and the **DivLevel** is a computed column. Statement 3 inserts the first row, the root, into the table. Take a close look at the **INSERT** statement. Instead of inserting a value into **DivNode**, the statement uses the name of the data type along with the **GetRoot** method. Of course, since the **DivLevel** is computed column, you do not insert anything into the column.

	DivisionID	DivLevel	Node	Name
1	1	0	/	State
2	2	1	/1/	Madison County

Figure 9-12. *The results of creating a hierarchy*

To insert the second and subsequent nodes, you have to use the **GetDescendant** method of the parent node. You also have to determine the last child of the parent. Statement 4 declares two variables needed to accomplish this. Statement 5 saves the parent into a variable. Statement 6 saves the last child of the parent into a variable. In this case, there are no children just yet. Statement 7 inserts the row using the **GetDescendant** method. If the second argument is **NULL**, the method returns a new child that is greater than the child node in the first argument. Finally, query 8 displays the data.

Using Stored Procedures to Manage Hierarchical Data

Working with **HIERARCHYID** can be pretty complicated, as shown in the previous section. If you decide to use this data type in your applications, I recommend that you create stored procedures to encapsulate the logic and make coding your application much easier. Listing 9-10 contains a stored procedure to add new rows to the table. Type in and execute the code to learn more.

Listing 9-10. *Using a Stored Procedure to Insert New Nodes*

```
USE tempdb;
GO

--1
IF OBJECT_ID('dbo.usp_AddDivision') IS NOT NULL BEGIN
    DROP PROC dbo.usp_AddDivision;
```

```
END;
IF OBJECT_ID('dbo.SportsOrg') IS NOT NULL BEGIN
    DROP TABLE dbo.SportsOrg;
END;
GO


--2
CREATE TABLE SportsOrg
    (DivNode HierarchyID NOT NULL PRIMARY KEY CLUSTERED,
    DivLevel AS DivNode.GetLevel(), --Calculated column
    DivisionID INT NOT NULL,
    Name VARCHAR(30) NOT NULL);
GO


--3
INSERT INTO SportsOrg(DivNode,DivisionID,Name)
VALUES(HIERARCHYID::GetRoot(),1,'State');
GO


--4
CREATE PROC usp_AddDivision @DivisionID INT,
    @Name VARCHAR(50),@ParentID INT AS

    DECLARE @ParentNode HierarchyID, @LastChildNode HierarchyID;

    --Grab the parent node
    SELECT @ParentNode = DivNode
    FROM SportsOrg
    WHERE DivisionID = @ParentID;

    BEGIN TRANSACTION
        --Find the last node added to the parent
        SELECT @LastChildNode = max(DivNode)
        FROM SportsOrg
        WHERE DivNode.GetAncestor(1) = @ParentNode;
        --Insert the new node using the GetDescendant function
        INSERT INTO SportsOrg(DivNode,DivisionID,Name)
        VALUES (@ParentNode.GetDescendant(@LastChildNode,NULL),
            @DivisionID,@Name);
    COMMIT TRANSACTION;
GO
```

```
--5
EXEC usp_AddDivision 2,'Madison County',1;
EXEC usp_AddDivision 3,'Macoupin County',1;
EXEC usp_AddDivision 4,'Green County',1;
EXEC usp_AddDivision 5,'Edwardsville',2;
EXEC usp_AddDivision 6,'Granite City',2;
EXEC usp_AddDivision 7,'Softball',5;
EXEC usp_AddDivision 8,'Baseball',5;
EXEC usp_AddDivision 9,'Basketball',5;
EXEC usp_AddDivision 10,'Softball',6;
EXEC usp_AddDivision 11,'Baseball',6;
EXEC usp_AddDivision 12,'Basketball',6;
EXEC usp_AddDivision 13,'Ages 10 - 12',7;
EXEC usp_AddDivision 14,'Ages 13 - 17',7;
EXEC usp_AddDivision 15,'Adult',7;
EXEC usp_AddDivision 16,'Preschool',8;
EXEC usp_AddDivision 17,'Grade School League',8;
EXEC usp_AddDivision 18,'High School League',8;

--6
SELECT DivNode.ToString() AS Node,
    DivisionID, SPACE(DivLevel * 3) + Name AS Name
FROM SportsOrg
ORDER BY DivNode;
```

Figure 9-13 shows the results. Code section 1 drops the stored procedure and table if they already exist. Statement 2 creates the table, and statement 3 inserts the root as in the previous section. Code section 4 creates the stored procedure to insert new nodes. The stored procedure requires the new DivisionID and Name values along with the DivisionID of the parent node. Inside the stored proc, an explicit transaction contains the code to grab the last child node and perform the insert. If this were part of an actual multiuser application, it would be very important to make sure that two users did not accidentally insert values into the same node position. By using an explicit transaction, you avoid that problem. Code section 5 calls the stored procedure to insert each node. Finally, query 6 retrieves the data from the SportsOrg table. The query uses the same technique from the previous section utilizing the SPACES function to format the Name column results.

	Node	DivisionID	Name
1	/	1	State
2	/1/	2	Madison County
3	/1/1/	5	Edwardsville
4	/1/1/1/	7	Softball
5	/1/1/1/1/	13	Ages 10 - 12
6	/1/1/1/2/	14	Ages 13 - 17
7	/1/1/1/3/	15	Adult
8	/1/1/2/	8	Baseball
9	/1/1/2/1/	16	Preschool
10	/1/1/2/2/	17	Grade School League
11	/1/1/2/3/	18	High School League
12	/1/1/3/	9	Basketball

Figure 9-13. *The partial results of using a stored procedure to insert new rows*

Deleting a node is easy; you just delete the row. Unfortunately, there is nothing built into the HIERARCHYID data type to ensure that the children of the deleted nodes are also deleted or moved to a new parent. You will end up with orphaned nodes if the deleted node was a parent node. You can also move nodes, but you must make sure that you move the children of the moved nodes as well. If you decide to include the HIERARCHYID in your applications, be sure to learn about this topic in depth before you design your application. See Books Online for more information about how to work with HIERARCHYID.

Spatial Data Types

In the previous section, you learned about the CLR data type HIERARCHYID. SQL Server 2008 has two other CLR data types, GEOMETRY and GEOGRAPHY, also known as the *spatial* data types. The GEOMETRY data type might be used for a warehouse application to store the location of each product in the warehouse. The GEOGRAPHY data type can be used to store data that can be used in mapping software. You may wonder why two types exist that both store locations. The GEOMETRY data type follows a "flat Earth" model, with basically X, Y, and Z coordinates. The GEOGRAPHY data type represents the "round Earth," storing longitude and latitude. These data types implement international standards for spatial data.

Using GEOMETRY

By using the GEOMETRY type, you can store points, lines, and polygons. You can calculate the difference between two shapes, you can determine whether they intersect, and you can do much more. Just like HIERARCHYID, the database engine stores the data as a binary value. GEOMETRY also has many built-in methods for working with the data. Type in and execute Listing 9-11 to learn how to use the GEOMETRY data type with some simple examples.

Listing 9-11. Using the GEOMETRY Data Type

```
USE tempdb;
GO


--1
IF OBJECT_ID('dbo.GeometryData') IS NOT NULL BEGIN
    DROP TABLE dbo.GeometryData;
END;

--2
CREATE TABLE dbo.GeometryData (
    Point1 GEOMETRY, Point2 GEOMETRY,
    Line1 GEOMETRY, Line2 GEOMETRY,
    Polygon1 GEOMETRY, Polygon2 GEOMETRY);

--3
INSERT INTO dbo.GeometryData (Point1, Point2, Line1, Line2, Polygon1, Polygon2)
VALUES (
    GEOMETRY::Parse('Point(1 4)'),
    GEOMETRY::Parse('Point(2 5)'),
    GEOMETRY::Parse('LineString(1 4, 2 5)'),
    GEOMETRY::Parse('LineString(4 1, 5 2, 7 3, 10 6)'),
    GEOMETRY::Parse('Polygon((1 4, 2 5, 5 2, 0 4, 1 4))'),
    GEOMETRY::Parse('Polygon((1 4, 2 7, 7 2, 0 4, 1 4))'));


--4
SELECT Point1.ToString() AS Point1, Point2.ToString() AS Point2,
    Line1.ToString() AS Line1, Line2.ToString() AS Line2,
    Polygon1.ToString() AS Polygon1, Polygon2.ToString() AS Polygon2
FROM dbo.GeometryData;

--5
SELECT Point1.STX AS Point1X, Point1.STY AS Point1Y,
    Line1.STIntersects(Polygon1) AS Line1Poly1Intersects,
    Line1.STLength() AS Line1Len,
    Line1.STStartPoint().ToString() AS Line1Start,
    Line2.STNumPoints() AS Line2PtCt,
    Polygon1.STArea() AS Poly1Area,
    Polygon1.STIntersects(Polygon2) AS Poly1Poly2Intersects
FROM dbo.GeometryData;
```

Figure 9-14 shows the results. Code section 1 drops the **dbo.GeometryData** table if it already exists. Statement 2 creates the table along with six **GEOMETRY** columns each named for the type of shape it will contain. Even though this example named the shape types, a **GEOMETRY** column can store any of the shapes; it is not limited to one shape. Statement 3 inserts one row into the table using the **Parse** method. Query 4 displays the data using the **ToString** method so that you can read the data. Notice that the data returned from the **ToString** method looks just like it does when inserted. Query 5 demonstrates a few of the methods available for working with **GEOMETRY** data. For example, you can display the X and Y coordinates of a point, determine the length or area of a shape, determine whether two shapes intersect, and count the number of points in a shape.

	Point1	Point2	Line1	Line2	Polygon1	Polygon2
1	POINT (1 4)	POINT (2 5)	LINESTRING (1 4, 2 5)	LINESTRING (4 1, 5 2, 7 3, 10 6)	POLYGON ((1 4, 2 5, 5 2, 0 4, 1 4))	POLYGON ((1 4, 2 7, 7 2, 0 4, 1 4))

	Point1X	Point1Y	Line1Poly1Intersects	Line1Len	Line1Start	Line2PtCt	Poly1Area	Poly1Poly2Intersects
1	1	4	1	1.4142135623731	POINT (1 4)	4	4	1

Figure 9-14. The results of using the GEOMETRY type

Using GEOGRAPHY

The **GEOGRAPHY** data type is even more interesting than the **GEOMETRY** type. With the **GEOGRAPHY** type, you can store longitude and latitude values for actual locations or areas. Just like the **GEOMETRY** type, you can use several built-in methods to work with the data. You can also extract the data in a special XML format that can be used along with Microsoft's Virtual Earth application. Unfortunately, integrating the **GEOMETRY** data with the Virtual Earth is beyond the scope of this book. To learn more about creating Virtual Earth applications with SQL Server Geometry data, see the book *Beginning Spatial with SQL Server 2008* by Alastair Aitchison (Apress, 2009).

The AdventureWorks2008 database contains one **GEOMETRY** column in the **Person.Address** table. Type in and execute the code in Listing 9-12 to learn more.

Listing 9-12. Using the GEOGRAPHY Data Type

```
USE AdventureWorks2008;
GO

--1
DECLARE @OneAddress GEOGRAPHY;

--2
SELECT @OneAddress = SpatialLocation
FROM Person.Address
WHERE AddressID = 91;
```

```
--3
SELECT AddressID,PostalCode, SpatialLocation.ToString(),
    @OneAddress.STDistance(SpatialLocation) AS DiffInMeters
FROM Person.Address
WHERE AddressID IN (1,91, 831,11419);
```

Figure 9-15 shows the results. Statement 1 declares a variable, **@OneAddress**, of the **GEOGRAPHY** type. Statement 2 assigns one value to the variable. Query 3 displays the data including the **AddressID**, the **PostalCode**, and the **SpatialLocation.ToString** method. The **DiffInMeters** column displays the distance between the location saved in the variable to the stored data. Notice that the difference is zero when comparing a location to itself.

	AddressID	PostalCode	(No column name)	DiffInMeters
1	1	98011	POINT (-122.164644615406 47.7869921906598)	25366.6874166672
2	91	98104	POINT (-122.391164430965 47.6176669267707)	0
3	831	06510	POINT (-72.9550181450784 41.3589413896096)	3924885.39255556
4	11419	98366	POINT (-122.72771089643 47.575135985628)	25748.07917586

Figure 9-15. *The results of using the GEOGRAPHY data type*

Viewing the Spatial Results Tab

When you select **GEOMETRY** or **GEOGRAPHY** data in the native binary format, another tab shows up in the results. This tab displays a visual representation of the spatial data. Type in and execute Listing 9-13 to see how this works.

Listing 9-13. *Viewing Spatial Results*

```
--1
DECLARE @Area GEOMETRY;

--2
SET @Area = GEOMETRY::Parse('Polygon((1 4, 2 5, 5 2, 0 4, 1 4))');

--3
SELECT @Area AS Area;
```

After running the code, click the "Spatial results" tab. Figure 9-16 shows how this should look. This tab will show up whenever you return spatial data in the binary format in a grid.

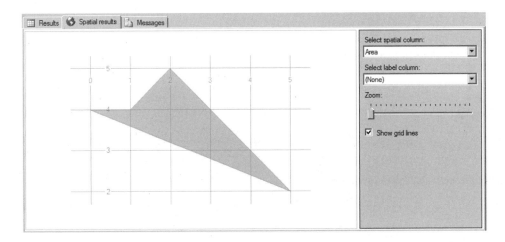

Figure 9-16. *The "Spatial results" tab*

Although the spatial data types are very interesting, they also require specialized knowledge to take full advantage of them. I encourage you to learn more if you think that your applications can benefit from these new data types.

Sparse Columns

Whenever you store fixed-length data, such as any of the numeric data types and some of the string data types, the data takes up the same amount of space in the database even when storing **NULL** values. By using the new sparse option, you can significantly reduce the amount of storage for **NULL** values. The trade-off is that the non-**NULL** values of sparse columns take up slightly more space than values stored in regular columns, and there is a small performance decrease when retrieving the non-**NULL** values. To use sparse columns, the option must be specified when creating the table. You can also include a special type of column, called a *column set*, to return all the sparse columns as XML. Type in and execute Listing 9-14 to learn more.

Listing 9-14. *Using Sparse Columns*

```
USE tempdb;
GO


--1
IF OBJECT_ID('dbo.SparseData') IS NOT NULL BEGIN
    DROP TABLE dbo.SparseData;
END;
GO
```

```
--2
CREATE TABLE dbo.SparseData
    (ID INT NOT NULL PRIMARY KEY,
    sc1 INT SPARSE NULL,
    sc2 INT SPARSE NULL,
    sc3 INT SPARSE NULL,
    cs XML COLUMN_SET FOR ALL_SPARSE_COLUMNS);
GO


--3
INSERT INTO dbo.SparseData(ID,sc1,sc2,sc3)
VALUES  (1,1,NULL,3),(2,NULL,1,1),(3,NULL,NULL,1);


--4
INSERT INTO SparseData(ID,cs)
SELECT 4,'<sc2>5</sc2>';


--5
SELECT * FROM dbo.SparseData;


--6
SELECT ID, sc1, sc2, sc3, cs FROM SparseData;
```

Figure 9-17 shows the results. Code section 1 drops the **dbo.SparseData** table if it exists. Statement 2 creates the table with a primary key column, **ID**; three sparse integer columns; and the XML column, **cs**. Statement 3 inserts three rows into the table, leaving out the **cs** column. Statement 4 inserts a row, but this time only providing values for **ID** and **cs**. Query 5 uses the asterisks to return all the columns and rows with surprising results. Instead of returning the individual sparse columns, the **cs** column provides the sparse data. Query 6 shows that you can still retrieve these columns individually if you need to and validates the **cs** column. Statement 4 provides a value only for the **cs** column and not the sparse columns. Query 6 proves that statement 4 inserted the data correctly into the sparse column.

	ID	cs		
1	1	<sc1>1</sc1><sc3>3</sc3>		
2	2	<sc2>1</sc2><sc3>1</sc3>		
3	3	<sc3>1</sc3>		
4	4	<sc2>5</sc2>		

	ID	sc1	sc2	sc3	cs
1	1	1	NULL	3	<sc1>1</sc1><sc3>3</sc3>
2	2	NULL	1	1	<sc2>1</sc2><sc3>1</sc3>
3	3	NULL	NULL	1	<sc3>1</sc3>
4	4	NULL	5	NULL	<sc2>5</sc2>

Figure 9-17. *The results of using sparse columns*

Because there is increased overhead when using sparse columns and because non-NULL values of sparse columns take a bit more space, Microsoft suggests that you use this feature only when the data will contain mostly NULL values. SQL Server Books Online contains a table in the "Using Sparse Columns" article showing the percentage
of NULL values the data should contain in order to make using the sparse columns beneficial.

To make it easier to work with the new sparse columns, Microsoft introduced a new type of index called a *filtered index*. By using a filtered index, you can filter out the NULL values from the sparse columns right in the index.

Summary

By practicing the skills taught in Chapters 1 through 8, you should become a very proficient T-SQL developer. This chapter introduced you to the new data types available in recent versions of SQL Server and how to work with them. You now know that you should not use TEXT, NTEXT, and IMAGE types going forward and that the new MAX data types should be used for very large columns. If you must store files, such as Microsoft Word documents or video, you know about a new option, FILESTREAM. You saw just a glimpse of the powerful XML data type and SQL Server support for XML. The new HIERARCHYID and the spatial types are available for special-purpose applications. You also have a new way to save space when working with tables that have many columns containing mostly NULLs. You now know what these types can do as well as the downsides of using these types. Because of this introduction, you can come up with solutions to challenging problems that others on your team may not think of.

Writing Advanced Queries

In Chapter 9 you learned about some exciting new data types that Microsoft introduced with SQL Server 2005 and 2008. In this chapter, you will learn about some of the new functions and advanced queries available with these most recent releases. For example, you will learn more about common table expressions (CTEs), how to write a pivot query, how to use the new ranking functions, and more. As a beginning T-SQL developer, you may or may not need this information right away. This chapter does not contain any exercises, but I encourage you to experiment and come up with your own examples for any of the features that you are interested in. Consider the information in this chapter as a head start in becoming an expert T-SQL developer.

Advanced CTE Queries

In Chapter 4 you learned to use common table expressions as one of the ways to combine the data from more than one table into one query. In Chapters 5 and 6 you learned how CTEs can simplify many statements. CTEs allow you to isolate part of the query logic or do things you could not ordinarily do, such as use an aggregate expression in an update. In these cases, you could use derived tables (see the "Derived Tables" section in Chapter 4), but now you will learn that CTEs are much more versatile. You can do several things with CTEs that are not possible with derived tables, such as write a recursive query. This section covers those advanced CTE features.

■ **Caution** The keyword WITH appears in many other statement types. Because of this, a statement containing a CTE must be the first statement in the batch, or the previous statement must end with a semicolon. At this point, Microsoft recommends using semicolons to end T-SQL statements, but it is not required. Some developers start all CTE definitions with a semicolon to avoid errors.

Using Multiple CTEs

You can use CTEs to organize and isolate query logic in order to write complicated queries efficiently. You cannot nest CTEs; that is, one CTE cannot contain another CTE. You can, however, add multiple CTEs to one query. You might want to do this just to make your query more readable or possibly because writing the query this way will let you avoid creating temp tables or views. Here is the syntax:

```
WITH <cteName1> AS (SELECT <col1> FROM <table1>),
    <cteName2> AS (SELECT <col2> FROM <table2>),
    <cteName3> AS (SELECT <col3> FROM <table3>)
SELECT <col1>, <col2>, <col3>
FROM <cteName1> INNER JOIN <cteName2> ON <join condition1>
INNER JOIN <cteName3> ON <join condition2>
```

Of course, your CTE definitions can contain just about any valid **SELECT** statement, and your outer query can use the CTEs in any way you need to use them. Type in and execute Listing 10-1 to learn more.

Listing 10-1. A Query with Multiple Queries in a CTE

```
USE AdventureWorks;
GO

WITH
Emp AS(
    SELECT e.EmployeeID, e.ManagerID,e.Title AS EmpTitle,
        c.FirstName + ISNULL(' ' + c.MiddleName,'') + ' ' + c.LastName AS EmpName
    FROM HumanResources.Employee AS e
    INNER JOIN Person.Contact AS c
    ON e.ContactID = c.ContactID
    ),
Mgr AS(
    SELECT e.EmployeeID AS ManagerID,e.Title AS MgrTitle,
        c.FirstName + ISNULL(' ' + c.MiddleName,'') + ' ' + c.LastName AS MgrName
    FROM HumanResources.Employee AS e
    INNER JOIN Person.Contact AS c
    ON e.ContactID = c.ContactID
    )
SELECT EmployeeID, Emp.ManagerID, EmpName, EmpTitle, MgrName, MgrTitle
FROM Emp INNER JOIN Mgr ON Emp.ManagerID = Mgr.ManagerID
ORDER BY EmployeeID;
```

Figure 10-1 shows the partial results. Each CTE must have a name, followed by the keyword **AS** and the definition in parentheses. Separate the CTE definitions with a comma. This query, from the AdventureWorks database, contains a CTE for the employees, **Emp**, and a CTE for the managers, **Mgr**. Within each CTE, the **HumanResources.Employee** table joins the **Person.Contact** table. By writing the query using CTEs, the outer query is very simple. You just join the **Mgr** CTE to the **Emp** CTE just as if they were regular tables or views.

	EmployeeID	ManagerID	EmpName	EmpTitle	MgrName	MgrTitle
1	1	16	Guy R Gilbert	Production Technician - WC60	Jo A Brown	Production Supervisor - WC60
2	2	6	Kevin F Brown	Marketing Assistant	David M Bradley	Marketing Manager
3	3	12	Roberto Tamburello	Engineering Manager	Terri Lee Duffy	Vice President of Engineering
4	4	3	Rob Walters	Senior Tool Designer	Roberto Tamburello	Engineering Manager
5	5	263	Thierry B D'Hers	Tool Designer	Ovidiu V Cracium	Senior Tool Designer
6	6	109	David M Bradley	Marketing Manager	Ken J Sánchez	Chief Executive Officer
7	7	21	JoLynn M Dobney	Production Supervisor - WC60	Peter J Krebs	Production Control Manager
8	8	185	Ruth Ann Ellerbrock	Production Technician - WC10	Andrew R Hill	Production Supervisor - WC10

Figure 10-1. The partial results of multiple CTEs in one statement

Calling a CTE Multiple Times

Just as you can have multiple CTE definitions within one statement, you can call a CTE multiple times within one statement. This is not possible with a derived table, which can be used only once within a statement. (See Chapter 4 for more information about derived tables.) A CTE could be used in a self-join, in a subquery, or in any valid way of using a table within a statement. Here are two syntax examples:

```
--self-join
WITH <cteName> AS (SELECT <col1>, <col2> FROM <table1>)
SELECT a.<col1>, b.<col1>
FROM <cteName> AS a
INNER JOIN <cteName> AS b ON <join condition>


--subquery
WITH <cteName> AS (SELECT <col1>, <col2> FROM <table1>)
SELECT <col1>
FROM <cteName>
WHERE <col2> IN (SELECT <col2>
    FROM <cteName> INNER JOIN <table1> ON <join condition>)
```

Type in and execute Listing 10-2 to see some examples. The self-join produces the same results as those in the previous section.

Listing 10-2. Calling a CTE Multiple Times Within a Statement

```
USE AdventureWorks;
GO


--1
WITH
Employees AS(
    SELECT e.EmployeeID, e.ManagerID,e.Title,
        c.FirstName + ISNULL(' ' + c.MiddleName,'') + ' ' + c.LastName AS EmpName
```

```
    FROM HumanResources.Employee AS e
    INNER JOIN Person.Contact AS c
    ON e.ContactID = c.ContactID
    )
SELECT emp.EmployeeID, emp.ManagerID, emp.EmpName, emp.Title AS EmpTitle,
    mgr.EmpName as MgrName, mgr.Title as MgrTitle
FROM Employees AS Emp INNER JOIN Employees AS Mgr
ON Emp.ManagerID = Mgr.EmployeeID;


--2
WITH Employees AS (
    SELECT e.EmployeeID, e.ManagerID,e.Title,
        c.FirstName + ISNULL(' ' + c.MiddleName,'') + ' ' +  c.LastName AS EmpName
    FROM HumanResources.Employee AS e
    INNER JOIN Person.Contact AS c
    ON e.ContactID = c.ContactID)
SELECT EmployeeID, ManagerID, EmpName, Title
FROM Employees
WHERE EmployeeID IN (SELECT EmployeeID
    FROM Employees AS e
    INNER JOIN Sales.SalesOrderHeader AS soh ON e.EmployeeID = soh.SalesPersonID
    WHERE soh.TotalDue > 10000);
```

Figure 10-2 shows the partial results. Statement 1 defines just one CTE, joining **HumanResources. Employee** to **Person.Contact**. The outer query calls the CTE twice, once with the alias **Emp** and once with the alias **Mgr**. Statement 2 defines the same CTE. In this case, however, the outer query uses the CTE as the main table and also within a subquery.

EmployeeID	ManagerID	EmpName	EmpTitle	MgrName	MgrTitle
1	16	Guy R Gilbert	Production Technician - WC60	Jo A Brown	Production Supervisor - WC60
2	6	Kevin F Brown	Marketing Assistant	David M Bradley	Marketing Manager
3	12	Roberto Tamburello	Engineering Manager	Terri Lee Duffy	Vice President of Engineering
4	3	Rob Walters	Senior Tool Designer	Roberto Tamburello	Engineering Manager
5	263	Thierry B D'Hers	Tool Designer	Ovidiu V Cracium	Senior Tool Designer
6	109	David M Bradley	Marketing Manager	Ken J Sánchez	Chief Executive Officer
7	21	JoLynn M Dobney	Production Supervisor - WC60	Peter J Krebs	Production Control Manager
8	185	Ruth Ann Ellerbrock	Production Technician - WC10	Andrew R Hill	Production Supervisor - WC10

EmployeeID	ManagerID	EmpName	Title
284	273	Amy E Alberts	European Sales Manager
278	268	Garrett R Vargas	Sales Representative
281	268	Shu K Ito	Sales Representative
275	268	Michael G Blythe	Sales Representative
276	268	Linda C Mitchell	Sales Representative
287	268	Tete A Mensa-Ann...	Sales Representative
279	268	Tsvi Michael Reiter	Sales Representative
290	288	Lynn N Tsoflias	Sales Representative

Figure 10-2. *The partial results of using a CTE twice in one statement*

Joining a CTE to Another CTE

Another very interesting feature of CTEs is the ability to call one CTE from another CTE definition. This is not recursion, which you will learn about in the "Writing a Recursive Query" section. Calling one CTE from within another CTE definition allows you to base one query on a previous query. Here is a syntax example:

```
WITH <cteName1> AS (SELECT <col1>, <col2> FROM <table1>),
    <cteName2> AS (SELECT <col1>, <col2>, <col3>
        FROM <table3> INNER JOIN <cteName1> ON <join condition>)
SELECT <col1>, <col2>, <col3> FROM <cteName2>
```

The order in which the CTE definitions appear is very important. You cannot call a CTE before it is defined. Type in and execute the code in Listing 10-3 to learn more.

Listing 10-3. Joining a CTE to Another CTE

```
USE tempdb;
GO


--1
IF OBJECT_ID('dbo.JobHistory') IS NOT NULL BEGIN
    DROP TABLE dbo.JobHistory;
END;


--2
CREATE TABLE JobHistory(
    EmployeeID INT NOT NULL,
    EffDate DATE NOT NULL,
    EffSeq INT NOT NULL,
    EmploymentStatus CHAR(1) NOT NULL,
    JobTitle VARCHAR(50) NOT NULL,
    Salary MONEY NOT NULL,
    ActionDesc VARCHAR(20)
 CONSTRAINT PK_JobHistory PRIMARY KEY CLUSTERED
(
    EmployeeID, EffDate, EffSeq
));

GO
```

```
--3
INSERT INTO JobHistory(EmployeeID, EffDate, EffSeq, EmploymentStatus,
    JobTitle, Salary, ActionDesc)
VALUES
    (1000,'07-31-2008',1,'A','Intern',2000,'New Hire'),
    (1000,'05-31-2009',1,'A','Production Technician',2000,'Title Change'),
    (1000,'05-31-2009',2,'A','Production Technician',2500,'Salary Change'),
    (1000,'11-01-2009',1,'A','Production Technician',3000,'Salary Change'),
    (1200,'01-10-2009',1,'A','Design Engineer',5000,'New Hire'),
    (1200,'05-01-2009',1,'T','Design Engineer',5000,'Termination'),
    (1100,'08-01-2008',1,'A','Accounts Payable Specialist I',2500,'New Hire'),
    (1100,'05-01-2009',1,'A','Accounts Payable Specialist II',2500,'Title Change'),
    (1100,'05-01-2009',2,'A','Accounts Payable Specialist II',3000,'Salary Change');

--4
DECLARE @Date DATE = '05-02-2009';

--5
WITH EffectiveDate AS (
        SELECT MAX(EffDate) AS MaxDate, EmployeeID
        FROM JobHistory
        WHERE EffDate <= @Date
        GROUP BY EmployeeID
    ),
    EffectiveSeq AS (
        SELECT MAX(EffSeq) AS MaxSeq, j.EmployeeID, MaxDate
        FROM JobHistory AS j
        INNER JOIN EffectiveDate AS d
            ON j.EffDate = d.MaxDate AND j.EmployeeID = d.EmployeeID
        GROUP BY j.EmployeeID, MaxDate)
SELECT j.EmployeeID, EmploymentStatus, JobTitle, Salary
FROM JobHistory AS j
INNER JOIN EffectiveSeq AS e ON j.EmployeeID = e.EmployeeID
    AND j.EffDate = e.MaxDate AND j.EffSeq = e.MaxSeq;
```

Figure 10-3 shows the results. I based this example on a system that I have worked with for several years. Many of the tables in this system contain history information with an effective date and an effective sequence. The system adds one row to these tables for each change to the employee's data. For a particular effective date, the system can add more than one row along with an incrementing effective sequence. To display information valid on a particular date, you first have to figure out the latest effective date before the date in mind and then figure out the effective sequence for that date. At first glance, you might think that just determining the maximum date and maximum sequence in one aggregate query should work. This doesn't work because the maximum sequence in the table for an employee may not be valid for a particular date. For example, the employee may have four changes and, therefore, four rows for an earlier date and only one row for the latest date.

	EmployeeID	Employment Status	Job Title	Salary
1	1000	A	Intern	2000.00
2	1100	A	Accounts Payable Specialist II	3000.00
3	1200	T	Design Engineer	5000.00

Figure 10-3. The results of calling one CTE from another CTE definition

Code section 1 drops the **JobHistory** table if it already exists. Statement 2 creates the **JobHistory** table including a primary key composed of **EmployeeID**, **EffDate**, and **EffSeq**. Statement 3 inserts several rows into the table. Notice that the statement inserts one row for each change even if the changes happen on the same date. Statement 4 declares and initializes a variable, **@Date**, which will be used in the **WHERE** clause in Statement 5. You can change the value of this variable to validate the results for different dates.

Statement 5 contains the **SELECT** statement. The first CTE, **EffectiveDate**, just determines the maximum **EffDate** from the **JobHistory** table for each employee that is valid for the **@Date** value. The second CTE, **EffectiveSeq**, joins the **JobHistory** table to the **EffectiveDate** CTE to find the maximum **EffSeq** for each employee for the date determined in the previous CTE, **EffectiveDate**. Finally, the outer query joins the **JobHistory** table on the **EffectiveSeq** CTE to display the valid data for each employee on the date stored in **@Date**.

Using the Alternate CTE Syntax

I prefer naming all the columns within the CTE definition, but you can also specify the column names outside the definition. There is no advantage to either syntax, but you should be familiar with both. Here is the syntax:

```
WITH <cteName> (<col1>, <col2>) AS (
    SELECT <col3>,<col4> FROM <table1>)
SELECT <col1>,<col2> FROM <cteName>
```

When using this technique, the column names defined outside the definition must be used in the outer query. If you have an expression within the definition, you do not have to give the expression an alias. Type in and execute the code in Listing 10-4 to practice this technique.

Listing 10-4. Writing a Query with the Alternate CTE Syntax

```
USE AdventureWorks;
GO

WITH Emp (EmployeeID, ManagerID, JobTitle,EmpName) AS
    (SELECT e.EmployeeID, e.ManagerID,e.Title,
        c.FirstName + ISNULL(' ' + c.MiddleName,'') + ' ' + c.LastName
    FROM HumanResources.Employee AS e
```

```
    INNER JOIN Person.Contact AS c
    ON e.ContactID = c.ContactID)
SELECT Emp.EmployeeID, ManagerID, JobTitle, EmpName
FROM Emp;
```

Figure 10-4 shows the partial results. All the columns must be listed in parentheses between the CTE name and the definition. Only the columns listed are valid. Either syntax will work; it is just a matter of preference.

	EmployeeID	ManagerID	JobTitle	EmpName
1	25	21	Production Supervisor - WC10	Zheng W Mu
2	26	108	Production Technician - WC20	Ivo William Salmre
3	27	87	Production Technician - WC40	Paul B Komosinski
4	24	184	Production Technician - WC30	David N Johnson
5	29	14	Production Technician - WC50	Kendall C Keil
6	30	140	Human Resources Manager	Paula M Barreto de Mattos
7	31	210	Production Technician - WC40	Alejandro E McGuel
8	32	184	Production Technician - WC30	Garrett R Young

Figure 10-4. *The partial results of using the named column CTE syntax*

Writing a Recursive Query

Recursive code, in any programming language, is code that calls itself. Programmers use this technique to follow paths in tree or directory structures. When following the paths in these structures, the code must start at the root, follow each path to the end, and back up again to the next path repeatedly. In T-SQL, you can use the same technique in a CTE. One common example is the **HumanResources.Employee** table in the AdventureWorks database. The self-join found in that table represents a hierarchical structure. To view the entire hierarchy, you must start at the root, the CEO of the company, and follow every possible manager-employee path down to the lowest person. Here is the syntax for writing a recursive CTE:

```
WITH <cteName> (<col1>, <col2>, <col3>, level)
AS
(
    --Anchor member
    SELECT <primaryKey>,<foreignKey>,<col3>, 0 AS level
    FROM <table1>
    WHERE <foreignKey> = <startingValue>
    UNION ALL
    --Recursive member
    SELECT a.<primaryKey>,a.<foreignKey>,a.<col3>, b.level + 1
    FROM <table1> AS a
    INNER JOIN <cteName> AS b
        ON a.<foreignKey>  = b.<primaryKey>
)
```

```
SELECT <col1>,<col2>,<col3>,level
FROM <cteName> [OPTION (MAXRECURSION <number>)]
```

To write the recursive CTE, you must have an anchor member, which is a statement that returns the top of your intended results. This is like the root of the directory. Following the anchor member, you will write the recursive member. The recursive member actually joins the CTE that contains it to the same table used in the anchor member. The results of the anchor member and the recursive member join in a **UNION ALL** query. Type in and execute the code in Listing 10-5 to see how this works.

Listing 10-5. A Recursive CTE

```
USE AdventureWorks;
GO

WITH OrgChart (EmployeeID, ManagerID, Title, Level,Node)
    AS (SELECT EmployeeID, ManagerID, Title, 0,
            CONVERT(VARCHAR(30),'/') AS Node
        FROM HumanResources.Employee
        WHERE ManagerID IS NULL
        UNION ALL
        SELECT a.EmployeeID, a.ManagerID,a.Title, b.Level + 1,
            CONVERT(VARCHAR(30),b.Node +
                CONVERT(VARCHAR,a.ManagerID) + '/')
        FROM HumanResources.Employee AS a
        INNER JOIN OrgChart AS b ON a.ManagerID = b.EmployeeID
    )
SELECT EmployeeID, ManagerID, SPACE(Level * 3) + Title AS Title, Level, Node
FROM OrgChart
ORDER BY Node;
```

Figure 10-5 shows the results. The anchor member selects the **EmployeeID**, **ManagerID**, and **Title** from the **HumanResources.Employee** table for the CEO. The CEO is the only employee with a **NULL ManagerID**. The level is zero. The node column, added to help sorting, is just a slash. To get this to work, the query uses the **CONVERT** function to change the data type of the slash to a **VARCHAR(30)** because the data types in the columns of the anchor member and recursive member must match exactly. The recursive member joins **HumanResources.Employee** to the CTE, **OrgChart**. The query is recursive because the CTE is used inside its own definition. The regular columns in the recursive member come from the table, and the level is one plus the value of the level returned from the CTE. To sort in a meaningful way, the node shows the **ManagerID** values used to get to the current employee surrounded with slashes. This looks very similar to the node used in the **HierarchyID** example in Chapter 9.

	EmployeeID	ManagerID	Title	Level	Node
1	109	NULL	Chief Executive Officer	0	/
2	6	109	Marketing Manager	1	/109/
3	12	109	Vice President of Engineering	1	/109/
4	42	109	Information Services Manager	1	/109/
5	140	109	Chief Financial Officer	1	/109/
6	148	109	Vice President of Production	1	/109/
7	273	109	Vice President of Sales	1	/109/
8	3	12	Engineering Manager	2	/109/12/
9	4	3	Senior Tool Designer	3	/109/12/3/
10	9	3	Design Engineer	3	/109/12/3/
11	11	3	Design Engineer	3	/109/12/3/
12	158	3	Research and Development Manager	3	/109/12/3/
13	263	3	Senior Tool Designer	3	/109/12/3/
14	267	3	Senior Design Engineer	3	/109/12/3/
15	270	3	Design Engineer	3	/109/12/3/
16	79	158	Research and Development Engineer	4	/109/12/3/158/

Figure 10-5. The partial results of a recursive query

The query runs the recursive member repeatedly until all possible paths are selected, that is, until the recursive member no longer returns results. In case of an incorrectly written recursive query that will run forever, the recursive member will run only 100 times by default unless you specify the MAXRECURSION option to limit how many times the query will run. To alter the query in Listing 10-5 to a potential unending loop, change a.ManagerID = b.EmployeeID to a.EmployeeID = b.EmployeeID.

Just because the default MAXRECURSION value is 100 doesn't mean that a recursive query will return only 100 rows. In this example, the anchor returns the CEO, EmployeeID 109. The first time the recursive member runs, the results include all employees who report to 109. The next call returns the employees reporting to the employees returned in the last call, and so on. The values from one call feed the next call.

Instead of filtering the anchor to find the CEO, you can supply any ManagerID value. If you specify a particular manager, instead of starting at the CEO, the results will start at the subordinates of the ManagerID supplied. On your own, change the criteria in the anchor member, and rerun the query to see what happens.

Writing recursive queries is an advanced skill you may or may not need right away. Luckily, if you do need to write a recursive query, you will know where to find a simple example.

The OUTPUT Clause

You learned how to manipulate data in Chapter 6. The OUTPUT clause, new with SQL Server 2005, allows you to see or even save the modified values when you perform a data manipulation statement. The interesting thing about OUTPUT is that data manipulation statements do not normally return data except for the number of rows affected. By using OUTPUT, you can retrieve a result set of the data in the same statement that updates the data. You can see the result set in the query window results or return the result set to a client application.

Using OUTPUT to View Data

When using **OUTPUT**, you can view the data using the special tables **DELETED** and **INSERTED**. You may wonder why there is not an **UPDATED** table. Instead of an **UPDATED** table, you will find the old values in the **DELETED** table and the new values in the **INSERTED** table. Here are the syntax examples for using the **OUTPUT** clause for viewing changes when running data manipulation statements:

```
--Update style 1
UPDATE a SET <col1> = <value>
OUTPUT deleted.<col1>,inserted.<col1>
FROM <table1> AS a

--Update style 2
UPDATE <table1> SET <col1> = <value>
OUTPUT deleted.<col1>, inserted.<col1>
WHERE <criteria>

--Insert style 1
INSERT [INTO] <table1> (<col1>,<col2>)
OUTPUT inserted.<col1>, inserted.<col2>
SELECT <col1>, <col2>
FROM <table2>

--Insert style 2
INSERT [INTO] <table1> (<col1>,<col2>)
OUTPUT inserted.<col1>, inserted.<col2>
VALUES (<value1>,<value2>)

--Delete style 1
DELETE [FROM] <table1>
OUTPUT deleted.<col1>, deleted.<col2>
WHERE <criteria>

--DELETE style 2
DELETE [FROM] a
OUTPUT deleted.<col1>, deleted.<col2>
FROM <table1> AS a
```

Probably the trickiest thing about using **OUTPUT** is figuring out where in the statement to include it. Type in and execute the code in Listing 10-6 to learn more about **OUTPUT**.

Listing 10-6. Viewing the Manipulated Data with OUTPUT

```
USE AdventureWorks2008;
GO


--1
IF OBJECT_ID('dbo.Customers') IS NOT NULL BEGIN
    DROP TABLE dbo.Customers;
END;


--2
CREATE TABLE dbo.Customers (CustomerID INT NOT NULL PRIMARY KEY,
    Name VARCHAR(150),PersonID INT NOT NULL)
GO


--3
INSERT INTO dbo.Customers(CustomerID,Name,PersonID)
OUTPUT inserted.CustomerID,inserted.Name
SELECT c.CustomerID, p.FirstName + ' ' + p.LastName,PersonID
FROM Sales.Customer AS c
INNER JOIN Person.Person AS p
ON c.PersonID = p.BusinessEntityID;



--4
UPDATE c SET Name = p.FirstName +
    ISNULL(' ' + p.MiddleName,'') + ' ' + p.LastName
OUTPUT deleted.CustomerID,deleted.Name AS OldName, inserted.Name AS NewName
FROM dbo.Customers AS c
INNER JOIN Person.Person AS p on c.PersonID = p.BusinessEntityID;



--5
DELETE FROM dbo.Customers
OUTPUT deleted.CustomerID, deleted.Name, deleted.PersonID
WHERE CustomerID = 11000;
```

Figure 10-6 shows the partial results. Unfortunately, you cannot add an **ORDER BY** clause to **OUTPUT**, and the **INSERT** statement returns the rows in a different order than the **UPDATE** statement. Code section 1 drops the **dbo.Customers** table if it already exists. Statement 2 creates the **dbo.Customers** table. Statement 3 inserts all the rows when joining the **Sales.Customer** table to the **Person.Person** table. The **OUTPUT** clause, located right after the **INSERT** clause, returns the **CustomerID** and **Name**. Statement 4 modifies the **Name** column by including the **MiddleName** in the expression. The **DELETED** table displays the **Name** column data before the update. The **INSERTED** table displays the **Name** column after the update. The

UPDATE clause includes aliases to differentiate the values. Statement 5 deletes one row from the table. The OUTPUT clause displays the deleted data.

CustomerID	Name
1	11000	Jon Yang
2	11001	Eugene Huang
3	11002	Ruben Torres
4	11003	Christy Zhu
5	11004	Elizabeth Johnson

CustomerID	OldName	NewName
1	29485	Catherine Abel	Catherine R. Abel
2	29486	Kim Abercrombie	Kim Abercrombie
3	29487	Humberto Acevedo	Humberto Acevedo
4	29484	Gustavo Achong	Gustavo Achong
5	29488	Pilar Ackerman	Pilar Ackerman

CustomerID	Name	PersonID
1	11000	Jon V Yang	13531

Figure 10-6. *The partial results of viewing the manipulated data with* OUTPUT

Saving OUTPUT Data to a Table

Instead of displaying or returning the rows from the OUTPUT clause, you might need to save the information in another table. For example, you may need to populate a history table or save the changes for further processing. Here is a syntax example showing how to use INTO along with OUTPUT:

```
INSERT [INTO] <table1> (<col1>, <col2>)
OUTPUT inserted.<col1>, inserted.<col2>
INTO <table2>
SELECT <col3>,<col4>
FROM <table3>
```

One drawback of using INTO along with OUTPUT is that you cannot specify the column names in the target table. You must have a value in the OUTPUT clause for each column of the target table. One way around this, for example, if the target table has an IDENTITY column, would be to create a view to receive the data. Type in and execute the code in Listing 10-7 to learn more.

Listing 10-7. *Saving the Results of* OUTPUT

```
USE AdventureWorks2008;
GO


--1
IF OBJECT_ID('dbo.Customers') IS NOT NULL BEGIN
    DROP TABLE dbo.Customers;
END;
```

```
IF OBJECT_ID('dbo.CustomerHistory') IS NOT NULL BEGIN
    DROP TABLE dbo.CustomerHistory;
END;


--2
CREATE TABLE dbo.Customers (CustomerID INT NOT NULL PRIMARY KEY,
    Name VARCHAR(150),PersonID INT NOT NULL)

CREATE TABLE dbo.CustomerHistory(CustomerID INT NOT NULL PRIMARY KEY,
    OldName VARCHAR(150), NewName VARCHAR(150),
    ChangeDate DATETIME)
GO


--3
INSERT INTO dbo.Customers(CustomerID, Name, PersonID)
SELECT c.CustomerID, p.FirstName + ' ' + p.LastName,PersonID
FROM Sales.Customer AS c
INNER JOIN Person.Person AS p
ON c.PersonID = p.BusinessEntityID;



--4
UPDATE c SET Name = p.FirstName +
    ISNULL(' ' + p.MiddleName,'') + ' ' + p.LastName
OUTPUT deleted.CustomerID,deleted.Name, inserted.Name, GETDATE()
INTO dbo.CustomerHistory
FROM dbo.Customers AS c
INNER JOIN Person.Person AS p on c.PersonID = p.BusinessEntityID;


--5
SELECT CustomerID, OldName, NewName,ChangeDate
FROM dbo.CustomerHistory;
```

Figure 10-7 shows the partial results. Code section 1 drops the **dbo.Customers** and **dbo.CustomerHistory** tables if they already exist. Code section 2 creates the two tables. Statement 3 populates the **dbo.Customers** table. Statement 4 updates the **Name** column for all of the rows. By including **OUTPUT INTO**, the **CustomerID** along with the previous and current **Name** values are saved into the table. The statement also populates the **ChangeDate** column by using the **GETDATE** function.

	CustomerID	OldName	NewName	ChangeDate
1	11000	Jon Yang	Jon V Yang	2009-06-14 14:34:23.517
2	11001	Eugene Huang	Eugene L Huang	2009-06-14 14:34:23.517
3	11002	Ruben Torres	Ruben Torres	2009-06-14 14:34:23.517
4	11003	Christy Zhu	Christy Zhu	2009-06-14 14:34:23.517
5	11004	Elizabeth Johnson	Elizabeth Johnson	2009-06-14 14:34:23.517
6	11005	Julio Ruiz	Julio Ruiz	2009-06-14 14:34:23.517
7	11006	Janet Alvarez	Janet G Alvarez	2009-06-14 14:34:23.517
8	11007	Marco Mehta	Marco Mehta	2009-06-14 14:34:23.517

Figure 10-7. *The partial results of saving the* OUTPUT *data into a table*

The MERGE Statement

The MERGE statement, also known as *upsert*, allows you to synchronize two tables with one statement. For example, you would normally need to perform at least one UPDATE, one INSERT, and one DELETE statement to keep the data in one table up-to-date with the data from another table. By using MERGE, you can perform the same work more efficiently, assuming that the tables have the proper indexes in place, and with just one statement. The drawback is that MERGE is more difficult to understand and write than the three individual statements. One potential use for MERGE, where taking the time to write the MERGE statements really pays off, is loading data warehouses and data marts. Here is the syntax for a simple MERGE statement:

```
MERGE <target table>
USING <source table name>|(or query>) AS alias [(column names)]
ON (<join criteria>)
WHEN MATCHED [AND <other critera>]
THEN UPDATE SET <col> = alias.<value>
WHEN NOT MATCHED BY TARGET [AND <other criteria>]
THEN INSERT (<column list>) VALUES (<values>) -- row is inserted into target
WHEN NOT MATCHED BY SOURCE [AND <other criteria>]
THEN DELETE -- row is deleted from target
[OUTPUT $action, DELETED.*, INSERTED.*];
```

At first glance, the syntax may seem overwhelming. Basically, it defines an action to perform if a row from the source table matches the target table (WHEN MATCHED), an action to perform if a row is missing in the target table (WHEN NOT MATCHED BY TARGET), and an action to perform if an extra row is in the target table (WHEN NOT MATCHED BY SOURCE). The actions to perform on the target table can be anything you need to do. For example, if the source table is missing a row that appears in the target table (WHEN NOT MATCHED BY SOURCE), you don't have to delete the target row. You could, in fact, leave out that part of the statement or perform another action. In addition to the join criteria, you can also specify any other criteria in each match specification. You can include an optional OUTPUT clause along with the $action option. The $action option shows you which action is performed on each row. Include the DELETED and INSERTED tables in the OUTPUT clause to see the before and after values. The MERGE statement must end with a semicolon. Type in and execute the code in Listing 10-8 to learn how to use MERGE.

Listing 10-8. Using the MERGE Statement

```
USE AdventureWorks2008;
GO


--1
IF OBJECT_ID('dbo.CustomerSource') IS NOT NULL BEGIN
    DROP TABLE dbo.CustomerSource;
END;
IF OBJECT_ID('dbo.CustomerTarget') IS NOT NULL BEGIN
    DROP TABLE dbo.CustomerTarget;
END;


--2
CREATE TABLE dbo.CustomerSource (CustomerID INT NOT NULL PRIMARY KEY,
    Name VARCHAR(150), PersonID INT NOT NULL);
CREATE TABLE dbo.CustomerTarget (CustomerID INT NOT NULL PRIMARY KEY,
    Name VARCHAR(150), PersonID INT NOT NULL);
GO


--3
INSERT INTO dbo.CustomerSource(CustomerID,Name,PersonID)
SELECT CustomerID,
    p.FirstName + ISNULL(' ' + p.MiddleName,'') + ' ' + p.LastName,
    PersonID
FROM Sales.Customer AS c
INNER JOIN Person.Person AS p ON c.PersonID = p.BusinessEntityID
WHERE c.CustomerID IN (29485,29486,29487,10299);


--4
INSERT INTO dbo.CustomerTarget(CustomerID,Name,PersonID)
SELECT CustomerID, p.FirstName  + ' ' + p.LastName, PersonID
FROM Sales.Customer AS c
INNER JOIN Person.Person AS p ON c.PersonID = p.BusinessEntityID
WHERE c.CustomerID IN (29485,29486,21139);


--5
SELECT CustomerID, Name, PersonID
FROM dbo.CustomerSource
ORDER BY CustomerID;
```

```
--6
SELECT CustomerID, Name, PersonID
FROM dbo.CustomerTarget
ORDER BY CustomerID;

--7
MERGE dbo.CustomerTarget AS t
USING dbo.CustomerSource AS s
ON (s.CustomerID = t.CustomerID)
WHEN MATCHED AND s.Name <> t.Name
THEN UPDATE SET Name = s.Name
WHEN NOT MATCHED BY TARGET
THEN INSERT (CustomerID, Name, PersonID) VALUES (CustomerID, Name, PersonID)
WHEN NOT MATCHED BY SOURCE
THEN DELETE
OUTPUT $action, DELETED.*, INSERTED.*;--semi-colon is required

--8
SELECT CustomerID, Name, PersonID
FROM dbo.CustomerTarget
ORDER BY CustomerID;
```

Figure 10-8 shows the results. Code section 1 drops the tables **dbo.CustomerSource** and **dbo.CustomerTarget**. Code section 2 creates the two tables. They have the same column names, but this is not a requirement. Statement 3 populates the **dbo.CustomerSource** with four rows. It creates the **Name** column using the **FirstName**, **MiddleName**, and **LastName** columns. Statement 4 populates the **dbo.CustomerTarget** table with three rows. Two of the rows contain the same customers as the **dbo.CustomerSource** table. Query 5 displays the data from **dbo.CustomerSource**, and query 6 displays the data from **dbo.CustomerTarget**. Statement 7 synchronizes **dbo.CustomerTarget** with **dbo.CustomerSource**, correcting the **Name**, inserting missing rows, and deleting extra rows by using the **MERGE** command. Because the query includes the **OUTPUT** clause, you can see the action performed on each row. Query 8 displays the **dbo.CustomerTarget** with the changes. The target table now matches the source table.

Results

	CustomerID	Name	PersonID
1	29485	Catherine R. Abel	293
2	29486	Kim Abercrombie	295
3	29487	Humberto Acevedo	297

	CustomerID	Name	PersonID
1	21139	Alex Adams	16724
2	29485	Catherine Abel	293
3	29486	Kim Abercrombie	295

	$action	CustomerID	Name	PersonID	CustomerID	Name	PersonID
1	DELETE	21139	Alex Adams	16724	NULL	NULL	NULL
2	UPDATE	29485	Catherine Abel	293	29485	Catherine R. Abel	293
3	INSERT	NULL	NULL	NULL	29487	Humberto Acevedo	297

	CustomerID	Name	PersonID
1	29485	Catherine R. Abel	293
2	29486	Kim Abercrombie	295
3	29487	Humberto Acevedo	297

Figure 10-8. *The results of using MERGE*

GROUPING SETS

You learned all about aggregate queries in Chapter 5. Another option, **GROUPING SETS**, when added to an aggregate query, allows you to combine different grouping levels within one statement. This is equivalent to combining multiple aggregate queries with **UNION**. For example, suppose you want the data summarized by one column combined with the data summarized by a different column. Just like **MERGE**, this feature is very valuable for loading data warehouses and data marts. When using **GROUPING SETS** instead of **UNION**, you can see increased performance, especially when the query includes a **WHERE** clause and the number of columns specified in the **GROUPING SETS** clause increases. Here is the syntax:

```
SELECT <col1>,<col2>,<aggregate function>(<col3>)
FROM <table1>
WHERE <criteria>
GROUP BY GROUPING SETS (<col1>,<col2>)
```

Listing 10-9 compares the equivalent **UNION** query to a query using **GROUPING SETS**. Type in and execute the code to learn more.

Listing 10-9. *Using GROUPING SETS*

```
USE AdventureWorks2008;
GO

--1
SELECT NULL AS SalesOrderID,SUM(UnitPrice)AS SumOfPrice,ProductID
FROM Sales.SalesOrderDetail
WHERE SalesOrderID BETWEEN 44175 AND 44180
```

```
GROUP BY ProductID
UNION
SELECT SalesOrderID,SUM(UnitPrice), NULL
FROM Sales.SalesOrderDetail
WHERE SalesOrderID BETWEEN 44175 AND 44180
GROUP BY SalesOrderID;

--2
SELECT SalesOrderID,SUM(UnitPrice) AS SumOfPrice,ProductID
FROM Sales.SalesOrderDetail
WHERE SalesOrderID BETWEEN 44175 AND 44180
GROUP BY GROUPING SETS(SalesOrderID,ProductID);
```

Figure 10-9 shows the partial results. Query 1 is a **UNION** query that calculates the sum of the **UnitPrice**. The first part of the query supplies a **NULL** value for **SalesOrderID**. That is because **SalesOrderID** is just a placeholder. The query groups by **ProductID**, and **SalesOrderID** is not needed. The second part of the query supplies a **NULL** value for **ProductID**. In this case, the query groups by **SalesOrderID**, and **ProductID** is not needed. The **UNION** query combines the results. Query 2 demonstrates how to write the equivalent query using **GROUPING SETS**.

	SalesOrderID	SumOfPrice	ProductID
1	NULL	3578.27	751
2	NULL	3578.27	752
3	NULL	3578.27	753
4	NULL	3399.99	774
5	NULL	6749.98	777
6	44175	3578.27	NULL
7	44176	3578.27	NULL
8	44177	3374.99	NULL
9	44178	3578.27	NULL

	SalesOrderID	SumOfPrice	ProductID
1	NULL	3578.27	751
2	NULL	3578.27	752
3	NULL	3578.27	753
4	NULL	3399.99	774
5	NULL	6749.98	777
6	44175	3578.27	NULL
7	44176	3578.27	NULL
8	44177	3374.99	NULL
9	44178	3578.27	NULL

Figure 10-9. The partial results of comparing UNION to GROUPING SETS

Pivoted Queries

Normally, a query displays the data in a way that is similar to how it looks in a table, often with the column headers being the actual names of the columns within the table.

A pivoted query displays the values of one column as column headers instead. For example, you could display the sum of the sales by month so that the month names are column headers. Each row would then contain the data by year with the sum for each month displayed from left to right. This section shows how to write pivoted queries with two techniques: **CASE** and **PIVOT**.

Pivoting Data with CASE

Before SQL Server 2005, many developers used the **CASE** function to create pivoted results. (See "The Case Function" section in Chapter 3 to learn more about **CASE**.) In fact, many still use this technique. Essentially, you use several **CASE** expressions in the query, one for each pivoted column header. For example, the query will have a **CASE** expression checking to see whether the month of the order date is January. If the order does occur in January, supply the total sales value. If not, supply a zero. For each row, the data ends up in the correct column where it can be aggregated. Here is the syntax for using **CASE** to pivot data:

```
CASE <col1>,SUM(CASE <col3> WHEN <value1> THEN <col2> ELSE 0 END) AS <alias1>,
    SUM(CASE <col3> WHEN <value2> THEN <col2> ELSE 0 END) AS <alias2>,
    SUM(CASE <col3> WHEN <value3> THEN <col2> ELSE 0 END) AS <alias3>
FROM <table1>
GROUP BY <col1>
```

Type in and execute Listing 10-10 to learn how to pivot data using **CASE**.

Listing 10-10. Using CASE to Pivot Data

```
USE AdventureWorks2008;
GO
SELECT YEAR(OrderDate) AS OrderYear,
ROUND(SUM(CASE MONTH(OrderDate) WHEN 1 THEN TotalDue ELSE 0 END),0)
    AS Jan,
ROUND(SUM(CASE MONTH(OrderDate) WHEN 2 THEN TotalDue ELSE 0 END),0)
    AS Feb,
ROUND(SUM(CASE MONTH(OrderDate) WHEN 3 THEN TotalDue ELSE 0 END),0)
    AS Mar,
ROUND(SUM(CASE MONTH(OrderDate) WHEN 4 THEN TotalDue ELSE 0 END),0)
    AS Apr,
ROUND(SUM(CASE MONTH(OrderDate) WHEN 5 THEN TotalDue ELSE 0 END),0)
    AS May,
ROUND(SUM(CASE MONTH(OrderDate) WHEN 6 THEN TotalDue ELSE 0 END),0)
    AS Jun
FROM Sales.SalesOrderHeader
GROUP BY YEAR(OrderDate)
ORDER BY OrderYear;
```

Figure 10-10 shows the results. To save space in the results, the statement calculates the totals only for the months January through June and uses the **ROUND** function. The **GROUP BY** clause contains just the **YEAR(OrderDate)** expression. You might think that you need to group by month as well, but this query doesn't group by month. It just includes each **TotalDue** value in a different column depending on the month.

OrderYear	Jan	Feb	Mar	Apr	May	Jun
1	2001	0.00	0.00	0.00	0.00	0.00	0.00
2	2002	1462449.00	2749105.00	2350568.00	1727690.00	3299799.00	1920507.00
3	2003	1968647.00	3226056.00	2297693.00	2660724.00	3866365.00	2852210.00
4	2004	3359927.00	4662656.00	4722358.00	4269365.00	5813557.00	6004156.00

Figure 10-10. *The results of using CASE to create a pivot query*

Using the PIVOT Function

Microsoft introduced the **PIVOT** function with SQL Server 2005. In my opinion, the **PIVOT** function is more difficult to understand than using **CASE** to produce the same results. Just like **CASE**, you have to hard-code the column names. This works fine when the pivoted column names will never change, such as the months of the year. When the query bases the pivoted column on data that changes over time, such as employee or department names, the query must be modified each time that data changes. Here is the syntax for **PIVOT**:

```
SELECT <groupingCol>, <pivotedValue1> [AS <alias1>], <pivotedValue2> [AS <alias2>]
FROM (SELECT <groupingCol>, <value column>, <pivoted column>) AS <queryAlias>
PIVOT
( <aggregate function>(<value column>)
FOR <pivoted column> IN (<pivotedValue1>,<pivotedValue2>)
) AS <pivotAlias>
[ORDER BY <groupingCol>]
```

The **SELECT** part of the query lists any nonpivoted columns along with the values from the pivoted column. These values from the pivoted column will become the column names in your query. You can use aliases if you want to use a different column name than the actual value. For example, if the column names will be the month numbers, you can alias with the month names.

This syntax uses a derived table, listed after the word **FROM**, as the basis of the query. See the "Derived Tables" section in Chapter 4 to review derived tables. Make sure that you only list columns that you want as grouping levels, the pivoted column, and the column that will be summarized in this derived table. Adding other columns to this query will cause extra grouping levels and unexpected results. The derived table must be aliased, so don't forget that small detail.

▓ **Tip** It is possible to use a CTE to write this query instead of a derived table. See the article "Create Pivoted Tables in 3 Steps" in *SQL Server Magazine*'s July 2009 issue to learn this alternate method.

Follow the derived table with the **PIVOT** function. The argument to the **PIVOT** function includes the aggregate expression followed by the word **FOR** and the pivoted column name. Right after the pivoted column name, include an **IN** expression. Inside the **IN** expression, list the pivoted column values. These will match up with the pivoted column values in the **SELECT** list. The **PIVOT** function must also have an alias. Finally, you can order the results if you want. Usually, this will be by the grouping level column, but you can also sort by any of the pivoted column names. Type in and execute Listing 10-11 to learn how to use **PIVOT**.

Listing 10-11. Pivoting Results with PIVOT

```
USE AdventureWorks2008;
GO


--1
SELECT OrderYear, [1] AS Jan, [2] AS Feb, [3] AS Mar,
    [4] AS Apr, [5] AS May, [6] AS Jun
FROM (SELECT YEAR(OrderDate) AS OrderYear, TotalDue,
    MONTH(OrderDate) AS OrderMonth
    FROM Sales.SalesOrderHeader) AS MonthData
PIVOT (
    SUM(TotalDue)
    FOR OrderMonth IN ([1],[2],[3],[4],[5],[6])
    ) AS PivotData
ORDER BY OrderYear;


--2
SELECT OrderYear, ROUND(ISNULL([1],0),0) AS Jan,
    ROUND(ISNULL([2],0),0) AS Feb, ROUND(ISNULL([3],0),0) AS Mar,
    ROUND(ISNULL([4],0),0) AS Apr, ROUND(ISNULL([5],0),0) AS May,
    ROUND(ISNULL([6],0),0) AS Jun
FROM (SELECT YEAR(OrderDate) AS OrderYear, TotalDue,
    MONTH(OrderDate) AS OrderMonth
    FROM Sales.SalesOrderHeader) AS MonthData
PIVOT (
    SUM(TotalDue)
    FOR OrderMonth IN ([1],[2],[3],[4],[5],[6])
    ) AS PivotData
ORDER BY OrderYear;
```

Figure 10-11 shows the results. First take a look at the derived table aliased as **MonthData** in query 1. The **SELECT** statement in the derived table contains an expression that returns the year of the **OrderDate**, the **OrderYear**, and an expression that returns the month of the **OrderDate**, **OrderMonth**. It also contains the **TotalDue** column. The query will group the results by **OrderYear**. The **OrderMonth** column is the pivoted column. The query will sum up the **TotalDue** values. The derived table contains only the columns and expressions needed by the pivoted query.

	OrderYear	Jan	Feb	Mar	Apr	May	Jun
1	2001	NULL	NULL	NULL	NULL	NULL	NULL
2	2002	1462448.8986	2749104.6546	2350568.1264	1727689.5793	3299799.233	1920506.6177
3	2003	1968647.184	3226056.1486	2297692.9898	2660723.7481	3866365.1263	2852209.8283
4	2004	3359927.2196	4662655.6183	4722357.5175	4269365.0103	5813557.453	6004155.7672

	OrderYear	Jan	Feb	Mar	Apr	May	Jun
1	2001	0.00	0.00	0.00	0.00	0.00	0.00
2	2002	1462449.00	2749105.00	2350568.00	1727690.00	3299799.00	1920507.00
3	2003	1968647.00	3226056.00	2297693.00	2660724.00	3866365.00	2852210.00
4	2004	3359927.00	4662656.00	4722358.00	4269365.00	5813557.00	6004156.00

Figure 10-11. The results of using PIVOT

The **PIVOT** function specifies the aggregate expression **SUM(TotalDue)**. The pivoted column is **OrderMonth**. The **IN** expression contains the numbers 1–6, each surrounded by brackets. The **IN** expression lists the values for **OrderMonth** that you want to show up in the final results. These values are also the column names. Since columns starting with numbers are not valid column names, the brackets surround the numbers. You could also quote these numbers. The **IN** expression has two purposes: to provide the column names and to filter the results.

The outer **SELECT** list contains **OrderYear** and the numbers 1–6 surrounded with brackets. These must be the same values found in the **IN** expression. Because you want the month abbreviations instead of numbers as the column names, the query uses aliases. Notice that the **SELECT** list does not contain the **TotalDue** column. Finally, the **ORDER BY** clause specifies that the results will sort by **OrderYear**.

The results of query 2 are identical to the results from the pivoted results using the **CASE** technique in the previous section. This query uses the **ROUND** and **ISNULL** functions to replace **NULL** with zero and round the results.

TOP Enhancements

Use the **TOP** keyword to limit the number or percentage of rows returned from a query. **TOP** has been around for a long time, but with the release of SQL Server 2005, Microsoft has added several enhancements. **TOP** originally could be used in **SELECT** statements only. You could not use **TOP** in a **DELETE**, **UPDATE**, or **INSERT** statement. The number or percentage specified had to be a hard-coded value. Beginning with SQL Server 2005, you can use **TOP** in data manipulation statements and use a variable to specify the number or percentage or rows. Here is the syntax:

```
SELECT TOP(<number>) [PERCENT] [WITH TIES] <col1>,<col2>
FROM <table1> [ORDER BY <col1>]

DELETE TOP(<number>) [PERCENT] [FROM] <table1>

UPDATE TOP(<number>) [PERCENT] <table1> SET <col1> = <value>

INSERT TOP(<number>) [PERCENT] [INTO] <table1> (<col1>,<col2>)
SELECT <col3>,<col4> FROM <table2>
```

```
INSERT [INTO] <table1> (<col1>,<col2>)
SELECT TOP(<numbers>) [PERCENT] <col3>,<col4>
FROM <table2>
ORDER BY <col1>
```

       The ORDER BY clause is optional with the SELECT statement, but most of the time, you will use it to determine which rows the query returns. The ORDER BY clause is not valid with DELETE and UPDATE. The WITH TIES option is valid only with the SELECT statement. It means that, if there are rows that have identical values in the ORDER BY clause, the results will include all the rows even though you now end up with more rows than you expect. Type in and execute the code in Listing 10-12 to learn how to use TOP.

Listing 10-12. Limiting Results with TOP

```
USE AdventureWorks2008;
GO


--1
IF OBJECT_ID('dbo.Sales') IS NOT NULL BEGIN
    DROP TABLE dbo.Sales;
END;


--2
CREATE TABLE dbo.Sales (CustomerID INT, OrderDate DATE,
    SalesOrderID INT NOT NULL PRIMARY KEY);
GO


--3
INSERT TOP(5) INTO dbo.Sales(CustomerID,OrderDate,SalesOrderID)
SELECT CustomerID, OrderDate, SalesOrderID
FROM Sales.SalesOrderHeader;


--4
SELECT CustomerID, OrderDate, SalesOrderID
FROM dbo.Sales
ORDER BY SalesOrderID;


--5
DELETE TOP(2) dbo.Sales


--6
UPDATE TOP(2) dbo.Sales SET CustomerID = CustomerID + 10000;
```

```
--7
SELECT CustomerID, OrderDate, SalesOrderID
FROM dbo.Sales
ORDER BY SalesOrderID;

--8
DECLARE @Rows INT = 2;
SELECT TOP(@Rows) CustomerID, OrderDate, SalesOrderID
FROM dbo.Sales
ORDER BY SalesOrderID;
```

Figure 10-12 shows the results. Code section 1 drops the **dbo.Sales** table if it exists. Statement 2 creates the table. Statement 3 inserts five rows into the **dbo.Sales** table. Using **TOP** in the **INSERT** part of the statement does not allow you to use **ORDER BY** to determine which rows to insert. To control which rows get inserted, move **TOP** to the **SELECT** statement. Query 4 shows the inserted rows. Statement 5 deletes two of the rows. Statement 6 updates the **CustomerID** of two of the rows. Query 7 shows how the data looks after the delete and update. Code section 8 shows how to use a variable with **TOP**.

	CustomerID	OrderDate	SalesOrderID
1	29825	2001-07-01	43659
2	29672	2001-07-01	43660
3	29734	2001-07-01	43661
4	29994	2001-07-01	43662
5	29565	2001-07-01	43663

	CustomerID	OrderDate	SalesOrderID
1	39734	2001-07-01	43661
2	39994	2001-07-01	43662
3	29565	2001-07-01	43663

	CustomerID	OrderDate	SalesOrderID
1	39734	2001-07-01	43661
2	39994	2001-07-01	43662

Figure 10-12. The results of using TOP

Ranking Functions

The ranking functions introduced with SQL Server 2005 allow you to assign a number to each row returned from a query. For example, suppose you need to include a row number with each row for display on a web page. You could come up with a method to do this, such as inserting the query results into a temporary table that includes an **IDENTITY** column, but now you can create the numbers by using the new **ROW_NUMBER** function. During your T-SQL programming career, you will probably find you can solve many query problems by including **ROW_NUMBER**. Recently I needed to insert several thousand rows into a table that included a unique ID. I was able to add the maximum ID value already in the table to the result of the **ROW_NUMBER** function to successfully insert the new rows.

Along with **ROW_NUMBER**, this section covers **RANK**, **DENSE_RANK**, and **NTILE**.

Using ROW_NUMBER

The ROW_NUMBER function returns a sequential numeric value along with the results of a query. The ROW_NUMBER function contains the OVER clause, which the function uses to determine the numbering behavior. You must include the ORDER BY option, which determines the order in which the function applies the numbers. You have the option of starting the numbers over whenever the values of a specified column change, called *partitioning*, with the PARTITION BY clause. One limitation with using ROW_NUMBER is that you cannot include it in the WHERE clause. To filter the rows, include the query containing ROW_NUMBER in a CTE, and then filter on the ROW_NUMBER alias in the outer query. Here is the syntax:

```
SELECT <col1>,<col2>,
    ROW_NUMBER() OVER([PARTITION BY <col1>,<col2>]
        ORDER BY <col1>,<col2>) AS <RNalias>
FROM <table1>

WITH <cteName> AS (
    SELECT <col1>,<col2>,
        ROW_NUMBER() OVER([PARTITION BY <col1>,<col2>]
            ORDER BY <col1>,<col2>) AS <RNalias>
    FROM <table1>)
SELECT <col1>,<col2>,<RNalias>
FROM <table1>
WHERE <criteria including RNalias>
```

Type in and execute Listing 10-13 to learn how to use ROW_NUMBER.

Listing 10-13. Using ROW_NUMBER

```
USE AdventureWorks2008;
GO

--1
SELECT CustomerID, FirstName + ' ' + LastName AS Name,
    ROW_NUMBER() OVER (ORDER BY LastName, FirstName) AS Row
FROM Sales.Customer AS c INNER JOIN Person.Person AS p
ON c.PersonID = p.BusinessEntityID;

--2
WITH customers AS (
    SELECT CustomerID, FirstName + ' ' + LastName AS Name,
        ROW_NUMBER() OVER (ORDER BY LastName, FirstName) AS Row
    FROM Sales.Customer AS c INNER JOIN Person.Person AS p
    ON c.PersonID = p.BusinessEntityID
    )
```

```
SELECT CustomerID, Name, Row
FROM customers
WHERE Row > 50
ORDER BY Row;

--3
SELECT CustomerID, FirstName + ' ' + LastName AS Name, c.TerritoryID,
    ROW_NUMBER() OVER (PARTITION BY c.TerritoryID
        ORDER BY LastName, FirstName) AS Row
FROM Sales.Customer AS c INNER JOIN Person.Person AS p
ON c.PersonID = p.BusinessEntityID;
```

Figure 10-13 shows the partial results. Query 1 assigns the row numbers in order of LastName, FirstName to the query joining the Sales.Customer table to the Person.Person table. Each row in the results contains a unique row number.

	CustomerID	Name	TerritoryID	Row
1	29485	Catherine Abel	4	1
2	29486	Kim Abercrombie	3	2
3	29487	Humberto Acevedo	2	3
4	29484	Gustavo Achong	5	4
5	29488	Pilar Ackerman	9	5

	CustomerID	Name	TerritoryID	Row
1	29030	Jeremy Adams	4	51
2	17172	Jesse Adams	4	52
3	28247	Jonathan Adams	1	53
4	16377	Jordan Adams	4	54
5	20387	Jordan Adams	4	55

	CustomerID	Name	TerritoryID	Row
3427	19552	Margaret Zhu	1	3427
3428	22192	Henry Zimmerman	1	3428
3429	29487	Humberto Acevedo	2	1
3430	29498	Kim Akers	2	2
3431	29501	Milton Albury	2	3

Figure 10-13. *The partial results of using ROW_NUMBER*

Query 2 demonstrates how you can include the row number in the WHERE clause by using a CTE. The CTE in query 2 contains the same code as query 1. Now the Row column is available to you to use in the WHERE clause just like any other column. By using this technique, you can apply the WHERE clause to the results of the ROW_NUMBER function, and only the rows with a row number exceeding 50 appear in the results.

Query 3 uses the PARTITION BY option to start the row numbers over on each TerritoryID. The results shown in Figure 10-13 show the end of TerritoryID 1 and the beginning of TerritoryID 2.

Using RANK and DENSE_RANK

RANK and DENSE_RANK are very similar to ROW_NUMBER. The difference is how the functions deal with ties in the ORDER BY values. RANK assigns the same number to the duplicate rows and skips numbers not used. DENSE_RANK doesn't skip numbers. For example, if rows 2 and 3 are duplicates, RANK will supply the values 1, 3, 3, and 4, and DENSE_RANK will supply the values 1, 2, 2, and 3. Here is the syntax:

```
--1 RANK exampple
SELECT <col1>, RANK() OVER([PARTITION BY <col2>,<col3>] ORDER BY <col1>,<col2>)
FROM <table1>

--2 DENSE_RANK example
SELECT <col2>, DENSE_RANK() OVER([PARTITION BY <col2>,<col3>]
    ORDER BY <col1>,<col2>)
FROM <table1>
```

Type in and execute the code in Listing 10-14 to learn how to use RANK and DENSE_RANK.

Listing 10-14. Using RANK and DENSE_RANK

```
USE AdventureWorks2008;
GO

SELECT CustomerID,COUNT(*) AS CountOfSales,
    RANK() OVER(ORDER BY COUNT(*) DESC) AS Ranking,
    ROW_NUMBER() OVER(ORDER BY COUNT(*) DESC) AS Row,
    DENSE_RANK() OVER(ORDER BY COUNT(*) DESC) AS DenseRanking
FROM Sales.SalesOrderHeader
GROUP BY CustomerID
ORDER BY COUNT(*) DESC;
```

Figure 10-14 shows the partial results. The query compares ROW_NUMBER to RANK and DENSE_RANK. In each expression, the count of the sales for each customer determines the order of the numbers.

	CustomerID	CountOfSales	Row	Ranking	DenseRanking
1	11091	28	1	1	1
2	11176	28	2	1	1
3	11185	27	3	3	2
4	11200	27	4	3	2
5	11223	27	5	3	2
6	11262	27	6	3	2
7	11276	27	7	3	2
8	11277	27	8	3	2
9	11287	27	9	3	2
10	11300	27	10	3	2
11	11330	27	11	3	2
12	11331	27	12	3	2
13	11711	27	13	3	2
14	11566	25	14	14	3
15	11211	17	15	15	4
16	11212	17	16	15	4
17	11203	17	17	15	4

Figure 10-14. *The partial results of using RANK and DENSE_RANK*

Using NTILE

While the other ranking functions supply a row number or rank to each row, the **NTILE** function assigns buckets to groups of rows. For example, suppose the AdventureWorks company wants to divide up bonus money for the sales staff. You can use the **NTILE** function to divide up the money based on the sales by each employee. Here is the syntax:

```
SELECT <col1>, NTILE(<buckets>) OVER([PARTITION BY <col1>,<col1>]
    ORDER BY <col1>,<col2>) AS <alias>
FROM <table1>
```

Type in and execute Listing 10-15 to learn how to use **NTILE**.

Listing 10-15. Using NTILE

```
USE AdventureWorks2008;
GO

SELECT SalesPersonID,SUM(TotalDue) AS TotalSales,
    NTILE(10) OVER(ORDER BY SUM(TotalDue)) * 10000/COUNT(*) OVER() AS Bonus
FROM Sales.SalesOrderHeader
WHERE SalesPersonID IS NOT NULL
    AND OrderDate BETWEEN '1/1/2004' AND '12/31/2004'
GROUP BY SalesPersonID
ORDER BY TotalSales;
```

Figure 10-15 shows the results. The AdventureWorks sales department has $10,000 to divide up in bonuses for the sales staff based on total sales per person. The query returns the sum of the total sales grouped by the **SalesPersonID** for 2004. The **NTILE** function divides the rows into 10 groups, or buckets, based on the sales for each salesperson. The query multiplies the value returned by the **NTILE** expression by 10,000 divided by the number of rows to determine the bonus amount. The query uses the **COUNT(*)** **OVER()** expression to determine the number of rows in the results. See "The OVER Clause" in Chapter 5 to review how this works.

	SalesPersonID	TotalSales	Bonus
1	285	29906.7517	588
2	287	111421.137	588
3	274	281123.5472	1176
4	278	642214.142	1176
5	280	732896.3491	1764
6	283	760254.2516	1764
7	286	811100.2789	2352
8	284	943376.5484	2352
9	288	955237.2485	2941
10	281	1212101.788	2941
11	279	1226631.9068	3529
12	282	1392757.701	3529
13	277	1546519.7757	4117
14	290	1549000.1782	4117
15	275	1732868.0076	4705
16	289	2037152.8042	5294
17	276	2126790.5635	5882

Figure 10-15. *The results of using* NTILE

The salespeople with the lowest sales get the smallest bonuses. The salespeople with the highest sales get the biggest bonuses. Notice that the smaller values have two rows in each bucket, but the last three buckets each have one row. The query must produce ten buckets, but there are not enough rows to divide the buckets up evenly.

Database Cleanup

Run the script in Listing 10-16 to clean up the tables used in this chapter. You can download the script from this book's page at **http://www.apress.com**. Alternately, you can reinstall the sample databases by following the instructions in the "Installing the Sample Databases" section in Chapter 1.

Listing 10-16. Demo Table Cleanup

```
USE AdventureWorks2008;
GO

IF OBJECT_ID('dbo.Customers') IS NOT NULL BEGIN
    DROP TABLE dbo.Customers;
END;
IF OBJECT_ID('dbo.CustomerHistory') IS NOT NULL BEGIN
    DROP TABLE dbo.CustomerHistory;
END;
IF OBJECT_ID('dbo.CustomerSource') IS NOT NULL BEGIN
    DROP TABLE dbo.CustomerSource;
END;
IF OBJECT_ID('dbo.CustomerTarget') IS NOT NULL BEGIN
    DROP TABLE dbo.CustomerTarget;
END;
IF OBJECT_ID('dbo.Sales') IS NOT NULL BEGIN
    DROP TABLE dbo.Sales;
END;
```

Summary

This chapter covered how to write advanced queries using some exciting new T-SQL features introduced with SQL Server 2005 and 2008. Starting with Chapter 4, you saw how CTEs, or common table expressions, can help you solve query problems without resorting to temporary tables or views. In this chapter, you learned several other ways to use CTEs, including how to display hierarchical data with a recursive CTE. With the OUTPUT clause, you can return or store the data involved in data manipulation statements. If you will be involved with loading data warehouses, you can use the MERGE and GROUPING SET features to improve performance. You learned two ways to write pivot queries, using CASE and using the new PIVOT function. You learned about the enhancements to TOP and the exciting new ranking functions.

Although the material in this chapter is not required knowledge for beginning T-SQL developers, it will be very beneficial to you to keep these techniques in mind. As you gain more experience, you will often find ways to take advantage of these features.

CHAPTER 11

▪ ▪ ▪

Where to Go Next?

I hope you have enjoyed learning about T-SQL as much as I have enjoyed writing about it. Not everyone is cut out to be a T-SQL developer; it helps to really enjoy writing code. Programming is not something you can just learn and be done with it. You will continue to learn new techniques as long as you are programming T-SQL. The other thing you can count on is that Microsoft will continue to add new features to SQL Server, including new T-SQL features, giving you more to learn about. At the time of this writing, Microsoft has just announced SQL Server 2008 R2 due out in 2010.

You may have read this book from cover to cover, typing in all the sample code and performing the exercises found in most of the chapters. If you are like me, you may have just skipped around looking for specific knowledge as you needed it, using the book as a reference. Either way, you would have found simple examples that showed you how to use a specific feature or solve a particular problem. Each chapter used techniques from the previous chapters to solve more complex query problems as the book progressed.

I began writing T-SQL queries 12 years ago. I had a book that was about four inches thick on my desk that contained just about everything I needed to know about SQL Server at the time, including T-SQL. I remember constantly looking up how to join tables, write aggregate queries, or perform updates until, eventually, I just knew the syntax. As I learned even more techniques, the syntax I knew continued to grow, and the syntax I had to look up constantly changed. Since then, Microsoft has introduced several new versions of SQL Server, expanding the feature set each time. I would probably need four or five books the size of my old reference to cover everything offered with SQL Server today.

Online Resources

Besides having a great reference book in your hands, what other ways can you learn? A wealth of knowledge is available for free on the Web. You can post questions on newsgroups and forums; read articles, blogs, and white papers; and even view videos explaining how to write T-SQL code. Someone else has already posted an answer, blog, or article to answer just about anything you could ever want to know.

Here are some of my favorite sites featuring SQL Server information:

```
http://www.sqlservercentral.com
http://www.sqlteam.com
http://www.microsoft.com/sqlserver/2008/en/us/community.aspx
http://www.sql-server-performance.com/
http://sqlblog.com/
http://sqlserverpedia.com/
http://www.sqlshare.com/
```

At the time of this writing, social networking sites such as Facebook, LinkedIn, and Twitter make the news every day. These sites provide yet another way to get answers to questions by discussing the issues with colleagues across the world.

Because of printing and shipping costs and the impact of online resources, publishers are moving print magazines to online services only. I suspect that over time we will see less and less paper and even more online subscription resources.

Conferences

If you get the chance to attend a conference such as Professional Association for SQL Server (PASS), DevTeach/SQLTeach, TechEd, or one of the other conferences featuring SQL Server presentations, be sure to take advantage of the opportunity. The great thing about attending conferences is that you get a chance to talk with the gurus and experts as well as listen to the presentations. You also get to meet other people who face many of the same issues that you do and learn about the solutions they have developed. Conferences can get you out of your day-to-day environment, get you refreshed, and get you excited about the future.

Just as more and more traditionally printed material now appears on the Internet, you can also attend virtual conferences via the Web. SQL Server World User Group hosts two or three virtual conferences each year (http://www.sswug.org/). The advantage to virtual conferences over in-person conferences is in cost savings and lack of travel. The disadvantage, of course, is not getting to meet the speakers and other attendees face to face. Either way, attending conferences is a great way to learn about SQL Server.

User Groups

Many metropolitan areas have user groups dedicated to programming languages or using certain software. These groups often provide food, usually pizza, prizes, and educational presentations at meetings held on a scheduled basis. To find a list of user groups that are associated with PASS, go to http://www.sqlpass.org. User group membership is usually free. A few dedicated volunteers run most user groups, and sponsors, such as recruiting firms or software vendors, often pay for the food and provide prizes. Not only is attending user group meetings a great way to learn T-SQL and other SQL Server topics, but you may also meet your next employer at a user group meeting!

Vendors

Even though they may have an ulterior motive, such as getting you to buy a product, vendors creating software for SQL Server developers and database administrators often provide a wealth of information. Vendors have educational web sites, webinars, newsletters, and online books all for free. Some of the software vendors employ high-profile SQL Server experts who speak at user group meetings and conferences and provide education to the SQL Server community.

Books

Even though you have many online resources available to you, nothing beats a great book that you can carry with you on an airplane or a bus. You now have the choice to buy the physical book, download the book as a computer file, or read book on a subscription device such as a Kindle. The great thing about books by Apress authors, regardless of how you access the books, is that they are written by developers and database administrators who have worked at real jobs just like you. Apress authors can pass along the benefit of their experience as well as their knowledge.

If you need to get started learning a language or need to really focus on a particular area, a well-organized book will save you a lot of time over hunting down resources on the Web. When learning a new programming language, follow the examples from cover to cover at first. Then, once you are familiar with the language, save your book as a reference for when you need more information about a particular topic.

Classes

If you live in a metropolitan area, many training centers offer SQL Server courses. These classes are a great way to get you started with new language, especially if you learn better in person than with a book or video. Another benefit is being able to ask the instructor questions, often even after the class is over by e-mail. Like conferences, getting out of the regular work environment helps you focus and learn. I encourage you to attend training classes, especially if your employer is willing to foot the bill.

SQL Server Books Online

Refer to SQL Server Books Online often. I am constantly surprised to learn new ways to use T-SQL features from taking a look at Books Online when I thought I already knew all there was to know about a feature. I often use Books Online as a starting point and then see how someone else explains the same concept in a book or article.

One thing that I do not like about Books Online is how the syntax is presented. The syntax examples include every possible option, making it, in my opinion, difficult to understand. I usually skip down to the example code to figure it out. I hope you learned a lot by the way this book presented the syntax examples, showing only what you needed to see to learn the particular topic at hand.

Practice, Practice, and More Practice

The only way to really learn T-SQL is by doing it. You can have an entire bookshelf filled with T-SQL books, attend conferences and classes, ask questions, and surf the Web, but you won't learn T-SQL without practicing it yourself. I am reminded of a recent TV episode of *The Big Bang Theory* where one of the characters thought he could learn to swim by just reading about swimming on the Web. The more you practice and experiment, the faster you will learn.

This book is full of examples and exercises that you can use to experiment. What will happen if you tweak this query, or how can you change that query so that it runs more efficiently? Keep working at it; keep learning.

Teach Someone Else

I am always amazed at how much I learn when I must explain a concept to another developer or write about a T-SQL topic. To use a feature, you have to understand it, but to teach it, you have to know it at an entirely different level. I have learned so much by writing this book, not only about the process of writing a book, but I have also learned more about writing T-SQL code. Sometimes I have been surprised that writing a query one way didn't really give me the performance increase I expected. Sometimes I have learned about an optional parameter that I didn't know about or a different way to use a particular feature. To explain a concept to you, I had to really think about how the query works, not just how to make it work.

I have learned a lot writing this book. Thank you for learning along with me.

Solutions to the Exercises

The appendix provides answers to the exercise questions in Chapters 2 through 8.

Chapter 2: Writing Simple SELECT Queries

This section provides solutions to the exercises on writing simple **SELECT** queries.

Solutions to Exercise 2-1: Using the SELECT Statement

Use the AdventureWorksLT2008 database to complete this exercise.

1. Write a **SELECT** statement that lists the customers along with their ID numbers. Include the last names, first names, and company names.

   ```
   SELECT CustomerID, LastName, FirstName, CompanyName
   FROM SalesLT.Customer;
   ```

2. Write a **SELECT** statement that lists the name, product number, and color of each product.

   ```
   SELECT Name, ProductNumber, Color
   FROM SalesLT.Product;
   ```

3. Write a **SELECT** statement that lists the customer ID numbers and sales order ID numbers from the **SalesLT.SalesOrderHeader** table.

   ```
   SELECT CustomerID, SalesOrderID
   FROM SalesLT.SalesOrderHeader;
   ```

4. Answer this question: Why should you specify column names rather than an asterisk when writing the **SELECT** list? Give at least two reasons.

   You would do this to decrease the amount of network traffic and increase the performance of the query, retrieving only the columns needed for the application or report. You can also keep users from seeing confidential information by retrieving only the columns they should see.

Solutions to Exercise 2-2: Filtering Data

Use the AdventureWorks2008 database to complete this exercise.

1. Write a query using a **WHERE** clause that displays all the employees listed in the **HumanResources.Employee** table who have the job title Research and Development Engineer. Display the business entity ID number, the login ID, and the title for each one.

   ```
   SELECT BusinessEntityID, JobTitle, LoginID
   FROM HumanResources.Employee
   WHERE JobTitle = 'Research and Development Engineer';
   ```

2. Write a query using a **WHERE** clause that displays all the names in **Person.Person** with the middle name J. Display the first, last, and middle names along with the ID numbers.

   ```
   SELECT FirstName, MiddleName, LastName, BusinessEntityID
   FROM Person.Person
   WHERE MiddleName = 'J';
   ```

3. Write a query displaying all the columns of the **Production.ProductCostHistory** table from the rows that were modified on June 17, 2003. Be sure to use one of the features in SQL Server Management Studio to help you write this query.

   In SQL Server Management Studio, expand the AdventureWorks2008 database. Expand Tables. Right-click the **Production.ProductCostHistory** table, and choose "Select table as." Select "Select to" and New Query Editor Window. Then type in the **WHERE** clause.

   ```
   SELECT [ProductID]
         ,[StartDate]
         ,[EndDate]
         ,[StandardCost]
         ,[ModifiedDate]
     FROM [AdventureWorks2008].[Production].[ProductCostHistory]
   WHERE ModifiedDate = '2003-06-17';
   GO
   ```

4. Rewrite the query you wrote in question 1, changing it so that the employees who do not have the title Research and Development Engineer are displayed.

   ```
   SELECT BusinessEntityID, JobTitle, LoginID
   FROM HumanResources.Employee
   WHERE JobTitle <> 'Research and Development Engineer';
   ```

5. Write a query that displays all the rows from the **Person.Person** table where the rows were modified after December 29, 2000. Display the business entity ID number, the name columns, and the modified date.

```
SELECT BusinessEntityID, FirstName, MiddleName, LastName, ModifiedDate
FROM Person.Person
WHERE ModifiedDate > '2000-12-29';
```

6. Rewrite the last query so that the rows that were not modified on December 29, 2000, are displayed.

```
SELECT BusinessEntityID, FirstName, MiddleName, LastName, ModifiedDate
FROM Person.Person
WHERE ModifiedDate <> '2000-12-29';
```

7. Rewrite the query from question 5 so that it displays the rows modified during December 2000.

```
SELECT BusinessEntityID, FirstName, MiddleName, LastName, ModifiedDate
FROM Person.Person
WHERE ModifiedDate BETWEEN '2000-12-01' AND '2000-12-31';
```

8. Rewrite the query from question 5 so that it displays the rows that were not modified during December 2000.

```
SELECT BusinessEntityID, FirstName, MiddleName, LastName, ModifiedDate
FROM Person.Person
WHERE ModifiedDate NOT BETWEEN '2000-12-01' AND '2000-12-31';
```

9. Explain why a **WHERE** clause should be used in many of your T-SQL queries.

    Most of the time the application or report will not require all the rows. The query should be filtered to include only the required rows to cut down on network traffic and increase SQL Server performance since returning a smaller number of rows is usually more efficient.

Solutions to Exercise 2-3: Filtering with Wildcards

Use the AdventureWorks2008 database to complete this exercise.

1. Write a query that displays the product ID and name for each product from the **Production.Product** table with the name starting with *Chain*.

```
SELECT ProductID, Name
FROM Production.Product
WHERE Name LIKE 'Chain%';
```

2. Write a query like the one in question 1 that displays the products with *helmet* in the name.

```
SELECT ProductID, Name
FROM Production.Product
WHERE Name LIKE '%helmet%';
```

3. Change the last query so that the products without *helmet* in the name are displayed.

```
SELECT ProductID, Name
FROM Production.Product
WHERE Name NOT LIKE '%helmet%';
```

4. Write a query that displays the business entity ID number, first name, middle name, and last name from the **Person.Person** table for only those rows that have *E* or *B* stored in the middle name column.

```
SELECT BusinessEntityID, FirstName, MiddleName, LastName
FROM Person.Person
WHERE MiddleName LIKE '[E,B]';
```

5. Explain the difference between the following two queries:

```
SELECT FirstName
FROM Person.Person
WHERE LastName LIKE 'Ja%es';
```

```
SELECT FirstName
FROM Person.Person
WHERE LastName LIKE 'Ja_es';
```

The first query will return rows with any number of characters replacing the percent sign. The second query will allow only one character to replace the underscore character.

Solutions to Exercise 2-4: Filtering with Multiple Predicates

Use the AdventureWorks2008 database to complete this exercise. Be sure to check you results to assure that they make sense.

1. Write a query displaying the order ID, order date, and total due from the **Sales.SalesOrderHeader** table. Retrieve only those rows where the order was placed during the month of September 2001 and the total due exceeded $1,000.

```
SELECT SalesOrderID, OrderDate, TotalDue
FROM Sales.SalesOrderHeader
WHERE OrderDate BETWEEN '2001-09-01' AND '2001-09-30'
    AND TotalDue > 1000;
```

2.   Change the query in question 1 so that only the dates September 1–3, 2001, are retrieved. See whether you can figure out three different ways to write this query.

```
SELECT SalesOrderID, OrderDate, TotalDue
FROM Sales.SalesOrderHeader
WHERE OrderDate BETWEEN '2001-09-01' AND '2001-09-03'
    AND TotalDue > 1000;
```

```
SELECT SalesOrderID, OrderDate, TotalDue
FROM Sales.SalesOrderHeader
WHERE OrderDate IN ('2001-09-01', '2001-09-02', '2001-09-03')
    AND TotalDue > 1000;
```

```
SELECT SalesOrderID, OrderDate, TotalDue
FROM Sales.SalesOrderHeader
WHERE (OrderDate >= '2001-09-01' AND OrderDate <= '2001-09-03')
    AND TotalDue > 1000;
```

3.   Write a query displaying the sales orders where the total due exceeds $1,000. Retrieve only those rows where the salesperson ID is 279 or the territory ID is 6.

```
SELECT SalesOrderID, OrderDate, TotalDue, SalesPersonID, TerritoryID
FROM Sales.SalesOrderHeader
WHERE TotalDue > 1000 AND (SalesPersonID = 279 OR TerritoryID = 6);
```

4.   Change the query in question 3 so that territory 4 is included.

```
SELECT SalesOrderID, OrderDate, TotalDue, SalesPersonID, TerritoryID
FROM Sales.SalesOrderHeader
WHERE TotalDue > 1000 AND (SalesPersonID = 279 OR TerritoryID IN (6,4));
```

5.   Explain when it makes sense to use the **IN** operator.

You will probably want to use the **IN** operator when you are checking a column for more than one possible value.

Solutions to Exercise 2-5: Working with Nothing

Use the AdventureWorks2008 database to complete this exercise. Make sure you consider how **NULL** values will affect your results.

1. Write a query displaying the **ProductID**, **Name**, and **Color** columns from rows in the **Production.Product** table. Display only those rows where no color has been assigned.

```
SELECT ProductID, Name, Color
FROM Production.Product
WHERE Color IS NULL;
```

2. Write a query displaying the **ProductID**, **Name**, and **Color** columns from rows in the **Production.Product** table. Display only those rows in which the color is not blue.

   Here are two possible solutions:

```
SELECT ProductID, Name, Color
FROM Production.Product
WHERE Color IS NULL OR Color <> 'Blue';
```

```
SELECT ProductID, Name, Color
FROM Production.Product
WHERE ISNULL(Color,'') <> 'Blue';
```

3. Write a query displaying **ProductID**, **Name**, **Style**, **Size**, and **Color** from the **Production.Product** table. Include only those rows where at least one of the **Style**, **Size**, or **Color** columns contains a value.

```
SELECT ProductID, Name, Style, Size, Color
FROM Production.Product
WHERE Style IS NOT NULL OR Size IS NOT NULL OR Color IS NOT NULL;
```

Solutions to Exercise 2-6: Performing a Full-Text Search

Use the AdventureWorks2008 database to complete the following tasks. Be sure to take advantage of the full-text indexes in place when writing the queries.

1. Write a query using the **Production.ProductReview** table. Use **CONTAINS** to find all the rows that have the word *socks* in the **Comments** column. Return the **ProductID** and **Comments** columns.

```
SELECT Comments,ProductID
FROM Production.ProductReview
WHERE CONTAINS(Comments,'socks');
```

2. Write a query using the **Production.Document** table. Use **CONTAINS** to find all the rows that have the word *reflector* in any column that is indexed with Full-Text Search. Display the **Title** and **FileName** columns.

```
SELECT Title,FileName
FROM Production.Document
WHERE CONTAINS(*,'reflector');
```

3. Change the query in question 2 so that the rows containing *seat* are not returned in the results.

```
SELECT Title, FileName
FROM Production.Document
WHERE CONTAINS(*,'reflector AND NOT seat')
```

4. Answer this question: When searching a **VARBINARY(MAX)** column that contains Word documents, a **LIKE** search can be used, but the performance will be worse. True or false?

False, you cannot use **LIKE** with **VARBINARY(MAX)** columns. Use Full-Text searching to search **VARBINARY(MAX)** columns.

Solutions to Exercise 2-7: Sorting Data

Use the AdventureWorks2008 database to complete the exercise to practice sorting the results of your queries.

1. Write a query that returns the business entity ID and name columns from the **Person.Person** table. Sort the results by **LastName**, **FirstName**, and **MiddleName**.

```
SELECT BusinessEntityID, LastName, FirstName, MiddleName
FROM Person.Person
ORDER BY LastName, FirstName, MiddleName;
```

2. Modify the query written in question 1 so that the data is returned in the opposite order.

```
SELECT BusinessEntityID, LastName, FirstName, MiddleName
FROM Person.Person
ORDER BY LastName DESC, FirstName DESC, MiddleName DESC;
```

Solutions to Exercise 2-8: Thinking About Performance

Use the AdventureWorks2008 database to complete this exercise. Be sure to turn on the Include Actual Execution Plan setting before you begin. Type the following code into the query window and then complete each question.

```
USE AdventureWorks2008;
GO

--1
SELECT LastName
FROM Person.Person
WHERE LastName = 'Smith';

--2
SELECT LastName
FROM Person.Person
WHERE LastName LIKE 'Sm%';

--3
SELECT LastName
FROM Person.Person
WHERE LastName LIKE '%mith';

--4
SELECT ModifiedDate
FROM Person.Person
WHERE ModifiedDate BETWEEN '2000-01-01' and '2000-01-31';
```

1. Highlight and run queries 1 and 2. Explain why there is no difference in performance between the two queries.

   Query 1 uses an index to perform an index seek on the **LastName** column to find the rows. Since the wildcard in query 2 begins after the beginning of the value, the database engine can also perform an index seek on the **LastName** column to find the rows in this query.

2. Highlight and run queries 2 and 3. Determine which query performs the best, and explain why you think that is the case.

   Query 2 performs the best. Query 2 takes advantage of the index by performing an index seek on the **LastName** column. Since Query 2 contains the wildcard at the beginning of the value, the database engine must check every value in the index.

3. Highlight and run queries 3 and 4. Determine which query performs the best, and explain why you think this is the case.

   Query 3 performs the best. Even though query 3 must scan every value in the index, no index exists to help query 4. The database engine must scan the clustered index, which is the actual table for query 4. Scanning the table performs worse than scanning a nonclustered index.

Chapter 3: Using Functions and Expressions

This section provides solutions to the exercises on using functions and expressions.

Solutions to Exercise 3-1: Writing Expressions Using Operators

Use the AdventureWorks2008 database to complete this exercise.

1. Write a query that displays in the "AddressLine1 (City PostalCode)" format from the **Person.Address** table.

   ```
   SELECT AddressLine1 + ' (' + City + ' ' + PostalCode + ')'
   FROM Person.Address;
   ```

2. Write a query using the **Production.Product** table displaying the product ID, color, and name columns. If the color column contains a **NULL** value, replace the color with *No Color*.

   ```
   SELECT ProductID, ISNULL(Color,'No Color') AS Color, Name
   FROM Production.Product;
   ```

3. Modify the query written in question 2 so that the description of the product is displayed in the "Name: Color" format. Make sure that all rows display a value even if the **Color** value is missing.

   ```
   SELECT ProductID, Name + ISNULL(': ' + Color,'') AS Description
   FROM Production.Product;
   ```

4. Write a query using the **Production.Product** table displaying a description with the "ProductID: Name" format. Hint: You will need to use a function to write this query.

   Here are two possible answers:

   ```
   SELECT CAST(ProductID AS VARCHAR) + ': ' +  Name AS IDName
   FROM Production.Product;
   ```

   ```
   SELECT CONVERT(VARCHAR, ProductID) + ': ' + Name AS IDName
   FROM Production.Product;
   ```

5. Explain the difference between the **ISNULL** and **COALESCE** functions.

   You can use **ISNULL** to replace a **NULL** value or column with another value or column. You can use **COALESCE** to return the first non-**NULL** value from a list of values or columns.

Solutions to Exercise 3-2: Using Mathematical Operators

Use the AdventureWorks2008 database to complete this exercise.

1. Write a query using the `Sales.SpecialOffer` table. Display the difference between the `MinQty` and `MaxQty` columns along with the `SpecialOfferID` and `Description` columns.

   ```
   SELECT SpecialOfferID, Description, MaxQty - MinQty AS Diff
   FROM Sales.SpecialOffer;
   ```

2. Write a query using the `Sales.SpecialOffer` table. Multiply the `MinQty` column by the `DiscountPct` column. Include the `SpecialOfferID` and `Description` columns in the results.

   ```
   SELECT SpecialOfferID, Description, MinQty * DiscountPct AS Discount
   FROM Sales.SpecialOffer;
   ```

3. Write a query using the `Sales.SpecialOffer` table that multiplies the `MaxQty` column by the `DiscountPCT` column. If the `MaxQty` value is null, replace it with the value 10. Include the `SpecialOfferID` and `Description` columns in the results.

   ```
   SELECT SpecialOfferID, Description, ISNULL(MaxQty,10) * DiscountPct AS Discount
   FROM Sales.SpecialOffer;
   ```

4. Describe the difference between division and modulo.

   When performing division, you divide two numbers, and the result, the quotient, is the answer. If you are using modulo, you divide two numbers, but the reminder is the answer. If the numbers are evenly divisible, the answer will be zero.

Solutions to Exercise 3-3: Using String Functions

Use the AdventureWorks2008 database to complete this exercise. Be sure to refer to the discussion of the functions to help you figure out which ones to use if you need help.

1. Write a query that displays the first 10 characters of the `AddressLine1` column in the `Person.Address` table.

   Here are two possible solutions:

   ```
   SELECT LEFT(AddressLine1,10) AS Address10
   FROM Person.Address;
   ```

   ```
   SELECT SUBSTRING(AddressLine1,1,10) AS Address10
   FROM Person.Address;
   ```

2. Write a query that displays characters 10 to 15 of the **AddressLine1** column in the **Person.Address** table.

```
SELECT SUBSTRING(AddressLine1,10,6) AS Address10to15
FROM Person.Address;
```

3. Write a query displaying the first name and last name from the **Person.Person** table all in uppercase.

```
SELECT UPPER(FirstName) AS FirstName, UPPER(LastName) AS LastName
FROM Person.Person;
```

4. The product number in the **Production.Product** contains a hyphen (-). Write a query that uses the **SUBSTRING** function and the **CHARINDEX** function to display the characters in the product number following the hyphen. Note: there is also a second hyphen in many of the rows; ignore the second hyphen for this question. Hint: Try writing this statement in two steps, the first using the **CHARINDEX** function and the second adding the **SUBSTRING** function.

```
--Step 1
SELECT ProductNumber, CHARINDEX('-',ProductNumber)
FROM Production.Product;

--Step 2
SELECT ProductNumber,
    SUBSTRING(ProductNumber,CHARINDEX('-',ProductNumber)+1,25) AS ProdNumber
FROM Production.Product;
```

Solutions to Exercise 3-4: Using Date Functions

Use the AdventureWorks2008 database to complete Exercise 3-4.

1. Write a query that calculates the number of days between the date an order was placed and the date that it was shipped using the **Sales.SalesOrderHeader** table. Include the **SalesOrderID**, **OrderDate**, and **ShipDate** columns.

```
SELECT SalesOrderID, OrderDate, ShipDate,
    DATEDIFF(d,OrderDate,ShipDate) AS NumberOfDays
FROM Sales.SalesOrderHeader;
```

2. Write a query that displays only the date, not the time, for the order date and ship date in the **Sales.SalesOrderHeader** table.

```
--Use any of the styles that return only date
SELECT CONVERT(VARCHAR,OrderDate,1) AS OrderDate,
    CONVERT(VARCHAR, ShipDate,1) AS ShipDate
FROM Sales.SalesOrderHeader;
```

3. Write a query that adds six months to each order date in the `Sales.SalesOrderHeader` table. Include the `SalesOrderID` and `OrderDate` columns.

```
SELECT SalesOrderID, OrderDate, DATEADD(m,6,OrderDate) Plus6Months
FROM Sales.SalesOrderHeader;
```

4. Write a query that displays the year of each order date and the numeric month of each order date in separate columns in the results. Include the `SalesOrderID` and `OrderDate` columns.

    Here are two possible solutions:

```
SELECT SalesOrderID, OrderDate, YEAR(OrderDate) AS OrderYear,
    MONTH(OrderDate) AS OrderMonth
FROM Sales.SalesOrderHeader;
SELECT SalesOrderID, OrderDate, DATEPART(yyyy,OrderDate) AS OrderYear,
    DATEPART(m,OrderDate) AS OrderMonth
FROM Sales.SalesOrderHeader;
```

5. Change the query written in question 4 to display the month name instead.

```
SELECT SalesOrderID, OrderDate, DATEPART(yyyy,OrderDate) AS OrderYear,
    DATENAME(m,OrderDate) AS OrderMonth
FROM Sales.SalesOrderHeader;
```

Solutions to Exercise 3-5: Using Mathematical Functions

Use the AdventureWorks2008 database to complete this exercise.

1. Write a query using the `Sales.SalesOrderHeader` table that displays the `SubTotal` rounded to two decimal places. Include the `SalesOrderID` column in the results.

```
SELECT SalesOrderID, ROUND(SubTotal,2) AS SubTotal
FROM Sales.SalesOrderHeader;
```

2. Modify the query in question 1 so that the `SubTotal` is rounded to the nearest dollar but still displays two zeros to the right of the decimal place.

```
SELECT SalesOrderID, ROUND(SubTotal,0) AS SubTotal
FROM Sales.SalesOrderHeader;
```

3. Write a query that calculates the square root of the **SalesOrderID** value from the **Sales.SalesOrderHeader** table.

```
SELECT SQRT(SalesOrderID) AS OrderSQRT
FROM Sales.SalesOrderHeader;
```

4. Write a statement that generates a random number between 1 and 10 each time it is run.

```
SELECT CAST(RAND() * 10 AS INT) + 1;
```

Solutions to Exercise 3-6: Using System Functions

Use the AdventureWorks2008 database to complete this exercise.

1. Write a query using the **HumanResources.Employee** table to display the **BusinessEntityID** column. Also include a **CASE** statement that displays "Even" when the **BusinessEntityID** value is an even number or "Odd" when it is odd. Hint: Use the modulo operator.

```
SELECT BusinessEntityID,
    CASE BusinessEntityID % 2 WHEN 0 THEN 'Even' ELSE 'Odd' END
FROM HumanResources.Employee;
```

2. Write a query using the **Sales.SalesOrderDetail** table to display a value ("Under 10" or "10–19" or "20–29" or "30–39" or "40 and over") based on the **OrderQty** value by using the **CASE** function. Include the **SalesOrderID** and **OrderQty** columns in the results.

```
SELECT SalesOrderID, OrderQty,
    CASE WHEN OrderQty BETWEEN 0 AND 9 THEN 'Under 10'
        WHEN OrderQty BETWEEN 10 AND 19 THEN '10-19'
        WHEN OrderQty BETWEEN 20 AND 29 THEN '20-29'
        WHEN OrderQty BETWEEN 30 AND 39 THEN '30-39'
        ELSE '40 and over' end AS range
FROM Sales.SalesOrderDetail;
```

3. Using the **Person.Person** table, build the full names using **Title**, **FirstName**, **MiddleName**, **LastName**, and **Suffix** columns. Check the table definition to see which columns allow **NULL** values, and use the **COALESCE** function on the appropriate columns.

```
SELECT COALESCE(Title + ' ','') + FirstName +
    COALESCE(' ' + MiddleName,'') + ' ' + LastName +
    COALESCE(', ' + Suffix,'')
FROM Person.Person;
```

4. Look up the **SERVERPROPERTY** function in Books Online. Write a statement that displays the edition, instance name, and machine name using this function.

```
SELECT SERVERPROPERTY('Edition'),
    SERVERPROPERTY('InstanceName'),
    SERVERPROPERTY('MachineName');
```

Solutions to Exercise 3-7: Using Functions in the WHERE and ORDER BY Clauses

Use the AdventureWorks2008 database to complete this exercise.

1. Write a query using the **Sales.SalesOrderHeader** table to display the orders placed during 2001 by using a function. Include the **SalesOrderID** and **OrderDate** columns in the results.

    ```
    SELECT SalesOrderID, OrderDate
    FROM Sales.SalesOrderHeader
    WHERE YEAR(OrderDate) = 2001;
    ```

2. Write a query using the **Sales.SalesOrderHeader** table listing the sales in order of the month the order was placed and then the year the order was placed. Include the **SalesOrderID** and **OrderDate** columns in the results.

    ```
    SELECT SalesOrderID, OrderDate
    FROM Sales.SalesOrderHeader
    ORDER BY MONTH(OrderDate), YEAR(OrderDate);
    ```

3. Write a query that displays the **PersonType** and the name columns from the **Person.Person** table. Sort the results so that rows with a **PersonType** of **IN**, **SP**, or **SC** sort by **LastName**. The other rows should sort by **FirstName**. Hint: Use the **CASE** function.

    ```
    SELECT PersonType, FirstName, MiddleName, LastName
    FROM Person.Person
    ORDER BY CASE WHEN PersonType IN ('IN','SP','SC') THEN LastName
            ELSE FirstName END;
    ```

Solutions to Exercise 3-8: Thinking About Performance

Use the AdventureWorks2008 database to complete this exercise. Make sure you have the Include Actual Execution Plan setting toggled on before starting this exercise.

1. Type in and execute the following code. View the execution plans once query execution completes, and explain whether one query performs better than the other and why.

    ```
    USE AdventureWorks2008;
    GO
    ```

```
--1
SELECT Name
FROM Production.Product
WHERE Name LIKE 'B%';


--2
SELECT Name
FROM Production.Product
WHERE CHARINDEX('B',Name) = 1;
```

Query 1 performs better because it performs an index seek on the **Name** column. Query 2 must scan the entire index, applying the function to each value of **Name**.

2. Type in and execute the following code. View the execution plans once query execution completes, and explain whether one query performs better than the other and why.

```
USE AdventureWorks2008;
GO


--1
SELECT LastName
FROM Person.Person
WHERE LastName LIKE '%i%';


--2
SELECT LastName
FROM Person.Person
WHERE CHARINDEX('i',LastName) > 0;
```

The queries have the same performance because both queries must scan the index. Query 1 contains a wildcard at the beginning of the search term, and query 2 has a function that takes the column name as an argument.

Chapter 4: Querying Multiple Tables

This section provides solutions to the exercises on querying multiple tables.

Solutions to Exercise 4-1: Writing Inner Joins

Use the AdventureWorks2008 to complete this exercise.

1. The **HumanResources.Employee** table does not contain the employee names. Join that table to the **Person.Person** table on the **BusinessEntityID** column. Display the job title, birth date, first name, and last name.

```
SELECT JobTitle, BirthDate, FirstName, LastName
FROM HumanResources.Employee AS E
INNER JOIN Person.Person AS P ON E.BusinessEntityID = P.BusinessEntityID;
```

2. The customer names also appear in the **Person.Person** table. Join the **Sales.Customer** table to the **Person.Person** table. The **BusinessEntityID** column in the **Person.Person** table matches the **PersonID** column in the **Sales.Customer** table. Display the **CustomerID**, **StoreID**, and **TerritoryID** columns along with the name columns.

```
SELECT CustomerID, StoreID, TerritoryID, FirstName, MiddleName, LastName
FROM Sales.Customer AS C
INNER JOIN Person.Person AS P ON C.PersonID = P.BusinessEntityID;
```

3. Extend the query written in question 2 to include the **Sales.SalesOrderHeader** table. Display the **SalesOrderID** column along with the columns already specified. The **Sales.SalesOrderHeader** table joins the **Sales.Customer** table on **CustomerID**.

```
SELECT c.CustomerID, StoreID, c.TerritoryID, FirstName, MiddleName,
    LastName, SalesOrderID
FROM Sales.Customer AS C
INNER JOIN Person.Person AS P ON C.PersonID = P.BusinessEntityID
INNER JOIN Sales.SalesOrderHeader AS S ON S.CustomerID = C.CustomerID;
```

4. Write a query that joins the **Sales.SalesOrderHeader** table to the **Sales.SalesPerson** table. Join the **BusinessEntityID** column from the **Sales.SalesPerson** table to the **SalesPersonID** column in the **Sales.SalesOrderHeader** table. Display the **SalesOrderID** along with the **SalesQuota** and **Bonus**.

```
SELECT SalesOrderID, SalesQuota, Bonus
FROM Sales.SalesOrderHeader AS S
INNER JOIN Sales.SalesPerson AS SP
    ON S.SalesPersonID = SP.BusinessEntityID;
```

5. Add the name columns to the query written in question 4 by joining on the **Person.Person** table. See whether you can figure out which columns will be used to write the join.

    You can join the **Person.Person** table on the **SalesOrderHeader** table or the **Sales.SalesPerson** table.

```
SELECT SalesOrderID, SalesQuota, Bonus, FirstName, MiddleName, LastName
FROM Sales.SalesOrderHeader AS S
INNER JOIN Sales.SalesPerson AS SP ON S.SalesPersonID = SP.BusinessEntityID
INNER JOIN Person.Person AS P ON SP.BusinessEntityID = P.BusinessEntityID;
```

```
SELECT SalesOrderID, SalesQuota, Bonus, FirstName, MiddleName, LastName
FROM Sales.SalesOrderHeader AS S
INNER JOIN Sales.SalesPerson AS SP ON S.SalesPersonID = SP.BusinessEntityID
INNER JOIN Person.Person AS P ON S.SalesPersonID = P.BusinessEntityID;
```

6. The catalog description for each product is stored in the **Production.ProductModel** table. Display the columns that describe the product from the **Production.Product** table, such as the color and size along with the catalog description for each product.

```
SELECT PM.CatalogDescription, Color, Size
FROM Production.Product AS P
INNER JOIN Production.ProductModel AS PM ON P.ProductModelID = PM.ProductModelID;
```

7. Write a query that displays the names of the customers along with the product names that they have purchased. Hint: Five tables will be required to write this query!

```
SELECT FirstName, MiddleName, LastName, Prod.Name
FROM Sales.Customer AS C
INNER JOIN Person.Person AS P ON C.PersonID = P.BusinessEntityID
INNER JOIN Sales.SalesOrderHeader AS SOH ON C.CustomerID = SOH.CustomerID
INNER JOIN Sales.SalesOrderDetail AS SOD
    ON SOH.SalesOrderID = SOD.SalesOrderID
INNER JOIN Production.Product AS Prod ON SOD.ProductID = Prod.ProductID;
```

Solutions to Exercise 4-2: Writing Outer Joins

Use the AdventureWorks2008 and AdventureWorks (question 7) databases to complete this exercise.

1. Write a query that displays all the products along with the **SalesOrderID** even if an order has never been placed for that product. Join to the **Sales.SalesOrderDetail** table using the **ProductID** column.

```
SELECT SalesOrderID, P.ProductID, P.Name
FROM Production.Product AS P
LEFT OUTER JOIN Sales.SalesOrderDetail
    AS SOD ON P.ProductID = SOD.ProductID;
```

2. Change the query written in question 1 so that only products that have not been ordered show up in the query.

```
SELECT SalesOrderID, P.ProductID, P.Name
FROM Production.Product AS P
LEFT OUTER JOIN Sales.SalesOrderDetail
    AS SOD ON P.ProductID = SOD.ProductID
WHERE SalesOrderID IS NULL;
```

3. Write a query that returns all the rows from the **Sales.SalesPerson** table joined to the **Sales.SalesOrderHeader** table along with the **SalesOrderID** column even if no orders match. Include the **SalesPersonID** and **SalesYTD** columns in the results.

```
SELECT SalesOrderID, SalesPersonID, SalesYTD
FROM Sales.SalesPerson AS SP
LEFT OUTER JOIN Sales.SalesOrderHeader AS SOH
    ON SP.BusinessEntityID = SOH.SalesPersonID;
```

4. Change the query written in question 3 so that the salesperson's name also displays from the **Person.Person** table.

```
SELECT SalesOrderID, SalesPersonID, SalesYTD, FirstName,
    MiddleName, LastName
FROM Sales.SalesPerson AS SP
LEFT OUTER JOIN Sales.SalesOrderHeader AS SOH
    ON SP.BusinessEntityID = SOH.SalesPersonID
LEFT OUTER JOIN Person.Person AS P
    ON P.BusinessEntityID = SP.BusinessEntityID;
```

5. The **Sales.SalesOrderHeader** table contains foreign keys to the **Sales.CurrencyRate** and **Purchasing.ShipMethod** tables. Write a query joining all three tables, making sure it contains all rows from **Sales.SalesOrderHeader**. Include the **CurrencyRateID**, **AverageRate**, **SalesOrderID**, and **ShipBase** columns.

```
SELECT CR.CurrencyRateID, CR.AverageRate, SM.ShipBase, SalesOrderID
FROM Sales.SalesOrderHeader AS SOH
LEFT OUTER JOIN Sales.CurrencyRate AS CR
    ON SOH.CurrencyRateID = CR.CurrencyRateID
LEFT OUTER JOIN Purchasing.ShipMethod AS SM
    ON SOH.ShipMethodID = SM.ShipMethodID;
```

6. Write a query that returns the **BusinessEntityID** column from the **Sales.SalesPerson** table along with every **ProductID** from the **Production.Product** table.

    ```
    SELECT SP.BusinessEntityID, P.ProductID
    FROM Sales.SalesPerson AS SP CROSS JOIN Production.Product AS P;
    ```

7. Starting with the query written in Listing 4-13, join the table **a** to the **Person.Contact** table to display the employee's name. The **EmployeeID** column joins the **ContactID** column.

    ```
    USE AdventureWorks;
    GO
    SELECT a.EmployeeID AS Employee,
        a.Title AS EmployeeTitle,
        b.EmployeeID AS ManagerID,
        b.Title AS ManagerTitle,
        c.FirstName, c.MiddleName, c.LastName
    FROM HumanResources.Employee AS a
    LEFT OUTER JOIN HumanResources.Employee AS b
    ON a.ManagerID = b.EmployeeID
    LEFT OUTER JOIN Person.Contact AS c ON a.EmployeeID = c.ContactID;
    ```

Solutions to Exercise 4-3: Writing Subqueries

Use the AdventureWorks2008 database to complete this exercise.

1. Using a subquery, display the product names and product ID numbers from the **Production.Product** table that have been ordered.

    ```
    SELECT ProductID, Name
    FROM Production.Product
    WHERE ProductID IN (SELECT ProductID FROM Sales.SalesOrderDetail);
    ```

2. Change the query written in question 1 to display the products that have not been ordered.

    ```
    SELECT ProductID, Name
    FROM Production.Product
    WHERE ProductID NOT IN (
        SELECT ProductID FROM Sales.SalesOrderDetail
        WHERE ProductID IS NOT NULL);
    ```

3. If the **Production.ProductColor** table is not part of the AdventureWorks2008 database, run the code in Listing 4-11 to create it. Write a query using a subquery that returns the rows from the **Production.ProductColor** table that are not being used in the **Production.Product** table.

```
SELECT Color
FROM Production.ProductColor
WHERE Color NOT IN (
    SELECT Color FROM Production.Product WHERE Color IS NOT NULL);
```

4. Write a query that displays the colors used in the **Production.Product** table that are not listed in the **Production.ProductColor** table using a subquery. Use the keyword **DISTINCT** before the column name to return each color only once.

```
SELECT DISTINCT Color
FROM Production.Product
WHERE Color NOT IN (
    SELECT Color FROM Production.ProductColor WHERE Color IS NOT NULL);
```

5. Write a **UNION** query that combines the **ModifiedDate** from **Person.Person** and the **HireDate** from **HumanResources.Employee**.

```
SELECT ModifiedDate
FROM Person.Person
UNION
SELECT HireDate
FROM HumanResources.Employee;
```

Solutions to Exercise 4-4: Exploring Derived Tables and Common Table Expressions

Use the AdventureWorks2008 database to complete this exercise.

1. Using a derived table, join the **Sales.SalesOrderHeader** table to the **Sales.SalesOrderDetail** table. Display the **SalesOrderID**, **OrderDate**, and **ProductID** columns in the results. The **Sales.SalesOrderDetail** table should be inside the derived table query.

```
SELECT SOH.SalesOrderID, SOH.OrderDate, ProductID
FROM Sales.SalesOrderHeader AS SOH
INNER JOIN (
    SELECT SalesOrderID, ProductID
    FROM Sales.SalesOrderDetail) AS SOD
    ON SOH.SalesOrderID = SOD.SalesOrderID;
```

2. Rewrite the query in question 1 with a common table expression.

```
WITH SOD AS (
    SELECT SalesOrderID, ProductID
    FROM Sales.SalesOrderDetail
    )
SELECT SOH.SalesOrderID, SOH.OrderDate, ProductID
FROM Sales.SalesOrderHeader AS SOH
INNER JOIN SOD ON SOH.SalesOrderID = SOD.SalesOrderID;
```

3. Write a query that displays all customers along with the orders placed in 2001. Use a common table expression to write the query and include the **CustomerID**, **SalesOrderID**, and **OrderDate** columns in the results.

```
WITH SOH AS (
    SELECT SalesOrderID, OrderDate, CustomerID
    FROM Sales.SalesOrderHeader
    WHERE OrderDate BETWEEN '1/1/2001' AND '12/31/2001'
    )
SELECT C.CustomerID, SalesOrderID, OrderDate
FROM Sales.Customer AS C
LEFT OUTER JOIN SOH ON C.CustomerID = SOH.CustomerID;
```

Solutions to Exercise 4-5: Thinking About Performance

Use the AdventureWorks2008 database to complete this exercise.

Run the following code to add and populate a new column, **OrderID**, to the **Sales.SalesOrderDetail** table. After running the code, the new column will contain the same data as the **SalesOrderID** column.

```
USE AdventureWorks2008;
GO
ALTER TABLE Sales.SalesOrderDetail ADD OrderID INT NULL;
GO
UPDATE Sales.SalesOrderDetail SET OrderID = SalesOrderID;
```

1. Make sure that the Include Actual Execution Plan is turned on before running the following code. View the execution plans, and explain why one query performs better than the other.

```
--1
SELECT o.SalesOrderID,d.SalesOrderDetailID
FROM Sales.SalesOrderHeader AS o
INNER JOIN Sales.SalesOrderDetail AS d ON o.SalesOrderID = d.SalesOrderID;
```

```
--2
SELECT o.SalesOrderID,d.SalesOrderDetailID
FROM Sales.SalesOrderHeader AS o
INNER JOIN Sales.SalesOrderDetail AS d
    ON o.SalesOrderID = d.OrderID;
```

Query 1, which joins the `Sales.SalesOrderDetail` table to `Sales.SalesOrderHeader` on the `SalesOrderID` column, performs better because there is a nonclustered index defined on the `SalesOrderID` column. There is not an index on the new `OrderID` column, so a clustered index scan is performed on the `Sales.SalesOrderDetail` table to join the tables in query 2.

2. Compare the execution plans of the derived table example (Listing 4-18) and the CTE example (Listing 4-19). Explain why the query performance is the same or why one query performs better than the other.

The performance of the two queries is the same. These two techniques are just different ways to do the same thing in this case.

Chapter 5: Grouping and Summarizing Data

This section provides solutions to the exercises on grouping and summarizing data.

Solutions to Exercise 5-1: Using Aggregate Functions

Use the AdventureWorks2008 database to complete this exercise.

1. Write a query to determine the number of customers in the `Sales.Customer` table.

```
SELECT COUNT(*) AS CountOfCustomers
FROM Sales.Customer;
```

2. Write a query that lists the total number of products ordered. Use the `OrderQty` column of the `Sales.SalesOrderDetail` table and the `SUM` function.

```
SELECT SUM(OrderQty) AS TotalProductsOrdered
FROM Sales.SalesOrderDetail;
```

3. Write a query to determine the price of the most expensive product ordered. Use the `UnitPrice` column of the `Sales.SalesOrderDetail` table.

```
SELECT MAX(UnitPrice) AS MostExpensivePrice
FROM Sales.SalesOrderDetail;
```

4. Write a query to determine the average freight amount in the **Sales.SalesOrderHeader** table.

```
SELECT AVG(Freight) AS AverageFreight
FROM Sales.SalesOrderHeader;
```

5. Write a query using the **Production.Product** table that displays the minimum, maximum, and average **ListPrice**.

```
SELECT MIN(ListPrice) AS Minimum,
    MAX(ListPrice) AS Maximum,
    AVG(ListPrice) AS Average
FROM Production.Product;
```

Solutions to Exercise 5-2: Using the GROUP BY Clause

Use the AdventureWorks2008 database to complete this exercise.

1. Write a query that shows the total number of items ordered for each product. Use the **Sales.SalesOrderDetail** table to write the query.

```
SELECT SUM(OrderQty) AS TotalOrdered, ProductID
FROM Sales.SalesOrderDetail
GROUP BY ProductID;
```

2. Write a query using the **Sales.SalesOrderDetail** table that displays a count of the detail lines for each **SalesOrderID**.

```
SELECT COUNT(*) AS CountOfOrders, SalesOrderID
FROM Sales.SalesOrderDetail
GROUP BY SalesOrderID;
```

3. Write a query using the **Production.Product** table that lists a count of the products in each product line.

```
SELECT COUNT(*) AS CountOfProducts, ProductLine
FROM Production.Product
GROUP BY ProductLine;
```

4. Write a query that displays the count of orders placed by year for each customer using the **Sales.SalesOrderHeader** table.

```
SELECT CustomerID, COUNT(*) AS CountOfSales, YEAR(OrderDate) AS OrderYear
FROM Sales.SalesOrderHeader
GROUP BY CustomerID, YEAR(OrderDate);
```

Solutions to Exercise 5-3: Using the HAVING Clause

Use the AdventureWorks2008 to complete this exercise.

1. Write a query that returns a count of detail lines in the **Sales.SalesOrderDetail** table by
   SalesOrderID. Include only those sales that have more than three detail lines.

   ```
   SELECT COUNT(*) AS CountOfDetailLines, SalesOrderID
   FROM Sales.SalesOrderDetail
   GROUP BY SalesOrderID
   HAVING COUNT(*) > 3;
   ```

2. Write a query that creates a sum of the **LineTotal** in the **Sales.SalesOrderDetail** table grouped by
   the **SalesOrderID**. Include only those rows where the sum exceeds 1,000.

   ```
   SELECT SUM(LineTotal) AS SumOfLineTotal, SalesOrderID
   FROM Sales.SalesOrderDetail
   GROUP BY SalesOrderID
   HAVING SUM(LineTotal) > 1000;
   ```

3. Write a query that groups the products by **ProductModelID** along with a count. Display the rows
   that have a count that equals 1.

   ```
   SELECT ProductModelID, COUNT(*) AS CountOfProducts
   FROM Production.Product
   GROUP BY ProductModelID
   HAVING COUNT(*) = 1;
   ```

4. Change the query in question 3 so that only the products with the color blue or red are included.

   ```
   SELECT ProductModelID, COUNT(*) AS CountOfProducts, Color
   FROM Production.Product
   WHERE Color IN ('Blue','Red')
   GROUP BY ProductModelID, Color
   HAVING COUNT(*) = 1;
   ```

Solutions to Exercise 5-4: Using DISTINCT

Use the AdventureWorks2008 database to complete this exercise.

1. Write a query using the **Sales.SalesOrderDetail** table to come up with a count of unique
   ProductID values that have been ordered.

   ```
   SELECT COUNT(DISTINCT ProductID) AS CountOFProductID
   FROM Sales.SalesOrderDetail;
   ```

2. Write a query using the **Sales.SalesOrderHeader** table that returns the count of unique **TerritoryID** values per customer.

```
SELECT COUNT(DISTINCT TerritoryID) AS CountOfTerritoryID, CustomerID
FROM Sales.SalesOrderHeader
GROUP BY CustomerID;
```

Solutions to Exercise 5-5: Using Aggregate Queries with More Than One Table

Use the AdventureWorks2008 database to complete this exercise.

1. Write a query joining the **Person.Person**, **Sales.Customer**, and **Sales.SalesOrderHeader** tables to return a list of the customer names along with a count of the orders placed.

```
SELECT COUNT(*) AS CountOfOrders, FirstName, MiddleName, LastName
FROM Person.Person AS P
INNER JOIN Sales.Customer AS C ON P.BusinessEntityID = C.PersonID
INNER JOIN Sales.SalesOrderHeader AS SOH ON C.CustomerID = SOH.CustomerID
GROUP BY FirstName, MiddleName, LastName;
```

2. Write a query using the **Sales.SalesOrderHeader**, **Sales.SalesOrderDetail**, and **Production.Product** tables to display the total sum of products by **ProductID** and **OrderDate**.

```
SELECT SUM(OrderQty) SumOfOrderQty, P.ProductID, SOH.OrderDate
FROM Sales.SalesOrderHeader AS SOH
INNER JOIN Sales.SalesOrderDetail AS SOD
    ON SOH.SalesOrderID = SOD.SalesOrderDetailID
INNER JOIN Production.Product AS P ON SOD.ProductID = P.ProductID
GROUP BY P.ProductID, SOH.OrderDate;
```

Solutions to Exercise 5-6: Isolating Aggregate Query Logic

Use the AdventureWorks2008 database to complete this exercise.

1. Write a query that joins the **HumanResources.Employee** table to the **Person.Person** table so that you can display the **FirstName**, **LastName**, and **HireDate** columns for each employee. Display the **JobTitle** along with a count of employees for the title. Use a derived table to solve this query.

```
SELECT FirstName, LastName, e.JobTitle, HireDate, CountOfTitle
FROM HumanResources.Employee AS e
INNER JOIN Person.Person AS p ON e.BusinessEntityID = p.BusinessEntityID
INNER JOIN (
    SELECT COUNT(*) AS CountOfTitle, JobTitle
    FROM HumanResources.Employee
    GROUP BY JobTitle) AS j ON e.JobTitle = j.JobTitle;
```

2. Rewrite the query from question 1 using a CTE.

```
WITH j AS (SELECT COUNT(*) AS CountOfTitle, JobTitle
    FROM HumanResources.Employee
    GROUP BY JobTitle)
SELECT FirstName, LastName, e.JobTitle, HireDate, CountOfTitle
FROM HumanResources.Employee AS e
INNER JOIN Person.Person AS p ON e.BusinessEntityID = p.BusinessEntityID
INNER JOIN j ON e.JobTitle = j.JobTitle;
```

3. Rewrite the query from question 1 using the **OVER** clause.

```
SELECT FirstName, LastName, e.JobTitle, HireDate,
    COUNT(*) OVER(PARTITION BY JobTitle) AS CountOfTitle
FROM HumanResources.Employee AS e
INNER JOIN Person.Person AS p ON e.BusinessEntityID = p.BusinessEntityID
```

4. Display the **CustomerID**, **SalesOrderID**, and **OrderDate** for each **Sales.SalesOrderHeader** row as long as the customer has placed at least five orders. Use any of the techniques from this section to come up with the query.

Here are three possible solutions:

```
--subquery
SELECT CustomerID, SalesOrderID, OrderDate
FROM Sales.SalesOrderHeader
WHERE CustomerID IN
    (SELECT CustomerID
    FROM Sales.SalesOrderHeader
    GROUP BY CustomerID
    HAVING COUNT(*) > 4);
```

```
--CTE
WITH c AS (
    SELECT CustomerID
    FROM Sales.SalesOrderHeader
    GROUP BY CustomerID
    HAVING COUNT(*) > 4)
SELECT c.CustomerID, SalesOrderID, OrderDate
FROM Sales.SalesOrderHeader AS SOH
INNER JOIN c ON SOH.CustomerID = c.CustomerID;

--derived table
SELECT c.CustomerID, SalesOrderID, OrderDate
FROM Sales.SalesOrderHeader AS SOH
INNER JOIN (
    SELECT CustomerID
    FROM Sales.SalesOrderHeader
    GROUP BY CustomerID
    HAVING COUNT(*) > 4) AS c ON SOH.CustomerID = c.CustomerID;
```

Solutions to Exercise 5-7: Thinking About Performance

Use the AdventureWorks2008 database to complete this exercise.

1. Make sure that the Include Actual Execution Plan setting is turned on before typing and executing the following code. Compare the execution plans to see whether the CTE query performs better than the **OVER** clause query.

```
USE AdventureWorks2008;
GO
--1
WITH SumSale AS
    (SELECT SUM(TotalDue) AS SumTotalDue,
        CustomerID
    FROM Sales.SalesOrderHeader
    GROUP BY CustomerID)
SELECT o.CustomerID, TotalDue,
    TotalDue / SumTotalDue * 100 AS PercentOfSales
FROM SumSale INNER JOIN Sales.SalesOrderHeader AS o
ON SumSale.CustomerID = o.CustomerID
ORDER BY CustomerID;
```

```
--2
SELECT CustomerID, TotalDue,
    TotalDue / SUM(TotalDue) OVER(PARTITION BY CustomerID) * 100 AS PercentOfSales
FROM Sales.SalesOrderHeader
ORDER BY CustomerID;
```

The performance is about the same for this example.

2. The following queries each contain two calculations: percent of sales by customer and percent of sales by territory. Type in and execute the code to see the difference in performance. Make sure the Include Actual Execution Plan setting is turned on before running the code.

```
USE AdventureWorks2008;
GO
```

```
--1
WITH SumSale AS
    (SELECT SUM(TotalDue) AS SumTotalDue,
        CustomerID
    FROM Sales.SalesOrderHeader
    GROUP BY CustomerID),
 TerrSales AS
    (SELECT SUM(TotalDue) AS SumTerritoryTotalDue, TerritoryID
     FROM Sales.SalesOrderHeader
     GROUP BY TerritoryID )
SELECT o.CustomerID, TotalDue,
    TotalDue / SumTotalDue * 100 AS PercentOfCustSales,
    TotalDue / SumTerritoryTotalDue * 100 AS PercentOfTerrSales
FROM SumSale
INNER JOIN Sales.SalesOrderHeader AS o ON SumSale.CustomerID = o.CustomerID
INNER JOIN TerrSales ON TerrSales.TerritoryID = o.TerritoryID
ORDER BY CustomerID;
```

```
--2
SELECT CustomerID, TotalDue,
    TotalDue / SUM(TotalDue) OVER(PARTITION BY CustomerID) * 100 AS
PercentOfCustSales,
    TotalDue / SUM(TotalDue) OVER(PARTITION BY TerritoryID) * 100 AS
PercentOfTerrSales
FROM Sales.SalesOrderHeader
ORDER BY CustomerID;
```

In this case, the CTE in query 1 performs better.

Chapter 6: Manipulating Data

This section provides solutions to the exercises on manipulating data.

Solutions to Exercise 6-1: Inserting New Rows

Use the AdventureWorksLT2008 database to complete this exercise.

     Run the following code to create the required tables. You can also download the code from this book's page at http://www.apress.com to save typing time.

```
USE AdventureWorksLT2008;
GO
IF  EXISTS (SELECT * FROM sys.objects
            WHERE object_id = OBJECT_ID(N'[dbo].[demoProduct]')
                AND type in (N'U'))
DROP TABLE [dbo].[demoProduct]
GO

CREATE TABLE [dbo].[demoProduct](
    [ProductID] [INT] NOT NULL PRIMARY KEY,
    [Name] [dbo].[Name] NOT NULL,
    [Color] [NVARCHAR](15) NULL,
    [StandardCost] [MONEY] NOT NULL,
    [ListPrice] [MONEY] NOT NULL,
    [Size] [NVARCHAR](5) NULL,
    [Weight] [DECIMAL](8, 2) NULL,
);
IF  EXISTS (SELECT * FROM sys.objects
            WHERE object_id = OBJECT_ID(N'[dbo].[demoSalesOrderHeader]')
                AND type in (N'U'))
DROP TABLE [dbo].[demoSalesOrderHeader]
GO

CREATE TABLE [dbo].[demoSalesOrderHeader](
    [SalesOrderID] [INT] NOT NULL PRIMARY KEY,
    [SalesID] [INT] NOT NULL IDENTITY,
    [OrderDate] [DATETIME] NOT NULL,
    [CustomerID] [INT] NOT NULL,
    [SubTotal] [MONEY] NOT NULL,
    [TaxAmt] [MONEY] NOT NULL,
    [Freight] [MONEY] NOT NULL,
```

```
    [DateEntered] [DATETIME],
    [TotalDue]  AS (ISNULL((([SubTotal]+[TaxAmt])+[Freight],(0)))),
    [RV] ROWVERSION NOT NULL);
GO

ALTER TABLE [dbo].[demoSalesOrderHeader] ADD  CONSTRAINT
[DF_demoSalesOrderHeader_DateEntered]
DEFAULT (GETDATE()) FOR [DateEntered];

GO
IF  EXISTS (SELECT * FROM sys.objects
    WHERE object_id = OBJECT_ID(N'[dbo].[demoAddress]')
    AND type in (N'U'))
DROP TABLE [dbo].[demoAddress]
GO

CREATE TABLE [dbo].[demoAddress](
    [AddressID] [INT] NOT NULL IDENTITY PRIMARY KEY,
    [AddressLine1] [NVARCHAR](60) NOT NULL,
    [AddressLine2] [NVARCHAR](60) NULL,
    [City] [NVARCHAR](30) NOT NULL,
    [StateProvince] [dbo].[Name] NOT NULL,
    [CountryRegion] [dbo].[Name] NOT NULL,
    [PostalCode] [NVARCHAR](15) NOT NULL
);
```

1. Write a SELECT statement to retrieve data from the SalesLT.Product table. Use these values to insert five rows into the dbo.demoProduct table using literal values. Write five individual INSERT statements.

    The rows you choose to insert may vary.

    ```
    SELECT ProductID, Name, Color,
        StandardCost, ListPrice, Size, Weight
    FROM SalesLT.Product;

    INSERT INTO dbo.demoProduct(ProductID, Name, Color,
        StandardCost, ListPrice, Size, Weight)
    VALUES (680,'HL Road Frame - Black, 58','Black',1059.31,1431.50,'58',1016.04);

    INSERT INTO dbo.demoProduct(ProductID, Name, Color,
        StandardCost, ListPrice, Size, Weight)
    VALUES (706,'HL Road Frame - Red, 58','Red',1059.31, 1431.50,'58',1016.04);
    ```

```
INSERT INTO dbo.demoProduct(ProductID, Name, Color,
    StandardCost, ListPrice, Size, Weight)
VALUES (707,'Sport-100 Helmet, Red','Red',13.0863,34.99,NULL,NULL);

INSERT INTO dbo.demoProduct(ProductID, Name, Color,
    StandardCost, ListPrice, Size, Weight)
VALUES (708,'Sport-100 Helmet, Black','Black',13.0863,34.99,NULL,NULL);
INSERT INTO dbo.demoProduct(ProductID, Name, Color,
    StandardCost, ListPrice, Size, Weight)
VALUES (709,'Mountain Bike Socks, M','White',3.3963,9.50,'M',NULL);
```

2. Insert five more rows into the **dbo.demoProduct** table. This time write one **INSERT** statement.

The rows you choose to insert may vary.

```
INSERT INTO dbo.demoProduct(ProductID, Name, Color,
StandardCost, ListPrice, Size, Weight)
VALUES (711,'Sport-100 Helmet, Blue','Blue',
        13.0863,34.99,NULL,NULL),
    (712,'AWC Logo Cap','Multi',6.9223,
     8.99,NULL,NULL),
    (713,'Long-Sleeve Logo Jersey,S','Multi',
     38.4923,49.99,'S',NULL),
    (714,'Long-Sleeve Logo Jersey,M','Multi',
     38.4923,49.99,'M',NULL),
    (715,'Long-Sleeve Logo Jersey,L','Multi',
     38.4923,49.99,'L',NULL);
```

3. Write an **INSERT** statement that inserts all the rows into the **dbo.demoSalesOrderHeader** table from the **SalesLT.SalesOrderHeader** table. Hint: Pay close attention to the properties of the columns in the **dbo.demoSalesOrderHeader** table.

Don't insert a value into the **SalesID**, **DateEntered**, and **RV** columns.

```
INSERT INTO dbo.demoSalesOrderHeader(
    SalesOrderID, OrderDate, CustomerID,
    SubTotal, TaxAmt, Freight)
SELECT SalesOrderID, OrderDate, CustomerID,
    SubTotal, TaxAmt, Freight
FROM SalesLT.SalesOrderHeader;
```

4. Write a SELECT INTO statement that creates a table, **dbo.tempCustomerSales**, showing every CustomerID from the SalesLT.Customer along with a count of the orders placed and the total amount due for each customer.

```
SELECT COUNT(ISNULL(SalesOrderID,0)) AS CountOfORders, c.CustomerID,
    SUM(TotalDue) AS TotalDue
INTO dbo.tempCustomerSales
FROM SalesLT.Customer AS c
LEFT JOIN SalesLT.SalesOrderHeader AS soh ON c.CustomerID = soh.CustomerID
GROUP BY c.CustomerID;
```

5. Write an INSERT statement that inserts all the products into the **dbo.demoProduct** table from the SalesLT.Product table that have not already been inserted. Do not specify literal **ProductID** values in the statement.

Here are two possible solutions:

```
INSERT INTO dbo.demoProduct (ProductID, Name, Color, StandardCost,
    ListPrice, Size, Weight)
SELECT p.ProductID, p.Name, p.Color, p.StandardCost, p.ListPrice,
    p.Size, p.Weight
FROM SalesLT.Product AS p
LEFT OUTER JOIN dbo.demoProduct AS dp ON p.ProductID = dp.ProductID
WHERE dp.ProductID IS NULL;


INSERT INTO dbo.demoProduct (ProductID, Name, Color, StandardCost,
    ListPrice, Size, Weight)
SELECT ProductID, Name, Color, StandardCost, ListPrice,
    Size, Weight
FROM SalesLT.Product
WHERE ProductID NOT IN (
    SELECT ProductID FROM dbo.demoProduct WHERE ProductID IS NOT NULL);
```

6. Write an INSERT statement that inserts all the addresses into the **dbo.demoAddress** table from the SalesLT.Address table. Before running the INSERT statement, type and run the command so that you can insert values into the **AddressID** column.

```
SET IDENTITY_INSERT dbo.demoAddress ON;

INSERT INTO dbo.demoAddress(AddressID,AddressLine1,AddressLine2,
    City,StateProvince,CountryRegion,PostalCode)
```

```
SELECT AddressID,AddressLine1,AddressLine2,
    City,StateProvince,CountryRegion,PostalCode
FROM SalesLT.Address;

--to turn the setting off
SET IDENTITY_INSERT dbo.demoAddress OFF;
```

Solutions to Exercise 6-2: Deleting Rows

Use the AdventureWorksLT2008 database to complete this exercise. Before starting the exercise, run code Listing 6-9 to re-create the demo tables.

1. Write a query that deletes the rows from the **dbo.demoCustomer** table where the **LastName** values begin with the letter *S*.

```
DELETE FROM dbo.demoCustomer
WHERE LastName LIKE 'S%'
```

2. Delete the rows from the **dbo.demoCustomer** table if the customer has not placed an order or if the sum of the **TotalDue** from the **dbo.demoSalesOrderHeader** table for the customer is less than $1,000.

   Here are two possible solutions:

```
WITH Sales AS (
    SELECT C.CustomerID
    FROM dbo.demoCustomer AS C
    LEFT OUTER JOIN dbo.demoSalesOrderHeader AS SOH
    ON C.CustomerID = SOH.CustomerID
    GROUP BY c.CustomerID
    HAVING SUM(ISNULL(TotalDue,0)) < 1000)
DELETE C
FROM dbo.demoCustomer AS C
INNER JOIN Sales ON C.CustomerID = Sales.CustomerID;

DELETE FROM dbo.demoCustomer
WHERE CustomerID IN (
    SELECT C.CustomerID
    FROM dbo.demoCustomer AS C
    LEFT OUTER JOIN dbo.demoSalesOrderHeader AS SOH
    ON C.CustomerID = SOH.CustomerID
    GROUP BY c.CustomerID
    HAVING SUM(ISNULL(TotalDue,0)) < 1000);
```

3. Delete the rows from the **dbo.demoProduct** table that have never been ordered.

Here are two possible solutions:

```
DELETE P
FROM dbo.demoProduct AS P
LEFT OUTER JOIN dbo.demoSalesOrderDetail AS SOD ON P.ProductID = SOD.ProductID
WHERE SOD.ProductID IS NULL;
```

```
DELETE FROM dbo.demoProduct
WHERE ProductID NOT IN
    (SELECT ProductID
    FROM dbo.demoSalesOrderDetail
    WHERE ProductID IS NOT NULL);
```

Solutions to Exercise 6-3: Updating Existing Rows

Use the AdventureWorksLT2008 database to complete this exercise. Run the code in Listing 6-9 to re-create tables used in this exercise.

1. Write an **UPDATE** statement that changes all **NULL** values of the **AddressLine2** column in the **dbo.demoAddress** table to *N/A*.

```
UPDATE dbo.demoAddress SET AddressLine2 = 'N/A'
WHERE AddressLine2 IS NULL;
```

2. Write an **UPDATE** statement that increases the **ListPrice** of every product in the **dbo.demoProduct** table by 10 percent.

```
UPDATE dbo.demoProduct SET ListPrice *= 1.1;
```

3. Write an **UPDATE** statement that corrects the **UnitPrice** with the **ListPrice** of each row of the **dbo.demoSalesOrderDetail** table by joining the table on the **dbo.demoProduct** table.

```
UPDATE SOD
SET UnitPrice = P.ListPrice
FROM SalesLT.SalesOrderDetail AS SOD
INNER JOIN dbo.demoProduct AS P ON SOD.ProductID = P.ProductID;
```

4. Write an **UPDATE** statement that updates the **SubTotal** column of each row of the **dbo.demoSalesOrderHeader** table with the sum of the **LineTotal** column of the **dbo.demoSalesOrderDemo** table.

```
WITH SOD AS(
    SELECT SUM(LineTotal) AS TotalSum, SalesOrderID
    FROM dbo.demoSalesOrderDetail
    GROUP BY SalesOrderID)
UPDATE SOH Set SubTotal = TotalSum
FROM dbo.demoSalesOrderHeader AS SOH
INNER JOIN SOD ON SOH.SalesOrderID = SOD.SalesOrderID;
```

Solutions to Exercise 6-4: Using Transactions

Use the AdventureWorksLT2008 database to this exercise. Run the following script to create a table for this exercise:

```
IF OBJECT_ID('dbo.Demo') IS NOT NULL BEGIN
    DROP TABLE dbo.Demo;
END;
GO
CREATE TABLE dbo.Demo(ID INT PRIMARY KEY, Name VARCHAR(25));
```

1. Write a transaction that includes two insert statements to add two rows to the **dbo.Demo** table.

    Here's a possible solution:

    ```
    BEGIN TRAN
        INSERT INTO dbo.Demo(ID,Name)
        VALUES (1,'Test1');

        INSERT INTO dbo.Demo(ID,Name)
        VALUES(2,'Test2');
    COMMIT TRAN;
    ```

2. Write a transaction that includes two insert statements to add two more rows to the **dbo.Demo** table. Attempt to insert a letter instead of a number into the **ID** column in one of the statements. Select the data from the **dbo.Demo** table to see which rows made it into the table.

Here's a possible solution:

```
BEGIN TRAN
    INSERT INTO dbo.Demo(ID,Name)
    VALUES(3,'Test3');

    INSERT INTO dbo.Demo(ID,Name)
    VALUES('a','Test4');
COMMIT TRAN;
GO
SELECT ID,Name
FROM dbo.Demo;
```

Chapter 7: Understanding T-SQL Programming Logic

This section provides solutions to the exercises on understanding T-SQL programming logic.

Solutions to Exercise 7-1: Using Variables

Use the AdventureWorks2008 database to complete this exercise.

1. Write a script that declares an integer variable called **@myInt**. Assign 10 to the variable, and then print it.

    ```
    DECLARE @myInt INT = 10;
    PRINT @myInt;
    ```

2. Write a script that declares a **VARCHAR(20)** variable called **@myString**. Assign **This is a test** to the variable, and print it.

    ```
    DECLARE @myString VARCHAR(20) = 'This is a test';
    PRINT @myString;
    ```

3. Write a script that declares two integer variables called **@MaxID** and **@MinID**. Use the variables to print the highest and lowest **SalesOrderID** values from the **Sales.SalesOrderHeader** table.

    ```
    DECLARE @MaxID INT, @MinID INT;
    SELECT @MaxID = MAX(SalesOrderID),
        @MinID = MIN(SalesOrderID)
    FROM Sales.SalesOrderHeader;
    PRINT 'Max: ' + CONVERT(VARCHAR,@MaxID);
    PRINT 'Min: ' + CONVERT(VARCHAR, @MinID);
    ```

4. Write a script that declares an integer variable called **@ID**. Assign the value **70000** to the variable. Use the variable in a **SELECT** statement that returns all the **SalesOrderID** values from the Sales.SalesOrderHeader table that have a SalesOrderID greater than the value of the variable.

```
DECLARE @ID INTEGER = 70000;
SELECT SalesOrderID
FROM Sales.SalesOrderHeader
WHERE SalesOrderID > @ID;
```

5. Write a script that declares three variables, one integer variable called **@ID**, an **NVARCHAR(50)** variable called **@FirstName**, and an **NVARCHAR(50)** variable called **@LastName**. Use a **SELECT** statement to set the value of the variables with the row from the **Person.Person** table with **BusinessEntityID = 1**. Print a statement in the "BusinessEntityID: FirstName LastName" format.

```
DECLARE @ID INT, @FirstName NVARCHAR(50), @LastName NVARCHAR(50);
SELECT @ID = BusinessEntityID, @FirstName = FirstName,
    @LastName = LastName
FROM Person.Person
WHERE BusinessEntityID = 1;
PRINT CONVERT(NVARCHAR,@ID) + ': ' + @FirstName + ' ' + @LastName;
```

6. Write a script that declares an integer variable called **@SalesCount**. Set the value of the variable to the total count of sales in the **Sales.SalesOrderHeader** table. Use the variable in a **SELECT** statement that shows the difference between the **@SalesCount** and the count of sales by customer.

```
DECLARE @SalesCount INT;
SELECT @SalesCount = COUNT(*)
FROM Sales.SalesOrderHeader;

SELECT @SalesCount - COUNT(*) AS CustCountDiff, CustomerID
FROM Sales.SalesOrderHeader
GROUP BY CustomerID;
```

Solutions to Exercise 7-2: Using the IF…ELSE Construct

Use the AdventureWorks2008 database to complete this exercise.

1. Write a batch that declares an integer variable called **@Count** to save the count of all the **Sales.SalesOrderDetail** records. Add an **IF** block that that prints "Over 100,000" if the value exceeds 100,000. Otherwise, print "100,000 or less."

```
DECLARE @Count INT;
SELECT @Count = COUNT(*)
FROM Sales.SalesOrderDetail;
```

```
IF @Count > 100000 BEGIN
    PRINT 'Over 100,000';
END
ELSE BEGIN
    PRINT '100,000 or less.';
END;
```

2. Write a batch that contains nested **IF** blocks. The outer block should check to see whether the month is October or November. If that is the case, print "The month is " and the month name. The inner block should check to see whether the year is even or odd and print the result. You can modify the month to check to make sure the inner block fires.

```
IF MONTH(GETDATE()) IN (10,11) BEGIN
    PRINT 'The month is ' + DATENAME(mm,GETDATE());
    IF YEAR(GETDATE()) % 2 = 0 BEGIN
        PRINT 'The year is even.';
    END
    ELSE BEGIN
        PRINT 'The year is odd.';
    END
END;
```

3. Write a batch that uses **IF EXISTS** to check to see whether there is a row in the **Sales.SalesOrderHeader** table that has **SalesOrderID = 1**. Print "There is a SalesOrderID = 1" or "There is not a SalesOrderID = 1" depending on the result.

```
IF EXISTS(SELECT * FROM Sales.SalesOrderHeader
    WHERE SalesOrderID = 1) BEGIN
    PRINT 'There is a SalesOrderID = 1';
END
ELSE BEGIN
    PRINT 'There is not a SalesOrderID = 1';
END;
```

Solutions to Exercise 7-3: Using WHILE

Use the AdventureWorks2008 database to complete this exercise.

1. Write a script that contains a **WHILE** loop that prints out the letters *A* to *Z*. Use the function **CHAR** to change a number to a letter. Start the loop with the value 65.

Here is an example that uses the **CHAR** function:

```
DECLARE @Letter CHAR(1);
SET @Letter = CHAR(65);
PRINT @Letter;

DECLARE @Count INT = 65;
WHILE @Count < 91 BEGIN
    PRINT CHAR(@Count);
    SET @Count += 1;
END;
```

2. Write a script that contains a **WHILE** loop nested inside another **WHILE** loop. The counter for the outer loop should count up from 1 to 100. The counter for the inner loop should count up from 1 to 5. Print the product of the two counters inside the inner loop.

```
DECLARE @i INTEGER = 1;
DECLARE @j INTEGER;

WHILE @i <= 100 BEGIN
    SET @j = 1;
    WHILE @j <= 5 BEGIN
        PRINT @i * @j;
        SET @j += 1;
    END;
    SET @i += 1;
END;
```

3. Change the script in question 2 so the inner loop exits instead of printing when the counter for the outer loop is evenly divisible by 5.

```
DECLARE @i INTEGER = 1;
DECLARE @j INTEGER;

WHILE @i <= 100 BEGIN
    SET @j = 1;
    WHILE @j <= 5 BEGIN
        IF @i % 5 = 0 BEGIN
            PRINT 'Breaking out of loop.'
            BREAK;
        END;
        PRINT @i * @j;
        SET @j += 1;
    END;
```

```
        SET @i += 1;
    END;
```

4. Write a script that contains a **WHILE** loop that counts up from 1 to 100. Print "Odd" or "Even" depending on the value of the counter.

```
DECLARE @Count INT = 1;
WHILE @Count <= 100 BEGIN
    IF @Count % 2 = 0 BEGIN
        PRINT 'Even';
    END
    ELSE BEGIN
        PRINT 'Odd';
    END
    SET @Count += 1;
END;
```

Solutions to Exercise 7-4: Handling Errors

Use AdventureWorks2008 to complete this exercise.

1. Write a statement that attempts to insert a duplicate row into the **HumanResources.Department** table. Use the **@@ERROR** function to display the error.

```
DECLARE @Error INT;
INSERT INTO HumanResources.Department(DepartmentID,Name,GroupName,ModifiedDate)
VALUES (1,'Engineering','Research and Development',GETDATE());
SET @Error = @@ERROR;
IF @Error > 0 BEGIN
    PRINT @Error;
END;
```

2. Change the code you wrote in question 1 to use **TRY…CATCH**. Display the error number, message, and severity.

```
BEGIN TRY
    INSERT INTO HumanResources.Department(DepartmentID,Name,GroupName,ModifiedDate)
    VALUES (1,'Engineering','Research and Development',GETDATE());
END TRY
BEGIN CATCH
    SELECT ERROR_NUMBER() AS ErrorNumber,ERROR_MESSAGE() AS ErrorMessage,
        ERROR_SEVERITY() AS ErrorSeverity;
END CATCH;
```

3. Change the code you wrote in question 2 to raise a custom error message instead of the actual error message.

```
BEGIN TRY
    INSERT INTO HumanResources.Department(DepartmentID,Name,GroupName,ModifiedDate)
    VALUES (1,'Engineering','Research and Development',GETDATE());
END TRY
BEGIN CATCH
    RAISERROR('You attempted to insert a duplicate!',16,1);
END CATCH;
```

Solutions to Exercise 7-5: Creating Temporary Tables and Table Variables

Use the AdventureWorks2008 database to complete this exercise.

1. Create a temp table called **#CustomerInfo** that contains **CustomerID**, **FirstName**, and **LastName** columns. Include **CountOfSales** and **SumOfTotalDue** columns. Populate the table with a query using the **Sales.Customer**, **Person.Person**, and **Sales.SalesOrderHeader** tables.

```
CREATE TABLE #CustomerInfo(
    CustomerID INT, FirstName VARCHAR(50),
    LastName VARCHAR(50),CountOfSales INT,
    SumOfTotalDue MONEY);
GO
INSERT INTO #CustomerInfo(CustomerID,FirstName,LastName,
    CountOfSales, SumOfTotalDue)
SELECT C.CustomerID, FirstName, LastName,COUNT(*),SUM(TotalDue)
FROM Sales.Customer AS C
INNER JOIN Person.Person AS P ON C.CustomerID = P.BusinessEntityID
INNER JOIN Sales.SalesOrderHeader AS SOH ON C.CustomerID = SOH.CustomerID
GROUP BY C.CustomerID, FirstName, LastName ;
```

2. Change the code written in question 1 to use a table variable instead of a temp table.

```
DECLARE @CustomerInfo TABLE (
    CustomerID INT, FirstName VARCHAR(50),
    LastName VARCHAR(50),CountOfSales INT,
    SumOfTotalDue MONEY);

INSERT INTO @CustomerInfo(CustomerID,FirstName,LastName,
    CountOfSales, SumOfTotalDue)
```

```
SELECT C.CustomerID, FirstName, LastName,COUNT(*),SUM(TotalDue)
FROM Sales.Customer AS C
INNER JOIN Person.Person AS P ON C.CustomerID = P.BusinessEntityID
INNER JOIN Sales.SalesOrderHeader AS SOH ON C.CustomerID = SOH.CustomerID
GROUP BY C.CustomerID, FirstName, LastName ;
```

3. Create a table variable with two integer columns, one of them an INDENTITY column. Use a WHILE loop to populate the table with 1,000 random integers using the following formula. Use a second WHILE loop to print the values from the table variable one by one.

```
CAST(RND() * 10000 AS INT) + 1
```

Here's a possible solution:

```
DECLARE @test TABLE (ID INTEGER NOT NULL IDENTITY, Random INT)
DECLARE @Count INT = 1;
DECLARE @Value INT;

WHILE @Count <= 1000 BEGIN
    SET @Value = CAST(RAND()*10000 AS INT) + 1;
    INSERT INTO @test(Random)
    VALUES(@Value);
    SET @Count += 1;
END;
SET @Count = 1;
WHILE @Count <= 1000 BEGIN
    SELECT @Value = Random
    FROM @test
    WHERE ID = @Count;
    PRINT @Value;
    SET @Count += 1;
END;
```

Chapter 8: Moving Logic to the Database

This section provides solutions to the exercises on moving logic to the database.

Solutions to Exercise 8-1: Creating Tables

Use the AdventureWorks2008 database to complete this exercise.

1. Create a table called **dbo.testCustomer**. Include a **CustomerID** that is an identity column primary key. Include **FirstName** and **LastName** columns. Include an **Age** column with a check constraint specifying that the value must be less than 120. Include an **Active** column that is one character with a default of **Y** and allows only **Y** or **N**. Add some rows to the table.

   Here's a possible solution:

```
IF OBJECT_ID ('dbo.testCustomer') IS NOT NULL BEGIN
    DROP TABLE dbo.testCustomer;
END;
GO

CREATE TABLE dbo.testCustomer (
    CustomerID INT NOT NULL IDENTITY PRIMARY KEY,
    FirstName VARCHAR(25), LastName VARCHAR(25),
    Age INT, Active CHAR(1) DEFAULT 'Y',
    CONSTRAINT ch_testCustomer_Age CHECK (Age < 120),
    CONSTRAINT ch_testCustomer_Active CHECK (Active IN ('Y','N'))
);
GO


INSERT INTO dbo.testCustomer(FirstName, LastName,Age)
VALUES ('Kathy','Morgan',35),('Lady B.','Kellenberger',14),
    ('Luke','Moore',30);
```

2. Create a table called **dbo.testOrder**. Include a **CustomerID** column that is a foreign key pointing to **dbo.testCustomer**. Include an **OrderID** column that is an identity column primary key. Include an **OrderDate** column that defaults to the current date and time. Include a **ROWVERSION** column. Add some rows to the table.

```
IF OBJECT_ID('dbo.testOrder') IS NOT NULL BEGIN
    DROP TABLE dbo.testOrder;
END;
GO
CREATE TABLE dbo.testOrder (CustomerID INT NOT NULL,
    OrderID INT NOT NULL IDENTITY PRIMARY KEY,
    OrderDate DATETIME DEFAULT GETDATE(),
    RW ROWVERSION,
    CONSTRAINT fk_testOrders FOREIGN KEY (CustomerID)
        REFERENCES dbo.testCustomer(CustomerID)
    );
GO
```

```
INSERT INTO dbo.testOrder (CustomerID)
VALUES (1),(2),(3);
```

3. Create a table called **dbo.testOrderDetail**. Include an **OrderID** column that is a foreign key pointing to **dbo.testOrder**. Include an integer **ItemID** column, a **Price** column, and a **Qty** column. The primary key should be a composite key composed of **OrderID** and **ItemID**. Create a computed column called **LineItemTotal** that multiplies **Price** times **Qty**. Add some rows to the table.

```
IF OBJECT_ID('dbo.testOrderDetail') IS NOT NULL BEGIN
    DROP TABLE dbo.testOrderDetail;
END;
GO
CREATE TABLE dbo.testOrderDetail(
    OrderID INT NOT NULL, ItemID INT NOT NULL,
    Price Money NOT NULL, Qty INT NOT NULL,
    LineItemTotal AS (Price * Qty),
    CONSTRAINT pk_testOrderDetail PRIMARY KEY (OrderID, ItemID),
    CONSTRAINT fk_testOrderDetail FOREIGN KEY (OrderID)
        REFERENCES dbo.testOrder(OrderID)
);

GO
INSERT INTO dbo.testOrderDetail(OrderID,ItemID,Price,Qty)
VALUES (1,1,10,5),(1,2,5,10);
```

Solutions to Exercise 8-2: Creating Views

Use the AdventureWorks2008 database to complete this exercise.

1. Create a view called **dbo.vw_Products** that displays a list of the products from the **Production.Product** table joined to the **Production.ProductCostHistory** table. Include columns that describe the product and show the cost history for each product. Test the view by creating a query that retrieves data from the view.

```
IF OBJECT_ID('dbo.vw_Products') IS NOT NULL BEGIN
    DROP VIEW dbo.vw_Products;
END;
GO
CREATE VIEW dbo.vw_Products AS (
    SELECT P.ProductID, P.Name, P.Color, P.Size, P.Style,
        H.StandardCost, H.EndDate, H.StartDate
    FROM Production.Product AS P
```

```
    INNER JOIN Production.ProductCostHistory AS H ON P.ProductID = H.ProductID
    );

GO
SELECT ProductID, Name, Color, Size, Style, StandardCost,
    EndDate, StartDate
FROM dbo.vw_Products;
```

2. Create a view called **dbo.vw_CustomerTotals** that displays the total sales from the **TotalDue** column per year and month for each customer. Test the view by creating a query that retrieves data from the view.

```
IF OBJECT_ID('dbo.vw_CustomerTotals') IS NOT NULL BEGIN
    DROP VIEW dbo.vw_CustomerTotals;
END;
GO
CREATE VIEW dbo.vw_CustomerTotals AS (
    SELECT C.CustomerID, YEAR(OrderDate) AS OrderYear,
        MONTH(OrderDate) AS OrderMonth, SUM(TotalDue) AS TotalSales
    FROM Sales.Customer AS C
    INNER JOIN Sales.SalesOrderHeader AS SOH ON C.CustomerID = SOH.CustomerID
    GROUP BY C.CustomerID, YEAR(OrderDate), MONTH(OrderDate)
    );
GO
SELECT CustomerID, OrderYear, OrderMonth, TotalSales
FROM dbo.vw_CustomerTotals;
```

Solutions to Exercise 8-3: Creating User-Defined Functions

Use the AdventureWorks2008 database to complete this exercise.

1. Create a user-defined function called **dbo.fn_AddTwoNumbers** that accepts two integer parameters. Return the value that is the sum of the two numbers. Test the function.

```
IF OBJECT_ID('dbo.fn_AddTwoNumbers') IS NOT NULL BEGIN
    DROP FUNCTION dbo.fn_AddTwoNumbers;
END;
GO

CREATE FUNCTION dbo.fn_AddTwoNumbers (@NumberOne INT, @NumberTwo INT)
RETURNS INT AS BEGIN
    RETURN @NumberOne + @NumberTwo;
END;
```

```
GO
SELECT dbo.fn_AddTwoNumbers(1,2);
```

2. Create a user-defined function called **dbo.Trim** that takes a **VARCHAR(250)** parameter. This function should trim off the spaces from both the beginning and the end of a string. Test the function.

```
IF OBJECT_ID('dbo.Trim') IS NOT NULL BEGIN
    DROP FUNCTION dbo.Trim;
END
GO
CREATE FUNCTION dbo.Trim (@Expression VARCHAR(250))
RETURNS VARCHAR(250) AS BEGIN
    RETURN LTRIM(RTRIM(@Expression));
END;
GO
SELECT '*' + dbo.Trim('  test  ') + '*';
```

3. Create a function called **dbo.fn_RemoveNumbers** that removes any numeric characters from a **VARHCHAR(250)** string. Test the function. Hint: The **ISNUMERIC** function checks to see whether a string is numeric. Check Books Online to see how to use it.

```
IF OBJECT_ID('dbo.fn_RemoveNumbers') IS NOT NULL BEGIN
    DROP FUNCTION dbo.fn_RemoveNumbers;
END;
GO
CREATE FUNCTION dbo.fn_RemoveNumbers (@Expression VARCHAR(250))
RETURNS VARCHAR(250) AS BEGIN
    DECLARE @NewExpression VARCHAR(250) = '';
    DECLARE @Count INT = 1;
    DECLARE @Char CHAR(1);
    WHILE @Count <= LEN(@Expression) BEGIN
        SET @Char = SUBSTRING(@Expression,@Count,1);
        IF ISNUMERIC(@Char) = 0 BEGIN
            SET @NewExpression += @Char;
        END
        SET @Count += 1;
    END;
RETURN @NewExpression;
END;
GO
SELECT dbo.fn_RemoveNumbers('abc 123 baby you and me');
```

4. Write a function called **dbo.fn_FormatPhone** that takes a string of ten numbers. The function will format the string into this phone number format: "(###) ###-####." Test the function.

```
IF OBJECT_ID('dbo.fn_FormatPhone') IS NOT NULL BEGIN
    DROP FUNCTION dbo.fn_FormatPhone;
END;
GO
CREATE FUNCTION dbo.fn_FormatPhone (@Phone VARCHAR(10))
RETURNS VARCHAR(14) AS BEGIN
    DECLARE @NewPhone VARCHAR(14);
    SET @NewPhone = '(' + SUBSTRING(@Phone,1,3) + ') ';
    SET @NewPhone = @NewPhone + SUBSTRING(@Phone,4,3) + '-';
    SET @NewPhone = @NewPhone + SUBSTRING(@Phone,7,4)
    RETURN @NewPhone;
END;
GO
SELECT dbo.fn_FormatPhone('5555551234');
```

Solutions to Exercise 8-4: Creating Stored Procedures

Use the AdventureWorks2008 database to complete this exercise.

1. Create a stored procedure called **dbo.usp_CustomerTotals** instead of the view from question 2 in Exercise 8-2. Test the stored procedure.

```
IF OBJECT_ID('dbo.usp_CustomerTotals') IS NOT NULL BEGIN
    DROP PROCEDURE dbo.usp_CustomerTotals;
END;
GO
CREATE PROCEDURE dbo.usp_CustomerTotals AS
    SELECT C.CustomerID, YEAR(OrderDate) AS OrderYear,
        MONTH(OrderDate) AS OrderMonth, SUM(TotalDue) AS TotalSales
    FROM Sales.Customer AS C
    INNER JOIN Sales.SalesOrderHeader AS SOH ON C.CustomerID = SOH.CustomerID
    GROUP BY C.CustomerID, YEAR(OrderDate), MONTH(OrderDate)

GO
EXEC dbo.usp_CustomerTotals;
```

2. Modify the stored procedure created in question 1 to include a parameter **@CustomerID**. Use the parameter in the **WHERE** clause of the query in the stored procedure. Test the stored procedure.

```
IF OBJECT_ID('dbo.usp_CustomerTotals') IS NOT NULL BEGIN
    DROP PROCEDURE dbo.usp_CustomerTotals;
END;
GO
CREATE PROCEDURE dbo.usp_CustomerTotals @CustomerID INT AS
    SELECT C.CustomerID, YEAR(OrderDate) AS OrderYear,
        MONTH(OrderDate) AS OrderMonth, SUM(TotalDue) AS TotalSales
    FROM Sales.Customer AS C
    INNER JOIN Sales.SalesOrderHeader AS SOH ON C.CustomerID = SOH.CustomerID
    WHERE C.CustomerID = @CustomerID
    GROUP BY C.CustomerID, YEAR(OrderDate), MONTH(OrderDate)

GO
EXEC dbo.usp_CustomerTotals 17910;
```

3. Create a stored procedure called **dbo.usp_ProductSales** that accepts a **ProductID** for a parameter and has an **OUTPUT** parameter that returns the number sold for the product. Test the stored procedure.

```
IF OBJECT_ID('dbo.usp_ProductSales') IS NOT NULL BEGIN
    DROP PROCEDURE dbo.usp_ProductSales;
END;
GO
CREATE PROCEDURE dbo.usp_ProductSales @ProductID INT,
    @TotalSold INT = NULL OUTPUT AS

    SELECT @TotalSold = SUM(OrderQty)
    FROM Sales.SalesOrderDetail
    WHERE ProductID = @ProductID;

GO
DECLARE @TotalSold INT;
EXEC dbo.usp_ProductSales @ProductID = 776, @TotalSold =  @TotalSold OUTPUT;
PRINT @TotalSold;
```

Index

■Special Characters

-- (two hyphens), 25
$action option, 357
% (modulo) operator, 85
% (percent) character, 53, 56
* (asterisk), 151–152, 235
/* and */ delimiters, 25
@@ERROR, 244–245
[ ] (square brackets), 41, 54
_ (underscore), 53, 56
+ (concatenation operator), 79
+ (plus symbol), 85
<> (not equal to) operator, 47, 61
!= (not equal to) operator, 47
" " (double quotes), 69
- (minus symbol), 85
' (single quote mark), 38
/ (slashes), 52, 85

■A

ABS function, 103
Account Provisioning tab, SQL Server
    Installation Center, 9–10
ad hoc DELETE statements, 198
admin functions, 110–111
AdventureWorks databases, 12–14, 16
aggregate functions
        main discussion, 151–152
        updating rows with, 210–212
aggregate queries, 151–181
        common table expressions (CTEs),
        173–175
        derived tables, 172–175

DISTINCT, 163–165
        within aggregate
expression, 164–165
                vs. GROUP BY, 163–164
                overview, 163
GROUP BY clause, 153–156
                grouping on columns,
153–155
                grouping on expressions,
155–156
                overview, 153
HAVING clause, 160–163
inline correlated subqueries, 170–172
with more than one table, 166–167
ORDER BY clause, 157–158
OVER clause, 176–177
overview, 151–168
performance, 178–180
WHERE clause
                main discussion, 159–160
                using correlated subquery
in, 168–170
aliases, 42–43
        defined, 42
        deleting rows, 203
ALTER TABLE command, 254, 270, 272
AND NOT operator, 67
AND operator, 58, 60, 67
applications, versus services, 27
arrays, 258
AS keyword, 42
asterisk (*), 151–152, 235
AVG function, 151

■Q

You Need the Companion eBook

Your purchase of this book entitles you to buy the companion PDF-version eBook for only $10. Take the weightless companion with you anywhere.

We believe this Apress title will prove so indispensable that you'll want to carry it with you everywhere, which is why we are offering the companion eBook (in PDF format) for $10 to customers who purchase this book now. Convenient and fully searchable, the PDF version of any content-rich, page-heavy Apress book makes a valuable addition to your programming library. You can easily find and copy code—or perform examples by quickly toggling between instructions and the application. Even simultaneously tackling a donut, diet soda, and complex code becomes simplified with hands-free eBooks!

Once you purchase your book, getting the $10 companion eBook is simple:

❶ Visit **www.apress.com/promo/tendollars/**.

❷ Complete a basic registration form to receive a randomly generated question about this title.

❸ Answer the question correctly in 60 seconds, and you will receive a promotional code to redeem for the $10.00 eBook.

THE EXPERT'S VOICE™

233 Spring Street, New York, NY 10013

Offer valid through 4/10.